AGINCOURT

A NEW HISTORY

AGINCOURT
A NEW HISTORY

ANNE CURRY

TEMPUS

Tempus Publishing Limited
The Mill, Brimscombe Port,
Stroud, Gloucestershire, GL5 2QG

ISBN 0 7524 2828 4

Typesetting and origination by Tempus Publishing Limited
Printed in the U.S.A.

Contents

Abbreviations

Unpublished materials are to be found in The National Archives, Kew, unless otherwise stated.

AD	Archives Départementales
AN	Archives Nationales, Paris
Basin	Thomas Basin, *Histoire de Charles VII*, ed. C. Samaran and H. De Saint-Rémy, 2 vols (Paris, 1934-44), vol. 1
Belleval	R. de Belleval, *Azincourt* (Paris, 1865)
Berry Herald	*Les Chroniques du roi Charles VII par Gilles le Bouvier dit le héraut Berry*, ed. H. Couteault and L.Celier (SHF, Paris, 1979)
BL	British Library, London
BN	Bibliothèque Nationale, Paris
Brut	*The Brut, or the Chronicle of England*, ed. F.W.D. Brie, Early English Text Society, original series, 131 and 136 (London, 1906–08), vol. 2
CCR	*Calendars of the Close Rolls*
CPR	*Calendars of the Patent Rolls*
CP	*Complete Peerage*
De Cagny	*Chronique de Perceval de Cagny*, ed. H. Moranville (SHF, Paris, 1902)
Des Ursins	Jean Juvenal des Ursins, *Histoire de Charles VI, roy de France, Nouvelle collection des mémoires pour servir à l'histoire de France*, ed. Michaud & Poujoulet, series 1 (Paris, 1836), vol. 2
Deseille	E. Deseille, 'Etude sur les relations des communes du nord lors du désastre d'Azincourt', *Mémoires de la société académique de l'arrondissment de Boulogne-sur-Mer* (1879)
Dynter	*Chronique des ducs de Brabant par Edmond Dynter*, ed. P.F.X. De Ram, 6 vols (Brussels, 1854–60), vol. 3

Famiglietti	R.C. Famiglietti, *Royal Intrigue. Crisis at the Court of Charles VI 1392–1420* (New York, 1986)
Foedera	T. Rymer, *Foedera, conventiones, litterae et cuiuscunque generis acta publica*, 3rd edn (The Hague, 1739–45)
French rolls	'Calendar of French Rolls' in *Annual Report of the Deputy Keeper of the Public Records* xliv (1883)
Fusoris	L. Mirot, 'Le process de maître Jean Fusoris', *Mémoires de la société de l'histoire de Paris et de l'île de France*, 27 (1900)
Gesta	*Gesta Henrici Quinti. The Deeds of Henry the Fifth*, ed. F. Taylor and J.S. Roskell (Oxford, 1975)
Gruel	*Chronique d'Arthur de Richemont par Guillaume Gruel*, ed. A. Le Vavasseur (SHF, Paris, 1890)
Hardyng	John Hardyng, *Chronicle (to 1461)*, ed. H. Ellis (London, 1812)
Le Fèvre	*Chronique de Jean Le Fèvre, Seigneur de Saint Rémy*, ed. F. Morand, 2 vols (SHF, 1876–81)
London Letter Book I	*Calendar of Letter Books preserved among the archives of the Corporation of the City of London. Letter Book I*, ed. R.R. Sharpe (London, 1909)
Monstrelet	*La Chronique d'Enguerran de Monstrelet*, ed. L. Douet-D'Arcq, 6 vols (SHF, Paris, 1857–62)
Nicolas	N.H. Nicolas, *History of the Battle of Agincourt*, 3rd edn (London, 1833)
Ordonnances	*Ordonnances des rois de France de la troisième race*, 21 vols (Paris, 1723–1849)
PPC	*Proceedings and Ordinances of the Privy Council*, ed. N.H. Nicolas (London, 1834)
Religieux	Le Religieux de Saint-Denis, *Histoire de Charles VI*, ed. L. Bellaguet, *Collection de documents inédits sur l'histoire de France*, 6 vols (Paris, 1839–52)
SHF	Société de l'Histoire de France
Sources	A. Curry, *The Battle of Agincourt. Sources and Interpretations* (Woodbridge, 2000)
Waurin	*Receuil des Croniques et Anchiennes istories de la Grant Bretagne a present nomme Engleterre par Jehan de Waurin*, ed. W.L. Hardy and E.L.C.P. Hardy, 5 vols, Rolls Series (London, 1864–91)

Acknowledgements

Over the years, many people have encouraged and assisted my work on Agincourt. I owe a particular debt of gratitude to M. Boulet, the mayor of the commune of Azincourt, to M. and Mme Delclusse of the Centre Historique and Eric Revet and Bertrand Klein, its architects, and to Siobhan Stevens of the Centre Verginaud and Southlands School, who have made me so welcome on my visits. I am also grateful to Philippe Cailleux and Richard Jones for information on Harfleur and its fortifications. Discussions with fellow enthusiasts Robert Hardy, Matthew Bennett and Clifford Rogers have always been stimulating and good fun even if we have had to agree to disagree. Laetitia Renault provided very useful assistance with sources in the Bibliothèque Nationale and Shelagh Mitchell with names of archers in the records of The National Archives. I am also grateful to the University of Southampton for providing financial support. Jonathan Reeve has been a constant source of encouragement and has displayed a patience well beyond that expected of a publisher. I am thankful also to Sophie Bradshaw for her diligence and assistance in preparing the text for publication. My husband and son have lived with Agincourt for almost as long as I have and have never failed to ask those difficult questions or to indulge my desire to retrace Henry V's steps 'just one more time'. My special thanks to them, and to all those who have helped and supported me in this project but must remain nameless here.

Introduction

The Letter Book of the City of London records that on Friday 25 October 1415 'a lamentable report replete with sadness and cause for endless sorrow' was circulating in the city. Such pessimism had arisen because no one knew what was happening to the English army and its king 'valorously struggling to gain the rights of his realm overseas… all particulars lay shrouded in mystery'.[1] On the same day, news arrived in Abbeville of a great French victory and a feast was arranged by the guild of silversmiths to celebrate.[2] Little did either place realise what was actually happening at Agincourt. But soon the truth was known. A marginal entry in the account of the Abbeville guild, with classic understatement, noted that news of the victory was 'not true'. By contrast, the entry in the London Letter Book went on to say that a trustworthy report arrived within a few days 'to refresh all the longing ears of the city'. King Henry had 'by God's grace, gained victory over the enemy who had united to resist his march through the midst of his territory towards Calais'. The majority of his opponents had been 'delivered to the arbitration of death or had submitted to his gracious might, praise be God'. This 'joyous news' arrived in London early on the morning of Tuesday 29 October. After proclamation outside St Paul's at 9 a.m., the bells of the city churches were rung and Te Deums sung. Later in the day, there was solemn procession to Westminster Abbey to offer thanks at the shrine of Edward the Confessor. Among those present was Joan of Navarre, the widowed queen of Henry IV, who doubtless had mixed emotions if she had already learned that her son by her first marriage, Arthur, Count of Richemont, brother of the Duke of Brittany, was among those who had submitted as prisoners to the 'gracious might' of her stepson, Henry V.

In an age of rapid and mass communication, it is hard to imagine a time when news travelled so slowly and uncertainly.[3] On the day the victory was announced in London, Henry V, his army and his prisoners arrived at Calais. Alongside Richemont were the French king's nephew, Charles, Duke of Orléans, the

Duke of Bourbon, the Counts of Eu and Vendôme, and the marshal of France, Boucicaut. Meanwhile at Agincourt, the servants of their erstwhile comrades-in-arms continued to search the piles of naked and disfigured dead in the hope of finding their masters. The contrast between fatalities on each side was immediately obvious by the roll call of the noble dead alone. The body of Henry's second cousin, Edward, Duke of York, had been boiled and placed in a barrel to bring home, as had the body of Michael de la Pole, Earl of Suffolk, who had inherited his title only six weeks earlier when his father died from dysentery at the siege of Harfleur. On the French side, the bodies of the constable of France, Charles, Sire d'Albret, the Dukes of Bar, Brabant, and Alençon, the Counts of Nevers, Vaudémont, Salm, Roucy, Marle and countless others of the flower of French chevalerie were found and carried off for burial.

Agincourt was an unmitigated disaster for the French as well as a blood bath. Harfleur, the town near the mouth of the Seine that Henry had taken after a siege of five weeks (17 August–22 September), remained in English hands and defeat in battle meant that there was no chance of an early attempt at its recovery. By contrast, Henry's star was in the ascendant. The parliament that opened at Westminster on 4 November while the king was still at Calais lasted only eight days – the shortest of any medieval parliament – and voted him customs duties for life. His victory was all the more amazing, since, as the London Letter Book notes, the French had delayed and harried his homeward march across Normandy for two-and-a-half weeks (8–25 October) and had forced him to engage against his will. Within one day, therefore, the world had changed for English and French alike.

Any battle like Agincourt, with such an imbalance of mortality rates between the protagonists, would be bound to attract attention at the time and for centuries to come. There has indeed been a vast amount of ink expended on the battle through a wide variety of genres.[4] Several key perceptions prevail: the victory of the few against the many; of the common man against the arrogant aristocrat; of Henry V's military genius against French royal incompetence. Myths have also developed, not least the supposed invention of the V-sign by victorious English archers. But can such interpretations be sustained? One danger is taking the battle out of its context. Agincourt took place within a dramatic and complex period in English and French history. Henry was the son of a usurper and still insecure on his own throne in 1415. France had a king who suffered from psychological illness, and in the years leading up to Henry's invasion had been troubled by civil war. The aim of this book is to examine Agincourt as the final stage of the whole campaign and to attempt a balanced treatment of Henry's aims and actions and of French responses to them.

In many ways a historian works like a detective, finding as much evidence as possible and assessing it critically to find the truth. A detective can interview those involved. We must make do with interrogating the eyewitness accounts.[5]

John Hardyng claimed to have served on the campaign but the accounts he gave in his verse chronicles are perfunctory and written over forty years later.[6] The Flemish chronicler Jean de Waurin was on his own admission fifteen years old at the time of the campaign, and accompanied the French army at the battle. He adds that he gained information from Jean Le Fèvre, who was later King-of-Arms of the Burgundian order of the Golden Fleece and who was 'at the time of the battle nineteen years old and in the company of the king of England in all the business of this time'. In what capacity Le Fèvre was with the English is not certain, although it was probably with the heralds rather than as a soldier. A second comment by Waurin suggests Le Fèvre was with the English on the march as well as the battle, but it is not certain whether he was present at the siege. Both men put together their chronicles later in life, Waurin in the 1440s and '50s and Le Fèvre in the '50s and '60s. They also drew on testimony of other heralds and of French soldiers such as Sir Hue de Lannoy and his brother, Sir Guillebert.[7] Our earliest eyewitness account is written from an English perspective. This is the anonymous *Gesta Henrici Quinti*, written by a chaplain who was with Henry's army for the whole campaign. This is therefore the most important narrative source we have, although it has its shortcomings and does not always answer the questions we would most like to ask.

There are also a number of works where information must have come from eyewitnesses. The *Vita Henrici Quinti* (*c.* 1438) was written by Titus Livius Forojuliensis, an Italian in the pay of Humphrey, Duke of Gloucester, Henry V's last surviving brother and a veteran of the battle. The *Vita et Gesta Henrici Quinti* (*c.* 1446–49) is an anonymous work commonly called the Pseudo-Elmham, which is known to have drawn on information from Sir (later Lord) Walter Hungerford, who also fought at Agincourt. Three texts, the *Chronique d'Arthur de Richemont* by Gruel (*c.* 1458), the *Chronique de Perceval de Cagny* (late 1430s), a family chronicle of the Dukes of Alençon, and Edouard Dynter's *Chronique des ducs de Brabant* (1440s) were linked to French lords who were present.

Since Agincourt was a major event, it found its way into contemporary monastic chronicles such as those of Thomas Walsingham (*c.* 1420–22) of St Albans, and of the Religieux of Saint-Denis (*c.* 1415–22), religious houses long associated with the writing of histories. Another monk, Thomas Elmham of St Augustine's, Canterbury, wrote the verse *Liber Metricus de Henrico Quinto* (*c.* 1418). When histories in English such as the *Brut* and the London-based chronicles became popular later in the century, the events of 1415 were recounted there too. In France, accounts of the battle were included in major works such as the *Chroniques* of Enguerran de Monstrelet (*c.* 1444); the *Histoire de Charles VI* (1430–40s) of Jean Juvenal des Ursins; the *Histoire de Charles VII* (1471–72) of Thomas Basin; the *Mémoires* (1430s) of Pierre de Fenin; the *Chroniques* of the Berry Herald (?1450s), as well as in lesser works such as the *Chronique de Ruisseauville* (?1420s–30s), a place close to Agincourt.

In a desire to tell a good story, modern commentators have tended to choose the juiciest bits from each chronicle to create one single account. But we do need to exercise some caution when using these chronicles, even those of our eyewitnesses, as 'evidence'. They give conflicting accounts and they were written to their own agenda, which makes it dangerous to take what they say at face value. For the French, Agincourt was such a disaster that someone had to be to blame. Its interpretation was politicised in the context of previous and ongoing tension between the Burgundian and the Armagnac (or Orléanist) factions. Even the Religieux of Saint-Denis, the nearest we come to an official court chronicler, and other non-aligned writers such as the Berry Herald, felt the need to emphasise the folly of those who advised on giving battle. For the English, the matter was simpler but equally loaded. Agincourt marked the triumph of Henry's Lancastrian kingship as well as of England's success against her ancient enemy. The *Gesta Henrici Quinti* was probably written to extol Henry's virtues as a Christian knight on the European stage, especially at the Council of Constance then deliberating the papal schism. Titus Livius wrote to eulogise not only Henry V but also Duke Humphrey at a time when the latter's political influence was on the wane. Later pro-Yorkist writers of the English vernacular chronicles ascribed the decision to place the English archers behind stakes not to Henry but to Edward, Duke of York, uncle of the Richard who claimed the throne in 1460.

In all cases, we have to interpret what the chronicles say, bearing in mind the difficulty of translating from their original languages and of understanding contemporary nuances. Where their narratives are close or identical, this is not necessarily confirmation of veracity but of copying and interdependence. This is particularly noticeable when looking at the three Burgundian writers, Monstrelet, Le Fèvre and Waurin, whose textual similarity is considerable and not yet fully understood. Similarly, the Pseudo-Elmham may be a more long-winded version of Titus Livius, and the *Liber Metricus* a verse version of the *Gesta*. As we have noted, many accounts, including those of eyewitnesses, were not put together until much later. Not only does memory fade but it becomes selective as a result of what happens in the meantime. All of our authors were writing with hindsight of Henry's victory of 1415 and the majority after the treaty of Troyes of 1420, which made the English king heir to the French throne. This contributes further to the patriotism of English accounts and the pessimism of French. In questioning our sources, we must be aware too that battles are intrinsically difficult events to describe even for eyewitnesses. Writers found it difficult to disentangle events that were happening simultaneously or to give any sense of timings. The author of the *Gesta* and other Latin chroniclers were heavily influenced by the classical texts they read. Indeed, all writers had a tendency to write battle accounts to a 'template'[8] and to invent numbers for effect. None the less, all of the works written within forty years or so of the battle remain valuable sources of evidence so long as they are used critically. Just like detectives, historians are constantly searching for new leads. Under Edward III a number of royal newsletters were sent back to England from the front, providing a more immediate insight into events and motive.[9] This is a source which is lacking for 1415, but we can deduce how decisions were reached by examining royal orders, records of councils and parliaments, and diplomatic documents, but even here we have to remember that propaganda and spin are not recent inventions. Where we are on more straightforward terrain is with the financial records of the period.[10] Since the armies of both countries were paid, we can ascertain their size, composition and even names of soldiers, thereby liberating ourselves from over-reliance on narrative accounts.

The overwhelming impression is that Henry's invasion was a personal obsession inspired by his views on kingship. His army of around 12,000 was one of the largest to enter France during the whole of the Hundred Years' War and contained the highest proportion of archers to date. Even with the losses incurred at Harfleur, the English still had a formidable and cohesive army at the battle. The scale of the English victory at Agincourt and the eulogising of Henry V that resulted have disguised both the potential insecurity of his position at home and the failure of his campaign up to the point of the battle. The disarray that defeat caused in France has likewise hidden the fact that, after years of turmoil, the French were reasonably united in their response. They brought Henry to battle while he gave every impression of trying to avoid it. They chose the battlefield – a 'scene of crime' which we can add to our forensic study along with other locations which feature in the campaign. Yet on the day they found themselves in confusion and without the numbers they had hoped for. Even then, Henry's response was symptomatic of panic and uncertainty as much as military genius. Agincourt was and is shocking and amazing. It needs no mythologising.

I

Henry V's Inheritance:
England and France, 1399–1413

enry V had called himself 'king of France' ever since his accession to the English throne on 21 March 1413. At the battle of Agincourt his surcoat bore the quartered arms of England and France and his helmet was encircled with a crown bearing the insignia of both kingdoms. Men from nearby Hesdin who pillaged his baggage during the heat of battle found two crowns, one to wear when appearing before the people of France, and the other with which to be crowned at the traditional crowning place of Reims.[1] The claim of English kings to the throne of France dates back to Henry's great-grandfather, Edward III, who started the Hundred Years' War by declaring himself king of France in 1340, as the rightful heir, albeit through the female line, to the late king, Charles IV.[2] Historians have long debated whether Edward was serious about acquiring this throne. Although he made for Reims with a crown in his baggage in 1359, in the following year he came to a treaty with the French king, John II, who was already in English captivity after his capture at the battle of Poitiers in 1356. The treaty of Brétigny of 1360, which became known as the Great Peace, gave Edward an enlarged Guienne (the great duchy of Aquitaine with its capital at Bordeaux), Poitou (the county based on Poitiers), Ponthieu (the county to the north of the Somme estuary) and the march of Calais in full sovereignty. In return, he agreed to stop calling himself king of France. It appears therefore that Edward had simply used his claim to the French throne to expand the extent and independence of the lands of English kings in France, the southern parts of which had been held since the marriage of Henry II to Eleanor of Aquitaine on condition of homage being paid to the French king. Ponthieu had come into English hands through the inheritance of Edward I's queen in 1279. Edward III had taken Calais in 1347. Edward might have asked for more in this Great Peace. In the negotiations of 1358–59 he had demanded other lands held by English kings in the past:

Normandy, whose link went back to 1066, and Anjou, Maine and Touraine, which were also part of Henry II's Angevin 'empire'. These had all been lost in the reign of John, but there was still a strong remembrance of their tenure.

By the time Henry was born in 1387,[3] the Great Peace had failed. Charles V had reopened the war in 1369 and his armies had quickly reduced the English to holding the coastal areas of Guienne, with an inland projection down the rivers Dordogne and Garonne, and the Calais march. Edward III retaliated by resuming the title 'king of France'. At his death in 1377, the title and claim passed to his grandson, Richard II, but the English found it impossible to recover their position. The last campaign occurred in 1388. In 1396 a long truce was agreed, to last until 1426, symptomatic of the impasse that had been reached. The truce was further cemented by the marriage of Richard to Charles VI's six-year-old daughter, Isabella. There things might have remained, and we would have all been writing books about the 'Sixty Years' War'. Likewise, Henry V's life could have turned out quite differently. At the sealing of the long truce he was simply Henry of Monmouth, the nine-year-old son of Henry Bolingbroke, Earl of Derby and Hereford, and grandson of John of Gaunt, Duke of Lancaster, third son of Edward III. He would have grown up to enjoy a typical noble lifestyle, much as his father had done, although had the long truce endured and led to permanent peace, his opportunities for military service in France would have been more limited. But neither were to be. In September 1399 Bolingbroke deposed Richard II. Henry of Monmouth was now Prince Henry, heir to the crown of England as well as a putative crown of France. Henry IV immediately bestowed on his son not only the traditional titles of Prince of Wales, Earl of Chester and Duke of Cornwall, but also Duke of Guienne. There were immediate plans to send the prince to Guienne at the nominal head of an army, but parliament advised that he should not leave the country 'at such a tender age until peace had been more securely established within the kingdom'.[4]

Prince Henry never did cross to France. There were repeated conspiracies against Henry IV in England, difficulties with the Scots, revolt and long-term war in Wales, and financial problems – all stemming at base from the fact of usurpation. At Epiphany 1400, leading nobles plotted to kill Henry and his sons. The new king's response was savage and swift, as it was throughout his reign. On this occasion it led to the execution of several leading nobles and the murder of the deposed king. In 1403 it was Henry's erstwhile friends, the Percys, who rebelled and whom he defeated in the bloody battle of Shrewsbury on 21 July 1403, at which the prince was wounded in the face by an arrow. Two years later, threats of revolt in the north led the king to execute Richard Scrope, Archbishop of York. In 1408, further rebellion brought the death of the Earl of Northumberland. The possibility of rival claims to the throne was never completely removed, as Henry V was to discover as he prepared to set sail in 1415.

As prince, he grew up in a context of insecurity and militarism. A whole book could be written on his military apprenticeship, but a few salient points must be emphasised here. Although warfare was a challenge to any king, it was also an extremely significant way of enforcing royal will and generating a practical demonstration of loyalty. Just as Henry V was to use this mechanism as king, through a massive invasion of France in 1415, so his father did the same within the first year of his own reign with an expedition against the Scots, who had taken advantage of the disarray caused by Richard's deposition to invade Northumberland, affronting the king by addressing him as 'Duke of Lancaster'.[5] The army that Henry IV raised, numbering at least 13,085, was one of the largest ever assembled in late-medieval England, larger than for Henry V's invasions of France in both 1415 and 1417. It called on the service of the nobility, knights and gentry, invoking their obligation to support the crown. This was therefore a very effective way of imposing and testing the rule of a new and disputed king, and for Henry to achieve immediate success. Faced with such military strength, the Scots not surprisingly chose to negotiate.

The expedition of 1400 also reveals how well developed the English military system and the royal powers of calling men to arms were. Should either Henry IV or his son wish to make a big showing in France, then there was no doubting the existence of a strong infrastructure and ample supply of manpower especially through the nobility, issues to which we shall return in Chapter 3. Furthermore, the royal family and household was central to the army of 1400 and to all of Henry IV's military endeavours. Many of these men, such as Sir Thomas Erpingham, continued in service to Agincourt and beyond. Although there is some uncertainty over the actual participation of Prince Henry in the campaign to Scotland, we do know that he was allocated a company of seventeen men-at-arms and ninety-nine archers.[6] When he was first appointed royal lieutenant in Wales in March 1403, the army assigned to him (although he was still under the tutelage of others) consisted of 500 men-at-arms and 2,500 archers. His real military independence came in January 1406, when he was assigned 1,100 men-at-arms and 3,800 archers for Wales.[7] These armies were intended for use in the field as well as to reinforce garrisons. The Welsh wars were a major contributor to the financial difficulties faced by Henry IV. They also had a direct impact on Prince Henry, in a way which previsaged problems faced in launching the 1415 expedition. In late May 1403, for example, the prince wrote to his father to explain how he had had to pawn his jewels to pay the troops, and how food for horses was in such short supply in Wales that his men had been forced to carry oats with them.[8]

With so much going on within the British Isles, it is easy to overlook Henry IV's concern for his French interests. It is clear, however, that he was equally determined to maintain his rights there and to extend them, should circumstances permit. The claim to the French crown was an important element of his legitimacy as king of England. Although he was never to cross to France during his reign, despite several plans to do so, his involvement in Anglo-French affairs was considerable, and the policies developed over his reign paved the way for those of his son. At the time of his accession, Henry IV may have anticipated that France would be his major headache, since there was a danger that the French would use his usurpation as an excuse to restart conflict. At first they rejected his approaches to confirm the state of truce, but there was a constraint on their actions since they needed to negotiate the return of Richard's widow, Isabella, to France. They refused to contemplate Henry IV's proposal that she should be married instead to the Prince of Wales. Had they agreed, there might have been no invasion in 1415! The French never acknowledged Henry IV as king of England, but confirmed the truce in June 1400 by agreeing that it had been made between the kingdoms and peoples of England and France and not between Charles and Richard as individuals.[9] Even so, they remained reluctant to hold meetings to settle infringements of the truce, which were increasing daily, especially at sea, until forced to do so by Henry's delaying of Isabella's return (and with her the repayment of part of her dowry). On 31 July 1401 the young queen was given back to the French.

The years that followed saw a 'cold war'. The French stirred up trouble for the English wherever and however they could, by symbols and by actions, while always stopping short of formally reopening the war. When the Dauphin Charles died aged nine in January 1401, his next brother, Louis (b.1397), then aged nearly four, was made Dauphin and also Duc de Guienne. It is by this latter title that he is referred to in most chronicles of the period, including those of the time of Agincourt, although he was not, despite Shakespeare, present at the battle. His elevation was intended as a deliberate slight to the English. It certainly made the parliament of the spring of 1401 fearful that the French were about to invade the duchy.[10] In response, on 5 July 1401 Henry IV appointed his cousin, Edward, Earl of Rutland (b.1373), as lieutenant in Guienne for three years, with a retinue of 100 men-at-arms and 1,000 archers.[11] Rutland became Duke of York in 1402 at the death of his father, Edmund of Langley, the last surviving son of Edward III. He played a prominent role in the Welsh campaigns alongside Prince Henry, who supported him even when the king had suspicions of his loyalty. He continued to play a prominent military role after 1413 and was the leading English peer killed at the battle of Agincourt.[12] English authority was restored in Guienne by the end of 1401, but there were continuing pressures on the frontiers, especially in Périgord which Charles VI had granted to his brother, Louis, Duke of Orléans. Although Louis had been a supporter of Bolingbroke when the latter had been exiled by Richard II, he had turned into his bitter enemy after the usurpation. Orléans was certainly behind an incursion into Guienne in October 1403 led by himself, the Count of Alençon (b.1385) and Charles, Sire d'Albret (b.1369), who had been constable since 1403. The two last-named met their end at Agincourt after many years of military experience.

This was a breach of the truce, but was one of many hostile acts against the English in the first years of Henry IV's reign. The French had continued in alliance with the Scots, sending armed support in 1402 under Jacques de Heilly. He was subsequently captured by the Percys, and was the subject of a dispute between them and Henry IV, which contributed to their revolt in 1403. De Heilly was subsequently imprisoned in Wisbech (Cambs.) until he broke prison. He was to fight against the English again in Guienne in 1413 and also in the Agincourt campaign.[13] From the time of Richard's deposition, English shipping found itself under constant attack from French-condoned acts of piracy, many of which were launched from Harfleur. In July 1404 the French even went so far as to recognise Owen Glendower as Prince of Wales and came to an alliance with him against their common enemy, 'Henry of Lancaster'.[14]

This was part of French plans to reopen the war on a larger scale. An estimate was drawn up of how much it would cost to fight against the English in Guienne, Calais and at sea.[15] Over the next two years, there was a pattern of attack and counter-attack. For instance, Waleran de Luxembourg, Count of Saint-Pol, who had married Richard II's half-sister, Margaret Holland, attacked Marck in the Calais march, and the English retaliated with an attack on Sluys. At sea they went on the offensive under the nominal command of Prince Thomas, later Duke of Clarence, making a landing at St-Vaast-la-Hougue on the eastern tip of the Cotentin, with burning and pillaging conducted thirty miles inland.[16] The French landed troops at Milford Haven to assist Glendower. Harlech fell, and it was there that Glendower held his second parliament in August 1405, where he arrogantly announced his intention to broker a peace between England and France which would involve acknowledgement of Welsh independence. D'Albret took outlying English fortifications in the Agenais and the French began to threaten the English heartlands of Guienne in October 1406, with the Duke of Orléans's siege of Bourg, the place that controlled the estuary of the Gironde. John the Fearless, Duke of Burgundy, threatened English possessions in the Calais march but the French decided that they could not afford war on two frontiers, so he was ordered to disband his troops. As it happened, Orléans's attempt to take Bourg failed and he was forced to lift the siege on 14 January 1407. The failure of these military initiatives, and also growing tensions between Orléans and Burgundy, led the French to allow English envoys to come to Paris for the first time. Once again the marriage of Prince Henry to one of Charles VI's daughters was proposed, as well as the establishment of a new long truce. Neither materialised, but a system of repeated short local truces was introduced for Picardy and Western Flanders, for Guienne, and for the sea. This remained in use for the rest of Henry IV's reign.[17]

It is significant that the first of the short truces for Guienne was only agreed after Louis of Orléans had been assassinated in Paris on 23 November 1407. It immediately became clear that the man who arranged his death was Duke John of Burgundy. This assassination was the culmination of a feud which had begun in the lifetime of the latter's father, Philip the Bold (d.1404), fanned by the mental illness of King Charles VI. The king's periodic incapacity made those closest to the king compete for power and influence, as they were to continue to do for the rest of his reign, eventually contributing to Charles's acceptance of Henry V as his heir, by the treaty of Troyes of 1420. This event was itself closely linked to the assassination of John the Fearless in September 1419 – a revenge killing for that of Louis of Orléans in 1407.

This is a gross simplification of three decades of extremely complicated French politics, from the king's first signs of instability in 1392. Charles VI was never totally incapable of ruling, however, and he remained closely involved in govern-ment whenever in a condition to do so. His illness was sporadic and there was considerable reverence of and obedience to the king within the French political system. In England, the king himself was under threat because of a usurpation, but this was never the case in France. The conflicts were between members of the royal family. In many respects, they stemmed from a battle to control the Dauphin in anticipation of his accession to power. By the time of the battle of Agincourt, Dauphin Louis was eighteen years old and had gradually been developing his own 'middle way' between the various factions but, as with his father, it is difficult to know which decisions were his alone and which the result of the influence of others.[18] Although there developed a basic divide between the Burgundians on the one hand and the Orléanists (later called Armagnacs) on the other, men were not permanently committed to one side or the other, and many remained neutral, or perhaps, more accurately, committed to what they perceived as the royal interest.

John the Fearless, Duke of Burgundy had a special interest in Anglo-French relations, since his county of Flanders, inherited from his mother, was England's principal trading partner. His landed interests were extensive and included the duchy and county of Burgundy (the latter lying within the Empire), as well as the counties of Artois, Charolais, Nevers and Rethel. The possessions of his great-aunt, Duchess Joan of Brabant, were also due to fall to his family, although there was an understanding that her duchy would be given to one of his younger brothers. When Joan died in December 1406, Brabant therefore passed to Anthony (b.1384), whom we shall encounter again at Agincourt where he met his death alongside John's youngest brother, Philip (b.1391), who was given the counties of Nevers and Rethel. The tenure of such vast lands gave the duke and his brothers a strong political and military base as well as a capacity for independent action. Louis, Duke of Orléans (1372–1407) had much less in the way of lands but was closer in blood to the king. Although he had failed to prevent the Dauphin Louis marrying John the Fearless's daughter, Margaret, he was able to persuade Charles VI to have Isabella, the widow of Richard II, marry his eldest son, Charles, Count of Angoulême (b.1394), then aged nine, who, as Duke of Orléans after his father's death, was to be taken prisoner at Agincourt.[19]

The feud between Louis of Orléans and John of Burgundy was also encour-aged by their rivalries in the war against England. Many thought that the latter's interest in attacking English-held Guines and Calais was to annexe them to his

county of Artois. In November 1406 Duke Louis of Orléans was keen to inten-
sify the war at sea, appointing as admiral Clignet de Brabant (who fought at
Agincourt and survived), but at the very same time Burgundy was negotiating a
twelve-month trade treaty with England. Significantly, Duke John did not submit
for Charles VI's approval all of the terms agreed with Henry IV, despite being
obliged by his vassalage to do so.[20] The ability, and desire, of Duke John to pursue
his own interests became increasingly important in Anglo-French relations over
the next nine years and beyond. An eternal triangle was brought into existence
– England, France and Burgundy – with all of the intrigues and complications
such a situation generates.

Crisis point came in the summer of 1407. By this stage Orléans and the royal
government as a whole were suffering widespread criticism, since the combined
costs of the court and war had proved unsustainable. On 28 April Charles VI
announced a reduction in the number of councillors, to save salaries. The twenty-
six left in place included only two Burgundian sympathisers. Those targeted for
removal included three of Duke John's close supporters, one of whom was David,
Sire de Rambures, master of the crossbowmen, who fought at Agincourt. Duke
John decided on a drastic solution: the assassination of Louis. That he was not
brought to book for the murder shows how strong the king and other dukes
considered him to be. To avoid civil war, the king had no choice but to accept his
justification for the murder and to issue a pardon on 9 March 1408. He was also
persuaded to dismiss Clignet de Brabant who had tried to arrest Duke John for
the crime. Although the king later changed his mind and withdrew the pardon,
Duke John was able to use his considerable power base in Paris to install himself
in the capital by late November, strengthened by his victory in battle at Othée on
22 September against the rebels of Liège. This forced the royal court once more
into the need for a rapprochement. On 9 March 1409, in the cathedral of Chartres,
the duke was again formally pardoned by the king. Allegedly, he approached the
new Duke of Orléans, Charles (b.1394), and his brother, Philip, Count of Vertus
(b.1396), in tears, asking for their forgiveness, but they did not respond until the
king ordered them to do so.[21] The Duke of Burgundy was now in power, having
the king's maître d'hôtel, Jean de Montaigu, whom he suspected of working against
him, arrested and executed for alleged treason, and becoming sole guardian of the
Dauphin Louis. There were some key appointments of the duke's supporters into
the Dauphin's household, most notably David, Sire de Rambures, as councillor
and chamberlain.

Between 1407 and 1409 there had been further diplomatic exchanges, raising the possibility of Prince Henry marrying one of Charles's daughters, but
they had been conducted by the king's last surviving uncle, the Duke of Berry
(1340–1416), and they came to an end once Burgundy was in control of the government. Although the trade agreement with his county of Flanders came into
operation in June 1407 and saw a series of renewals up until 1419,[22] there were

signs that, once in control of the government, Duke John favoured a revival of French aggression towards England.[23] But in the eighteen months following the reconciliation at Chartres, the consensus in France broke down into civil war and both sides looked to the English for military assistance. As a result, in both 1411 and 1412 armies were sent, the first time to assist the Burgundians, the second the Armagnac/Orléanist group. These last years of Henry IV's reign are therefore extremely important in ushering in a new phase in Anglo-French relations and setting the scene for Henry V's aggressive line. By 1409 Henry IV was increasingly suffering from ill health. When he responded to parliament's demands in May 1410 to know the names of his councillors, it was Prince Henry who headed the list.[24] Also there was the king's half-brother, Henry, Bishop of Winchester (later Cardinal Beaufort), Thomas, Earl of Arundel (b.1381), one of the prince's closest friends who had served with him in Wales and was to die at the siege of Harfleur in 1415, and Henry, Lord Scrope (b.1373), the royal treasurer, who had also served the prince in Wales and who contracted to serve in 1415 but was executed for his role in the Southampton plot as the expedition prepared to depart. Shortly afterwards, Richard, Earl of Warwick (b.1382) was added to the list of councillors, another man who had served in Wales and who was to play a prominent role in the later conquest of Normandy, although he was not at Agincourt since he was designated to the defence of Calais.

This council appears to have remained in place until November 1411. Historians have therefore portrayed 1410–11 as the period of the prince's ascendancy during which 'he adopted an aggressive attitude towards France and Plantagenet claims there'.[25] At the parliament that met in the spring and summer of 1410, the issue of the maintenance of strong defences was uppermost. Sizeable sums were diverted to Wales, now mainly subdued although Glendower remained at large, as well as to Guienne and Calais. It was thought likely that Burgundy would attack the latter, prompting the appointment of Prince Henry as captain, although he never visited the Calais march, exercising control through deputies. These measures were not a new, prince-inspired policy but rather a standard response to French threats – threats which did not materialise because the French fell to fighting among themselves.

Although young Duke Charles of Orléans had little choice but to forgive his father's murderer at the ceremony in Chartres on 9 March 1409, it was unlikely that he would not, at a more conducive time, attempt to secure his revenge. This time came in the spring of 1410. On 15 April, the Dukes of Berry, Brittany and Orléans, along with the Counts of Alençon, Armagnac and Clermont, came to an alliance commonly known as the League of Gien after its place of sealing, which lies 60km to the east of Orléans.[26] A series of marriages was simultaneously arranged between the group of lords, the most important being that of Orléans to Bonne, daughter of Bernard, Count of Armagnac.[27] It was from this marital link that the anti-Burgundian group became known in due course as the

Armagnacs. The initial driving force behind this League was the Duke of Berry, who had decided that he could tolerate the ascendancy of Duke John no longer. The expressed aim of the League was 'to fight against those who were damaging the welfare and honour of the king and the kingdom'. Berry was the last surviving uncle of Charles VI, and Orléans was the king's nephew, but who were these other lords? It may be helpful to say a little more about them, since the majority feature at Agincourt. John, Count of Clermont (b.1381) was the eldest son of Louis, Duke of Bourbon and was to inherit the duchy at his father's death on 19 August 1410. He was taken prisoner at Agincourt alongside Orléans. John, Count of Alençon (b.1385) also held the county of Perche and was thus a leading landowner in southern Normandy. He was elevated to the status of duke on 1 January 1415 but met his death at Agincourt later in the year. John, Duke of Brittany (b.1389) had become duke at the age of ten. Ever since Edward III's support in a succession war, the Dukes of Brittany had close links with England. John's mother, Joan of Navarre, had married Henry IV in 1403 as part of the king's policy to find friends in Europe against France and to formalise international acceptance of his usurpation. In July 1407, a one-year truce for Anglo-Breton trade was sealed. It was renewed regularly, being extended in 1412 for a further ten years.[28] The duke responded to Charles VI's request for aid against the English in 1415, but had only reached Amiens by the time of the battle. His younger brother, Arthur, Count of Richemont (b.1393), led the Dauphin's troops and was taken prisoner. Bernard, Count of Armagnac (b.1367), whose lands bordered English-held Guienne, was defending the south in 1415, but was made constable after the death of d'Albret at Agincourt. Others subsequently associated with the League included Charles of Artois, Count of Eu (b.1394), grandson of the Duke of Berry. He was taken prisoner at the battle.

As soon as the League was formed it turned to raising troops, as did Burgundy once he knew of its existence. So many troops were being assembled that, according to the Religieux of Saint-Denis, the people thought that an English invasion was expected.[29] Being in control of the royal government, Duke John could easily portray the League as a revolt against the king. Charles VI therefore issued orders to ban it and to disband its armies. When the lords refused, the king went so far as to issue the arrière-ban on 28 August, which obliged all to act against the League. Towards the end of September Charles sent for the *oriflamme*, the sacred banner kept in Saint-Denis, and announced his intention to march to war himself.[30] On 1 November, the members of the League, with the exception of Brittany, renewed their oath, this time adding an explicit promise that they would each support the other against the Duke of Burgundy, and that none of them would come to an alliance with him without the consent of the others. Within a few days, however, peace was apparently established (the peace of Bicêtre). The lords had got cold feet when faced with confiscation of their lands. Differences of opinion had also emerged within the League. Berry made efforts to dissociate himself from the desire for retribution for the murder of Louis of Orléans, but Duke Charles was not prepared to accept this. On 30 January 1411 he took the law into his own hands, capturing John, Sire de Croy, chamberlain and councillor of the Duke of Burgundy, and even resorting to torture to ascertain his role in the assassination of Duke Louis. (De Croy was to die at the battle of Agincourt.) In March he wrote to the University of Paris requesting a formal condemnation of the justification put forward in March 1408 for the murder. Despite efforts of the king and Dauphin to prevent military action by both Orléans and Burgundy, it was too late. On 31 July 1411 Orléans sent his herald to Duke John with a letter of defiance, announcing that he would do all in his power to harm him.[31]

Duke John began to install his supporters into key military commands. The Count of Saint-Pol replaced d'Albret as constable. David, Sire de Rambures and Jacques de Longroy were appointed masters of the crossbowmen. On 3 October the royal council declared d'Albret, Orléans, Bourbon, Alençon and Armagnac to be rebels, thereby permitting subjects of the king to make war against them.[32] Berry was added to the list on 14 October. But it was Orléans who seized the military initiative, sending his troops to the frontier of the Duke of Burgundy's county of Artois. Orléans' men occupied Ham and harried the area, but the Burgundians took the place along with Roye and Nesle. (The last-named was threatened again by Henry V four years later.) The Orléanists also began to advance on Paris, easily taking Saint-Denis and the bridge at Saint-Cloud. But on 9 November, the Duke of Burgundy retook the latter. That he was able to do so was the result of military assistance from the English. In August 1411 the Duke of Burgundy approached Henry IV for an alliance 'by way of marriage between my lord the prince and the eldest daughter of the duke'. The English set a high price for any armed assistance they might give – reciprocal military aid in recovering lands and possessions in Guienne. If there was to be an alliance with Burgundy, then the duke would not be allowed to make an exclusion clause for the king of France.[33] In other words, the English wanted Duke John's full commitment to fight against his own sovereign in the English cause. There is no evidence, however, that any alliance was agreed on these terms.[34]

All we can prove is that troops under the Earl of Arundel were sent to join the Duke of Burgundy at Arras on 3 October. The status of this English army remains unclear. There are indications that Henry IV had intended leading troops himself to France, possibly for an invasion of Guienne. In mid-August he had ordered all those holding royal annuities to muster in London on 23 September, a tactic of recruitment repeated by Henry V in 1415.[35] But in early September the king (or else Prince Henry on his behalf) seems to have changed his mind, presumably because Duke John had not been prepared to agree to the terms the English wanted.[36] The protection for the Earl of Arundel, dated 28 October 1411, speaks of his going to Picardy in the *retinencia* (retinue) of the Prince of Wales.[37] This has led historians to conclude that this was a private expedition sponsored by

the prince against his father's will, although there is no evidence that Henry IV
was opposed to the sending of troops to Burgundy. Arundel's army was not contracted in the customary fashion nor did it receive pay in England, so it should
be seen as simply a mercenary force. Yet an episode in Monstrelet suggests that it
was perceived in France as representative of English official policy. It claims that
an English knight called Clifford, who had come from Bordeaux with 100 men-
at-arms and 200 archers to serve the Duke of Orléans, asked for leave to depart
when he heard that King Henry had sent Arundel with an army, since he was sure
that the English king would take a dim view of him staying in Orléans' service.
The duke granted his wish, but on condition that Clifford did not take up arms
against him. Clifford accepted this and returned to England.[38]

The numbers we have for Arundel's force are derived solely from chronicles.
According to the Religieux of Saint-Denis, the deal was that the English should
send 800 men-at-arms and 1,000 archers, but that in practice 600 men-at-arms
and 2,000 archers were sent. Monstrelet suggests rather that the English troops
numbered 1,200, 'mounted and foot, all well equipped'.[39] Chroniclers mention
the presence of Sir William Bardolf, lieutenant at Calais, with 300 men from the
garrison, Sir Francis Court, Sir Robert Umfraville, Gilbert Umfraville, Sir John
Grey, Sir John Oldcastle, John Phelip and William Porter, as well as the Earls of
Pembroke and Kent,[40] although neither title was held at this date. What is most
fascinating is that those fighting alongside English troops at Saint-Cloud were
Burgundy's youngest brother, the Count of Nevers, Jacques de Heilly, and many
others from Picardy and elsewhere in northern and eastern France, men whom
they were to fight against at Agincourt. Perhaps the most famous of these was
Jean le Meingre, Marshal Boucicaut (b. 1366), appointed marshal in 1391, who had
been captured by the Turks at the battle of Nicopolis in 1396 and had subsequently
been sent to assist the French allies of Genoa. He had only returned to France
in February 1411. He was to be captured at Agincourt.[41] English troops subsequently assisted in the sieges of Etampes and Dourdan, towns held by the Duke
of Berry. This was part of a major military offensive in the last months of 1411 by
the Burgundian-controlled royal government, which succeeded in driving the
Armagnacs out of the Paris region. At Etampes, Arundel and his men may even
have come across the Dauphin Louis for whom this was a first taste of military
activity, at a siege that deployed the same offensive techniques as Henry V used at
Harfleur – cannon bombardment, mining, burning of structures to hasten their
collapse.[42] How long the English soldiers remained in French service is unclear.
They seem to have returned to Paris in late December, where they received their
pay. While most probably returned to England via Calais in the New Year, the
Umfravilles may have remained in the pay of Burgundy for some time longer.[43]

Some important points need to be made about their service in the light of
supposed English policy and, in particular, of the 'pro-Burgundian' stance of
Prince Henry. Since the Duke of Burgundy was in control of the French royal

government, the English had been fighting *for* Charles VI against Armagnac rebels. This makes it impossible that a deal had been struck with Burgundy along the lines of instructions given to the English envoys in September. Even if the duke had agreed secretly to assist the English in recovering their lands in Guienne, there is no indication that he did anything to implement such a promise. If the English had agreed to send troops in the hope of gaining some advantage in their own quarrel with France, they had both deluded themselves and been tricked by the Duke of Burgundy. By extension, if this policy had been undertaken at the behest of the prince as chief councillor, then it was a failure. The English had not succeeded in exploiting French divisions as they had hoped. It is difficult to know what place the prince had in government after November 1411. The council set up in May 1410 was disbanded at that point, as the king was enjoying a better state of health.

Burgundian envoys were again in England between 1 February and 4 March 1412, pursuing the matter of the marriage and meeting both the king and the prince. In late January 1412, Berry, Bourbon, Orléans and Alencon also decided to approach the English for aid. Their strategy was 'to outbid the duke of Burgundy'.[44] The offers their envoys brought to Henry IV were very generous.[45] In return for a promise that he would not enter into any alliance with Burgundy but would send them 1,000 men-at-arms and 3,000 archers to serve at their expense, they recognised the whole duchy of Guienne as his and offered to assist him in its recovery and in his 'just quarrels' more generally. They accompanied this with offers of marriage between his sons and their female relatives. Shortly afterwards, the Count of Armagnac and the Sire d'Albret added their consent to these offers. King Henry delayed a response to the Armagnac lords while a Burgundian marriage was still under consideration, but on 18 May he ratified their offers in the treaty of London. His decision may have been based on a rumour that the Duke of Burgundy planned to move against the English in Guienne once he had smashed the Armagnacs. On the same day, by the treaty of Bourges, the Dukes of Berry, Orléans and Bourbon and the Count of Alençon gave their formal adherence to the terms on behalf of themselves and their allies. Some of their own lands were the very territories to be transferred to the English under the terms of the Great Peace. Berry therefore agreed to pay homage for the county of Poitou and Orléans for Angoulême, with the proviso that at their death these areas would revert to Henry. In return, Henry promised to send the 4,000-strong army.[46]

The Armagnac lords had acted totally *ultra vires*. They had no royal authority to give Henry the territories or the tenurial conditions promised. Furthermore, the effecting of the treaty depended on their success in the war against Burgundy but, as we have seen, that war, which was now also Henry's, was against the French king. This was therefore a defining moment in English foreign policy. When Charles VI heard of the offer that the Armagnac lords had made to Henry, he immediately ordered a tax levy of 600,000 francs to make war on them in person. This was probably his own decision, since their independent approach in foreign policy struck at the very heart of his royal authority. It was also intended that the Dauphin should join the king in this war. It was he who went to Saint-Denis to collect the *oriflamme*.[47] Towards the end of May the French royal army crossed the Loire and laid siege to Berry's town of Fontenay. By 11 June, the duke's principal seat at Bourges was surrounded.

Since it was Henry IV's initial intention to lead the English army to France, this could have been a war between kings as in 1415. The king again ordered those who held royal annuities to assemble in London by the middle of the next month. He also agreed that Prince Henry should join him with his own company.[48] But the king subsequently decided not to cross in person, presumably due to his failing health. As for the prince, he was offended by the small size of the retinue assigned to him. This is evidenced in a letter which he wrote to his father on 17 June 1412.[49] Here Prince Henry claimed that although arrangements had been made to discuss the problem, while he was making his way to Coventry, 'certain sons of iniquity… desiring, with something of the guile of the serpent, to disturb the line of succession', had suggested to the king that his eldest son had tried to obstruct the expedition to Guienne and was also plotting to depose his father. The prince was adamant that none of this was true. By this time, however, his eldest brother, Prince Thomas (b.1389), had been contracted to lead the expedition, entering into his indenture on 8 June.

In contrast with the troops sent under Arundel in 1411, the army sent to assist the Armagnacs in 1412 was a properly indented and paid royal army. The period of service was set at five months, with the Exchequer issuing pay at the outset for the first two months, but in the anticipation that 'the lords of France' would pay wages thenceforward. Prince Thomas's company, set at 500 men-at-arms and 1,500 archers, was to constitute half of the army. The king's half-brother, Thomas Beaufort (b.1377), was to bring 240 men-at-arms and 700 archers, with his cousin, Edward, Duke of York, raising 260 men-at-arms and 800 archers, and Sir John Cornwall (the king's brother-in-law) bringing 90 men-at-arms and 270 archers. On 5 July, Beaufort was created Earl of Dorset, with Prince Thomas being made Duke of Clarence and Earl of Aumale four days later. These elevations parallel the peerages made by Edward III in 1337 as war with France loomed. Among those engaged to serve within the three main companies were Richard (later Earl of Cambridge), younger brother of the Duke of York, Richard de Vere, Earl of Oxford, James Butler, Earl of Ormond, Thomas Montague, Earl of Salisbury, Robert, Lord Willoughby, and a number of prominent knights.[50] All these men save Butler were to serve in 1415.

The main English offensive was preceded by a sea raid from Calais to burn Berck and a land expedition from Guines to take Balinghem near Ardres, a useful conquest. As a result the Count of Saint-Pol mounted a counter-attack on Guines, but was driven back to Boulogne.[51] These preliminaries deluded the French into thinking that Clarence would land in Picardy.[52] In reality, an embarkation from Southampton and a landing at St-Vaast-la-Hougue on the tip of the Cotentin (Edward III's landing place in 1346) had been chosen, in order to combine a short sea crossing with ease of access to the defence of the Armagnac lands. The army landed on 10 August. Chronicles suggest that it ravaged its way through Normandy into Maine and Anjou. By 16 September, it was at Blois. Henry IV had already intended that Clarence should continue to Guienne once his services to the Armagnacs had been fulfilled. The wage rates for the first two months were therefore those accustomed for use in Guienne, and Clarence had been appointed lieutenant of the duchy on 11 July – an unsurprising decision, given the offers of the Armagnac lords to allow the restoration of the duchy in full sovereignty.

By the time Clarence landed, however, the lords had made peace with the king and with Burgundy. The volte-face had been led by the Duke of Berry, who delivered the keys of Bourges to the king on 15 July, and the Dauphin seems to have played an important role in mediation between the parties.[53] At a great assembly held at Auxerre on 22 August, all (save Alençon who gave his adherence in November) agreed to abide by the terms of the Peace of Chartres of March 1409 and to forsake any further requests to punish those responsible for the death of Louis of Orléans. In addition they were to renounce all alliances they had made with each other or with England, and to swear to assist Charles VI against the king of England or any other English person.[54] The treaty of Auxerre was also binding on the Duke of Burgundy. Duke John put in writing his renunciation of any alliance that he might have with the sons or allies of Henry IV, or with King Henry himself. This was probably a precautionary move engineered by the king and Dauphin in order to allay Armagnac suspicions. Burgundy had already claimed orally that he had no alliance with the English. The truth of this seems to be confirmed by a letter written around this time by Clarence, which expressed surprise at the duke's gesture since 'there was no alliance between Henry IV and Burgundy'.[55]

Clarence made this remark in a letter which he despatched to the Armagnac dukes from a location close to Blois on 16 September. He was displeased at the renunciation of their earlier promises, not least as his army now had no guarantee of pay for an extended stay in France. Not surprisingly, he took to attacking the lands of the Dukes of Orléans and of Berry. There was now a real threat of full war between England and France. On 8 October Charles VI ordered his vassals to Chartres to make war on the English, but on 14 November, Clarence was bought off by an agreement struck at Buzançais. He undertook to withdraw by 1 January without causing any further devastation. The Armagnac lords were to pay him 150,000 *écus* by Christmas, but as they could not raise the sum quickly enough, the obligation was raised to a total of 210,000 *écus* but with only 75,000 to be paid immediately and securities to be given for the rest. The sum paid and due was

allocated in proportion to each of the English commanders. This was an embarrassing and costly climb-down for the French. Jewels and *objets d'art* were given
in lieu of part of the first instalment, including some valuable religious artefacts
from the Duke of Berry's inestimable collection. As guarantee for payment of
the rest, seven hostages were given, including the youngest brother of the Duke
of Orléans, John, Count of Angoulême, only eight years old at this point, who
remained in England until 1445. It was in relation to the handover of the young
count that Clarence and Orléans came to what has been described as a brother-
hood-in-arms agreement on 14 November, whereby Clarence undertook to be
'a true and good kinsman, brother, companion in arms and friend' to Orléans and
to 'serve, aid, console and comfort him'.[56] This agreement could not override any
duty to fight in an English royal army against Orléans, of course. Clarence was to
lead the largest retinue in the army of 1415, although he was invalided home from
Harfleur and therefore was not at Agincourt.

On 16 November 1412 Charles VI issued a safe conduct to Clarence, guaranteeing immunity from attack on his march to Bordeaux. The French remained
alarmed at the prospect of renewed military action by the duke on the frontiers of English-held Guienne in the spring.[57] Clarence did indeed conduct some
pillaging raids into Saintonge but was constantly short of supplies and money,
despite some materials being sent from England. He appealed to the Estates to
vote a levy to support his army, which he claimed was there for the protection of
Guienne, and on 13 February he came to an arrangement whereby he agreed to
lend Bernard, Count of Armagnac and Charles d'Albret, now once again constable
of France, troops for their attack on the Count of Foix,[58] but before long he heard
of his father's death, and set out from Bordeaux to England on 6 April.

On the face of it, Henry IV and his sons had been too easily seduced by the
false promises made by both parties in the French civil war. The Peace of Auxerre
now formally united the French princes in an anti-English stance, but nobody
could tell what might happen in the future, since Orléans had still not achieved
the revenge he desired for his father's murder and had been forced to accept
terms by the defection of the Duke of Berry. Henry IV and his sons, as well as the
troops sent in 1411 and 1412, must have been all too well aware of the gravity of
the Armagnac/Burgundian feud. After all, the Armagnac princes had been desperate enough to offer restoration of the Great Peace, and John the Fearless had
entertained discussion on military assistance in a war against Charles VI, even if
nothing had materialised. As a result, a new era of English involvement in France
had begun. While Henry IV was totally on the defensive in the earlier parts of his
reign, by the time of his death England had already moved on to the offensive.

Prince Henry had been intimately involved in this change of direction, since
he had been in control of the council when negotiations were entered into with
Burgundy. Henry IV was not hostile to making deals with Duke John on the
right terms, but the Armagnacs made what seemed to him a better offer. This

placed the prince in an embarrassing position, since he was forced to write to the Duke of Burgundy on 22 and 31 May 1412 admitting that he had offered help in the previous year but that he had now to accept his father's decision to support the Armagnacs.[59] The prince therefore lost face abroad and also at home, since his father had chosen his brother to lead the campaign. This led to a serious breach between father and son. In retrospect, Henry IV's decision was wise, since the king died while the campaign was still underway, but Prince Henry could not have anticipated this.

By 1412 he was desperate to make his mark. His career in Wales had not been particularly successful. The king had been reluctant to give him his head and had only been forced to do so because of conflicting demands on his own time. The Welsh had outwitted the English forces on many occasions and the war had dragged on for much longer than it should have done. One reason for this was Prince Henry's responsibility for a serious military failure at the siege of Aberystwyth in the late summer of 1407. The king had intended to conduct the siege in person and had ordered the prince to join him, but later gave the prince full command in what was intended to be not only a coup de grâce against Glendower but also a coup de théâtre.[60] Large quantities of siege engines, cannons, arrows and gunpowder were brought in from Bristol and Haverfordwest. This was the first time the prince had been involved in a major siege and he had with him many of his associates including York, Warwick, Lords Furnivale and Carew, and Sir John Oldcastle. On 17 September 1407 Prince Henry agreed to one of the strangest compositions for surrender ever seen. He agreed to abandon the siege and let the defenders have free entry and exit for more than a month, in return for arranging that battle might be given by the king or his lieutenant against Glendower between 24 October and 1 November. If no battle ensued then the defenders would surrender the place without the need to give hostages. This was clemency at its most extreme. For the oath-taking ceremony to this treaty of composition, the prince had relics brought to the siege by Richard Courtenay. The latter was a close friend of the prince, and was elevated to the bishopric of Norwich shortly after Henry became king. The king entrusted him with negotiations with the French in 1414 and 1415 and with the distribution of royal jewels to fund the 1415 campaign. Courtenay accompanied the expedition but died at the siege of Harfleur on 13 September.

In making the composition at Aberystwyth, Prince Henry was moved by his devotion to St John of Bridlington and a desire to avoid the shedding of human blood. That was why he was prepared to lift the siege conditions in anticipation of a showdown with Glendower. He hoped to be the one to bring Glendower to battle and to win a glorious victory but his decision turned out to be a ghastly mistake. No royal army was arranged. As a result Glendower was able to enter Aberystwyth at the beginning of November and to expel those who had made the agreement with Prince Henry. Aberystwyth was not taken until September of the following year, and by others, not the prince. From 1408 onwards the prince continued in nominal command in Wales but was rarely present in person. His role in government was not extensive until May 1410. Although he was appointed Warden of the Cinque Ports and constable of Dover on 28 February 1409 and of Calais in March 1410, these were titular appointments exercised through lieutenants. In the last year of Henry IV's reign he was in the political wilderness.[61] His letter of 17 June 1412 effectively accused the king of listening to those who accused the prince of undermining royal policy and of plotting even to depose his father. This suggests that he had powerful enemies at court, likely including Thomas Arundel, Archbishop of Canterbury and royal chancellor. In September there were accusations that Prince Henry had not distributed to his Calais garrison all the sums he had received for their pay. After examination of the accounts in mid-October, these charges were found to be unsubstantiated, but they add to the evidence that the prince was neither trusted nor popular among his father's advisers.[62]

The impression one gets is that Prince Henry was a 'rebel without a cause'. The stories of a misspent youth have never been proven, but nor have they been disproved. A lack of application may therefore be a further factor contributing to his reputation towards the end of his father's reign. From his own perspective, he had not been given the role he felt was rightly his. As Prince of Wales he had military experience, but this consisted of small-scale, inconclusive campaigns against guerrillas, the uncertainty of garrisoning, and the constant strain of underfunding. He had not been allowed to flex his muscles against the French, a proper enemy, and he had lost face at home and abroad in his diplomatic and military plans. Furthermore, he had come to adulthood in an atmosphere of fear and insecurity. At the battle of Shrewsbury in 1403, he had fought against men who had been his friends and mentors. Even in 1412 he suspected men of plotting to prevent his inheritance of the crown. These experiences coloured his own approach to kingship and fanned his ambitions to prove himself and to prove his critics wrong. He was desperate for fame and success and would stop at nothing to achieve it.

2

Henry V and the Reopening of War, March 1413–August 1415

The coronation of Henry V as king of England took place at Westminster Abbey on Sunday 9 April 1413. He was anointed with special oil which, according to tradition, the Virgin had given to Thomas Becket, with a promise that all kings blessed by it would recover the lands lost by their predecessors, including Guienne and Normandy. For the last two years of his reign Richard II had carried this oil in an eagle-shaped container hung around his neck. The same oil had been used at the coronation of Henry IV.[1] Like them, Henry V also called himself king of France. With hindsight we know that he came close to making this title a reality, being recognised by Charles VI as his heir in 1420. His invasion in 1415 was the largest since the Great Peace of 1360, and the first time since that date that an English king had set foot in France.

During the first year of the new reign there was a dramatic turn in French politics. Duke John of Burgundy fell from grace as a result of his implication in the Cabochien revolt of the summer of 1413. By the middle of February 1414 he had been declared a traitor, and from April to September of that year, Charles VI and the Dauphin, with the aid of the Armagnac lords, conducted a full-scale war against him in Picardy and Artois. There is every reason to suppose that Henry V's interest in France was encouraged by its internal divisions but we must also look to his own desire to prove himself. Henry took his kingly duties seriously, even obsessively. The picture that Shakespeare painted of a change in demeanour at his accession has a root in reality. Richard Courtenay, a close friend who was made Bishop of Norwich soon after the accession, told a Frenchman early in 1415 that he did not believe that Henry had sexual relations with any woman after he became king.[2] It was not that Henry 'found God' but that he considered God integral to the way he wished to rule. Take, for example, the reburial of Richard II at Westminster Abbey on 4 December 1413 and, in 1415, the foundation of the Carthusian house of Jesus of Bethlehem at Sheen and the double monastery of St Saviour and St Brigit of Syon. These fulfilled promises made by Henry IV to the Pope to expiate the murders of Richard and of Archbishop Scrope. The new king responded swiftly and co-operatively to the English Church's desire to repress heresy: within a few months of his accession he gave permission for the heresy trial of Sir John Oldcastle, despite the latter's previously close connections during the Welsh wars.

Henry's religiosity went hand in hand with his policies at home and abroad. This is well expressed in the *Gesta*, although the author was obviously influenced by the memory of Agincourt, the victory that had revealed God's approval of the king in a way and to an extent that no other event could: 'The king applied his mind with all devotion to encompass what could promoted the honour of God, the extension of the church, the deliverance of his country, and the peace and tranquillity of kingdoms, and especially the peace and tranquillity of the two kingdoms of England and France.'[3] A further feature of the early years of the reign was Henry's commitment to improving law and order.[4] Overall, there is a strong impression that he wanted his reign to be a new beginning. He wanted to outdo his father in all respects and to prove the detractors of 1412 wrong.

This ambition is revealed by a desire to cut an important figure on the European stage. Henry's interest in the Council of Constance, then attempting to solve the problem of the papal schism, demonstrates this. There was a flurry of diplo-matic interactions with other European states, often related to a desire to isolate the French. That was certainly the point of his truce with the Duke of Brittany, which was put in place from 3 January 1414 for ten years. Henry immediately exploited this to proclaim the duke his ally. This may have played a role in the latter's uncertainty over participation in French resistance to the English inva-sion in 1415.[5] Henry moved negotiations with the French themselves on to a new level. While his father had simply responded to French approaches, Henry V made the running himself, sending two great embassies to France, the first since the early 1390s. Henry wanted to prove himself by being the king who solved once and for all the problem of English claims in France and who brought lasting peace. In this context it is interesting to note that Hoccleve's *Regimen of Princes*, which the poet dedicated to the prince in 1412, urged that the rulers of England and France should work for peace to avoid the shedding of Christian blood and to make possible a war against the enemies of the faith. The king's diplomatic endeavours focused on this end, employing a strongly religious tone. His invasion of 1415 was also based on the premise that this was 'war to end war'. It too was justified in crusading terms, as well as by invocation of the laws of Deuteronomy, which gave a lord rights to act with violence against his supposed rebels.[6]

Henry was motivated not only by these personal ambitions and by his high regard for kingship, but also by insecurity. There were lingering anxieties over the Lancastrian title to the throne and fears of plots and risings. According to the *Religieux*, it was rumoured in France that some Englishmen were saying shortly after the accession that the crown should belong to the Earl of March and not Henry.[7] At a council meeting on 29 June 1413 it was recommended that the king should spend the summer close to London, so that news of all areas could easily be reported to him and so that he could more easily raise loans and make provision for the defence of the realm.[8] Henry was right to be fearful. Historians have tended to downplay the significance of Oldcastle's rebellion of January 1414 and of the Southampton plot of July 1415. Yet both aimed to kill the king and both were led by erstwhile friends. It is not surprising that Henry should act harshly against the Southampton plotters, since their actions threatened his invasion of France, but his action against his friend Henry, Lord Scrope, whose offence was not involvement in the plot but the failure to reveal it to the king, was verging on arbitrary rule. The headstrong nature of the prince became, in the king, arrogance and obsession with royal prerogatives.

The campaign of 1415 was intended as an expression of his kingship, just as Henry IV's campaign against the Scots had been in 1400. We cannot say, however, that Henry V had committed himself to a great military endeavour against the French from the moment of his accession. As with his father, there were ample distractions closer to home. Fears of Scottish hostilities loomed large again, fanned by fears of French aid. On 2 April 1413 the Earl of Douglas came to a deal with the Duke of Burgundy, a reminder that Duke John was not naturally pro-English. Indeed, when he had been in control of the French government in 1409 he had pursued a blatantly aggressive line, as he now seemed to be doing in the wake of Henry V's accession. In return for Scottish troops being despatched to Artois and Flanders, presumably for use against Calais, the duke was to send 300 soldiers to Scotland.[9]

With regard to France, two matters needed the king's early attention: the governance of Guienne and the renewal of the truces. Although Clarence had returned home as soon as he heard of his father's death, Thomas, Earl of Dorset had stayed behind in the English duchy. Henry soon appointed him lieutenant of Guienne, empowering him to take oaths of the inhabitants on behalf of the new king and allowing him pay for a force of 240 men-at-arms and 1,000 archers.[10] Henry made no move to unpick the agreement that Clarence had struck at Buzançais nor, at this stage, to resurrect claims based on the territorial offers that the Armagnac lords had made in 1412, although this was not to prevent him exploiting the memory of the treaty of Bourges as part of justification for invasion in 1415. The campaign that Dorset was ordered to conduct into Saintonge continued the style of Clarence's actions into the Angoumois. Both had the same objective – to attack territory held by the perfidious Armagnacs. This campaign was the only military activity undertaken against the French by Henry until the invasion of 1415 and is therefore worth a few comments. The earl first advanced towards the north-east, taking Ribérac and Aubeterre on the Dronne, before moving north-west to Montandre and Barbezieux-Saint-Hillaire in the Angoumois. Entering Saintonge, he crossed the Charente, taking Taillebourg, just to the north of Saintes, and Soubise, at the mouth of the river, before threatening Rochefort. Up to this point he had avoided large places, taking instead small fortifications which controlled river crossings and estuaries. The French responded by sending guns, arrows and pavises from Paris to fortify Saint-Jean-d'Angely (just as artillery was sent to Harfleur as the English prepared to lay siege), as well as detailing a company under Jacques, Sire de Heilly, captain of Talmont in Saintonge, whom we shall meet again at Agincourt. A letter which Heilly wrote at Parthenay on 22 July spoke of 'smashing the English and chasing them out of the country',[11] but the English intercepted his company in late July, killing many and taking important prisoners to Bordeaux. For several months, the English controlled the entrance to the Charente and harried shipping off La Rochelle.

In the autumn the Duke of Bourbon came south with an army of 1,300 men-at-arms and 800 archers. He recovered Soubise on 22 November 1413, then being held by around 500-600 English and Gascon troops. Bourbon went on to retake Taillebourg and to attack English garrisons on the Dronne. It does not seem that the English made any effort to rescue these places or to launch any attacks outside their existing territories, but nor did the French follow up their successes. Bourbon was appointed on 1 December captain-general of Languedoc, and a few weeks later captain-general of Guienne beyond the Dordogne, a title that implied that the French were intending to strike at the heartlands of English control in the spring of 1414. This never happened, since a twelve-month truce was agreed from 2 February.[12] Dorset's efforts had been constantly limited by shortage of pay for his troops. Immediately after the truce, he toured Guienne to persuade communities to pay the hearth tax which had been granted to Clarence. We might ponder whether the experience of Dorset's brief war served to discourage Henry from pursuing war in this theatre in 1415. Guienne had too many frontiers. This was both an advantage, in that it made it difficult for the French to 'chase the English out of the country', and a disadvantage, since it proved difficult to maintain isolated conquests made outside the area of traditional English control around Bordeaux and Bayonne.

Henry V had inherited the campaign in Guienne from his father. He had also inherited a system of short truces with the French but these would need to be renewed at the change of ruler.[13] The record of the council of 29 June 1413 shows that Henry Chichele, Bishop of St David's, soon to be elevated to the Canterbury archbishopric following the death of Archbishop Arundel, prepared a 'remembrance' for the king. The precise content of this is not known, but on 14 July various commissions for negotiations with France were issued, including towards a truce. The envoys included Chichele, Warwick and Lord Scrope,[14] who were also given power to treat with the Duke of Burgundy and to redress infractions of the truce. Wylie assumed that the negotiations with Burgundy were separate from those with the king of France.[15] Since the same envoys were charged with both and since, at the time of their appointment, Burgundy was in control of the French royal government, it is unlikely that Henry intended a

separate agreement with Duke John other than confirmation of the trade truce
concerning Flanders. By the time the English envoys arrived on the continent,
however, Burgundy was no longer in control of the government, so that separate
meetings with his representatives occurred in Bruges and Lille in September
and October 1413. A marriage between Henry and one of the duke's daughters
was discussed, although Duke John denied this to Charles VI's envoys. The duke
was still at this stage hoping to redeem his position at the French court. Full
negotiations between Burgundy and England did not occur until the spring of
1414, following the complete breakdown of relations between the duke and the
French king.

English envoys began their perorations before the French king's representatives
with mention of the English claim to the French throne and English rights by
the Great Peace. Henry required this diplomatic posturing in order to emphasise that as a new king he had no intention of casting aside the long-standing
quarrels of the past. Even so, at this stage his desire was for a renewal of the truce.
On 25 September, that for Picardy and Western Flanders was extended until
1 June 1414.[16] On 16 October, a general truce was agreed but only until Easter.[17]
These short truces were intended to offer opportunity for fuller negotiation. As
a result, on 8 October safe conducts were given for French envoys, including the
constable of France, Charles d'Albret, to come to England. Their negotiations with
the Bishop of Durham and the Earl of Warwick led to agreement on 24 January
1414 to a new truce from 2 February, for one year.[18] This was a marked difference
from the time of Henry IV, since this one truce covered all areas simultaneously.
This was a diplomatic triumph for Henry.[19] By this stage, the now Armagnac-
dominated French court was fearful that the Duke of Burgundy was planning to
restore his position by military force and that he would seek an English alliance to
help him. As a result, they were also willing to continue negotiations of a broader
nature once the truce was in place. A further set of English envoys, led by Scrope,
was empowered on 28 January to treat for peace with France. The focus of this
was to be a marriage between Henry and Charles VI's daughter, Catherine. On
the same day Henry promised that until 1 May he would not contract marriage
with anyone else and gave his ambassadors, who arrived in Paris in early March,
power to extend this period.[20]

Contacts between the French and English courts were facilitated by the visits
of Edward, Duke of York to settle his financial claims arising out of the Buzançais
agreement with the Armagancs. According to the Religieux:

> as it was known that he had come to seek a partner for his master among the
> princesses of France, they let him see Lady Catherine, daughter of the king,
> then aged 13, dressed in a robe of cloth of gold and silk, studded with precious
> stones and jewels and followed by a glittering escort of ladies, so that he could
> give a favourable report on her beauty, grace, and good demeanour.[21]

This was in August 1413. By the time of York's visit, the Duke of Burgundy had fled Paris. Many thought that Henry had sent his cousin to ascertain the impact of the divisions in the government,[22] and there may be some truth in this. Although York had no official commission to negotiate a marriage, his impressions of Catherine, and even more of French enthusiasm for the marriage, no doubt influenced Henry further. Although there were diplomatic flirtations with other European powers for the king's bride, marriage to Princess Catherine remained a central tenet of Henry's diplomacy throughout these years and beyond. He was undoubtedly the most eligible bachelor in Europe. As king, the need to marry was firmly in his mind. He was probably influenced by remembrance of Richard II's marriage to Isabella in 1396 as part of a greater diplomatic plan to solve Anglo-French relations and as a way of securing useful funds through a dowry. From the perspective of the French court, negotiations for an English marriage were worth fostering, in the hope that they would serve to pre-empt any approach that the Duke of Burgundy might make to Henry to negotiate a marriage with his own daughter, also called Catherine.[23]

The French factions had ostensibly been reconciled by the Peace of Auxerre of 22 August 1412, but new problems had arisen over the following year. Orléans still harboured desire for revenge against Burgundy for the murder of his father, and the Dauphin was increasingly keen to break free of Duke John's control. The crown was faced with major financial difficulties as a result of the campaign against the Armagnac lords, and had to call an Estates General in late January 1413. This led to demands for reform, which Burgundy encouraged with the support of his Parisian allies, especially the butchers' guild known as the Cabochiens, from the name of their leader, Simon Caboche. When the Dauphin attempted to reduce the duke's influence by appointing Pierre des Essarts as *prévôt* of Paris in late April 1413, the Cabochiens rioted and seized members of Louis's entourage. This may have been stage-managed by Duke John so that he could then appear as the saviour of the day and remove all those he mistrusted within the Dauphin's company. As with many 'popular' rebellions, however, the Cabochiens went too far, even forcing the king, when he attended Notre Dame on 18 May to give thanks for his recovery to health, to wear the white hood which was a symbol of their cause. Eight days later, Charles announced wide-ranging ordinances for reform of government and royal revenues, commonly known as the Cabochien Ordinance.[24] Many of these were sensible, but the cause of reform was not assisted by the growing violence of the Cabochiens. This included the public beheading of the corpse of the Dauphin's chamberlain, who had allegedly committed suicide in prison by hitting his head repeatedly with a wine jug.[25] The Cabochiens were also keen to continue the war against the English in Guienne – a significant insight into the views on the matter held outside the court – and so ordered heavy taxation to be levied on the wealthiest citizens of Paris and on the University.

Burgundy began to lose control of the Cabochiens. The king and Dauphin appealed to the Armagnac lords for assistance. Seven hundred men were sent to Paris under Clignet de Brabant and Louis de Bosredon. At Pontoise the princes of the blood swore mutual loyalty and promised to refrain from acts of war against each other.[26] The Cabochien revolt was put down on 4 August but Burgundy now thought that the Dauphin was planning his arrest. Thus he fled from Paris on 23 August. Eight days later, the Duke of Orléans and his brother, the Count of Vertus, along with the Duke of Bourbon and the Count of Alençon, made a triumphal entry to Paris. It was only a matter of time before they sought vengeance. Despite the pleas for unity that Jean Gerson of the University of Paris made in a sermon to the court on 4 September, the purge of Burgundian office holders began. Significantly, Gerson had pleaded that a good treaty should be made with England and that no one should make alliance with his country's enemies without the king's permission.[27] The danger of possible English exploitation of French divisions was all too apparent.

Over the winter, suspicions of Burgundy's intentions mounted but divisions also began to appear within the other royal dukes. Monstrelet speaks of a dispute between the Dukes of Orléans and Brittany over precedence. The Count of Alençon charged the latter with cowardice, claiming that 'if he had a lion in his heart it must be only the size of a baby'.[28] This led to the Duke of Brittany leaving the court, never to return, although his brother, Arthur, Count of Richemont, remained with the Dauphin as one of his leading retainers. Equally significant was the deterioration in relations between the Dauphin and the Duke of Orléans. Orléans was determined to seek vengeance for his father's murder, but the Dauphin was keener on reconciliation as the way to peace and was increasingly feeling that he had simply replaced Burgundian tutelage with that of the Armagnac lords. It is possible that at the end of the year he wrote to Burgundy inviting him to come to his rescue.[29] In January 1414 Duke John began to march to Paris, much to the alarm of the Armagnacs and of the queen, who feared that he would once more try to control the Dauphin and the government, since at this time Charles VI's state of health was erratic. On 8 February Isabeau presided over a council which proclaimed the arrière-ban, calling men to the defence of Paris. Two days later, the Duke of Burgundy was declared a rebel who was not to be assisted.[30] As the gates of the city remained closed to him, he had little choice but to retreat. On 17 February he was formally banished from the kingdom as a false traitor and murderer, as were his followers. All their possessions were declared confiscate. On the same day, Duke John's justification for the murder of Louis of Orléans was condemned by the Bishop of Paris. The text was publicly burned outside Notre Dame on 25 February.[31]

The result was civil war in France, a mirror image of that of 1412. On that occasion the king, with the support of the Duke of Burgundy, had led an army against the Armagnacs. Now, in the spring of 1414, preparations were made for

a royal campaign against Burgundy in which the Armagnacs fought alongside
the king. On 2 April Charles VI took the *oriflamme* at Saint-Denis and handed
it to Guillaume Martel, whom he had appointed two weeks earlier as its keeper,
in place of the recently deceased Lord of Aumont. Martel, Lord of Bacqueville-
en-Caux, was over sixty, and was probably the same man who had controlled
the king in his first outbreak of mental difficulty in 1392. It was to him that the
oriflamme was again entrusted in the face of Henry V's invasion in 1415, and he
died at Agincourt.[32] The Dauphin was retained on 31 March as commander of
3,000 men-at-arms and 1,500 archers, who were to be placed under the control
of Arthur, Count of Richemont, as his marshal.[33] The Duke of Orléans and other
Armagnac lords joined with the king's forces to destroy Burgundy once and for
all. A total army size of 10,000 men-at-arms and 4,500 archers was aimed for.[34]

The chronicle of the Religieux of Saint-Denis provides us with a full eyewitness
account of the royal campaign. From Senlis the army moved to the Burgundian-
controlled city of Compiègne, which the constable, d'Albret, had already tried
but failed to take.[35] After its submission on 7 May, the royal army then moved on
to Soissons. Chroniclers tell us that the captain of English troops serving in the
Burgundian garrison connived with English members of the royal host to open
one of the gates, thereby letting the men of the Count of Armagnac into the town.
The town surrendered on 21 May but suffered an exceptionally violent sacking,
in which prisoners were slaughtered, nuns raped, and townspeople drowned as
they tried to escape. Allegedly, English mercenaries in the Burgundian garrison
joined in this attack on the civilians they had been paid to protect. The sacking of Soissons by the Armagnacs became a symbol of violence in war for many
years to come. In addition, the Burgundian captain of the town, Enguerrand de
Bournonville, was publicly executed as an act of private vengeance by the Duke of
Bourbon.[36] Burgundy's position at this point was precarious. His brother, Philip,
Count of Nevers, had submitted to Charles VI on 3 June, and his Flemish towns
had also signalled their loyalty to the king. The duke despatched his other brother,
Duke Anthony of Brabant, and his sister, the Countess of Hainault, to the king,
with terms for peace. Since these requested full restoration of the duke's honour
and a pardon to all his followers, including the Cabochiens, they were rejected.[37]
The royal army moved to Péronne on 29 June and laid siege to Bapaume. The
duke ordered the town to surrender, but this was not enough to prevent the king
making preparations to besiege Arras at the end of July.

Such dramatic events were bound to have a profound impact on English policies towards France. They encouraged Henry to a more aggressive stance over the
course of 1414 and into 1415. Their impact is seen in the terms of reference of a
new embassy appointed on 31 May 1414, which included the Earl of Salisbury,
Richard, Lord Grey of Codnor, and Richard Courtenay, Bishop of Norwich. It
was empowered to pursue not only 'the way of matrimony and affinity' but also
'the way of provision of justice and the restoration of our rights and inheritances'.[38]

In other words, Henry had now decided to press the French king for his territorial claims. On 4 June other envoys, including Lord Scrope, were appointed to treat with the Duke of Burgundy. They were empowered to negotiate an alliance with the duke and also to receive his homage, as well as to discuss the possible marriage of Henry to the duke's daughter, Catherine.[39] Henry was now double-dealing.

Burgundian envoys had been present at Leicester during the parliament held there between 30 April and 29 May, the very month that Charles's army started to move against the duke's strongholds.[40] It is at this stage that there is the first indication of a possible English invasion of France. We have evidence of proposals put forward by the duke's envoys, questions which English representatives put to them and replies given.[41] What the Burgundians wanted was an offensive alliance whereby each side provided 500 men-at-arms and 1,000 archers for three months to assist the other. The duke would be prepared to help Henry conquer lands held by the Armagnac lords (although Berry was excluded from the list), but he was not prepared to come to alliance against the French king or Dauphin. The English asked who would command the duke's troops if Henry did cross in person. (That this was not certain at this stage is indicated by questions about what would happen if Henry sent one of his brothers or another noble captain.) The reply was 'the duke of Burgundy himself'. His envoys were sure that 'he would rather lead 1,000 men in person than send 500'. (These figures are interesting because the duke was asked for 500 men-at-arms by Charles VI against the English in 1415 but claimed to be insulted, since he could send more.[42]) They gave rather obfuscating replies to English questions about what the duke would do if Charles VI ordered him to make peace, or if the French king attacked the joint army, or if Henry decided to attack a royal castle or troops. No alliance was agreed at this stage. There were, however, further discussions conducted by Scrope and his associates when they arrived in Ypres. A draft agreement dated 7 August 1414 states that the duke would not offer any opposition to Henry's effort to take the crown of France and would be prepared to fight with him against Charles.[43] This marked a distinct change from his reluctance in May to go to war against his king. This had come about because by early August one of his major cities, Arras, was about to be besieged by the royal army. Historians have long debated whether this Anglo-Burgundian offensive alliance was ever ratified. There is no evidence that it was and Burgundy's subsequent negotiations for peace with Charles VI rendered it a dead letter anyway.

The negotiations of the summer of 1414 with the French king and with Burgundy indicate that Henry was becoming deeply interested in exploiting French divisions to his advantage. One version of the *Brut* chronicle claims that before the parliament at Leicester Henry held a great council at Westminster, 'where it was treated and spoken of his title that he had to Normandy, Gascony and Guienne which was his inheritance of right', and that at the parliament he decided 'by the advice of all the lords of his council and of the commons of his land' to send an embassy to France, 'requiring them to yield up his inheritance or else let them know that he would get it with the sword by the help of Jesus Christ'.[44] Although there is no proof in the parliament rolls that the idea of an invasion was discussed in the Leicester assembly, an embassy to Charles VI was appointed, as we have seen, on 31 May, two days after it ended.

This embassy met with Charles VI and his Armagnac advisers between 8 August and late September, exactly the same period that the English embassy was in discussions with the Duke of Burgundy. At the outset the English demanded restitution of all their rights, including the crown and realm of France, but then condescended to lower their terms, although without prejudice to the royal claim. They asked for the restitution of all of the lands offered in the Great Peace as well as homage, superiority and lordship over the duchy of Normandy, the counties of Touraine, Maine and Anjou, and the homage of Brittany and Flanders. The payment of 1.6 million *écus*, the remainder of John II's ransom, was also required. To this end, a copy of John's liability was made for the English ambassadors on 5 July.[45] Catherine's dowry was set at 2 million *écus*. There were also smaller demands which derived from the king's Lancastrian ancestry. These were the castles of Beaufort (now Montmorency, Aube) and Nogent (Nogent l'Artaud, near Château-Thierry), which had come to Edmund Crouchback, first Earl of Lancaster, through his marriage to Blanche of Artois, and the moiety of Provence, which was believed to have fallen to Crouchback's mother, Eleanor, queen of Henry III, as co-heiress of her father, Raymond, Count of Provence. Louis IX, married to Eleanor's sister, had seized the whole of the county and given it to his brother, whose descendents now held it.

These were extensive demands which raked up every possible claim Henry might have to land in France even if he set aside his claim to the throne. Henry hoped that the king and his Armagnac allies would be so alarmed at the prospect of his allying with Burgundy that they would be prepared to negotiate, as indeed they were, but they did not go far enough. Their offer consisted of much the same as had been offered to Henry IV in the treaty of Bourges, along with the marriage to Catherine and a dowry of 600,000 *écus*.[46] The English rejected these offers and returned to England in early October. The members of the embassy, several of whom served on the 1415 campaign, passed through Harfleur on their return thereby gaining useful familiarity with the port.[47]

For the first month that the English embassy was in Paris, the siege of Burgundy's town of Arras proceeded. Royal troops were also active in the hinterland, penetrating as far as Hesdin close to Agincourt.[48] But dysentery began to take its toll. The French army had 'evidently been kept in the field much too long for military efficiency and, above all, for its good health',[49] a salutary reminder of the dangers of siege-based campaigns, as Henry V was to find to his cost at Harfleur. For his part, the Duke of Burgundy made little effort to raise the siege and again sent his brother, the Duke of Brabant, and his sister, the Countess of Hainault, to negotiate. A preliminary peace was agreed on 4 September although the promise of pardons for Duke John and his supporters was kept vague at this stage and was to be subject to further discussion. The duke's brother and sister 'certified that their brother had made no alliance with England', but they promised on his behalf that he would make no treaties with the English against the interests of the king or his kingdom.[50]

This situation raises some interesting issues. If Duke John was telling the truth about his relations with England, then it would confirm that no treaty with Henry had been made in August. Certainly Henry had made no preparations to send him troops. If Duke John was lying and there *was* an alliance, then we must ask whether there was a master plan to which he and Henry were working? Were they, for instance, intending to let the civil war come to an end so that the Armagnacs would disband their army, and planning to launch a combined attack in the future when Burgundy's enemies were ill-prepared? Was that why Henry's ambassadors in Paris had not been prepared to entertain or discuss French offers during the negotiations of the summer? That Charles VI's government still feared Anglo-Burgundian rapprochement is suggested by the fact that they wished to keep open negotiations with Henry for a marriage even after the English embassy had returned home. For his part, Henry continued to promise that he would entertain no marriage with no one other than the French king's daughter.

French desire to keep diplomatic channels open was also a way of keeping an eye on Henry's activities, and they had every reason to wish to do so. When parliament opened on 19 November, the chancellor, Henry Beaufort, Bishop of Winchester, declared:

> how our most sovereign lord the king desires especially that good and wise action should be taken against his enemies outside the realm, and that he will strive for the recovery of the inheritance and right of his crown outside the realm which has for a long time been withheld and wrongfully kept since the time of his progenitors, kings of England, in accordance with the authorities who wish that 'unto death shalt thou strive for justice'.[51]

In other words, Henry was now determined on war, or at least intending to use the threat of it to maximum advantage. The chancellor went on to say that just like the tree which germinates, flowers and bears fruit at the right time, 'so too man is given a time of peace and a time of war and of toil'. The king, he claimed, 'understands that a suitable time has now come for him to accomplish his purpose with the aid of God'. Furthermore, the king knew that the realm of England was now itself blessed with peace and tranquillity 'by God's grace', and had considered the truth of his quarrel (with France) – which were together 'the most necessary things for each prince who has to make war on his enemies abroad'.

To this end, Henry needed money – lots of it. He had the chancellor suggest that 'if the prince has a greater increase in his patrimony', meaning by success in France, the burden on his lieges at home would be less. Furthermore, 'when these things have been accomplished, great honour and glory must necessarily follow from them'. A double lay subsidy was requested and granted, the first instalment to be paid on 2 February 1415 and the second a year later.[52] However, the lords and commons were unanimous in their opinion that Henry should send a further embassy to France, although they agreed that in the meantime 'all the works or readiness' for the expedition considered necessary by Henry and his council might be undertaken. They ended their advice by saying that they would be ready 'with their bodies' to provide the service to the king, which they were obliged to offer and which their ancestors had performed to his predecessors in the past. More detailed discussion took place between Henry and the lords on the possible size of their retinues.[53]

These were important discussions which suggest that the political nation did not wholly share the king's increasing obsession with France. The lords and commons had not been able to go against Henry's proposal for war – a king could not be directly challenged in this respect – but they wanted further negotiations with France. Although they voted a generous tax, its collection was not speedy and certainly would not generate enough income to fund a campaign of the scale Henry envisaged. Henry would need recourse to large loans on security of the future tax income. Even then, as we shall see, he was forced to exploit the royal jewel collection to meet the lords' demands concerning payment of wages for the campaign. Furthermore, Henry's hands were tied until the return of the second embassy. This was appointed on 5 December 1414 and was given two sets of powers, first to treat with the French for a final peace, and secondly to discuss the marriage and dowry.[54] It did not cross until February. In order to facilitate discussions, the truce, which was due to expire at the end of January 1415, was extended until May.

The reasons for the delay in the embassy going to France are not certain. Most likely it was because the French government delayed in allowing safe conducts to the English envoys until the situation concerning Burgundy had been made clearer. Although Charles VI's war on the duke had come to an end in September, a fully negotiated peace was many months in coming. The Dauphin was trying desperately to avoid fulfilling the promises for full pardon that had been made to Duke John's brother and sister at Arras. This encouraged the Armagnacs to conduct further attacks on Burgundian supporters in Paris, but their activities were brought to an end when on 2 February 1415 the king, probably on his own initiative in order to avoid further conflict, issued a letter announcing that he had taken Duke John back into his good grace, thereby restoring his honour. This still left 500 Burgundians outside the general pardon. Duke John's initial inclination was to reject the deal but his representative in Paris, the Duke of Brabant, decided that it was too dangerous to do otherwise.[55] Thus the treaty of Arras was publicly pro-claimed on 22 February. On 13 March the Dukes of Berry, Bourbon and Orléans, the Counts of Alençon, Vertus and Eu, along with the Duke of Brabant and other Burgundian representatives, swore to uphold its terms.[56] These included a royal ban on any alliances being made with the English which would be prejudicial in any way to the crown or which were contrary to the peace that the princes had made at Chartres in 1409. In theory, therefore, both Duke John and the Armagnac lords had accepted peace including a ban on any treaties with the English.

On 2 February, the very day that Charles VI declared his pardon for Duke John, the second English embassy was allowed to enter Paris. Bishop Courtenay was again among their number, as was Thomas Beaufort, Earl of Dorset, Richard, Lord Grey of Codnor, and three of Henry's household esquires, William Bourchier, John Phelip and William Porter, all men who were to serve on the campaign of 1415. The English demands were put forward on 13 March, the day the French lords had gathered to swear to uphold the treaty of Arras. The marriage to Catherine was discussed separately. A dowry of 2 million *écus* was requested, although the English expressed their willingness to accept a reduction to 1.5 million *écus* so long as any second son born of the marriage had rights restored in Ponthieu. The French refused to admit any such rights at this stage but offered 800,000 *écus* in dowry, at which point the English responded with a request for 1 million *écus*. On the marriage, therefore, the two sides were coming very close to agreement. At Bordeaux on 10 March, the town council were of the belief that the mar-riage had been settled and that the Earl of Dorset and the constable, d'Albret, would soon make a joint visit to Guienne to effect a peaceful settlement there.[57] As for territorial demands, Henry's embassy asked only for the lands transferred to the English in the Great Peace of 1360 along with the Lancastrian interests in Provence, Beaufort and Nogent. The French, however, expressed doubts about the justice of these claims and were only prepared to offer lands in Guienne to be held as fiefs. This would be conditional on the English dropping their claims to outstanding payments of John II's ransom.

Given Henry's desire to go to war as expressed in the chancellor's speech to the parliament in November, it is striking that Henry had toned down his demands in March 1415 compared with his first embassy, and was prepared to negotiate on the marriage separately. What was going on here? The delay in entering into negotiations had certainly not worked in Henry's favour, since by the time they began, peace had officially been restored in France. It was now unlikely that the French would see any need to entertain a territorial settlement even though they could continue to contemplate the marriage, as this would make it difficult for Henry to wage war. One way of interpreting this is that Henry had been out-witted by the French. But there is another possibility. Diplomatic intelligence would have already made him aware of the likelihood of political reconciliations within France.[58] Henry could therefore pitch his demands lower yet know that they would be rejected. That way, he could satisfy the requirements of the lords and commons at the parliament that he had made efforts to 'moderate' his claims in order to achieve peace. It would then be possible to justify an invasion both at home and abroad, since it was the French who had behaved unreasonably in the face of Henry's willingness to compromise. This is precisely what happened.

It was the English who withdrew from negotiations, claiming that they did not have enough authority to accept the final French offers. They were back in England by 29 March but Henry had already anticipated that the talks would break down and had on 20 February sent out summons to a great council of the lords to assemble on Monday 15 April.[59] The king was able to announce that he had fulfilled the advice given in the last parliament about sending an embassy to France: in an attempt to put an end to all 'debates, disputes and wars between the kingdoms of England and France', the king had offered to let his adversary keep the greater part of what belonged by right to him. It was announced that because the enemy had refused to do justice, the king intended to carry out his expedition. At this point, therefore, Henry formally committed himself and his nation to war. Indentures for the army were drawn up and sealed on 29 April.

By this time, however, the French had themselves become more bombastic because of the formal reconciliations between the princes. Indeed, it was quite a coup for them to have this performed on 13 March, the very day the English embassy submitted its claims. The famous story of the tennis balls is easily dismissed, but there is reason to believe that the Dauphin did send an insulting message to Henry on behalf of the French royal government at the time of the failure of the negotiations of March 1415.[60] Henry had pursued an aggressive tone towards the French but so far his threats had been empty. Indeed, he had also shown himself apparently willing to step down his demands in the negotiations. There were even rumours that he was willing to pay homage.[61] This made it possible for the French to call his bluff. In this context, it is entirely credible that the Dauphin would remind him of his pusillanimity, although it is equally credible that the insult strengthened Henry's resolve to go to war. The Dauphin had spent the whole of the previous summer in arms and was now in control of royal finances and the nomination of officials.[62] He was calling the tune in relations with Burgundy by continuing to refuse to grant full pardons to the duke's supporters. Charles VI was enjoying a period of relatively good health, witnessed by his participation in jousts during the hospitality afforded to the second English embassy.[63] There was already fear of French raids and attacks on shipping. On 18 February Sir Thomas Carew and Gilbert, Lord Talbot were appointed captains of an armed fleet containing 110 men-at-arms and 520 archers for a period of forty days.[64]

As Henry started to prepare for war, therefore, he faced the prospect of united French resistance. He had not been successful in exploiting French divisions. His invasion would be undertaken with a considerable degree of risk. We might have, however, a lingering suspicion that he and the Duke of Burgundy were in a secret pact negotiated in August 1414 and that the reconciliation within France was a sham. After all, the duke had not come to Paris in person to ratify the treaty of Arras and was continuing to lobby for full pardons for his men. Envoys were sent to the duke by Henry in March. In late May he again assigned a group of emissaries to deal with the 'instruction to be made for the duke of Burgundy'.[65] The duke's envoys arrived in London in July. Henry despatched Philip Morgan to Burgundy on 10 August, the day before his fleet set sail, in 'certain secret discussions'. An emissary was sent to the Duke of Brittany at the same juncture.[66] Although Henry gave every impression of being keen to come to an arrangement with Burgundy, it is unlikely that there was any understanding in place at the time of the expedition. Furthermore, Duke John did raise troops in response to Charles's request. It is significant that a copy of the duke's order to his marshals exists in the English royal records.[67] How it came there is not certain, but it is tempting to believe that English spies fed it to Henry as proof of the duke's duplicity. As we shall see, the duke's absence from the battle can be explained by events within France. Moreover, large numbers of the Burgundian faction fought and died at the battle, including the duke's brothers of Brabant and Nevers.

The French court still feared, however, that there might be an Anglo-Burgundian understanding. This was one reason why they decided to send an embassy to England after the breakdown of the negotiations in March. Henry could not refuse their request, since his envoys had broken off discussions, saying that they needed to refer back to Henry on the French proposals. The French were also keen to keep an eye on Henry's preparations. It is unlikely that they were desperate to avoid war, as has been argued. They had started to make preparations even while the English ambassadors were still in Paris, indicating that they were as disinclined to make concessions for peace as Henry was to make any sacrifices on his part. On 13 March, the same day as the treaty of Arras was ratified and the English put their case, Charles VI ordered a levy of taxation to protect the kingdom on the grounds that Henry V was levying a war tax and assembling ships and men.[68] Although the French had arranged to send an embassy almost as soon as the English envoys had returned home they did not rush to do so. They needed to delay the invasion as much as they could for their own sake since the tax collections were not due until 1 June and 1 August.

Henry tried to put pressure on the French to despatch their envoys quickly. On 7 April he sent Charles a letter expressing surprise that no French embassy had been sent.[69] Further delay was not in his interests now that he and his realm were preparing for war. As soon as he knew the negotiations in Paris had failed, there was a flurry of activity to raise an army, but he could not launch his invasion while the French were still expressing their wish to negotiate. Given the emphasis on a just war, to have done so would have opened Henry to criticism at home and abroad. If the French could force him to postpone the invasion, or if they could use their time in England to spy out his preparations, this would be a propaganda victory for themselves. Their embassy finally left Paris on 4 June and arrived in London on 17 June, the day after Henry had made his ceremonial departure with his leading peers following a service at St Paul's. The French envoys finally met the king at Winchester on 30 June.[70]

It has been assumed that Henry deliberately delayed meeting them, but this does not fit with his plan that the army should muster on 1 July, the date given in the indentures sealed on 29 April. The French had already been successful, therefore, in causing some disruption but they could only keep the talks going for a week. What exactly was said by either party is uncertain since there is no official record. As the king was conducting discussions in person, no instructions were given to ambassadors. We have to rely on chronicle accounts which were written long after the event and which are not necessarily reliable.[71] The impression is that both sides were indulging in diplomatic posturing, offering what seemed to be compromises, for instance over Catherine's dowry, but then holding back. The chroniclers suggest that Henry finally lost his temper, shouting that he was the rightful king of France and that he was determined to have the crown of the fleur de lys. In response, the Archbishop of Bourges said that he did not even have a right to the crown of England and that they should really be negotiating with the heirs of Richard II. At this, talks broke down, and Bishop Beaufort, as chancellor, told the French that if they did not surrender forthwith all of the lands of the Great Peace, as well as Normandy, Anjou, Maine and Touraine, Henry would invade to recover them all and to seize the crown. As God knew, he had been forced to this position because the French had denied him justice.

The French embassy left Winchester on 7 July and reached Calais by 14 July, arriving in Paris on 26 July. In their company was a canon of Notre Dame de Paris, Jean Fusoris, who already had links with Bishop Courtenay. During the siege of Harfleur the bishop enticed a clerk of Montivilliers captured by the English to take secret letters to Fusoris, asking for information on the movements of the French king and the likely size of his army.[72] The priest and the letters fell into the hands of the French garrison at Montivilliers. As a result Fusoris was arrested in Paris on 6 September for treason. We have full transcript of his own testimony and that of various witnesses. Courtenay had apparently first made contact with Fusoris in Paris, during the embassy of the summer of 1414. It is possible, therefore, that the latter had worked as a spy for the English for some time, although he denied the charge at his trial. His claim was that he had come to England with the French envoys in June simply because Courtenay owed him money for scientific instruments and books which the bishop had purchased while in Paris. The truth of the matter will never be known but it gives us a unique insight into what was going on outside the formal negotiations. If the English were using spies then we can be certain that the French were too. This suspicion explains the order sent out on 3 July to the main English ports not to allow aliens to leave the country until further notice.[73]

Particularly interesting is the testimony Fusoris gave about his meeting with an unnamed esquire of the king at the town the French envoys reached three days after they withdrew from Winchester.[74] This esquire had brought the customary departing gifts for the ambassadors. He asked to speak to Fusoris, ostensibly on the grounds that Courtenay had sent him with part of the money owed. In the conversation that ensued, the esquire asked Fusoris why the embassy had not come earlier since had they done so the royal marriage might have materialised. Fusoris replied that he had heard 'a doctor' in Henry's household say that a marriage would have been better than a war for the king. A marriage would have made him secure in his kingdom, since it might also have given him access to French military support from the French in the future, should he need it. And well he might, since there were many who favoured his brother Clarence or the Earl of March. If he went ahead with his invasion he might well find, as Richard II had done, that there would be a rising against him while he was absent from England. Furthermore, if he was to effect a march (*unum cursum*) into France and then come home quickly without achieving anything for all of the expense that had been incurred, he would not be received with thanks at his return. On the other hand, if he stayed in France longer, say for two or three months, and the French gathered against him, the king would be in great danger. The French were much more practised in military matters than they used to be ('magis exercitati in armis quam solebant') and the lords of France were believed to be united and in harmony. The English were afraid of this, not least because they had already gone to France in the past and done nothing. This is a reference to the campaign of 1412, where the French had united and therefore removed any hope of the English army exploiting their divisions.

It would be easy to dismiss this evidence save for two reasons. The first is that Fusoris did not give this testimony until the end of March 1416, by which time the opinions expressed by the doctor were irrelevant. Secondly, neither Henry's preparations for the campaign nor his position in England were wholly secure. The delay caused by negotiations with the French had not helped. The intended date of assembly had been 1 July but musters did not begin until over a week later. The order to muster Clarence's large company was not issued until 20 July, suggesting that his troops had only just assembled. It was not until mid-August that the expedition set sail. In the interim, therefore, the troops were in royal pay but kicking their heels in and around Southampton.[75] There was difficulty in providing enough shipping to transport the army. On 27 July orders went out to bring more vessels for the crossing from the port of London to Southampton and to collect more bows, arrows and bowstrings from the arsenal at the Tower.[76] A further problem was money. Between 11 and 24 July the king made further securities from his jewels to repay loans and to pay for military service.[77] The soldiers also needed to procure food supplies. On 24 July Henry ordered the sheriff of Hampshire to proclaim that those about to depart on campaign should provide victuals for three months. This was not easy to achieve given the large numbers of troops involved.[78]

The dating of these various orders, and the fact that both the king and several of his lords drew up their wills around the same time, indicates that Henry intended to depart soon. On 28 July he sent a letter to Charles VI from the seaside ('sur le bord de la mer') at Southampton.[79] This was a final ultimatum which invoked several religious images, including the law of Deuteronomy. A man who planned an attack first offered peace but if the enemy refused him justice then he was permitted to have recourse to arms. Henry's letter offered Charles one last chance to restore his inheritance in order to avoid the spilling of Christian blood. It even offered to reduce the demand for Catherine's dowry by 50,000 écus. These were not genuine offers but simply formal justifications for invasion. The French reply was not written until two weeks after Henry landed. Charles likewise emphasised how he had continually sought peace by reasonable means and stated that he was not afraid of Henry's menaces. If his kingdom was attacked then it would be ready to repulse him by force of arms.

On Tuesday 29 July the king, now at Portchester, ordered his army to be ready for embarkation two days later, on 1 August. This may have been Henry's chosen date for departure all along, for reasons we shall investigate towards the end of this chapter.[80] Departure was in fact delayed for a further week because of the revelation of the Southampton plot. Reconstruction of this is not easy since it is based on forced confessions.[81] These tell of various meetings in and around Southampton following Sir Thomas Grey's arrival in the town on 21 July. On 26 July Henry, Lord Scrope and the Earl of Cambridge allegedly met on the Itchen ferry and talked about setting fire to the ships to prevent the expedition. The plan was to kill the king on 1 August and to replace him with his cousin, the Earl of March. This was a deliberate and highly significant coincidence of dates. The plotters not only intended to end Henry's life and reign but also his campaign. This tallies closely with what Fusoris's informant had told him. We must ask ourselves why men close to the king chose to attempt his deposition in 1415 as he prepared to depart for France. Surely this was the moment least likely to generate success since Henry was surrounded by a huge army? Did the plotters deliberately choose this occasion because they anticipated many would defect to them with their troops, and that it would therefore be easier to kill the king and the two brothers with him, and then to march on to London against his remaining brother? Henry had done little to make himself popular with those outside his inner circle over the first years of his reign. His obsession with a French war was not fully shared. But Henry had to be obeyed. He was not a man to question.

There has been speculation that there was no plot to kill the king at all. By a savage act against men who were close to him and of high status in the realm, Henry was ensuring that there would be no risings against him during his absence, nor would there be any criticism from those on the campaign. In this

context, it is significant that the *Gesta* claims that the plotters had been cor-
rupted 'by the stench of French promises or bribes'.[82] This was not included in
the formal charges against them but was a rumour, perhaps fanned by the king
himself. Whether it existed or was set up by Henry, the Southampton plot reveals
his obsessive and cruel nature, made worse by the fact that he was constantly
riddled with uncertainties, a characteristic that was to emerge again during the
campaign. On 31 July the Earl of March disclosed the plot to the king. The Earl of
Cambridge, Henry, Lord Scrope and Sir Thomas Grey were arrested, convenient-
ly confessed their guilt, and were executed on 5 August after a summary trial. On
7 August March was pardoned. On the same day the king left Portchester Castle
and boarded his ship, the *Trinite Royal*, which was probably moored between the
Hamble and the entrance to Portsmouth harbour. The sail was raised to half-mast
as the signal for the other ships to set sail. The expedition had begun.

What did Henry intend it to achieve? His final ultimatum to Charles spoke of
his 'rights and inheritance' but it also mentioned the restitution of 'at least what we
asked you for on several occasions through our ambassadors'. The last demand put
forward in the second embassy was for the fulfilment of the terms of the Great Peace.
The speech of Bishop Beaufort at the end of the failed negotiations at Winchester
also emphasised that Henry's ambassadors had not insisted on 'the great issues, such
as the crown of France, Normandy, Touraine, Anjou, Maine, and the suzerainty
of Flanders and Brittany', but on the settlement achieved by Edward III.[83] This
settlement was essentially what the Armagnac princes had agreed that the English
should have in the treaty of Bourges. Around 10 July, Henry ordered copies of this
agreement to be made and sent to the Council of Constance, Emperor Sigismund
and other princes, 'that all Christendom might know what great acts of injustice
the French in their duplicity had inflicted on him' and which had forced him 'as it
were reluctantly and against his will' to raise his standards 'against rebels'.[84]

Yet Henry invaded Normandy and called it 'his duchy'. He laid siege to Harfleur
which he called 'his town'. He then marched homewards across the northern part
of the duchy, as well as through Ponthieu and Calais. Both of these areas were part
of Edward's lands according to the treaty of Brétigny, but Normandy was not.
Indeed, Edward had explicitly surrendered his right to it in this settlement, thereby
confirming the treaty of Paris of 1259, where Henry III had given up the claim to
the duchy and other Angevin lands in the north. In terms of a just war, therefore,
Henry could only attack Normandy because of his claim to the French crown.
That does not mean that his hope was to become king of France or even Duke of
Normandy. The *Gesta* interpreted his crossing, however, as 'in order first to recover
his duchy of Normandy, which belonged to him by right from the time of William
the first, the conqueror'.[85] There is no doubt that Henry's second campaign of 1417
was aimed at the systematic conquest of Normandy and was conducted with a
deliberate emphasis on the king's Norman ducal inheritance. The king even started
calling himself Duke of Normandy once he had landed in the duchy on 1 August

1417, and began to revive ancient ducal institutions. In 1415, however, there is no mention of the 'Norman inheritance' save in the *Gesta*. In the opening speech of the November 1415 parliament, Harfleur was specifically stated to be 'in France' and Henry's march from there to Calais was described as being 'through the heart of France'.[86] The *Gesta*'s comment may therefore reflect the way Henry's ambition had turned in 1417 more than the actual situation in 1415.

More likely, at this stage his plan was to take land in Normandy in order to strengthen his bargaining position with the French on the Brétigny terms. It was much cheaper and quicker to transport a large army across the Channel than to Bordeaux. Had Henry conquered more of Normandy on the 1415 campaign he could have added that to his demands. The size of his army made it feasible to capture further towns and to install garrisons. It is easy to see why he should target Harfleur first. It gave him a useful bridgehead on the Seine through which supplies and reinforcements could be brought, and subsequent invasions launched. In the late fourteenth century the French crown had created there a fortified naval base (the *clos des galées*) from which raids on English coasts and shipping had subsequently been launched. Its capture therefore served to damage French naval power and to protect England. The town also lay on a river leading directly to Paris, through an area that was held directly by the French king and that contributed substantially to French royal revenues. By contrast, an invasion of the hinterland of English Guienne, as pursued by Clarence and Dorset in 1412–13, put no real pressure on the French and was a much less provocative act than invading close to the jugular.

That said, there are some indications that he was interested in a campaign in Guienne. The army indentures of 29 April spoke of an expedition 'into his duchy of Guienne or into his kingdom of France', but the majority of advance wage payments were made at the higher rates customarily given for Guienne. Wylie suggested that the payment of the higher Guienne rate was simply to encourage men to serve.[87] In other words, it was a pretence which also fitted well with public focus on restoration of the Great Peace. This could also explain the *Gesta*'s comment that Henry kept the destination of the army secret save to his closest advisers, although the truth of this remark is not certain.[88] Entries in the Issue Rolls between 16 April and mid-May 1415 for expenditure on military preparations speak of the king's expedition (*viage*) to Harfleur.[89] In order to accommodate both theatres, some historians have suggested that once he had taken Harfleur Henry intended to march south to Guienne.[90] This possibility cannot be ruled out, although it was awkward to land north of the Seine if such a southward move was envisaged. Unless Henry intended to take his army across the mouth of the Seine by boat, he would have had to take it to Rouen to find the first bridge over the river. His army was certainly large enough to contemplate a siege of the Norman capital (it was larger than the army that took the place in 1419, although only after a six-month siege). Rouen is certainly mentioned as one of his intentions in a letter written by Jean Bordiu at Harfleur on 2 October.[91]

This letter also mentions Paris as an objective. Another possibility is that Henry invaded Normandy to emulate Edward III's attack of 1346, which penetrated close to Paris and which brought the French to battle. Henry could not know what response the French would make to his invasion but he would certainly have envisaged that battle was a strong possibility. This brings us back to the strong religious tone of his justifications for war and to his likely choice of 1 August as the departure date in 1415. That this had been chosen some months earlier is suggested by a royal order of 27 May to the sheriff of Hampshire that the people of the county should bake and brew 'against the coming of the king to those parts with his retinue', from that date to 1 August.[92] It may be that Henry's astrologers had told him that this was a propitious date for embarkation. He did after all avoid being killed by the Southampton plotters on that day, but it is also significant that they had timed the intended murder for then. In the religious context 1 August was the feast of St Peter ad Vincula, which commemorated the angel rescuing St Peter by loosening his chains. Was Henry intending to symbolise the release of the Normans, or perhaps even the French as a whole, from the chains of the Valois? Diplomatic documents all emphasise that the French had withheld (*detentus*) lands that were rightly Henry's. Now was the time to liberate. Henry chose exactly the same date in 1417 to make his second landing in Normandy, a landing that led to the conquest of the whole duchy and, by the summer of 1419, an advance on Paris.

As he departed in 1415 Henry was also hoping to liberate himself from the failures and humiliations of the past. But as Fusoris's informant had told him, should Henry fail then he would face trouble at home. He had only been able to launch his expedition by force of royal will and by dealing savagely with his opponents. The execution of his second cousin (and the brother of one of his leading commanders still on the campaign) and his close friend cannot have boosted morale at this crucial moment. On 7 August, as the king joined his ship, an order went out that special watch should be kept at night in several towns in England.[93] He feared trouble while he was away. With the advantage of hindsight, we know that it worked out well, but neither the king nor his men could know that as they set sail. A short voyage, yes, but a voyage into the unknown.

3

The Raising of Henry V's Army,
April–August 1415

Raising a large army and preparing for war was a huge and costly undertaking. That it could happen at all was due to the crown's inherent authority over its subjects and their resources. Henry invoked and exploited this to the full to achieve his ambitions and also to demonstrate his kingship. The scale of the enterprise and his intention of being present in person could not fail to have a distinct impact, but the methods deployed followed the well-worn systems that had enabled the English to launch expeditions in the past.[1] Once war was decided upon, the crown entered into contracts with individual peers, knights and others which committed them to provide companies of an agreed size and composition.[2] For ease of discussion, we shall call all of those who entered into a contract 'captains' and the men who served under their command 'retinues'. Save for some important exceptions, which we shall note later, the crown did not recruit men directly but did so through the captains. The contracts are known as 'indentures' because they were written out by the Chancery in duplicate and then cut down the middle so that each party had a record. The cut was made in zig-zag form to prevent either party making fraudulent changes. Indentures for a campaign were standardised in form and content. Almost all of those for the 1415 campaign were sealed on 29 April. The indenture noted the length of the contracted service, which started on the day the captain mustered his troops before royal officials at the port ready for embarkation. In 1415 this length was twelve months and the assembly date was set as 1 July. The king undertook to inform the captains within the month of May as to where the muster would take place.

The indenture also defined the number and type of troops that the captain had contracted to provide. These were commonly expressed as so many men-at-arms and so many archers. The contracts also noted numbers of dukes, earls, barons and knights intended to be within the retinue. Although men of these social ranks mustered and fought as men-at-arms, they received higher pay to cover the costs of their expected lifestyle. All men were paid. The wage rates used in 1415 were the standard levels paid by the crown since the early stages of the Hundred Years' War. All of the wages for a retinue were paid to the captain who was then responsible for disbursing it to his men at his own behest. Part was paid to the captain at the point he entered into his indenture as a way of helping him recruit his men. The indentures then detailed the arrangements for the payment of remaining instalments. As we shall see, it is in this respect that the 1415 indentures contain several unique clauses which reflect the fact that Henry did not have enough money at his disposal. The indentures also laid down rules concerning gains of war. As was standard practice, all important prisoners taken by a captain or the members of his retinue were to be handed over to the crown in return for compensation. Since the invasion was of France, the king of France, his close relatives and kings of any other kingdoms were placed into this category. As for gains such as booty, money, gold, silver, jewels and other prisoners, precedent was again followed. For anything worth more than 10 marks (£6 13s 4d) the captain had a right to the third share of gains taken by his men. The crown took a third part of the captain's gains and a third of a third of the gains of his men.[3]

The indenture was the first of a series of documents concerning the captain and his retinue. The Chancery put the royal seal to the captain's half of the indenture, which the latter then kept in his possession, and the captain put his seal on the crown's half. Each side was mutually bound to uphold the terms of the contract. The next stage was for the Chancery to send a 'Warrant for Issue' to the Exchequer, authorising the first instalment of pay. Since these warrants recited the main terms of the indenture, especially the numbers and types of troops the captain contracted to provide, they are a very useful source of information where indentures do not survive. All monies paid out by the crown were listed on the Issue Rolls, so that the disbursement of army wages usually appears alongside other royal expenses. In 1415, however, a special Issue Roll was drawn up to record the payment of wages for the campaign, presumably because there were so many to be made and it was thought helpful to keep them together on a separate roll.[4]

When the troops were brought to the coast they were mustered by officials of, or appointed by, the Exchequer. This was to check whether the captains had provided the number and type of men for which they had contracted. The muster rolls are perhaps the most fascinating documents at our disposal, since they give the names of individual soldiers within the retinues of the captains. After the campaign, the captains were obliged to submit an account to the Exchequer which showed how much they had received and which gave details of the service of their retinue.[5] Since the crown had paid wages, it had to know whether a captain's retinue had been kept up to strength or whether it had lost men. It also had to know what gains had been made where it had the right to a share. The post-campaign accounts for the 1415 expedition were often presented many years later but the information they contain is extremely valuable for showing how many men were put into the garrison of Harfleur, how many died at the siege or were invalided home, and how many went on to fight at Agincourt. It is not uncommon for these post-campaign accounts to be accompanied by a retinue list showing the fate of each man. These lists add to the pool of names we have for soldiers on the campaign.

Public pronouncement on a possible expedition was made at the parliament of November 1414. The lords and commons advised that further negotiations with the French should be pursued, but agreed that in the meantime preparations for the king's expedition should be undertaken as necessary. It was obvious to all concerned that many months would be needed to prepare for a large-scale enterprise. Those present further expressed their willingness to be 'ready with their bodies' to provide service to the king, as their ancestors had done to the king's predecessors.[6] The lay peers told the king that they were ready to serve on his expedition 'with whatever retinue it pleased him to assign'.[7] From the proposals Henry made for payment of wages at this point, it was already apparent that he intended at least a nine-month campaign. The first quarter (a year was divided into four periods of ninety-one days, i.e. approximately three months) would be paid before the quarter began. The wages for the second and third quarters would be issued at the end of the second quarter.

Given the desire of parliament for further peace negotiations, the king could not make full military preparations for war while his embassy was still in France. This did not prevent 'strategic planning' in mid-February on the defence of the sea, the English frontiers and Calais during any expedition the king might make.[8] These discussions involved the Duke of York, the Earl of Dorset, Henry, Lord Scrope and Sir Thomas Erpingham, all highly experienced military men who were to indent to serve on the campaign. The king did not do everything single-handedly. Materials such as this indicate how much of the detail was left to his trusted inner circle. Setting aside the king's brothers and his closest friend, the Earl of Arundel, the men present at this council were likely to be the leading commanders, a point which makes Scrope's execution for treason on the eve of departure all the more significant. These discussions also show how much concern there was about internal peace during a possible royal absence. Owen Glendower had never been captured and the parliament of November 1414 had expressed concerns that Welsh rebels were troubling the border counties 'as if they were a land in war'.[9] York and his fellow advisers recommended that 180 troops should be placed in North Wales and 120 in South Wales before the king departed, and that private castles in Wales should also be well defended.[10] Over 300 troops were advised for Berwick and the marches, and 300 were recommended for Guines, in addition to 900 in Calais. Before the expedition sailed, however, the numbers for Calais and the sea were reduced but an extra 120 men were detailed to North Wales, again reflecting fears of trouble in that area.[11] Within England, concern for internal security led to the holding of shire and clerical arrays in the months before the king set sail: on 27 May the beacon system was ordered to be put in place.[12] Once again we are reminded of how insecure Henry considered himself to be. Remember that Fusoris's informer told him that Henry might find there would be risings against him in his absence, as there had been against Richard II in 1399.[13]

Since the king intended to lead the expedition in person, there was a need for all the necessary trappings of the court, as well as a larger quantity of military equipment than would already be held in the royal arsenal at the Tower. Thus an order went out on 5 February to the king's tentmaker to set men to work. Over the following weeks, stocks of iron, bows and gunpowder ingredients began to be collected, and the king signed up a number of German gunners.[14] Not surprisingly, the king's advisers were already worried whether royal funds were adequate to cover the likely costs of a major expedition and asked the treasurer to produce a statement of available revenues and commitments.[15] The hope was that before the king departed adequate provision could be made for each 'cost centre'. By this means, as Henry's advisers put it, the king's mind could be set at rest and he could depart as a 'well-governed Christian prince' and carry out his campaign 'to the pleasure of God and to the comfort of all his true subjects'. Although the parliament had granted a double subsidy in December 1414 worth around £76,000 to the king, only half was due for collection by 2 February 1415, the rest a year later. As was customary, and as would be necessary if troops were to receive money before leaving England, loans would be sought on the security of forthcoming income from the clergy, nobility, towns and 'substantial men of the realm'.

Since London was a major source of credit, the king summoned the mayor and aldermen to his presence in the Tower of London on 10 March 1415 and 'disclosed to them the purpose of his excellent intention… how that, God our reward, we do intend with no small army to visit the parts beyond the sea in order to duly reconquer the lands pertaining to the inheritance and crown of our realm'.[16] This wording suggests that Henry was publicising his aim as the restoration of the Great Peace. Since Henry anticipated that the city would be more likely to offer loans 'the more immediately that the purpose of out intention redounds to the manifest advantage of the whole realm', he had decided to send his council-lors to explain the situation more fully. Thus on 14 March his brothers, Bedford and Gloucester, along with Bishop Beaufort, Archbishop Chichele and the Duke of York, went to the Guildhall. What is evident here is a strategy to flatter the city into co-operation. At the meeting, the royal dukes were careful to allow the mayor to have the centre seat since he claimed to hold vice-regal authority. The city and its merchants did agree to lend money to the crown. A huge loan of 10,000 marks was secured on 16 June by the king's deposit of a great golden collar in the form of crowns and antelopes, set with precious stones.[17]

Once it was publicly known that negotiations had failed, military preparations for the raising of a large army moved on apace. On 12 April the Mayor and
aldermen of London were ordered to proclaim in the city that the price of arms
and armour should be lowered,[18] in anticipation of increased demand as men
signed up to serve. The Issue Rolls reveal other expenditure over April and May
in preparation for the campaign. Over £5,200 was paid to Roger Leche, keeper
of the wardrobe, to purchase victuals and war gear for the royal household.[19] Most
importantly in terms of drawing up indentures, the king called the lords to a
great council at Westminster on 16 April.[20] In addition to bishops and abbots, we
find that four dukes, eight earls and fourteen barons were present. The king told
them that since the French had refused to do him justice, he had determined to
launch an expedition in person 'to recover his inheritance and the rights of his
crown'. He thanked the clergy for their generous grants to him in convocation
and urged loans to be made. He had to admit, however, that since the lay subsidy
could not be collected quickly enough, he could not maintain the payment terms
outlined at the parliament. Although the first quarter could be paid in advance as
before, further payments would follow at the end of each quarter in turn. After
discussion among themselves, the lords told the king that they needed sufficient
guarantee that the end-of-quarter sums would be paid. This led to the king's offer
to give out the royal jewels as security.

Two days later the king declared to the lords his intention of an expedition lasting a whole year and also announced the daily wage rates, which would be paid
depending on where he decided to campaign. These rates were in line with past
precedent. For Guienne they were expressed as annual figures: 40 marks (£26
13s 4d) for men-at-arms and 20 marks (£13 6s 8d) for archers, equivalent to
18d and 9d per day respectively. For France daily rates were given: 12d for men-
at-arms and 6d for archers, with an additional regard of 100 marks per quarter
for every thirty men-at-arms. In both theatres, knights bachelor would be paid
2s per day, barons and knights banneret 4s, earls 6s 8d, dukes 13s 4d. All men
of title would serve as men-at-arms and therefore were counted in the
calculations for the regard in France. The regard had developed in the 1370s to replace
compensation payments for loss of horses, since that system, necessitating detailed
scrutiny and evaluation of each horse, had proved over-cumbersome once all
troops were mounted.[21]

Over the next two weeks the indentures were drawn up, with 29 April being
the standard date on which they were sealed, although additional contracts
continued to be made over ensuing months.[22] By the terms of the indentures,
captains were to be paid half of the first quarter's wages at the sealing of the indenture using the Guienne rates,[23] with the second half at the time of the muster. If
the king had decided by that point to go to France then the second instalment
would be adjusted accordingly to take account of the lower rates of pay. For
surety of payment for the second quarter, the indentee would have delivered to

him by 1 June jewels worth as much as the wages for the second quarter. These
were to be redeemed by the beginning of 1417. For the third quarter, pay was to
be made within six weeks of its start. For the fourth and last quarter, if the king
did not give surety by halfway through the third quarter then the captain would
be released from his obligation to serve beyond the three quarters.

These terms must reflect talks between the king and nobles over the last
two weeks of April. The conditions finally agreed gave the king potential service for a full twelve months but also gave captains some safeguards concerning
receipt of pay. In other words, a compromise had been reached. Discussion of
the king's plans is also evidenced by an entry in the Issue Rolls for 19 April,
where William Hoklyst was paid almost £24 for the cost of a jantaculum at the
palace of Westminster with the Duke of Clarence and other lords, so that the king
could be advised 'on his present expedition towards Harfleur and the region of
Normandy'.[24] Further entries in the Issue Rolls from 16 April to mid-May also
speak of an expedition to Harfleur. There can be no doubt that Henry's closest
circle knew of his intended target even if he was keeping his options open publicly.[25] His talk of a campaign to Guienne may have been a ploy to encourage men
to indent,[26] since the higher wage rates, as issued in the first instalment following
indenting, could be seen as compensating for the lack of certainty over prompt
cash payment for later stages of the expedition. The king also ensured that jewels
as security for the second quarter were made available as soon as possible. On
13 May he commanded Richard Courtenay, Bishop of Norwich and keeper of
the royal jewels, to hand over jewels to the treasurer, Thomas, Earl of Arundel, so
that they might be given out to the indenting captains as agreed.[27] (In practice,
however, the distribution of jewels did not meet the 1 June deadline and was
still going on in the weeks before the expedition sailed.) A further incentive for
recruitment was given later in May when the general assize was suspended for the
duration of the campaign, thereby freeing men from anxiety over any property
suits.[28]

During the parliament of November 1414 the lords and knights had invited the
king to indicate the size of retinues he desired. This implies that targets were set
by the king, a position supported by the fact that retinue sizes were almost always
rounded and commonly in a ratio of one man-at-arms to three archers, as for
instance in Clarence's retinue of 240 + 720. Furthermore, there is an impression
of banding according to rank. Many of the barons and knights banneret contracted to bring thirty men-at-arms and ninety archers. Knights bachelor often
contracted for 20 + 60. Those lords with the greatest military experience were
also expected to bring larger retinues. A 'kalendar' of intended retinues was held
by the keeper of the privy seal and there also survives a small piece of paper in
the king's own hand ordering indentures to be made as in the past, mentioning
specifically the royal share in gains.[29] Lords must also have sounded out potential
recruits for their retinues over the months between the parliament and the actual

drawing up of the indentures, since the latter stated the actual numbers of men of rank a captain would bring. Clarence, for instance, contracted to bring an earl, two bannerets and fourteen knights within his total retinue size of 960. Gilbert, Lord Talbot indented for thirty men-at-arms but subsequently asked that he might be allowed to have two knights bachelor in his company.[30] Such changes had implications for the costs of the army, since knights were paid at a higher rate. The musters and post-campaign accounts reveal that almost all captains achieved the numbers in their contracts. If the king had allocated targets, then these were realistic. It does not appear to have been difficult, therefore, to find captains or indeed soldiers as a whole.

In all, there is evidence in the Exchequer records for 320 men indenting to serve on the campaign, although sixty did so jointly with others (Appendix D).[31] This is a very high number compared with the other expeditions to France which had been launched since the indenture system became dominant. The norm had been for few captains, but with each contracting for large numbers. Take, for instance, the 4,000-strong army sent under the Duke of Clarence in 1412. This comprised only three retinues: 2,000 under Clarence, 1,060 under the Duke of York and 940 under the Earl of Dorset. As we have seen, the retinues for which these three men indented in 1415 were notably smaller. The difference arose from the fact that the king was campaigning in person. In 1412 the crown had delegated the raising of the army to the three noble captains, who would then enter into sub-indentures with other men to bring troops. In 1415 a much larger number of men indented directly with the crown. This produced a diverse group of indentees and a wide range of retinue sizes.

Not surprisingly, the king's brothers of Clarence and Gloucester indented for the largest retinues (960 and 800 men respectively), with the next largest (all at 400) under the king's relatives, York and Dorset, and his closest friend, Thomas, Earl of Arundel. After that came the other earls of the royal family: the Earl of March with 220, Richard, Earl of Cambridge with 210 and the Earl of Norfolk (the Earl Marshal) with 200, and then the other earls, Suffolk (160), Oxford (140) and Salisbury (120). The relatively small companies of Henry Percy, Earl of Northumberland (24) and John Holland, Earl of Huntingdon (80) may be explained by the fact they had not been fully restored to their possessions following the treasonable activities of their forebears. The retinues of knights lay between 40 and 120 men, with leading esquires contracting for companies of 12 or more. What was a distinctive feature of the Agincourt campaign was the very large number of tiny retinues. At least 122 men contracted to serve with fewer than 10 men, some even for their own service alone. The only parallel in recent times was the army raised by Henry IV in 1400 for Scotland, which he led in person.[32] Both this army and that of 1415 were raised early in a reign against an ancient enemy as the most effective way of creating a sense of national unity behind a king with an uncertain title. Raising an army confirmed royal authority and forced men of all ranks to demonstrate their loyalty in practical manner. What we are seeing on both occasions, therefore, is a major call to arms where the king required and encouraged everyone who should or could offer service to do so. It was only by this form of direct recruitment that such a large army could be raised. Furthermore, it is clear that when kings campaigned in person they wished to be accompanied by a large army for the sake of show and to make success more easily achieved. Henry wanted to impress the French and other European rulers.

A further reason why there were so many small retinues was the putting into arms of the royal household. Even on campaign kings expected to travel in style, with the trappings of royalty and the rituals of service. Henry was accompanied by a large number of men from his household. These included the knights and esquires of his chamber who waited upon him personally, his household officials such as the cofferer and almoner, as well as the administrators and staff of the various parts of the household. These indented and were paid either as men-at-arms or archers for the campaign. Some brought along further men-at-arms and archers. Many indented in a group, bringing two or three archers each. The result was that the costs of the king's household on the campaign were transferred to the war budget under the control of John Everdon as clerk for the wars. In addition, there were lower servants, such as the *garciones*, who went on the campaign but did not receive military wages. We can detect the presence of this last group in the records concerning those invalided home after the siege of Harfleur. Henry was so concerned to avoid desertion that all those given permission to return to England, not only those in military wages, had to be recorded. All of the major offices were represented on the campaign in order to preserve the royal lifestyle and to provide the kernel of an army: kitchen, pantry, buttery, napery, spicery, poultry, scullery, bakehouse, as well as hall, chamber and wardrobe. The king also had his chapel, headed by its dean, Edmund Lacy, and seventeen minstrels.

There were also those giving technical support to the royal household: the sergeant of the pavilions with his company of tent-erectors; grooms and stable-men; cordwainers; wheelwrights; fletchers; bowyers; saddlers; armourers. It is likely that their numbers had been increased for the purpose of the campaign. We can also see non-household groups being retained by the king for special purposes. Thus we find the engagement of Nicholas Colnet as physician, with three archers, and Thomas Morstede and William Bradwardine as surgeons, along with their assistant surgeons and six archers. For Morstede we have the petition he put to the king requesting money for equipment and appropriate transport (a chariot and two sumpter horses), but leaving it to the king to make an offer on wages. This gives an intriguing, and strikingly modern, impression of the role of Henry in decision making. Someone else read the petition first, writing on it all the king needed to decide: 'what wages of war Morsted should have for himself, and his men and what number during the voyage according as it best seems to your excellent noblesse'.[33] The king also called up two clerks to serve as counsel

and to draft correspondence: Richard Hals, treasurer of Exeter Cathedral, and
Jean Bordiu, Archdeacon of the Médoc, who has been proposed as the author of
the *Gesta*.[34] William Tropenell, master tailor, indented with two valet tailors and
four archers.[35] The crown was also responsible for recruitment of larger specialist companies. Thirty or so gunners were raised as the months went on, all of
continental origin, such as Hayne Joy, Frederik Colle, Martin van Okest, William
Gerardesson, Peter Gascon.[36] This suggests that there was not enough English
expertise in this dangerous and still relatively novel occupation. There were also
six master miners and their 113 assistants under Sir John Greyndore, a sixty-
year-old knight with lands in and around the Forest of Dean, the area that was the
likely source of his company.[37] On 6 June orders went out for the impressments
of 100 stonecutters, 120 carpenters and turners, 40 smiths and 60 waggoners.[38]
The latter were to be ready with collars, halters and pipes of leather for the carriage of the king's ordnance, which was itself under the command of the master
of ordnance, Nicholas Merbury. We would dearly like to know more about the
guns themselves but on this the records are silent.

Henry's household had no choice but to follow its master to war. There was
a sense of obligation for other groups too in his efforts to raise as large an army
as possible. Like his father, Henry called on men who held annuities and offices
of the crown, even though by no means all were held on terms that required
military service. On 22 March the king summoned them to meet in London on
24 April.[39] Indentures were entered into a few days later. Exceptions were allowed,
as in the case of John Stafford of Derbyshire who was constable of Lincoln Castle
and collector of the lay subsidy in the Peak District. He was also a good age, since
his annuity had been granted by the king's grandfather, John of Gaunt.[40] Henry IV
and Henry V had continued to exploit the Lancastrian inheritance to the same
end. As prince, Henry had also created annuities out of his revenues in Wales,
Cheshire and Cornwall, and as king, he could draw on the whole of the royal
demesne. In this way, the crown had its own retainers on which to draw as did
the other lords. A further group associated with Henry and overlapping with the
annuitants and office holders were the king's knights and esquires and others who
had served the regime in various capacities, often for many years. Into this group
fit men such as Sir Thomas Erpingham, who had an important role to play at the
battle in giving the signal to attack.[41]

Since Wales, Lancashire and Cheshire had a special relationship with the crown,
each was also required to provide companies of archers. The Cheshire archers
were raised from each of the hundreds of the county and paid by the chamberlain
of the county palatine, William Troutbeck, out of local taxation. His accounts indicate payments to 247 archers from the county serving on the campaign.[42] It may
be that this was a shortfall on original intentions: Rymer and Sanderson claimed
that Troutbeck was supposed to provide fifty men-at-arms and 650 archers.[43]
From Lancashire 500 archers were raised grouped into companies of fifty, each

under the command of a local knight or esquire who often had his own company of men-at-arms and archers in addition. These seem to have been recruited
around 20 June.[44] Since the loyalty of North Wales was suspected, no special
company of archers was recruited from there. In South Wales, the chamberlain,
John Merbury, raised from the counties of Carmarthen and Cardigan ten men-
at-arms, thirteen mounted archers and 327 foot archers, and from the lordship of
Brecon ten men-at-arms, thirteen mounted archers and 146 foot archers, making
500 archers in all, as for Lancashire.[45] Whether these volunteered or were 'chosen'
is not certain. The muster list for the company suggests that many of those who
were supposed to serve sent substitutes. This implies that there was some means
by which men were obliged to serve. We have a possible insight into this in a petition of the king's tenants of Kidwelly against his receiver, Hugh Edon, concerning
recruitment for the siege of Rouen in 1418. Edon told four men that they had
been assigned to go as men-at-arms and another five as archers, but that they
could be excused if they paid him fines of 16s 8d and 6s 8d respectively. Since one
of those allegedly picked for service was seventy years old, the tenants smelled a
rat and reported Edon for extortion.[46]

For the 1418 campaign Henry sent out commissions to the sheriffs to enlist
prisoners, following procedures used in Edward III's early campaigns where men
would serve in return for a promised pardon. There was no direct recruitment
of this type in 1415 but it is notable that several men who had been indicated in
King's Bench in Henry's efforts to restore law and order in 1413–14 did serve on
the campaign. Three former Welsh rebels pardoned in 1413, for instance, led the
archers from Cardigan and Carmarthen.[47] Edward III had also relied much on the
shire levies for raising archers and infantry more generally.[48] Henry issued commissions of array for twenty counties on 29 May 1415.[49] In almost every case the
commissioners included at least one knight or esquire who had already indented
to serve on the campaign. This may suggest that the arrays were a method of alert-
ing potential soldiers, but if any were recruited, they would have done so within
the retinue of an indentee. More likely the arrays were carried out to ensure that
sound national defence was in place before the king left the country. Shire levies
had not been used for service abroad since the 1350s.

Although the days of feudal service had long gone, Henry expected all of the
peers to accompany him unless there was good reason why they should not. The
Earl of Devon, for instance, was blind, but his son Sir Edward Courtenay indented
with thirty men-at-arms and ninety archers.[50] Henry, Earl of Somerset, Clarence's
stepson, was only fourteen and so did not indent, but was included within his
stepfather's retinue, being invalided home with him from Harfleur. Alongside him
was Humphrey, Lord Fitzwalter, aged sixteen, who likely died at the siege on
1 September. What we see here, therefore, is the blooding of young noblemen
who had not yet come into their inheritances. The Earl of Suffolk's elder son,
Michael, indented with his own company of 20 + 60, but his younger brother

William probably served within his father's retinue and was invalided home from Harfleur.[51] The Earl of Warwick did not indent for the campaign, since he was captain of Calais.

The king had decided by 17 April that his middle brother, John, Duke of Bedford, would act as keeper of the realm in his absence. This choice was likely based on two considerations. Clarence already had much military experience and was the only one of the royal brothers, counting even Henry himself, who had campaigned in France. The youngest brother, Humphrey, Duke of Gloucester, had had limited military exposure to date, and therefore the campaign was intended to blood him in the arts of war. It was also decided that a few peers should remain in England as royal councillors. Those earmarked were Ralph Neville, Earl of Westmorland, Reginald, Lord Grey of Ruthin,[52] Thomas, Lord Berkeley, Sir John Grey of Heton (known as Lord Powis by virtue of his marriage) and Thomas, Lord Morley. Although Grey of Heton (b. after 1384) was around the same age as the king, Grey of Ruthin (b.1362), Berkeley (b.1352) and Morley (b.1354) were all men over fifty and perhaps deemed too old for overseas service. Given the fragility of the frontier with Scotland, Westmorland (also aged fifty or so) was detailed to take charge of the marches, assisted by Lord Morley and a local peer, Thomas, Lord Dacre. On 16 May Richard, Lord Grey of Codnor (b.1371)[53] was appointed warden of the East March in the stead of Edward, Duke of York, and on 5 August was commissioned to negotiate a truce with the Scots. Westmorland's son, Sir John de Neville, was appointed warden of the West March by 24 June.[54]

Other than gunners, there was little effort to recruit any foreign soldiers. A request did go to the Gascon Sire de Saint-Pierre for twenty mounted men-at-arms and twenty mounted crossbowmen.[55] Pierre Lowat, who indented to serve with six men-at-arms and eighteen crossbowmen, was probably a foreigner, but his origins are not known.[56] Janico Dartas, an esquire of Navarre, indented to serve with ten men-at-arms and thirty archers but his position was much like that of the Robessarts from Hainault, Lewis and John. All were foreigners who had already established themselves in the service of the English king before 1415.[57] This was therefore a home-grown army, with captains drawn from the whole of England and also from South Wales. Davy Gam, esquire, of Brecon indented with three archers, one of whom was his son-in-law, Roger Fychan of Brodorddyn. At least one Welshman, Henry, son of William Gwyn of Carmarthenshire, possibly a supporter of Glendower, died on the French side.[58]

It is relatively easy to see how captains were recruited, but what of the men in their retinues? As we noted, Clarence contracted to bring an earl, two bann-erets and fourteen knights within his total retinue size of 960 men. The young Somerset and Fitzwalter provided the earl and one of the bannerets but neither brought any troops with them.[59] The second banneret was Sir John Lumley (b.1383), who died alongside Clarence at the battle of Baugé in March 1421. He brought along nine-teen men-at-arms and forty-eight archers. Clarence managed to recruit only ten knights, each of whom brought a group of men-at-arms and archers, from 20 + 66 under Sir John Daubridgecourt to 4 + 8 under Sir John Pudesay.[60] Fifty-nine esquires had also brought along men; twenty had both men-at-arms and archers, the remainder archers only (at an average of six archers each). The largest company (10 + 31) headed by an esquire was that of Brian Stapulton, who was probably knighted during the campaign, where he took eight prisoners.[61] Clarence also provided a company of 149 archers. In other words, the duke's retinue was made up of men recruited by himself and seventy other men. Lumley and the ten knights provided 42 per cent of the total, the esquires 44 per cent, with the duke providing the rest. The Duke of Gloucester's retinue can be similarly dissected.[62] He had indented for six knights, 193 men-at-arms and 600 archers. Together the six knights brought 222 men, with 105 of these in the company of Sir Henry Husee. Twenty-six esquires brought mixed retinues, twenty-four archers only. The duke contributed 128 archers. In his retinue, therefore, the knights provided 22 per cent, the esquires 62 per cent and the duke the remaining 16 per cent through his 128 archers.

The best insight into the retinue of a peer is provided by the example of John Mowbray, Earl Marshal (b.1392). He indented to serve with four knights, forty-five men-at-arms and 150 archers. There is no surviving muster at the point of embarkation, but we do have a list of those invalided home with the earl as well as a list of the earl's men at the battle. We can look at these names against the account of the earl's receiver-general, which notes the distribution of *vadia guerrae* (wages of war) to those who were to serve on the expedition.[63] The conclusion is again that the earl's retinue of 200 was made up of a number of smaller companies. For instance, Sir Thomas Rokeby, a retainer of the earl, provided another man-at-arms and nine archers. A later reference in the messenger section of the account indicates that the earl sent an envoy from London to the Yorkshire home of Sir Thomas with the first instalment of wages 'and to provide that the said Thomas would be with the earl at Bosham on 1 July 1415'.

The receiver-general's account shows that another knight, Sir Nicholas Colfox, provided a further two men-at-arms and seven archers. Six men brought mixed companies between seven and twenty-one men, eleven brought two archers each, fifteen brought three archers. Forty-three men brought only their own service as archers. One of these, Thomas Trompette, had been transferred from the retinue of Henry, Lord Scrope after his arrest. His surname suggests that he was a 'trompette', used for sounding military instructions as well as for taking messages.[64] We know that others of Scrope's company had been transferred to the charge of Sir Roland Lenthale.[65] What is most striking is how many of the earl's soldiers were already his 'employees', including his steward, the master of his horse, his minstrels, his baker, armourer, yeoman of his robes, even his barber. Another of his household, Thomas Lyons, was responsible for buying food and drink for the campaign, and for riding from Bosham to Midhurst to speak to Sir John Barre about an order concerning the campaign.[66] In other words, like the king, the earl had transferred his household to military wages. We can also see that he took with him at his own expense two chaplains, fourteen Welshmen whose function is not given, and several sumpter men and carters.

Men who brought troops within the larger retinues also drew on their own employees. Richard Lacon, Robert Corbet and Roger Corbet, who all served within the Earl of Arundel's company, were accompanied by men known, from the evidence of their joint criminal activity previously, to have been their servants.[67] At the core of all retinues, therefore, was a household, as had always been the case in medieval English armies. This was expanded for war by adding in servants of servants, tenants, neighbours, friends.[68] It is interesting to see the term *socii* (friends or associates) used to describe those within retinues in this period as, for instance, in the Earl Marshal's account. For the Earls of Dorset and Salisbury, sub-indentures were entered into with men who then promised to bring troops.[69] This may have been common practice for those who did not have a household or tenurial connection and may reveal the existence of freelance soldiers who allied themselves with anyone who needed their service.

Save for the specialist groups and the archer companies drawn from Cheshire, Lancashire and Wales, all retinues were mixed in that they contained both men-at-arms and archers. Generally speaking these groups were described as *homines ad arma* and *sagittarii*, but it is interesting to note other names used in the records. Men-at-arms were sometimes called lances (*lanceae*), reminding us of the expectation that they would be adept at the use of the foot lance in the mêlée. All were mounted and could be used in cavalry squadrons with couched lances where necessary, but for over a century it had become standard practice to fight primarily on foot in battle situations. Other terms found are *armiger* and *scutifer*, both of which can be translated as 'esquire', or *gentielx* (gentlemen).[70] This reminds us that men who were recruited as men-at-arms had an enhanced status as a result and also tended to come from families of 'gentle' status. They were expected to have a full suit of plate, with additional mail defences at vulnerable points and all the necessary under-padding. Bascinets with detachable visors were the most popular form of headwear. In terms of weapons, swords, lances, staff weapons of 2m–2.5m which combined the spear with an axe, hammer or other devices (such as halberd, pole-axe, billhook, guisarme), shorter-handled axes, war hammers and maces might be expected. Costs were met by the man himself, which restricted service to those who could afford it, although those in the lordly households might be provided with some armour and equipment. The Earl Marshal, for instance, purchased *pavises* (large wooden shields) for all his men-at-arms for the expedition. In addition, men-at-arms were expected to be fully trained in the use of weapons and in handling a horse. Much of this came as a natural corollary of their social rank and was a sign of status.

By contrast, archers were often described as *valetti*, which was in Middle English 'yeomen', a term increasingly being applied to the upper ranks of the peasantry.

The term also meant 'servant'. In the retinue of the Earl Marshal, the higher-ranking members of his household served as men-at-arms (and brought along their own servants as their archers), his lower servants as archers. This was also the case in the royal household companies. Indeed, this can raise problems in counting those invalided home, since the same term is used for archers as well as servants within the royal household who were not in military wages. For archers outside households, there are considerable problems in identification. Some shared a surname with men-at-arms in the retinue, suggesting that they were junior members of 'gentle' families serving their military apprenticeship.[71] Their equipment needs were substantially lower than for men-at-arms. They were required to have some body protection, such as the reinforced leather armours in the form of brigandines, jacquets or palletoqs. Head protection was also useful, but an iron or leather skull cap or any other form of non-visored helmet was suitable. The Burgundian chroniclers speak of archers being without armour and bare-headed at the battle, or else having 'hunettes or cappelines of boiled leather and some of osier on which they had a binding of iron'.[72] They were also expected to have a bow, quiver, sword and dagger. Given that very large quantities of arrows would be needed for siege, skirmish or battle, these (or often their constituent parts) were provided by their lords or the crown. This explains why so much effort was put into collecting large quantities of these objects over the months preceding the campaign. The Earl Marshal took on campaign a supply of bowstrings and 100 bundles of arrows, as well as chests in which to store and transport them whose descriptions match well the chests full of bow staves found on the Mary Rose. Archers were expected to have competence with the bow but not all needed to be sharpshooters, since the main use of arrow fire was *en masse*. As with all sports and martial arts, however, some men would have been more accomplished than others. Those in the lord's retinues would be expected to show their skills in the hunt. Furthermore, any facility at all with the long bow required practice and training, especially in the pace of reloading and directional fire.

As already noted, the ratio of men-at-arms to archers in retinues was generally 1:3, although there were some retinues with 1:2. In addition, there were at least 1,247 archers raised from Wales, Lancashire and Cheshire. The overall proportion of archers can be calculated as about 80 per cent. A comparative study is useful here, because it reveals the changing importance accorded to the two kinds of troops. The expeditions departing for France from 1369 to 1389 had equal or near equal numbers of men-at-arms and archers.[73] From April 1406 onwards, a ratio of 1:3 was established in the armies for Wales and also in garrisons. This ratio predominated through to the end of the occupation of Normandy in 1450, in all forms of military organisation. We can therefore argue that it was considered an optimum for English military endeavours. Indeed, since it came into being at the point when Prince Henry was in effective sole command in Wales, it is tempting to see him as linked to its creation. It is all too easy to jump to the conclusion that

the ratio was instituted with battle formation in mind, but since its origins in the
Welsh wars were not related to the likelihood of pitched battle, and it is seen in
both defensive and offensive provision thenceforward, there must be other explanations. That is not to say, of course, that archers were not deemed useful in battle
situations. At Shrewsbury arrow power had been significant on both sides, as the
prince found to his cost, since he had to be operated on to remove an arrow
head from his face. Two suggestions can be made on why the ratio of 1:3 predominated. The first is that archers were cheaper than men-at-arms: 50 per cent
cheaper. They could also be raised more easily, since they needed less specialised
equipment and multi-faceted training. Therefore, by increasing the proportion of
archers, a larger army could be achieved without any extra charge or delay. Since
the Lancastrian kings were frequently short of funds, this was a useful ploy. It did
not lead to military weakness. Most campaign activity in any theatre consisted
of raids, skirmishes and sieges, where archers were just as useful as men-at-arms.
At a siege, for instance, there was little function for men-at-arms save for countering
sorties. Furthermore, since archers were commonly mounted in this period (in
the sense that they were expected to bring along a horse), their presence did not
slow down an army or restrict their use to fixed-point warfare. In 1415 archers
were expected to have mounts unless specified otherwise and all were paid at the
rate for mounted archers, at 6d per day: only the special companies of archers
were mainly on foot.[74]

Even within the larger retinues it was common for archers to be assigned to
particular men-at-arms. This reflects recruitment methods but also had implications for discipline, since the men-at-arms were sometimes described as 'masters',
appropriate when archers were also their servants. There is some suggestion that
pay went from the captain to the man-at-arms, who then paid his archers. In pay
terms, the army remained in mixed retinues (save for the archer and specialist
companies). How this translated into military action is uncertain. Were men-
at-arms and archers of a retinue kept together at the siege of Harfleur, and in
the three marching battles into which Henry divided his men on the march?
Or was there a separation according to armaments, so that archers from different
retinues were put together? We are faced with the same questions when looking
at the battle, where the situation is made even more complex thanks to the way
chroniclers describe the English formation. A lack of certainty over this matter
is frustrating. It is noticeable that several retinues were mustered together at a
particular location before embarkation. A good number of the small retinues lay
within the royal household and therefore would have been grouped within the
battle of the king, but others were surely amalgamated into larger units.

Moving down to the level of the individual, we have the names of several
thousand soldiers on the campaign (Appendix E). Most come down to us in
the muster rolls drawn up as the army gathered to embark or in the retinue lists
returned by captains with post-campaign accounts. These can be supplemented

by protections and letters of attorney taken out by men before they departed, thereby safeguarding themselves against any legal actions in their absence. These are enrolled on the French (often called Treaty) rolls.[75] They were taken out from around 22 April onwards, with the majority between May and August, although some are found in September and October, adding to a possibility that reinforcements were sent after the siege had ended. In all, around 500 appear to relate to the campaign. In some cases occupations are given, such as butchers, fishmongers, drovers, bakers and brewers, as well as the occasional priest, tailor, armourer, bladesmith and barber. Some of these men were serving as soldiers. Occasionally musters note archers as having a particular occupation, as for instance: James Finch, dyer, in the retinue of Hugh, Lord Bourchier. But it was also the case that men accompanied the army in support functions without necessarily being part of the paid force. Geographical origin is also sometimes given for those taking out protections. It is difficult to come to any conclusions here, since most counties are represented at least once, but there are larger concentrations for London and the Home Counties than elsewhere, as well as a good number for the maritime counties of the south coast. There is no doubt that additional servants accompanied their masters. A list for the return shipping of the retinue of the Earl of Oxford shows that almost all of his thirty-nine men-at-arms, although none of his archers, had a page.[76] We do not have full information on how many men crossed with the expedition in addition to those in receipt of military wages. As we have seen, it was not uncommon for household servants to be serving as archers. If the situation on Oxford's retinue was replicated throughout the army, we would be talking about as many pages as men-at-arms (hence over 2,000) but there may have been a difference between retinues of the great lords and those of men of lesser social status.

Why were men willing to serve? As we have seen, some had no choice. It was part of their job to serve their king or lord. Others were professional soldiers who had served on previous campaigns and in garrisons. Historians have been reluctant to consider patriotism within a common cause as a stimulus in this period, but given the emphasis Henry placed on the recovery of his rights and on the perfidy of the French, it is hard to believe that it did not play a role. For many it was surely a great adventure acted out alongside comrades and relations, and with the possibility of forging new friendships and associations. The commitment was not for long. As it turned out, it was for less than half of the intended duration of twelve months. It was also lucrative. Ransoms were the equivalent of winning the lottery, since for the majority of the population there was no other way that a large sum could be gained overnight. Very few soldiers would ever make such a killing, but we must remember that pay rates in the army were high in comparison with other occupations. A man-at-arms at 12d (a shilling) a day could, with a year's service, earn the equivalent of the income of a small manor. Since captains received half of the first quarter's pay in advance, we can imagine that they used at least some of it to entice men to commit themselves to service – a forerunner of the 'king's shilling'. However, because the pay always went to the captain for him to pay out to his men, we cannot be sure how much actually came into the pockets of the troops themselves. It was customary for captains to keep money back to provide for food and accommodation.[77] But we must remember that recruiting a retinue was also a financial burden for captains. This was all the more so in the case of the 1415 campaign, since they would not receive cash but rather jewels for the second quarter. They had a choice: they could keep the jewels, pay their troops out of their own pockets and then collect the cash from the crown when the jewels were redeemed. Or they could pawn the jewels before the campaign for ready cash, on the understanding that they would be able to retrieve them with the promise of the crown's payment later. Given the arrangements, it is not surprising to find that there were many petitions by captains in the early part of Henry VI's reign concerning the moneys outstanding for their services in 1415. While Henry V lived, the lid had been kept on this particular can of worms, since the king had never been able to afford to keep his promise on redemption. In 1437 the crown abandoned efforts to retrieve jewels that it had not yet redeemed.[78]

Paying the army was one problem, feeding it was another. On the campaign there was strict list of 101 people entitled to *bouche de court* (the right to be fed within the royal household). These included household officials and the king's personal servants as well as men such as the surgeon, Thomas Morstede.[79] Before the expedition sailed, the royal household exploited its rights of pre-emption and control of markets within a designated radius of where it was lodged not only to feed itself while waiting to depart but also to gather foodstuffs for the campaign. On 27 May the council discussed the provision of victuals in the area around the king's intended embarkation point.[80] As a result, an order went out immediately to the sheriff of Hampshire to proclaim that, in Winchester, Southampton and other towns and villages, bakers and brewers should work under the direction of the under-sheriff to prepare for the coming of the king and his army.[81] There were also orders issued to sheriffs of several counties in southern England to provide live animals for the expedition.[82] After being brought to a number of places including Titchfield, Southwick, Southampton, Beaulieu, Leamington, Romsey, Alresford and Fareham, they were to be sold to the captains, since each was responsible for the victualling of his own retinue. We can see in the account of the Earl Marshal's receiver-general how beer, cider, salted meats and fish, as well as live animals, many from the earl's own estates, were collected at Bosham for transportation to Portsmouth and then to Harfleur.

On 24 July, a week before the expedition was due to sail, the king ordered the sheriff of Hampshire to proclaim that those going on the expedition should take enough victuals for a quarter.[83] This was no mean feat, since there had already been a drain on resources to feed the army as it gathered in the area. The solution was to distribute the troops between various locations. In early May the Earl of Salisbury had already been assigned Christchurch, Canford and Poole for the lodging and feeding of his retinue, since it was initially planned that he should go to Guienne.[84] Other locations are revealed by the musters, which were made from 13 July. Clarence's retinue was placed at St Catherine's Hill 'near the New Forest' (this may mean the hill close to Winchester but this is not certain), and Gloucester's at Romsey. The Earl of Oxford was at Wallopforth (presumably in the vicinity of Over and Middle Wallop). On Swanwick Heath was Huntingdon, along with Botreaux, Grey of Ruthin, Roland Lenthale and much of the royal household contingent. Sir Thomas Erpingham, Sir John Robessart and others were at Southampton Heath (now Common). Nicholas Horton and others were at Hampton Hill.[85] Every effort was made to ensure good relations with the local population. The order of 24 July had been accompanied by an invitation for any who had suffered molestation from soldiers to lodge their complaints before the steward or controller of the household. Four days later, hearing that English and Welsh soldiers passing through Warminster had taken goods without paying, the king, concerned at the bad example they had set, ordered that if they refused to pay then the sheriff should compel them to do so by calling out his posse.[86] That the passage of troops caused disruption is revealed in the archives of the city of Salisbury, which note an assault on 4 August by a group of men from Lancashire under James Harrington on some of its citizens, in which four Salisbury men were killed.[87]

Much preparation went into the expedition in terms of the provision of men and equipment. It is interesting to note that not only were materials taken over, such as bowstaves, carts, horseshoes etc., but also men who could see to their construction and repair during the expedition. There were also personal preparations, as revealed in the account of the Earl Marshal's receiver-general. These included several items bearing his arms: a costly surcoat, trappings for his horses, a mainsail for his ship, and flags. An old pavilion was repaired to use as his 'garderobe' and a new iron seat for a latrine was also purchased, as well as a bed, a mattress and equipment for his chapel. A number of medications was also provided, although the 'electura' against the bloody flux cannot have proved effective in protecting the earl from dysentery, since he had to be invalided home.

The earl also procured a tent for his stable. This reminds us that, in addition to men and equipment, large numbers of horses were taken across to France. We do not have information on this at the point of embarkation, although it is interesting to note that Dorset's sub-indentures specified the number of horses the contracted men-at-arms and archers should bring.[88] The only way we can count horses is through the post-campaign accounts, where numbers shipped back to England are given. This disguises losses during the campaign and also the fact that those invalided home seem to have left some of their horses behind. Even so, some interesting figures emerge. The Earl Marshal, for instance, had taken at least twenty-four horses and his knights six each. Sir John Grey of Ruthin fought at the battle with forty-four men. They returned with ninety-six horses between them.[89] The muster roll of the Duke of York for the second quarter of service, the only such roll to survive, shows that most of his men-at-arms had two horses, and 65 per cent of his archers one horse.[90] All in all, the number of horses must have exceeded the number of men. All had to be loaded onto ships, where they would have been placed in canvas hoops suspended from the beams of the hold so that they did not suffer from the movement of the ship.

Transporting men, horses and equipment to France required a large quantity of shipping. The crown's own fleet of thirteen ships was detailed to this: Henry himself crossed in the 540-tun *Trinite Royal* which had been commissioned soon after his accession.[91] The crown also had powers to requisition merchant vessels, although their owners had to be paid. Although there was arrest of English ships and sailors, as well as a call out of the fleet of the Cinque Ports, this was not on a scale seen in earlier or later campaigns. Instead, it had been decided to hire ships from Holland and Zealand at a cost of over £2,000.[92] Two explanations for this can be suggested. The first is that impressment was extremely unpopular with the English merchant community and the scale of this expedition would have interfered considerably with their interests. Secondly, larger ships were in greater abundance in the Low Countries for long-distance trade, perhaps already fitted out to transport horses and other livestock and large quantities of supplies. By 27 July it was realised that the shipping was not enough and orders went out to bring more vessels from London to Southampton.[93] Some men had to be left behind at the outset, although they may have been able to cross later, since there is evidence of replacements in retinues after the siege of Harfleur.[94]

There can be no doubt that the king tried to raise as large an army as possible for his invasion, but how large was it? Given the survival of so many financial records for the army that Henry raised, it is possible to be fairly certain of its size.[95] Altogether, twenty-six peers entered into indentures to provide 5,222 men. We have evidence of fifty-seven knights (both banneret and bachelor, and including Michael de la Pole junior, who inherited the duchy of Suffolk during the campaign) who contracted for a further 2,573 men. Those who indented below knightly rank produce a total of 1,306 men. A thousand archers were provided from Lancashire and South Wales. The figure for Cheshire is problematic, since only 247 seem to have received pay yet 650 archers and fifty men-at-arms may have been intended. Around 900 men, mainly serving as archers, were raised from the offices of the royal household. That gives a total of 11,248 soldiers, of whom 2,266 were men-at-arms (20.1 per cent). If the higher Cheshire figures are used, then the total would be 11,791, with 2,316 men-at-arms (19.6 per cent). The eighteenth-century list of indentures printed by Nicolas suggests that others indented for whom we now have no information surviving. For instance, he notes 250 men-at-arms and 250 archers under Sir John Devereux (possibly a

Gascon, since the ratio is more typical of that area than England) which cannot be traced in any of the documentation in The National Archives. He also gives 20 + 60 under William de la Pole, younger son of Suffolk, but the retinue list of the earl suggests that he served within his company. The total number of combatants likely exceeded 12,000 and was boosted by the non-military groups such as the miners and carpenters.

We know also that some captains had recruited more men than their indenture required. These men are listed in the musters as 'men beyond the number' (*oultre le nombre*).[96] Although these were only small numbers, they were useful in filling vacancies as they arose. In some companies, most notably the archers from South Wales and the retinue of the Earl of Arundel, almost all of those invalided home were replaced by others, as will be discussed in Chapter 5. This again suggests that these supernumeraries were with the army or else crossed later, since there is a reference in the council minutes of March 1417 to the fact that not all troops were able to find shipping at the outset.[97] There is also evidence of 560 support men (120 miners, 124 carpenters, 150 stonemasons, forty smiths, sixty waggoners, and 120 labourers). In addition, Sir John Tiptoft crossed to Bordeaux in mid-August with eighty men-at-arms and 400 archers.[98] While we cannot count these troops into the king's campaign, it is important to bear them in mind, as also the troops in Wales, the Scottish marches and Calais, in order to gain a full impression of the military investment of Henry at this point. Even if the paid troops did not much exceed 12,000, this was still a very large army by the standard of English expeditions to France, although larger forces had been raised for Scotland, as in 1400. Henry's army was three times the size of the army sent under Clarence in 1412. No expedition between 1369 and 1389 had exceeded 6,000 men. That of 1359 may have numbered 10,000, but to find larger armies, we need to go back to the pre-Black Death period. Recent research has suggested that the army that Edward III took to France in 1346 totalled 14,000 troops.[99]

A popular image is that the French army was much more lustrous in its aristo-cratic component. In fact, the English army contained almost all of the active peers. The participation of the royal family is distinctive (see Table 5). Men such as Dorset, York and Arundel had already enjoyed lengthy careers in arms and enjoyed the trust of the king. Some of the men on the campaign, such as Sir Thomas Erpingham, had experience that stretched back into the wars of the 1380s. Others, like Sir Walter Hungerford, had already show their prowess in the tournament.[100] England had been highly militarised since the usurpation of 1399. There was no difficulty in finding suitable commanders or troops, although the army size was so great that many must have had no previous military experience. By far the largest number of troops was provided by the nobility: the figure would be over 50 per cent of the whole army if knights banneret such as Erpingham were included within this group. As we have seen, households were at the centre of it all. The English army of 1415 was raised largely through existing connections and networks of service. Only the special archer and support companies came from a broader base. The army was dominated by men who shared common ideals of gentility and honour and whose status in society derived from their role as the 'fighting classes'. In that respect, it was little different from the French army save in two important respects – a very high number and proportion of archers, although many of these had close connections of service with their masters, and the presence of a king determined to prove himself at home and abroad.

4

The Siege of Harfleur,
13 August–22 September 1415

Although the French engineered a final set of negotiations in the summer of 1415, the die was cast on 13 March. On that day the treaty of Arras was ratified, formalising an end to the war against Burgundy. With the prospect of unity, the offers of the English envoys could be rejected. It is no coincidence, therefore, that on the very same day Charles VI ordered a tax levy to protect his kingdom. This he justified on the grounds that Henry V was himself raising funds as well as assembling ships and men.[1] At this stage, however, the French did not know when or where the invasion would come. Their strategy was to delay it for as long as possible, since the tax renders were not due until 1 June and 1 August. As in England, large-scale armed force could not be mounted until there was money to pay for it. No doubt in the light of intelligence of English activities from the middle of April onwards, the French started to make their own outline preparations. At the end of the month the Dauphin was appointed royal lieutenant and captain general of all frontiers, with powers to call up as many soldiers as necessary.[2] On 3 June the royal council at Paris, attended by the king, the Dauphin, d'Albret, the Count of Vendôme, the Seneschal of Hainault, the Sires de Gaucourt and de Torcy and others, wrote to the *baillis* of Normandy in the light of preparations of the English 'to enter into our kingdom and make war with all their might by both land and sea'.[3] The letter ordered proclamations that the nobility and others accustomed to offer military service should hold themselves in readiness. Not only were they to be on their guard day and night, but they were also to ensure that they possessed the necessary war gear. In addition, inhabitants of towns and captains of both urban and castle garrisons were to maintain the watch and carry out repairs and defensive improvements as necessary.

The Duke of Alençon was already in office as captain-general for war in Normandy by mid-July.[4] On 28 July Boucicaut was given special commission as the king's lieutenant and captain general.[5] Des Ursins claimed that this appointment was for Normandy and that the marshal went off to Rouen with the constable, 'which made the duke of Alençon very upset'. This comment may be a symptom of the culture of blame that developed in the wake of the defeats of 1415, in which both Alençon and d'Albret met their deaths while Boucicaut was captured. The surviving pay records for the French army certainly show Alençon in command, although largely in Lower Normandy. The official position of d'Albret is uncertain. Des Ursins claims that the constable was given military full authority but no formal appointment is known. As we shall see, he was certainly in command of companies in the *pays de Caux* during the siege. The chronicler also suggests that Clignet de Brabant, the admiral, was appointed to command of Picardy. The truth of this is also uncertain although he too was involved in naval activity against the English blockade of Harfleur.[6] Following a well-worn precedent, these regional commanders would be assigned companies which could be deployed as mobile patrols and as garrison reinforcements.[7]

It is important to remember that the French could only operate in response mode. Because of difficulties in communications, the initial advantage lay with Henry as aggressor. Although Normandy was seen as the likely venue for a landing, with such a length of coastline it was impossible to keep watch and defend everywhere. According to des Ursins, the inhabitants of Upper Normandy (the *pays de Caux*) thought that the landing would be in Lower Normandy (south of the Seine), and as a result their cattle were easy pickings for the English when they landed north of the river. The most likely invasion point was considered to be St-Vaast-la-Hougue on the north-eastern tip of the Cotentin, since this was where Edward III had landed in 1346 and Clarence in 1412. Army pay records reveal concentrations of troops kept in Valognes and Carentan from mid-July onwards, and there were also repairs to fortifications in the area of Coutances at the south-western end of the peninsula. By early August reinforcements were also installed at Falaise, Caen, Honfleur and Montivilliers. The French were spreading their resources thinly to cover all possibilities.[8] In August 1413 the English had launched a raid on St Aubin-sur-Mer near Dieppe, which made inhabitants fearful of a landing there.[9] There was also an expectation that the English would attack from the Calais march, as indeed they did once the truce ended in late July. Immediately, the Calais garrison launched a series of sorties into the area around Boulogne. According to Monstrelet, the French responded by sending 500 soldiers to the area under David, Sire de Rambures, master of the crossbowmen, and Jacques de Longroy. These were men of the area who held their main seigneuries in the Vimeu, the territory between the Bresle and the Somme. Both men had extensive military and administrative experience and served at Agincourt. Longroy had recently been appointed captain of Ardres, a French garrison on the frontier of the Calais march, and lieutenant of Picardy.

The first alert of Henry's invasion was raised by the fishermen of Boulogne, who spotted some of the English ships on their crossing to France. The town did not delay in warning their neighbours, despatching Jacques Roquelin le Jeune to Étaples, at the estuary of the Canche, and to Le Crotoy and Saint-Valéry, which stood on opposite sides of the mouth of the Somme. As soon as Roquelin had returned to Boulogne, he was sent off again, this time to Abbeville (the first bridging point of the Somme), Dieppe and Honfleur. In particular, he was instructed to seek out d'Albret, then believed to be at Honfleur, to give him letters about the English fleet, which by this time was known to be heading for the Seine.[10]

There is general agreement that the English set sail from the Solent on Sunday 11 August.[11] According to the *Gesta*, the king's ship entered the mouth of the Seine on Tuesday 13 August at 5 p.m. and dropped anchor off a village called 'Kidecaus', which lay about three miles from Harfleur, at which location Henry proposed that landing should be made. The wording implies that the spot had been chosen in advance. The coast would have been well known to English merchant and fishing fleets, and a number of men who had served as ambassadors to France and were now on the campaign had passed through Harfleur in the past. The supposed spy, Jean Fusoris, also mentioned during his trial that he saw a merchant of Harfleur at the house of Richard Courtenay, Bishop of Norwich.[12] With such a large army and fleet, Henry could not have left the landing point to chance. It was already known that this stretch of coastline was not customarily guarded. The French had relied on natural features reinforced by man-made 'walls of earth', probably erected against piratical raids.

The *Gesta*'s description of the landing place as 'very stony with large boulders which were dangerous to ships' would fit the coastline north of the current lighthouse at Cap de la Hève, which is the headland known as the Chef de Caux. It is unlikely that a landing of a large army, with all its horses and equipment, could have been made north of this point, since there is no easy access at any point along this coast. Most likely the landing was within the lee of the hill at Sainte-Adresse, where there is a col between two hills. This would fit the chronicler's descriptions of the army moving up a steep valley from the shore onto a flat high hill, across which they could approach Harfleur. This hill, at around 300 feet above sea level, now forms the northern residential areas of Le Havre – Bléville, Santivic and Frileuse. The manor and lordship of Frileuse, held by Guy Malet, Seigneur de Graville, was one of the first land donations made by Henry in Normandy, being granted on 29 January 1416 to John Fastolf. He was among those who made the landing in mid-August in the retinue of the Earl of Suffolk. Although he was invalided home after the siege, he subsequently returned to join the garrison of Harfleur, where he was at the time of the grant of Frileuse.[13]

The *Gesta* includes unique comment on how the landing was controlled by the king. After dropping anchor, the king called a meeting. The captains were summoned to his ship by a visual signal – the unfurling of the banner of the council.

After this meeting a proclamation was issued throughout the fleet that all should make ready to land on the morning of the next day (i.e. Wednesday 14 August) but that none should land before the king. The fear was that if there was a hap-hazard disembarkation the troops might disperse in search of plunder and so leave the king's own landing exposed. This provides an insight into perceptions of the priorities of soldiers and of the king's anxiety. A landing with so many men and so much equipment was a hazardous thing. The location was by no means as shel-tered as St-Vaast-la-Hougue. There again, it would be unlikely that the French could have done much to harry the disembarkation since they had been unable to predict where it would be made.

The date of landing had been deliberately chosen by Henry since it was the Vigil of the Assumption. This theme is emphasised by Titus Livius. There the king falls to his knees as he lands, praying that God will give him justice against his enemies. Then his troops rush to climb up to the high ground so that the feast can be properly celebrated on the next day. The author adds that Henry also created knights and bannerets at the landing. He gives no names, but Sir Thomas Erpingham's post-campaign account reveals that two of those dubbed were men-at-arms of his retinue, Thomas Geney and John Calthorp.[14] The *Gesta* gives a rather more prosaic account of the landing. Here, while still at sea and before dawn, the king sent the Earl of Huntingdon with a mounted patrol to reconnoitre inland.[15] Hardyng notes the presence of Gilbert Umfraville, John Cornwall, William Porter and John Steward in this action, and adds in his prose account that they reported back that there were no enemies to be seen at the top of the hill where the king hoped to pitch camp.[16] Huntingdon was only nineteen or twenty at this point and is unlikely to have had any previous military experience. In this period it was considered necessary for a man of high status to hold overall, if sometimes nominal, command, especially when interactions with the native population were possible, since such men were acting in a vice-regal capacity. It is noticeable that trusted veterans close to the king accompanied the young earl on this important manoeuvre. A further task given to Huntingdon and his party was to find a suit-able lodging place for the king. Armies of this period, as in later centuries, were very status-conscious. The king and the nobles tried to preserve as much as they could of their noble lifestyle on campaign. Finding an appropriate place for the king was important throughout the campaign and was a task assigned to the royal herbergers (or harbingers), who also acted in this capacity when the king moved around England.

The king with the majority of his army landed in the early afternoon of Wednesday 14 August. The unloading of all equipment was only complete, according to the *Gesta*, by Saturday 17 August. This chronicle claims that the king spent his first night ashore on the high ground towards Harfleur, between the wooded areas that lay on the southern slopes towards the Seine and the culti-vated lands on the landward side. Further detail is given by Titus Livius and the

Pseudo-Elmham, who claim that Henry ordered a 'tented city' to be built on the hill above the town towards Montivilliers (Mont Leconte), where his priests carried out the daily office 'just as they were accustomed to do in time of peace'. The Burgundian chroniclers, however, have the king lodge immediately at the priory of Graville, while his brothers of Clarence and Gloucester lodged nearby and the rest of the army 'found what they could'.[17] That further reconnaissance was carried out is suggested in the Pseudo-Elmham, which speaks of well-armed men being sent to explore the town of Harfleur. The *Gesta* comments that the king discussed with his advisers how best to lay the siege and also how to deploy detachments of foragers and maintain the night watch.

English chronicles provide further interesting insights into the likely organisation and disciplinary control of the army at this point. The *Gesta* has Henry put his army into three 'battles' (*acies*) as it moved to Harfleur. This formation was not simply for the battlefield but was also used to organise the army on the march, and here, as it arrayed on the high ground to the west of Harfleur. The king's battle was the centre, as at Agincourt. The vanguard to the right was almost certainly under the command of the Duke of Clarence, who was sent on the night of Sunday 18 August to the eastern side of Harfleur. According to Titus Livius, the rearguard on the left was under Michael de la Pole, Earl of Suffolk. It also appears that the king issued disciplinary ordinances just before siege was laid to Harfleur. Although chroniclers give only indicative clauses, there is enough to suggest that these were based on earlier codes issued by Edward III and Richard II. The most fundamental clause was that protecting churches and religious property. (The assumption must be, therefore, that if Henry had requisitioned the priory of Graville, he did not occupy the sacred parts of the building.) There was also the standard clause banning attacks on women, or on priests and other religious unless they were armed. In addition, it was ordered that there should be no more setting fire to places. Interestingly, the *Gesta* adds here 'as there had been to begin with', implying that while the landing was being effected, military considerations had taken precedence over the protection of civilians. With Henry's troops now poised to have their first formal contact with the king's supposed subjects in Harfleur, it is not surprising that the king should issue some disciplinary ordinances to control behaviour. We shall look at these in more detail in Chapter 7.

Even with the accretion of ring roads and modern buildings, the geographical position of Harfleur remains striking. The land to the west rises sharply, that to the north and east less so but still leading to the feeling that the place is hemmed in by a circle of high ground on three sides. To the south of the town is flat land leading down towards the Seine, which at the time of the siege was marshland, through which the river Lézarde meandered its way. The Lézarde, which comes down the narrow valley from Montivilliers 4km to the north, runs through the town. The townspeople were able to control the flow of the river by raising or lowering water gates. This gave them a defensive advantage, since by damming the river at its entry point to the town they could flood the lands that lay between the walls and the high ground to the west. The *Gesta* claims that they did this as soon as they heard of the English landing and that by the time the army reached the town the water was up to a man's thighs. In order for Clarence to take his men to the eastern side of the town, he had to make a detour of 16km or so, skirting round to the north of the town. The presence of the water had the advantage of making it possible for communications to be maintained between the king and his brother by boat, but also contributed to the unhealthy conditions in the royal siege camp to the west of the town and to the outbreak of dysentery.

Both Thomas Elmham and the author of the *Gesta* considered Harfleur to be a 'town of no great size'. This is rather dismissive, since its walled area was relatively extensive at over 21 hectares. Based on evidence of the hearth tax (*fouage*) there may have been as many as 1,600 families living there,[18] which indicates a total population of at least 5,000. Whether any civilians had left before siege was laid is not certain. Under normal circumstances, Harfleur would not have had a large garrison. Places without castles did not generally have large numbers of troops, since there was a reluctance on the part of the inhabitants to have troops billeted in a town. On 10 August, companies totalling thirty-four men-at-arms (called esquires in the French system) under the then captain, Sir Lyonnet de Bracquemont, Sir Olivier de Bracquemont and Sir Jean Bufreuil mustered in the town. There was also an unknown number of crossbowmen under Roland de Géraut, divided between Montivilliers and Harfleur.[19] According to the *Gesta*, 300 lances under Raoul de Gaucourt[20] came in from the east on Sunday 18 August, before it was possible for Clarence to establish his siege camp on that side of the town. We know that de Gaucourt had mustered on 14 August within the company of d'Albret, although the location of the muster is not given.[21]

There is some confusion over who the captain of Harfleur was during the siege. Titus Livius and the Pseudo-Elmham name Lyonnet de Bracquemont and have him conduct the negotiations for surrender. The *Gesta* claims that de Gaucourt was 'sent to take charge of the town by the French council', and later says that he was 'acting as captain', in which capacity he was involved in the negotiations for surrender. One version of the *Brut* chronicle gives the captain as Jacques de Harcourt.[22] The Burgundian chroniclers name the Sire d'Estouteville as captain, with de Gaucourt among those who brought in reinforcements. Pay records for the French army show d'Estouteville on 8 August in charge of companies at Montivilliers, under the general command of Alençon, but his movements after this point are not known.[23] A later dispute between the Gaucourt and Estouteville families over ransom payments (both men were taken to England as prisoners after the campaign) suggests that both were signatories to the surrender of Harfleur, but does not clarify which held superior command.[24] That the culture of blame continued to loom large for decades to come between these two prominent Norman families is also revealed in the chronicle of Jean Juvenal des Ursins.

Here it is de Gaucourt who is alleged to have gone 'two or three times a week' to discuss terms with the English and who decides that his men will not offer further resistance. Estouteville and his men have to agree to this against their will, even though there is enough food, allegedly, to hold out for longer: 'And so it is said that the town was sold and betrayed'.[25]

The exact number of troops in Harfleur during the siege cannot be established with precision. At the surrender, the *Gesta* notes that the king gave permission for de Gaucourt to leave 'along with many prisoners from the town who, citizens apart, numbered about sixty knights (*milites*) and more than 200 other gentlemen (*generosi*), almost all of the nobility from that part of Normandy up to the marches of Picardy'. The figure of 200 is also found in the Religieux, which also gives the names of a number of leading members of the garrison. Names of defenders are also found in the *Great Chronicle of London* and the *Brut*, based on lists of prisoners subsequently taken to England, although these are in rather garbled form as their English authors try to anglicise French names.[26] Putting all of the evidence together, however, there is a significant observation to be made. They were all men from Normandy and Picardy, as the *Gesta* said.[27] The townspeople would also be expected to assist by keeping watch and working on additional fortification measures. Note that the *Gesta* says that it was the townspeople (*oppidani*) who dammed the river when they heard of the king's landing. Henry was to install a garrison of 1,200 after the place fell; this was only achieved by driving out a good number of the population. When the area became more peaceful in the early 1420s the size of the garrison was reduced by the English to 120 men.

The defenders were considerably assisted by the town fortifications as well as the water defences. The walls were constructed between 1344 and 1361 and contained twenty-four mural towers. The route of the walls is still traceable today. The Porte de Rouen to the south-east also survives, although of mainly later fifteenth-century construction. The other two gates, the Porte de Montivilliers to the north, and the Porte de Leure to the south-west, are no longer extant. There were ditches all around the walls. Those to the north still survive and are around 4.5 metres deep, with stone walls on top of a steep-sided bank. An assault against these would not be easy, especially with deep water in the ditches. It is always difficult to know what condition walls were in, but repairs in the late fourteenth century are evidenced.[28] The three gates, which were intrinsically the 'softest' part of the defences since they needed to allow ingress and egress, were protected by outworks. The author of the *Gesta* calls these 'barbicans', adding that common people call them 'bulwarks'. That on the king's side (i.e. the Porte de Leure) is carefully described. It was constructed by means of tree trunks as high as the walls which were lashed together and driven into the ground. Inside there was further reinforcement of earth and wood, and openings had been made through which small guns, crossbows and other missiles could be fired. The constructions were circular, thus facilitating shot from several directions. These specially constructed outworks were a common feature of towns in this period, and presented a challenge for besiegers since they had to be taken in order to threaten the town itself. Given their circular projections, besiegers placed themselves in a vulnerable position when mounting an attack.

It was common for towns to house an arsenal of guns, large catapults (*balistae*) and large crossbows, as well as a stock of small arms. As we shall see, this artillery was put to good use in resisting attack. In addition, there seems to have been an ample supply of timber and stones in the town in anticipation of attack. Monstrelet and Waurin claim that, before the English arrived, the defenders had broken up the causeway between Montivilliers and Harfleur and carried the paving stones into the town. This may also have contributed to causing the Lézarde to flood the land to the west. Also helpful for the defenders of the town was the harbour (*le clos des galées*) and its defences, since these together also protected the southern flank of the town. This area is well described in the *Gesta* but little remains today. The harbour was itself walled with inter-mural towers. At the entrance there were two towers, between which chains could be stretched in order to prevent access. This was a common device, put to good use by Henry during his later siege of Rouen when, by driving piles into the Seine, he was able to place chains across the river to prevent ships bringing food to the city. As with the gates of the town, the harbour of Harfleur was further protected by timber works, in the form of tree trunks leaning outwards so that the English could not get close enough to mount an attack. All in all, therefore, Harfleur was a well-defended place which would be a challenge to take, although it was unlikely to occasion a very lengthy siege, as with great cities such as Rouen and Orléans.

Henry began his investment of Harfleur on 17 August. By 23 August, the inhabitants had sent word to d'Albret, then at Rouen, that they could no longer make contact by land. They requested that a boat be sent to help them bring in food and other necessities from Honfleur and elsewhere, and to ferry out messengers with news of what was happening in the besieged town. D'Albret commissioned a small galley (*galiot*), complete with a newly painted royal standard, and sent it downstream from Rouen to Harfleur under the command of Jean la Guette, a mariner based in the city.[29] As an oared vessel it was appropriate for crossing the estuary, since it could be taken against the river current and sea tides.

Not surprisingly, d'Albret was subsequently blamed for not preventing the English from laying siege. The Religieux claims that the constable had troops with him but made no effort to prevent the English landing. The chronicler adds that there were plenty of sailors and coastal inhabitants who could have prevented the initial landing, since this had been difficult and had taken time to achieve. This last observation has some truth in it. An army is vulnerable as it lands, especially in circumstances where men and equipment needed to be transported in dribs and drabs from ships to the shore. It is unfair to claim, however, that the local people would have been able to make a successful attack had they not foolishly put their trust in the nobility and the troops of the constable. Henry's army was large, well-equipped and made up of professional warriors against whom the local population would have been no match. The Religieux also notes that d'Albret was accused of forbidding resistance to the English, telling the men-at-arms who came to him for orders that they should stay put in the villages around Harfleur. It was even said that he had promised Henry, when a member of a French embassy, that he would not act against him. But the Religieux admitted that he heard counter-claims, that, for instance, the constable had divulged to his own king information he had discovered about the size and commanders of the English army, and that he had done all he could to speed up the response to the English attack. What we are seeing here is another example of the blame culture which came to surround the French defeats of 1415.

From around 12 August onwards, companies deployed for war against the English can be found serving under Boucicaut, d'Albret, Jean de Ligne, Sire de Bailleul, and the Duke of Alençon.[30] D'Albret was in charge of those placed in the *pays de Caux*, some of which were at Montivilliers a few kilometres to the north of Harfleur. The Berry Herald claims that both d'Albret and Boucicaut were based at Caudebec during the siege, with 1,500 men each. This is an exaggeration in terms of numbers but troops were certainly at Caudebec under the marshal during the siege.[31] Administrative records suggest that d'Albret was often at Rouen, seeing to its defences, since it was thought that the English intended to go on to make an attempt against the Norman capital.[32] At the surrender of Harfleur Boucicaut was, according to des Ursins, responsible for meeting at Lillebonne those driven out of the town and arranging their transport to Rouen. There is very little surviving information on him in the administrative and pay records. A document of 23 August ordering payment for messengers and other costs, including the commissioning of the *galiot* to send help by sea, was issued on the authority of both the constable and marshal, suggesting that they acted in collaboration. This letter also shows that Sir Robert de Hellande, *bailli* of Rouen, had been sent to Paris to the king, the Dauphin and the council in order to inform them about the 'descent and coming of the English' and what provision d'Albret considered necessary for the rescue of Harfleur and its locality.[33] Nothing was put in writing. The *bailli* was to present the constable's instruction 'by mouth' (*par bouche*), no doubt because it was feared that any written instructions might fall into the hands of the enemy. In the early days of the siege, letters requesting news and passing on information winged their way to and from Rouen, linking the Norman capital with Boulogne and Abbeville as well as Paris.

The first phase of Henry's attack was to lay siege by land. The *Gesta* implies only two commands: the king in the west and south and Clarence to the east. Titus Livius adds that the king gave control of one part of his sector of the siege to his other brother, Humphrey, Duke of Gloucester, and another to Edward, Duke of York, who was also marshal of the army. The Pseudo-Elmham elsewhere claims that Gloucester presided over cases in the military court, although he also names York as marshal and constable. Hardyng places the Earl of Huntingdon, Cornwall, Grey, Porter and Steward in a bastion, a wooden defensive structure built by the English carpenters for the siege. This was positioned facing the French outwork at the Porte de Leure, within the king's area of command. Hardyng adds also the name 'Earl of Kent', but since there was no peer of that title, it is likely that Gilbert Umfraville, styled Earl of Kyme, is meant. Note that this is the same group as detailed to the initial reconnaissance. He also mentions Clarence's position 'on the far side', adding also the name 'Earl of Mortain'. Again, no peer held that title in 1415, and it is not clear who Hardyng meant. We can assume that the various commanders had their own retinues with them. This is confirmed by the incidence of disease. In the company of the Earl of Arundel, who was himself invalided home to die soon afterwards, nineteen of the ninety men-at-arms and sixty-eight of the archers also went home sick. By contrast, there were apparently no men hit by disease in York's retinue and relatively few in Clarence's (forty-seven, but these included servants).[34] This information can also be used to suggest the distribution of men between the siege camps. The retinues that suffered high rates of dysentery, such as those of Arundel and of the royal household, were with the king in his large siege camp to the west of the town. The siege camp under Clarence to the east was smaller, but may also have contained York's retinue.

It is unclear whether Henry issued a formal summons to surrender at his first arrival or after he had laid siege. No text is extant, but its content is implied by passages in the *Gesta* and the *Liber Metricus*. The king sought war not peace. To this end he offered peace to the besieged, in accordance with Deuteronomic law, if they would open their gates to him and restore to him their town which was rightly his. This invocation of biblically based rules of engagement was commonplace in medieval sieges. The relevant passage in Deuteronomy was seen to give the right not only to lay siege if a city refused the besieger's offer of peace, but also to put the male population to the sword and carry off the women and property as spoil once God had delivered the place to him. The law was invoked in later negotiations with the town. Whenever the summons was made, it was rejected. The *Gesta* tells us that Henry then decided on a 'mild attack', in an effort to persuade the enemy to surrender while at the same time not exposing his own men to too much danger. While we can dismiss this as priestly hyperbole, the drawing up of the English artillery against the defences was itself an act that was aimed at frightening the enemy even before a shot was fired. This tactic worked at Mantes in 1449, when, faced with the sight of Charles VII's guns and the anticipation of the damage they would cause to the walls on which they had lavished so much money and effort over the last years, the town council decided to surrender without offering any resistance.[35]

In this case, however, it did not have the desired effect. Henry did use his guns and other stone-throwing engines. The Religieux, presumably reflecting French perceptions after the siege, claims that Henry had some 'machines' of tremendous size which threw enormous stones through a haze of dense smoke and with such a frightening noise that one might have thought they were 'disgorged from hell'. He adds that there were continuous bombardments, achieved by means of a shift system for the troops responsible for the firing. The *Gesta* suggests that Henry deliberately launched a lengthy bombardment during the night before a threatened assault of the town, in order to keep the inhabitants awake and anxious and persuade them to surrender. The exact quantity and nature of Henry's artillery is not documented in the administrative records, so that it is difficult to tell whether there is anything out of the ordinary about it. What we can be certain about, since it is confirmed by archaeology and by financial records of rebuilding costs in the decades to come, is that Henry's artillery caused considerable damage to the fortifications and to structures within the town.[36] This in itself is important. If Henry wished to use Harfleur as a base for himself in the war with France, he was already heaping up the expense of repairs, as well as the danger of having defences so ruinous that they could render the place vulnerable to French siege for years to come. It was indeed the case that the rebuilding of fortifications took years and needed special tax levies. Furthermore, the ruinous nature of the housing in the town was a disincentive for living there, despite Henry's efforts to attract English settlers once the place was in his hands. In order to achieve his ambition of taking Harfleur, therefore, Henry caused too much damage to it.

This brings us to a fundamental point, and that is that the siege of Harfleur was problematic for the English. This was partly because Henry had too large an army for the purpose. This raised issues of victualling, since there were horses and other live animals to be fed. Keeping 12,000 soldiers, their servants and their horses adequately housed and fed cannot have been easy. It was common in sieges for the besiegers to suffer as much deprivation in food supplies as the besieged. Anticipation of the difficulties of victualling explains why the king had been so keen to ensure that soldiers took enough food with them on the campaign. The *Gesta* also tells us that at the very outset of the siege Henry had discussion on how detachments might be sent out to get food and fodder.

Food supplies remained an issue as the siege continued. On 3 September Henry wrote to Bordeaux asking for victuals and wine. Given how long it would take for the message to be received and responded to, it implies that at this point Henry considered the siege might be even lengthier than it turned out to be. On the same day, Jean Bordiu, Archdeacon of the Médoc, who was with the English at the siege, also wrote to the city of Bordeaux saying that at present the fields were providing enough corn but that this could not go on meeting the future requirements of the great army which Henry had with him and which – an important remark – was 'increasing every day'. He too asked for wine to be sent, but predicted more optimistically that Harfleur would be in the king's hands within eight days at most.[37] Burgundian chroniclers also claim that the food the

English had brought with them soon ran out. They mention victualling raids
into the area, as does also des Ursins, noting particularly the taking of cattle. The
Burgundian writers add uniquely that the English tried to take other places in
the area but that they were prevented from doing so by French troops. Further
conquests in the hinterland of Harfleur would have been sensible in terms of
securing food supplies and also in acting as outer defences for the town after the
siege. It is perhaps surprising that no attack was made on Montivilliers.

It is evident that Henry did not want to divide his army at this time. He did
however send out foraging parties as well as reconnaissance patrols. A fascinat-
ing insight into this is seen in evidence presented at the trial of Jean Fusoris.
Raoul le Gay, the priest who agreed to take Courtenay's letters to Fusoris in
Paris, told how he had been captured by English soldiers between Epretot and
Saint-Romain, 12km east of Harfleur, on 17 August. He described how they had
surrounded him, but he did not understand any of them as they did not speak
French. He was tied up and taken to Santivic, a league away from Harfleur, to an
English knight who did speak French and who put him to ransom for 100 *écus*.
When he said he could not pay he was put into a tent and taken the next day
to the English camp before Harfleur.[38] There he was asked the state of Harfleur,
how many men were there and under which captains. He was held for ten days,
before being released in return for twenty nobles to take the letters to Fusoris. In
addition Courtenay told him to tell Fusoris that Henry had come with 50,000
men, 4,000 barrels of flour and the same of wine, as well as twelve guns. He was to
ask Fusoris whether the French king had set out and, if so, whether the Dauphin
and the Duke of Burgundy were in his company (another indication that Henry
was not sure of Burgundy's intentions), and how many other lords, men-at-arms
and archers accompanied them. Le Gay went instead to Montivilliers, where he
was arrested and interrogated.

The Burgundian writers add that the French kept the English under close sur-
veillance during their raids into the countryside and that this contributed to their
lack of food. It is likely that the French carried out a scorched earth policy in
the nearby areas of the *pays de Caux*, so again depriving the English of success
in their foraging raids. This reminds us that d'Albret and Boucicaut, and possibly
Alençon too, made efforts to harry the English during the siege and to bring
what relief they could to the besieged town. Henry had ordered a blockade by
positioning ships on the Seine and smaller boats in the area flooded by the river.
In this he used some of the smaller vessels that had transported troops across and
whose masters had been paid for six weeks' service from 1 August. We can also
see that the French commanders made serious efforts to counteract the blockade,
both under the direction of Clignet de Brabant, the admiral,[39] and of d'Albret
and Boucicaut. The Duke of Burgundy was approached for ships from Flanders,
with Jean Piquet being sent to Sluys to find galleys and rowers. Jean de Calleville,
Sire de Deauville was also sent to the Duke of Brittany requesting vessels to use

against the English at the siege. By the middle of September a small fleet of armed baleniers was prepared and gathered at Rouen. An attack on the English block-ade was made between 14 and 16 September.[40] For this purpose large quantities of *glues* and *bourées* (lines and protective hoardings) were purchased.[41] It does not seem, however, that this was successful, nor that any assistance had come from Flanders or Brittany. The failure of this attack may have been one factor in the decision of the town to enter into negotiations to surrender on 18 September.

A further problem facing the English was living conditions. Henry had not appreciated the risk of concentrating such a large force in wet and inhospitable conditions. All the right conditions were in place for dysentery, a disease char-acterised by diarrhoea containing blood ('the bloody flux'). The opening of the sluices polluted the freshwater supply of the Lézarde, and human waste from the army made this worse. There was little firm ground in which to bury both this and other waste. Walsingham speaks of fetid corpses of animals slaughtered by the army, which were thrown with other rubbish into the tidal waters, causing a terrible stench. Streeche's comments on the bad effects of eating unripe grapes, other fruit and shellfish also tally with the outbreak of gastro-enteric disease.[42] The Pseudo-Elmham tells us that it was unseasonably warm, which may then have fanned the disease, although Walsingham ascribes illness to very cold nights. Furthermore, illness continued even after the siege ended, as is shown by the dates of deaths and invalidings home, which continue into early October. Disease hit the besieged as well as the besiegers. This is noted by the Pseudo-Elmham and confirmed by later testimony of de Gaucourt,[43] but since the English army was so much larger, the effects of disease were more marked, particularly for those in the royal siege camp.

Henry lost several of his closest friends and advisers as a result. On 15 September, Richard Courtenay, the Bishop of Norwich, died, and three days later the Earl of Suffolk. The Duke of Clarence and the Earl Marshal fell ill and were among those invalided home after the fall of the town. They survived but Thomas, Earl of Arundel, died on 13 October within a short while of reaching England. It is always difficult to identify past diseases. There are two types of dysentery, both with similar symptoms. Only in its *shigella dysenteria* form does it cause an epidemic through direct person-to-person infection. As we shall see in the next chapter, the English mortality rates seem too low in comparison with modern-day outbreaks of this form. Therefore it is more likely that the dysentery at the siege was amoebic in form. In other words, each person caught it individually, although it could be passed on indirectly by a sufferer not washing his hands before prepar-ing food or by polluting water supplies through his waste. Dysentery was always a problem at sieges. We have already seen it disrupt French plans at the siege of Arras, in August 1414. It is important to remember, however, that given the large numbers with which Henry had set out, there was no danger that it would ever prevent him from taking Harfleur. None the less, he had to continue the campaign without the presence of some of his key supporters.

Reconstructing the chronology of events at the siege is not easy. Even the *Gesta*, which provides the most dates, gives none between 20 August and 10 September, the latter being the day on which Courtenay became ill, dying five days later. Jean Bordiu's letter of 3 September claims that by then the landward side had been breached and much destruction caused inside the town. In addition, the English had managed to cut off the flow of water below Montivilliers (a further indication of activity by English soldiers in the vicinity), which the Harfleurais had previously dammed. The subsiding of the water would have allowed the English to approach closer to the town on the western and southern sides, although by removing any flow of water, the English may have unwittingly increased the pre-conditions for dysentery. On 3 September Bordiu had predicted that a further eight days were all that was needed to subdue the town. It was not until 18 September, however, that a treaty of composition was made, which brought about a ceasefire and an agreement that if the French king did not send relief by 22 September, the place would surrender.

Assuming that Henry had laid an effective blockade from 23 August, that produces four weeks of full siege. This is therefore not a long siege but it was more time- and effort-consuming than Henry had anticipated. At the outset, the king had discussed with his advisers the establishment of watches against enemy sorties and ambushes. Although the *Gesta* mentions only one sortie launched from Harfleur, the Burgundian chroniclers imply that there were more, arguing that the firepower of English archers drove the French back into the town. As we shall see in a moment, the English spent much time and effort in protecting their positions from enemy attack. According to Titus Livius and the Pseudo-Elmham, Clarence's company suffered losses in an attack from the defenders or from the garrison of Montivilliers as he made his detour to reach the eastern flank of the town. In the *Gesta*, however, he met with good fortune on this occasion, capturing carts containing guns, powder, missiles and catapults, which had been sent from Rouen for the use of the town. The comment that the manoeuvre was at night suggests that the French hoped to smuggle in materials under cover of darkness, and that the English would not have spotted them had it not been for Clarence's time-consuming detour to reach his destination.

Although English guns and stone-throwing machines caused damage to structures, the enemy carried out repairs at night. This they did with timber and also tubs filled with earth, dung, sand, stones, or anything else they could put their hands on. Walls were shored up with bundles of faggots and earth, clay and dung. Streets were covered with sand and other materials so that cannon balls would not splinter on impact. When fortifications such as the barbicans were no longer in a fit state to protect the town guns, they were moved inside the ruins, being fired from other locations where, as the *Gesta* puts it, 'shelter would not have been thought possible'. In other words, the besieged took the war to the besieger. Jars were placed on the walls, full of burning powders, sulphur and quicklime, which could be thrown in the eyes of the English as they attacked. Larger vessels were filled with inflammable powders and burning fat, in order to set fire to the English siege towers when these were brought close to the walls.

The author of the *Gesta* was clearly fascinated by these stratagems, as he was by English counter-measures. When he has Henry set up his guns in order to try to force the town into an early surrender, he tells us how they were given protective screens made of planks, arranged so that when the top was pulled down the bottom was lifted up so as to give a view of the town. This reference, and the comments on protection given to the town guns, reminds us that early artillery took a great deal of time to load and reload, leaving its users vulnerable in the meantime. Trenches were also dug out and faggots placed along their edge to protect the guns and other engines, and also to protect those assigned to their guarding, since they were an obvious target for enemy sorties, and to create cover for the troops watching the barbicans. According to Titus Livius, Henry himself conducted nightly inspections of the English lines, 'praising those who performed their tasks well and correcting and punishing others'. The king's visits are also noted in Le Fèvre and Waurin, but with specific mention that they were to seek out the best places to put the *gros engines*, with Waurin adding that he was also looking for the easiest places to try to gain entry.

Although some companies were sent out into the hinterland, the main task for soldiers at the siege was digging. The *Gesta* tells us that 'those appointed to the guard-duty dug ceaselessly day after day, gaining ground towards that barbican' until the water stopped them getting any nearer. There were further trenches dug to protect the position of the troops under Clarence. They were seen as particularly vulnerable, given their position at the foot of a hill which kept them too close to the walls and thus exposed to enemy fire, as well as being isolated from the main part of the army. He too dug a trench on royal orders, using the earth to form a rampart to defend his men, which he further fortified by driving in trucks and stakes and by mounting guns and throwing engines. The *Gesta* mentions that all of this was 'in accordance with the theory of Master Giles'. This has been taken to mean that Henry knew Giles of Rome's *De regimine principum*, but this cannot be proved from the author's wording. More likely the author himself was acquainted with it. He also gives an interesting insight into how the digging was organised: masters of works were appointed to oversee the men-at-arms and archers, who were each allocated a certain length of trench to dig. There was also digging to be done on Clarence's side, in the creation of a mine intended to run under the walls to weaken them, which implies that the bombardment was less extensive or less effective on the eastern side of the town. A relative shortage of skilled gunners might also be suggested. As we have seen, those recruited for the campaign were all foreigners. Although the Burgundian chroniclers give a more positive account of the success of what they call 'three mines', English writers consider the mining operation to be a complete failure. Because there was so little space, the diggers had to operate within full sight of the defenders. The latter responded with countermines and a sortie against Clarence's men, which again led to losses. The plan was thus abandoned and the mine was filled in during the first years of the English occupation. The Pseudo-Elmham adds an interesting observation that the English had lost the knack of mining because of the long period of military inaction and truces in the recent past, and that some of the nobility were not keen on fighting underground. There were, therefore, some shortcomings in the way the siege was conducted.

We could well describe the siege as a 'war of trenches'. As we saw, the town was well defended by ditches, which made access to the walls difficult. Yet Henry had to get near if he intended to launch an assault. He thus ordered bundles of faggots to be fabricated and then taken by the soldiers to fill up the ditches, at the same time preparing wooden towers and belfries and ladders which could be taken across the faggot infill. On Clarence's side, large numbers of faggots were prepared for the same purpose, although no siege towers are noted. The duke discovered that the enemy planned to set fire to the faggots while his soldiers were trying to fill the ditches, and so he had to abandon this plan also. Luckily, the men who had been guarding the miners were able to take possession of one of the outer ditches of the town, from which they discharged missiles from catapults and stone throwers (not, it seems, gunpowder artillery). This was a useful break-through, but it was balanced by the sortie of the enemy from the main barbican on 15 September, which set fire to English defences facing the trenches opposite. According to Hardyng, this attack was against the wooden siege bastion held by Huntingdon, Umfraville, Cornwall, Grey, Porter and Steward, and William Bourchier.[44] No serious losses were incurred but it led to enemy taunts at the lack of English watchfulness. Wars of words were common at sieges. The event had occurred on a Sunday, the day on which Courtenay died, so the king and his men may have allowed other preoccupations to distract them.

This is the only sortie that the *Gesta* records, although there are clear state-ments that the English trenches, especially those constructed facing the barbican, were constructed to protect soldiers against the enemy when they sallied out. If the ordering of events in the *Gesta* is correct then the sortie and damage to the English camp appears to have stimulated both sides to more aggressive action. Remember too that this was around the same time that the French had tried to mount an attack on the naval blockade. It is tempting to think that they had been aiming at co-ordinated actions against the English both on land and sea. Overnight, the king had faggots laid over the ditch in front of a barbican. In the morning, the French sallied out again, but the Earl of Huntingdon (here described by the *Gesta* as 'a knight brave and high spirited though young') engaged them. He then went on to set fire to their barbican through the use of flaming arrows as well as by men stuffing burning material through the holes that had been made by previous bombardment. The flames were fanned by inflammable powder (presumably sulphur). The earl secured control of the barbican, erecting his banner over it as a sign of his victory. The French retreated into their inner barbican which was now treated to the same fire treatment. They were thus forced to abandon the barbicans and retreat within the walls, blocking the entrance (presumably a breach made in the walls earlier rather than a gate) with timber, stone, earth and dung to prevent the English getting through. The day was Henry's, although the fire continued to rage in the main barbican for three days and the no doubt foul-smelling smoke from the dung took a fortnight to subside – another health hazard for defender and attacker alike.

As was common practice, Henry made several attempts at negotiation during the siege. After all, it was in his interests to achieve a quick victory, as well as to have ample opportunity to remind the Harfleurais of their predicament. The Religieux speaks of Henry inviting de Gaucourt to his camp to treat, only to find the Frenchman asserting that his own king would not leave the place to be besieged for too long but would come soon with a large army. The same chronicle tells us that on several occasions the besieged sent representatives to the Dauphin, even giving us their supposed words. There was much rejoicing when news was brought back to Harfleur that the lords of France had assembled in large number and were occupying almost all of the area from Paris to Normandy. According to des Ursins, the envoys had left Harfleur on 1 September and gave their message to the Dauphin while he was at Saint-Denis on 3 September. On 13 September Mountjoye Herald acknowledged receipt of 4 *livres tournois* for having taken in his company from Rouen to Vernon (where the Dauphin then was) a man named Joven Lescot.[45] The latter had been put out of Harfleur secretly by de Gaucourt in order to inform Constable d'Albret of the state of the town so that help might be given. The exact date of Lescot's mission is not clear, but this gives an interesting insight into how a herald might be used as cover for a secret mission. It is also possible that this was how co-ordinated action by land and sea was achievable.

The *Gesta* has Henry issuing a further summons to surrender on 17 September, once again citing Deuteronomy with its threat of worse punishments should resistance continue. A letter which Henry sent to London on the day of the actual surrender (22 September) suggests rather that it was the men of the town who had approached him but that the king had rejected their proposals and determined on an assault on 18 September.[46] By contrast, in the *Gesta* it was the negotiators, named as the Sire de Gaucourt and the leading members of the town council, who refused to treat, thereby forcing the king's decision that an assault would be launched the next day. This was to be a major effort, using not only all of the soldiers but also the sailors. This is surely confirmation that the French attempt against the English shipping had failed by this point. This would have made Henry more confident that French resistance was now waning. On the night of 17 September proclamation was made 'by sound of the trumpet' that all should make themselves ready under their captains' direction to storm the walls

under the next day. To worry the enemy further, Henry maintained a bombardment all night.

The *Gesta* implies that there was no assault on 18 September but that the
defenders of Harfleur decided the time had come to treat. Their spirit had been
broken by the loss of their outer defences and by bombardment, and they were
frightened at the thought of an assault where they would be completely at
the mercy of their attackers. Furthermore, they had despaired of receiving any
help from their own side. Both the Religieux and Walsingham claim that they
first approached the Duke of Clarence, who reported their wishes to the king.
Walsingham then claims that Henry sent the Earl of Dorset, Lord Fitzhugh and
Sir Thomas Erpingham to discuss terms. His account suggests that the terms of
the treaty of composition – that they would surrender at 1 p.m. on the following
Sunday, 22 September (the feast of St Maurice), if Charles VI or Dauphin, being
informed of the treaty, did not raise the siege by force of arms by that point –
were initially rejected by Henry, who wanted a surrender on the morrow, but that
he then generously conceded their wishes. In negotiations of this kind Henry
maintained an aloof majesty, as he was to do at the siege of Rouen in 1419. Thus,
Walsingham tells us, the king was not present at the ceremony whereby hostages
of townsmen and some members of the garrison were handed over, and it was
arranged that the Sire de Hacqueville should take the ultimatum to the king
and Dauphin. The choice of de Hacqueville, whose seat lay close to Etrépagny
in the Norman Vexin, is confirmed in the letter that Henry sent to London on
22 September. According to Le Fèvre, de Hacqueville took the message to Louis
at Vernon, saying that rescue needed to be made within three days.

The treaty of composition appears to be no longer extant, but its terms are
noted in several chronicles and in the letter which Henry sent to the city of
London on 22 September. In this he announced that the town had surrendered
on that day, since no French army had appeared. In the Burgundian chronicles
there is a comment that the two towers guarding the harbour held out for a
further two days (Monstrelet increases this to ten) but this is dubious. There is
no doubt that Harfleur surrendered by composition. Yet that is not the explanation given in the Religieux. According to this chronicler, on the day appointed
for full surrender the besieged gave the impression of being reluctant to put the
agreement into effect. As a result, at midday Henry launched a vigorous assault
against the town for three hours, at the end of which those charged with defending the 'other part of the town' opened the gates to the English. So the besieged
surrendered themselves and the town to the English. The Religieux claims that
this information came from the Sires d'Estouteville and de Gaucourt, and follows
the passage with a diatribe against the inaction of those who let the place fall. He
claims that their pusillanimity made the French military a laughing stock in other
countries. But he was keen to excuse the king, whose courage, he claimed, would
have prevented this disaster had it not been that ill health prevented him from

acting. This account was written with the hindsight of the disaster of Agincourt. Just as a blame culture developed around the battle, so we can see that it did also for the siege. French chroniclers emphasise that the inhabitants of Harfleur were displeased at being forced to surrender.

While the treaty of composition had been negotiated on behalf of Henry, he received the full surrender in person, sitting in a pavilion on the top of Mont Lecomte, well away from the mess of the siege and the smelly smoke! The *Gesta* gives us a splendid account of the ceremonial, with Gilbert Umfraville standing to the right holding the king's helm adorned with a crown. De Gaucourt and the town representatives approached Henry and surrendered the keys of the town. The king handed the keys to the Earl Marshal. Henry spoke graciously to de Gaucourt, subsequently entertaining him and others to a banquet, in the company of his English lieges. This show of magnanimity was an intrinsic element in medieval kingship at war. It offered the king the opportunity to show his good lordship as well as to emphasise his victory. English standards were set up within Harfleur and the Earl of Dorset was appointed captain of the town.

The Burgundian chroniclers state that Henry made ceremonial entry into Harfleur on 23 September. He rode to the gates and then dismounted and went on foot to the church of St Martin, where he made his obligations, thanking God for this good fortune. This demeanour is reminiscent of the entry to London two months later. Henry deliberately eschewed triumphalism for emphasis on God's will, fully in keeping with the religious tone with which he had declared war. This may be why the *Gesta* omits any mention of a ceremonial entry at all, saying simply that Henry went into Harfleur on 23 September with his closest advisers to inspect the town. Likewise, the *Gesta* omits any mention of the booty taken from the town, whereas other English chroniclers, as well as the Burgundians, say that there was a large quantity of stuff taken by the king, with some being distributed 'according to merit', and that goods were also shipped back to England. In their post-campaign accounts, captains were obliged to detail the gains of war they and their men had made and to which the crown was entitled to its share. None of the accounts that survive mention any profits from this stage of the campaign, which suggests that there had been little of value to take.

Henry's treatment of the town was fully consistent with custom and practice. It was usual to allow the defeated soldiers to depart on the condition that they would not bear arms against the king again during the campaign.[47] The *Gesta* tells us that agreements made with de Gaucourt and his fellow members of the garrison were written up and put into one of the books of record, but no such texts have been discovered. The only condition we can prove to have been applied was that these soldiers took an oath to submit themselves at Calais on 11 November. The implications of this and the additional task apparently given to de Gaucourt in carrying a challenge to the Dauphin will be discussed in the next chapter. As for civilians, the king ordered a segregation of the population as soon as he arrived in the town. Those who had sworn fealty and those to be kept in custody against ransom were retained. Chroniclers diverge over whether these town hostages were taken to England. The *Gesta* claims that of the remaining population, 2,000 women, children, poor and helpless (defined also as the sick and elderly in other sources) were expelled on 24 September. This was partly a humanitarian act. It would have been impossible for these groups to have stayed in Harfleur given its physical state and the continuing war. The treatment of women was standard practice: they were allowed to depart with their clothing and all they could carry, and may also have been given 5 *sous* each. Des Ursins suggests that, numbering 1,500, they were escorted to Lillebonne by the English, where they were met by Boucicaut, who gave them food and drink. On the next day he had them taken to Rouen by boat. Churchmen were also given permission to leave.[48] The Religieux suggests that young men were forced to stay in order to assist with the defence of the town. We cannot be certain how many of the native population remained.

Henry's intention was to create a second Calais. The 300 men-at-arms and 900 archers installed as garrison under Dorset reflected the standard establishment in the Calais march.[49] His expulsions, attempts to encourage English settlement, and his replacement of French institutions were a direct parallel to the policies of Edward III in 1347. A charter granted to Harfleur by Charles VIII in 1492 claims that that Henry had the municipal records and existing title-deeds burned in the market place, and that he henceforward restricted the purchase and inheritance of properties to Englishmen, so that the remaining natives were reduced to the status of lessees of their new English masters.[50] On 5 October 1415 the keeper of the realm, John, Duke of Bedford, sent an order to the sheriffs of London to proclaim that all merchants, victuallers and artificers who were willing to reside in the town of Harfleur should go there with all speed with goods and equipment, and that the captain of the town would provide them with houses. Once installed, the king would grant them a charter of liberties.[51] We do not know how many settlers came to the town in these early stages. Only one grant of a house is documented before the second invasion in August 1417. In December 1415, Richard Bokeland of London was granted the *hostellerie* in Harfleur called the Peacock, in reward for his having provided two vessels to assist the king during the siege of the town.[52] But the many grants made between 1417 and 1422 – 497 in all – often refer to previous holders with English names, implying that there had indeed been earlier settlement. No charter of liberties was granted until 1444, by which time the town had been lost to the French and then recaptured. That charter reiterated Henry's initial intention 'immediately after his conquest' to populate the place with English, and sought once more to offer incentives, which included trade concessions and the right to elect a mayor and town council. Intriguingly, the elections were to be carried out on the anniversary of Henry V's taking of the town (22 September) or within six days thereafter.[53]

Harfleur was also intended as a military base and a point of entry for supplies from England. Another proclamation was made in London between 22 September and 5 October inviting merchants to make haste to the king at Harfleur with all kinds of victuals, clothing and armour.[54] That there was some response to this is shown by a commission issued on 12 October to John Laweney, citizen and grocer of the city, to take victuals, armour and other items for the provision, safekeeping and relief of Harfleur.[55] Because Harfleur was an outpost in enemy territory, it had to rely wholly on revictualling from England, both now and for a considerable time to come. Furthermore, there were many repairs to make on the structures damaged in the siege. Waurin says that Henry started on this as soon as he entered the town. Gunners, carpenters and masons recruited for the campaign were detailed into Harfleur for its defence and rebuilding, and it is therefore extremely likely that Henry left all of his guns and other siege artillery at Harfleur.[56]

Its defence remained a costly nightmare even after the victory at Agincourt. The parliament of November 1415 voted taxation for its upkeep, and shortly after the king's return, the council encouraged a full inspection of the town's defences and artillery.[57] Further craftsmen were raised for repairs, and foodstuffs were sent across, including 1,000 quarters of oats for the soldiers' horses. By the end of the year a proper financial administration was set up in the town under Thomas Barneby, whose powers were identical to those of the treasurer of Calais. When the French began to make preparations to attempt recovery of the town in the New Year, large quantities of wine, wheat, malt, bacon and live animals were sent across. By April 1416 the situation was serious, not only in terms of food supplies but also artillery. Men and many horses had been lost in abortive vict-ualling sorties into the locality in the previous month. Dorset therefore wrote to Henry warning that if no help came he and his garrison would have to evacuate Harfleur.[58] The situation was assisted by English victory at the battle of the Seine on 15 August 1416, a victory which the *Gesta* emphasises as a further expression of divine support, won as much, if not more, through the prayerfulness of the king as the bravery of Bedford as commander.[59]

Henry's choice of Thomas Beaufort, Earl of Dorset, as captain of his new conquest was not surprising given the earl's experience and his royal blood, albeit on the other side of the blanket, since the earl was the son of John of Gaunt by his mistress, Katherine Swynford, although he and his siblings had later been legitimised. Nor was it surprising that the king should consider a garrison of 1,200 men necessary, even though this removed at a stroke at least a tenth of his army from further action on the campaign.[60] The defences of the town had been damaged to such a degree that a large number of defenders was necessary and much money had to be spent on repairs.[61] Furthermore, military intelligence had revealed that the French were gathering in strength upriver at Rouen.

Henry had scored a success in his first military action in France, but at a considerable price. The siege had taken too long for the size of army he had deployed. Dysentery had developed much more quickly than usual and was still lingering in the weeks that followed the surrender. The loss of his closest friends and of many soldiers to illness, death and evacuation home cannot have boosted the morale of the army. Significantly, however, Henry did not repeat the mistakes he had made at Aberystwyth in 1407. At Harfleur he allowed only the shortest of time between the treaty of composition (18 September) and the required surrender (22 September). With only four days' notice, the French could not possibly send an army. Arguably, however, Henry's only real stroke of genius was to decide to move away from Harfleur as quickly as possible. He reckoned, correctly, that the French would seek to chase him since he was the prize they sought. Harfleur would have to wait until he had been defeated, since it would then be easy pickings.

5

To Fight or Not to Fight,
22 September–8 October 1415

As the siege of Harfleur drew to a close, both sides had important decisions to make. For the French the question was whether to make efforts to relieve the town. If not, what should they do next to counter Henry's actions? Their answer to this second question depended, of course, upon what he decided to do. As at the initial invasion, therefore, the French were at a disadvantage and could only respond to English moves. Yet Henry too was faced with dilemmas. What should he do next? Had the siege taken such a toll on his army that he needed to rethink his initial plans? We need now to turn to the issues facing each side, beginning with the French.

Why had the French not sent an army to relieve Harfleur? Why did they not accept the opportunity offered by the composition of 18 September to give battle to save the town? The explanation is simple. They could not raise in time an army large enough to guarantee success. Henry V had invaded with a large army. Even if dysentery had diminished his manpower – and it is not certain that the French would have known about this or that the disease had taken its full toll by this point – the force at his disposal on the day appointed for the *journée* (22 September) would have been formidable. The French were not in a position to take up the challenge. To understand this fully we need to examine their actions since the time of the English landing in mid-August. At that time the king and Dauphin were in Paris and the leading nobles were in their own dominions, to which they had been ordered after the formalising of peace with Burgundy on 13 March.[1] Although there had been preparatory moves made over the months preceding the English landing and in response to the siege, the French could not issue a call to arms on a large scale until the English landed. Within a few days of Henry laying siege, d'Albret sent the *bailli* of Rouen to Paris to the king, the Dauphin and council, to inform them about the 'descent and coming of the English'. The *bailli* was also instructed to pass on 'par bouche' what d'Albret considered necessary for the rescue of Harfleur and its locality.[2] We cannot know precisely what he reported, but the royal government responded as swiftly as it could.

On 28 August a *semonce des nobles* was ordered to be proclaimed in Normandy and adjoining areas.[3] This followed up the proclamation ordered in early June that all nobles and others accustomed to follow the pursuit of arms should make ready in anticipation of invasion.[4] Now it was possible to announce that the English had indeed landed and laid siege to Harfleur and that, to offer resistance and to safeguard the kingdom, the king had sent the Dauphin as lieutenant and captain general to Normandy. The king intended to follow soon after, in order to raise the siege and to fight against the enemy with the aid of God. What we see in the wording of this text is a mirror image of the English justification for war. The French had sent envoys to England in the hope of coming to a peace which would avoid the spilling of human blood and all the inconvenience and damage that war would bring. They had done all that God and reason required, yet the enemy had invaded none the less, threatening not only Harfleur but also the whole of Normandy with destruction and loss. The *baillis* were ordered to have proclaimed throughout their jurisdictions 'by sound of the trumpet' that 'all nobles and men of the area who had power to arm themselves and who were accustomed to follow war', as well as archers and crossbowmen, should go in person, accompanied by as many adequately armed and mounted men as they could provide, to join the Dauphin at Rouen as quickly as possible. The *baillis* were also to ensure that towns and castles remained adequately fortified and protected and that churchmen also fulfilled the obligations incumbent upon them relating to their duty to provide transport in the form of carts and carters. The *baillis* were also to tell the troops that they would receive pay once they came to the assembly point, and that they would also receive protection for six months from any legal cases pending against them. As they journeyed to Rouen or elsewhere as ordered, they were to wear a white cross and were under obligation not to carry out any pillaging, nor were they to stay more than one night in any one place at the expense of the local inhabitants.

In Paris, this proclamation was issued on 30 August 'before dinner'.[5] Within Normandy we can trace the reading of the order at various locations, including the market of Bayeux on 8 September and of Thury on 9 September. It was not proclaimed outside Picardy, Normandy and the Ile-de-France, nor was it, as Famiglietti claimed, an *arrière-ban*. The latter type of call-out, which invoked complete loss of lands in the case of disobedience, had been used during the civil wars of 1410–14, no doubt as a test of loyalty to the crown.[6] As a means of raising troops against an external enemy, it was obsolescent and had not been used at all since 1356. What was needed to face the English in 1415 was a professional army. Hence a *semonce des nobles* was used, focusing on the nobility and others accustomed to follow the profession of arms – in other words, those groups in society that were exempt from taxation because they were expected to provide military service to the crown instead. The purpose of the *semonce* was twofold: first, to alert experienced soldiers to the fact that the king was recruiting an army and, secondly, to notify those who were obliged to provide service by virtue of their tenure or office. These men would join with the companies raised or about to be raised under the constable, marshal, Duke of Alençon and other nobles, as well as those within the households of the Dauphin and king. The kernel of the French army was the households of the crown and nobility, supplemented by smaller retinues of knights and esquires. In this respect it was very similar to that of the English, although it contained a preponderance of men-at-arms rather than archers. Troops raised by the *semonce* would form their own small retinues under the direction of the local *bailli*. As with the English, all troops were paid, with the money given to the captain to pass on to his men. The French also had an equivalent of indentures in the *lettres de retenue*.[7] None are known to exist for the campaign and therefore it seems unlikely that this system was used. This may be because the lettres specified a time period for service, whereas the French obviously needed to have men in arms for as long as was necessary to counter the English threat.

It was difficult to anticipate how long this threat would last or what form it would take, but whatever materialised, the costs of mounting resistance would be substantial, since Henry had invaded in force. A meeting of the council in Paris on 31 August decided that the tax grants ordered in mid-March would not suffice for the pay of the army, the provision of artillery and all other impending royal expenditure. As a result, a further levy of 24,000 *livres tournois* (about £4,000 sterling) was ordered to be collected by 20 September.[8] The record of this decision again recites how the French had made every effort to come to peace with England, but that the enemy had laid siege to Harfleur and intended to continue their 'damnable enterprise' by sending troops into other parts of the kingdom. More importantly, it indicates the size of army that the French were proposing – 6,000 men-at-arms and 3,000 archers. There was no money to raise more. It may seem that the French kings had an advantage over their English counterparts, in that they could raise taxation when they needed it without reference to a representative body. But they did not have access to the same sources of credit as did the English crown. Parliamentary taxation was secure, and therefore it was possible to raise funds based on guarantee of its future collection. The French crown had already suffered financial pressures as a result of civil war. The new pressures they were now under in attempting to resist the English were considerable. The tax ordered to be collected by 1 June and 1 August had been slow in coming in, although there is evidence of moneys being taken from the localities to Paris throughout the summer.[9] Once Rouen had been fixed as the point of rendezvous, tax levies within Normandy were taken there instead, so that they could be directly applied to military expenditure. By mid-September, one of the

treasurers of war, Macé Heron, was in the Norman capital.[10] Charles also obtained
from the Pope at Avignon a bull which permitted him to levy taxation from
the clergy to contribute to the costs of war.[11] The tax burdens were unpopular.
According to the Bourgeois of Paris, the king had levied 'the heaviest tax that had
ever been seen in the whole age of man', an obvious exaggeration but one which
was coloured by his hindsight of knowing that 'it did no good for the kingdom
of France'.[12] Similar comments are found in the Religieux, who noted that the
perception of the French population was that there was not much to choose from
between the French officials and the English in terms of extortion.

A further problem that the French faced was one of leadership. Since Henry
had invaded to challenge Charles's kingship, it was essential that the king himself
should play some role in resistance. This was first symbolised by his presence in
a procession to mass in Notre Dame de Paris on 9 September. On the following day he was present at mass at Saint-Denis, at which the relics of the saint, the
special patron of France, were shown and the *oriflamme* handed to the king, as it
had been at the outset of the war against Burgundy in February 1414.[13] As on that
occasion, the king entrusted the banner to Guillaume Martel, Sire de Bacqueville,
whose lordship lay in the *pays de Caux* north of Harfleur. Martel was probably
one of those who had controlled the king in his first outbreak of madness in 1392,
and was now himself over sixty. He met his death at Agincourt. King Charles had
accompanied the royal army in the war against Burgundy in the summer of 1414,
but the appointment of the Dauphin as captain general on 26 April 1415 implied
that formal military command would on this occasion be vested in him. As we
saw, the *semonce* had ordered troops to join the Dauphin at Rouen. The Dauphin
duly left Paris on 1 September and at the same point letters were despatched to
the royal dukes. Like his father a week later, Louis went to pay his devotions at the
abbey of Saint-Denis. According to des Ursins, it was while there, on 3 September,
that he received a message from Harfleur that the garrison was in desperate need
of reinforcements.[14] By 13 September he had reached Vernon-sur-Seine where
Joven Lescot, smuggled out of Harfleur, had been sent by the constable in the
company of Mountjoye Herald.[15] According to the Religieux, it was at first difficult for the envoys from Harfleur to gain access to the Dauphin (this may be, of
course, an expression of the later blame culture) but when they did, Louis gave
assurances that his father the king would provide for the rescue of the town. The
chronicler claims that there was much rejoicing when news was taken back to
Harfleur that the lords of France had assembled in large number and were occupying almost all of the area from Paris to Normandy.[16]

It is easy to dismiss this as an exaggeration but it can be seen to contain some
truth. An army was assembling. The chronicle of Bec Hellouin, the Benedictine
abbey on the Risle to the south-west of Rouen, comments on the damage to
the monastery and to the whole area by the French army, 'which had gathered
there against the king of England'. They stayed there continually devastating and

destroying the whole region from the month of August right through to the battle. It had also been necessary to have munitions in the fortress of the monastery at the expense of the Church 'against the English invasion'.[17] On 22 September, the Dauphin issued an order from Vernon banning his officers from molesting the monks or taking foodstuffs from their estates.[18] A more prosaic insight into the gathering of troops is provided by the records of the French *chambre des comptes*, the equivalent of the English Exchequer. Although survival of records is much more random and incomplete than for the English army, there is enough to show that the French did make every effort to respond to the English threat.[19]

In the month of July, the Duke of Alençon, a leading landholder in Lower Normandy and 'capitaine general sur le fait de la guerre au pays de Normandie' under the overall aegis of the Dauphin as overall royal lieutenant and captain general, was based in Valognes with various companies.[20] During the siege, several companies were based at Touques, Honfleur and Caen under his command. It is from around 12 August onwards that companies under Boucicaut, d'Albret and Jean de Ligne, Sire de Bailleul and the Seneschal of Hainault, begin to appear in the records, operating from Rouen and in the *pays de Caux*. We know the total size of the company of the Sire de Ligne – 120 *escuiers* (men-at-arms) and sixty *gens de trait* (bowmen) – based first in the area around Harfleur and then from 24 August at Amiens.[21] By 11 September, the Count of Vendôme had a company of 300 men-at-arms and 150 archers.[22] Later in the month, there are references to the Duke of Berry having 1,000 men-at-arms and 500 archers, although he did not himself arrive in Rouen until 12 October.[23] Alençon continued to command troops over September, but these were now described as being for service in the *pays de Caux* against the English.

The companies of these commanders were made up, like the retinues of their English counterparts, of smaller units, usually numbering ten to fifteen men, under individual knights and esquires. Some of their members had probably turned up for service in Rouen as a result of the *semonce* issued at the end of August. Certainly there are a good number of Norman names among the leaders of the units. Each unit leader received pay directly for his men from the treasurer general, rather than through their overall commander as in England. Therefore we have to be careful not to double-count the troops evidenced in the pay records. Most of the units under knights and esquires consisted solely of men-at-arms, but some included a few longbowmen (*archiers*), often mounted. The remaining *gens de trait* were made up of separate companies of crossbowmen, such as the fifty-seven-strong company of Jean de Seville within the overall retinue of the Count of Vendôme.[24] It is difficult to know how many men there were in royal pay by the time Harfleur surrendered on 22 September, but the pay records suggest that it cannot have been more than a few thousand. There were definitely not enough to face Henry's army in battle to settle the fate of Harfleur. Furthermore, they had been deliberately dispersed, since the French strategy was to keep troops in various locations against possible English movements. Boucicaut, d'Albret and Rambures were based at Rouen but also operating into the *pays de Caux* against the English; Alençon was largely, but not exclusively, based south of the Seine, and de Ligne at Amiens.

The treaty of composition for Harfleur was agreed on 18 September. Notification of it was brought to the Dauphin at Vernon by one of the garrison, the Sire de Hacqueville. According to Le Fèvre and Waurin, the latter was told that the full strength of the French king's army had not yet assembled and that therefore no assistance could be given.[25] Since de Hacqueville's journey to Vernon would probably have taken two days, it was impossible that a French army, whatever its then size, could have appeared outside the town of Harfleur on 22 September. Henry knew this well and had deliberately given a very short time between the composition and surrender. He had chosen the feast of St Maurice for the actual surrender. This saint was a third-century soldier martyr who had refused to sacrifice to pagan gods for military success or to take part in the killing of Christians. He was considered the patron saint of soldiers and had been invoked in earlier centuries alongside St George as a protector of English armies.[26] Whether Henry was keen at this stage to give battle is a moot point. He was already certain that such a denouement was unlikely to materialise at this stage, but it served his purpose to express his readiness to do so.

The Dauphin was still at Vernon when Henry V's personal challenge of 26 September was brought to him, a challenge which will be discussed in more detail later in this chapter. What is striking is that neither the Dauphin Louis nor King Charles VI rushed to reach Rouen. The Dauphin stayed put at Vernon after Harfleur fell. After his visit to Saint-Denis on 10 September, the king also made slow progress down the Seine. On 17 September he dined at Poissy and slept at Meulan, before journeying on to Mantes by 19 September.[27] It was while there that he heard news of the surrender of Harfleur, although at Paris uncertainty prevailed for at least a week on whether the place had fallen or not.[28] Charles joined the Dauphin at Vernon on 7 October. Both were still there on 9 October but had moved to Rouen by 12 October.[29]

What is the explanation for this slow progress? The answer is again simple. There was great concern that Henry would move on from Harfleur to besiege Rouen. This had already been feared even before the landing. On 10 July the captain of Rouen, Guillaume de Melun, Count of Tancarville, was ordered to ensure that the city was well defended and that any necessary repairs were carried out in order to resist any English invasion.[30] By early October loans were being levied in the city for the costs of increased fortification and the provision of artillery. Money was also having to be spent on preparing accommodation for the king in anticipation of his arrival. Repairs were carried out at Pont-de-l'Arche to contribute to an outer ring of French defences for the city.[31] This plan is also apparent in the appointment on 7 October of Guillaume Martel, Sire de Bacqueville, keeper of the *oriflamme*, as captain of Château-Gaillard, a fortress on the Seine to the east of Rouen.[32] Rouen may indeed have been in the English king's sights. A letter sent from the siege camp at Harfleur to Bordeaux on 3 September by Jean Bordiu had it that Henry would move on to Montivilliers, Dieppe, Rouen and then Paris.[33] It would have been a complete disaster for the French if Henry laid siege to Rouen with the king and Dauphin inside the city. Charles and Louis did not move from the safety of Vernon to Rouen until it was clear that Henry had chosen a northward route towards the Somme.

This information must have reached the French at Vernon around 9 October, the day after Henry left Harfleur. Three days later, on 12 October, the French king and his son entered Rouen. By this point, French forces had already set off to shadow Henry's march and to intercept him at the Somme. The records of the *chambre des comptes* reveal large numbers of men in military pay between 23 September and 8 October, a major increase compared with the position during the siege. Over 230 companies are in evidence by 8 October. All of the commanders known to have had troops in their charge before the surrender continued to do so after this date and new commanders also begin to appear. Companies under the Count of Marle, for instance, were mustering at Rouen in the first week of October.[34] As will be discussed in the following chapter, the troops in arms by 8 October rushed north once it was known that Henry was making for the Somme. It is also extremely likely that some of the Dauphin's men had moved directly from Vernon to the north of the Somme under the command of Richemont and Guichard Dauphin, royal *maître d'hôtel*. Troops under the latter are also evidenced in the pay records from the first week of October.[35] In all, it is likely that at least 6,000 men were in royal pay by the time Henry left Harfleur.

The Duke of Berry entered Rouen on the same day as Charles, although his troops had already entered service before this date.[36] The Duke of Bourbon arrived by 17 October, at which point his troops also begin to appear in the pay records.[37] Louis II, Duke of Anjou, was still in Orléans on 12 October but had reached Rouen by 20 October.[38] The movements of the Duke of Orléans are problematic. That he was preparing for military service is indicated by his purchase of a new suit of armour in mid-September at a cost of over 83 *livres tournois*.[39] He was at his seat of Cléry near Orléans on 17 October,[40] and it is uncertain whether he ever joined the king in Rouen. Even though Henry's march northwards had taken pressure off Rouen, the king continued to be surrounded by an ample number of soldiers. According to the chronicle of Tournai, the crossbowmen from that place, who claimed the right to be the special guard of the king, left Tournai on 17 September with twenty-five shield-bearers (*paviseurs*) and their food supplies, and met with Charles at Mantes before going on with him to Rouen.[41] There is no evidence that a large army left Rouen after the arrival of the king and Dauphin in the city. The principal French army had already left to intercept

Henry, and only smaller contingents under Bourbon and Orléans moved north to join them at a later date.

The princes of the blood had been written to on 1 September. According to des Ursins, the request was that they should send '500 of their best lances'.[42] The chronicler mentions, in particular, letters being taken to the Duke of Burgundy, his brother, the Count of Nevers, and the Duke of Orléans. By the time des Ursins was writing, a lance was a three-strong unit of the mounted man-at-arms and two supporters. It is clear, however, that the actual request was for 500 men-at-arms and 300 archers. This is stated in a letter of the Duke of Burgundy dated 24 September, where he recites the royal request to him.[43] Before we consider the duke's response, it is worth noting that the Dauphin had already been concerned about the possible loyalty of Burgundy in the face of English invasion. At the end of July he sent two of his envoys, Guichard Dauphin and Jean de Vailly, to Duke John at Rouvres (south of Dijon) asking him to swear to abide by the terms of the peace. Although it is unlikely that there was any understanding between Henry V and Duke John, the French government could not be certain of this. Duke John immediately tried to turn their fears to his advantage. Although he agreed to abide by the peace, his oath was contingent upon fulfilment of the Dauphin's promise to include all of the duke's supporters in a general pardon. Not surprisingly, therefore, the Dauphin considered it wise to send the letter requesting troops with notice of two further decisions made by the council on 31 August. The first confirmed the restoration of the duke's honour and the second modified exclusions to the pardon while continuing to omit the leading Cabochiens.

The duke's reply to the request for troops is given in full by des Ursins and dated 24 September.[44] The most important point revealed in his letter is that although the duke had been asked to send troops, it was requested that he should not come in person. This indicates that the Dauphin and the other royal advisers were afraid Duke John's presence alongside the other lords might reopen old quarrels, and that his loyalty was still in doubt. On the assumption that we can trust the letter included verbatim by des Ursins, the reason why the duke was not at Agincourt was because he had been told to stay away from any action against the English.

Not surprisingly, Duke John displayed offence at this, emphasising his close link especially as the Dauphin's father-in-law. He also expressed annoyance that he had been asked to provide such a small number of troops. His letter reads:

> Do not doubt that the seriousness of the enterprise launched against you [by the English] makes the provision you have requested far too small… I am saddened by the lack of resistance which is being offered… everyone will know that I do not want to lose this kingdom but to put my loyalty to good use… I have no intention to let the kingdom fall… I hope that the other nobles of your kingdom will do their duty. I will never cease to do so, towards the glorious and much desired goal that you seek against your enemy.

According to the duke's letter, Duke Charles of Orléans had also been requested not to come in person 'because the peace was still new'. Duke John assured the king that he should not imagine 'that either Orléans or myself would ever wish to commit any great damage to God, yourself or the kingdom'.

Since des Ursins was a supporter of Charles VII and anti-Burgundian in stance, we might suspect him of fabricating Duke John's reply, were it not for a letter to the king from the nobles of the duchy of Burgundy, dated 24 September 1415. This arose out of a meeting with the duke at Argilly, his castle near Dijon. The nobles complained that the king had ordered the duke to send troops against the English, yet had not given him command of these troops.[45] Not surprisingly, the tone was similar to that of the duke's letter. The nobles expressed themselves amazed that there had been a delay in asking the duke for troops, and that he had been asked for so few and to refrain from coming in person. Did they not realise that the duke could find a very fine company of nobles, knight, esquires, archers and other men of war, 'both in the kingdom and from beyond'? Did they not realise the level of danger that the kingdom was now in, thanks to the English threat? As with the duke, the nobles indulged in delaying tactics. While reassuring the king of their loyalty and reminding him that he needed their help, they asked that the requests made of the duke should be reconsidered.

Was this any more than political posturing aimed at gaining full pardon for the duke's supporters? There is evidence that the duke had already started to raise his contingent. On 15 September he commissioned his marshals, includ- ing David, Sire de Brimeu, to carry out the mustering of companies which he had been ordered by the king to provide 'to serve the lord king in the matter of his adversaries who had invaded his kingdom'.[46] On 10 October, the duke's son, Philip, Count of Charolais, wrote to the *gens des comptes* at Lille saying that his father had sent news of his departure 'with all his power to advance against the English'. Around the same time, an observer in Paris also reported to the same *gens des comptes* that the duke had written to the king saying he would come in person, and that these letters had been read in the royal council and approved. A further reference in the archives of the duke suggests that he sent an embassy to the king on 12 October, saying that he was mobilising and intending to set out.[47] As we shall see in later chapters, there were many of the Burgundian alle- giance in the army at Agincourt. There is no reason to believe, therefore, that the duke refused to give aid against the English. We have no proof, however, that the French court changed its mind on his service in person. As a result, we cannot know precisely why the duke did not serve in person at Agincourt. Likewise, we cannot know what it was that made Orléans participate, if he too had been discouraged from coming in the initial letters of summons. If the king and his advisers changed their minds about his participation late in the day, this would explain why Orléans was still in his own duchy as late as 17 October. Burgundy's letter of 24 September implies that Orléans had been asked for the same number of troops, but we do not know how many men the duke actually brought with him to the battle.

According to des Ursins, additional requests were made to Duke John of Burgundy by the Dauphin's envoys.[48] These are not dated and therefore may pre-date his letter to the king of 24 September. It is possible that they derive rather from negotiations following the Dauphin's approaches of late July, before the duke had been told that his personal service was not wanted. These requests included, firstly, that he should allow his son, the Count of Charolais, to join the army (Charolais had recently been appointed governor of Flanders and is known to have been at Ghent on 1 September); secondly, that he should arrange for ships to be provided from Sluys (this request would suggest that the negotiations were made during the siege of Harfleur); and thirdly, that he should ensure that cannon and other military equipment within his lands should be sent for royal use. The duke's replies to these requests were on the whole positive. He agreed to tell the governor of Arras to deliver to royal officials all the artillery and equipment in the city. He also agreed to give full assistance in order that a large navy would be ready for royal service, but noted that he would have to write to his son, the Count of Charolais (as governor of Flanders), about this. He also stated that he would allow the latter to take the field with as large a company as possible. That the duke was trying to exploit the situation to his own advantage, however, is revealed by further content in his letter. He argued that the nationwide levy of taxes should not apply within his county of Artois, since this area lay on the frontier and the English had already come out of Calais to damage it. He therefore announced his intention of placing a large number of his troops in Artois to defend it against the English. Furthermore, since his lands had already been damaged by the passage of troops in previous years – a direct reference to the behaviour of royal armies in the civil war of 1414, such as at Soissons – and his towns had been burdened by repairs and the need to maintain permanent watch, they had petitioned him to ask the king to desist from collecting the tax and to allow the duke to raise funds himself.

Whether the duke had stirred up his subjects in Artois or whether the request did genuinely come from them is difficult to know. Equally worrying for the king and Dauphin was whether the duke's vassals would fight against the English, given the insult to their lord. We have already noted their letter of 24 September. Monstrelet also suggests that when the *semonce des nobles* was issued, letters were also sent to various named lords in Picardy requiring them to join the Dauphin with their troops, but they had delayed in doing so because the Duke of Burgundy had instructed them to 'hold themselves in readiness to march with him when he should summon them and not to attend the summons of any other lord, whatever might be his rank'.[49] This order would fit with the duke's supposed concern for the defence of his own lands in Artois as well as his attempt to gain political advantage from the situation. The episode also reminds us how strong bonds of loyalty and obedience could be between a lord and his subjects, even potentially against the royal interest.

Monstrelet goes on to include the text of a new royal order sent to the *bailli* of Amiens which he dates to 20 September, when the king was at Meulan.[50] This noted the initial proclamation ordering 'all nobles and others accustomed to bear arms and all other men of war and archers living in your *bailliage* and on its borders' to join the Dauphin. It went on to say that the king had been forced to surrender Harfleur because this order had been disobeyed. This makes the dating problematic, although not impossible, since the composition for surrender had been entered into on 18 September. The *bailli* was commanded to make proclamation again so that no one could plead ignorance of it but instead come before the king and his son to assist in expelling the English from the kingdom. If they refused, then the *bailli* was to put them under arrest, seize their property and force the billeting of troops on them. In addition, he was to order the towns to send artillery and other equipment, 'which we promise to restore at the end of the war'.

All of this suggests that there was strong suspicion at the French court about the intentions of Burgundy and concern that he might take advantage of a royal absence from Paris to restore his own power in the city. This helps to explain why the king and Dauphin had delayed so long in moving down the Seine. On 3 October an order was issued to repair the walls and ditches of the capital.[51] If it was thought possible that the English might advance as far as Paris then it demonstrates how afraid the French were in the weeks following the surrender of Harfleur. Burgundy's replies of 24 September cannot have been reassuring. A week later, the *prévot des marchands* and four *echevins* were replaced by pro-Armagnac men.[52] Although the Bourgeois of Paris claims that this was done without the knowledge of the citizens and without royal orders, it is further evidence that a Burgundian attempt on the city was anticipated. Troops from the city did not participate at Agincourt. The explanation usually given is that Jean de Beaumont, one of the knights of the Duke of Berry, cast aspersions on having military assistance from 'these rude mechanics'.[53] More likely the government was reluctant to draw troops from Paris when Burgundian intentions remained suspect, and when the king had left the capital. From 1 October onwards, there are several references to the payment of troops in Paris under the royal *prévot*, Tanneguy du Chastel, as well as others at Charenton-le-Pont, to the east of the city at the junction of the Seine and Marne.[54]

Equally problematic for the king and Dauphin was whether Duke John of Brittany would offer resistance to the English. He had entered into a truce with Henry V early in 1414, which the English king certainly interpreted as making him an ally.[55] On 19 August 1415 an English envoy was sent to the duchy charged with ensuring that Duke John did not renege upon his agreement. This envoy was present when Charles VI's letters requesting military support were received at the Breton ducal court,[56] and apparently reminded the duke of his obligations to Henry. The duke's response was a model of prevarication. He prepared to join Charles, advancing to the town of Falaise, south of Caen. While there, the king, Dauphin and Duke of Berry sent news of the fall of Harfleur and of Henry's march towards Calais, ordering the duke to join the other lords as soon as possible. Duke John continued to dally at Falaise for eight days before coming to Rouen, but may have been present at a meeting there on 20 October. According to Perceval de Cagny, he then refused to do more until the king had granted him the town of Saint-Malo. De Cagny was the chronicler of the Dukes of Alençon, who did not themselves enjoy good relations with the Duke of Brittany. It is possible, therefore, that the lack of co-operation of Duke John is exaggerated in his account. Even so, although the duke did march north with his troops, by 25 October he had only reached Amiens.

The pre-existing political situation in France contributed to uncertainties over the response to the English. It had not, however, prevented troops being raised. As we shall see in the next chapters, they were able to harry Henry's march northwards. The French had not been able to raise a large enough army to save Harfleur. This was not because of political divisions but because of the difficulty in raising a large enough army in the time needed. The French were aware that Henry had invaded in force. They had kept his activities in and around Harfleur under observation, using their limited military resources during the siege to best effect, but they could not risk engagement until they had gathered a large army. The French wanted to be certain of success if they were to bring him to battle. The *journée* of the siege, set by Henry for 22 September, was not the opportune moment for this.

As historians, we are in the enviable position of knowing what both sides were up to. The French could not be sure of Henry's next move, nor could he be sure of theirs. With the taking of Harfleur, he had achieved the first objective of his expedition to France, but what was he going to do next?[57] After the surrender of Harfleur on 22 September, he sent a letter to the city of London reporting the successful outcome of the siege. As for future plans, he merely indicated his intention 'by the fine power and the good labour and diligence of our faithful people over here to do our duty to achieve as soon as possible our rights in this area'.[58] This vagueness may reveal his own uncertainty about what to do next, or else a desire to keep his plans secret. The wording reminds us, however, that justification for invasion and conquest was still at the forefront of his mind. His next major move was no less aggressive in tone. On 26 September he issued a challenge to the Dauphin Louis.[59] The tone of this was reminiscent of his initial declarations of war, placing recurrent emphasis on the bad effects of war – 'the deaths of men, the destruction of countries, the lamentations of women and children and so many general evils that every good Christian must lament it and have pity'. Henry declared himself committed to seeking ways of avoiding such evils, 'and to acquire the approbation of God, and the praise of the world'. His quarrel was, he admitted, with Charles VI, but since 'it had pleased God to visit our said cousin your father with infirmity', Henry suggested that it might be decided 'at the will of God between our person and yours'.

Anticipating that the Dauphin would refuse on the grounds that his father's interest in the crown could not be put to one side, Henry proposed that, whatever happened, Charles should continue to enjoy his royal position for the rest of his days. So if Henry won what was presumably to be some form of personal combat, 'the crown of France shall be immediately rendered to us without difficulty after his decease':

> For it is better for us, Cousin, to decide this war for ever between our two persons than to suffer the unbelievers by means of our quarrels to destroy Christianity, our mother the Holy Church to remain in division and the people of God to destroy one another.

This again fitted with Henry's earlier declarations, in suggesting that Anglo-French peace would help to end the papal schism and facilitate crusades.

The *Gesta* tells us that the summons was carried to the Dauphin by Guienne Herald (William Bruges, who was to become the first Garter King of Arms) and Raoul de Gaucourt, who had led the defence of Harfleur. The chronicler's account is verbally reminiscent of the wording of the summons, suggesting that he had seen or heard the original text. For instance, both noted the need for the councils of Charles VI, Henry and the Dauphin to agree the intended outcome of the challenge. The chronicler adds two important dimensions. First, while the summons contained no ultimatum, the *Gesta* has Henry tell the Dauphin that he had already been waiting for him at his town of Harfleur and would continue to do so for eight days in anticipation of an answer. The second is that the duel is expressed in the *Gesta* as an alternative to another solution, namely that within the eight days the Dauphin, moved by compunction at the shedding of human blood, 'might cause his [Henry's] right to be conceded to him without further rigours of war and to reach peace with him'. It will come as no surprise that the Dauphin did not reply, but Henry did wait at Harfleur until around 6–8 October, thereby permitting the eight-day period to pass, as well as time for the message to be taken to the Dauphin. This was a useful breathing and thinking space while Henry planned the next stage of campaign. We shall consider in a moment why he decided to move northwards to Calais, but first we must consider further his challenge to the Dauphin.

The issuing of a challenge for personal combat was not common in this period. More usual, although not hugely so, was a group fight. The Duke of Rothesay had suggested to Henry IV during the Scottish campaign of 1400 that to avoid shedding Christian blood they should contest their dispute between 100 to 300

chosen warriors.[60] Henry knew that the Dauphin would not accept the challenge
and that he would not even reply. The advantages therefore all lay with Henry.
Since an English and French envoy were together charged with taking the summons to the Dauphin, there was no way that it could not be delivered and made
public at the French royal court. The Dauphin could not formally refuse the challenge for fear of loss of face. So a non-reply was his only option, but even this
was a victory for Henry since it implied refusal to fight, for himself and on behalf
of his people. If the Dauphin had sent tennis balls and an insulting message to
Henry earlier in the year, then this challenge was Henry's riposte. We must dismiss
the idea that Henry had suggested personal combat because the Dauphin had a
reputation for not being warlike. Louis was still only eighteen but had spent two
previous summers on campaign. At his death on 18 December 1415, Nicholas de
Baye, greffier of the Paris parlement, spoke of him as large and not very agile.[61]
He also noted that 'recently' the Dauphin had taken to staying up at night and
sleeping through the day, and that he spent money on fine clothes and his chapel.
Historians have misread this as meaning he was debauched, but de Baye's comments are in the standard mode of criticism of the court at a time of financial
difficulties for the nation as a whole and may also relate to the Dauphin's illness
which brought his premature death. Baye also says that the prince was 'handsome in features' and that he liked organ music. Dauphin Louis had worked hard,
despite his youth, to create peace between Burgundian and Armagnac lords and
to form a middle party around him. Fenin says of him that 'he earnestly wished
to preserve his people in peace'.[62] Since the Dauphin died within a few months
of Agincourt, it is more likely that he was already in poor health. But then Jean
Fusoris had been told by Courtenay that Henry V suffered from the same illness
as himself, being fat and complaining of weakness, especially when rising.[63]

There is a further point to make about the challenge. The proposal that Charles VI
should remain king for life even if Henry won is precisely what was agreed in
the treaty of Troyes of 1420. There is evidence that Henry was behind this part
of the treaty. It is intriguing to think that he may already have had the idea in
mind in 1415. The gesture also reveals an important element in Henry's religious
conception of kingship, namely, the impropriety of deposing an anointed king.
The summons to the Dauphin specifically speaks of Charles as a 'sacred person',
meaning a person who had been marked apart by an act of anointing. A similar concern may have lain behind Henry's reburial of Richard II in Westminster
Abbey shortly after his own accession. However, whereas in 1420 Henry was in
a strong position to become heir of France by treaty, thanks to his alliance with
Duke Philip of Burgundy after the assassination of the latter's father in September
1419, the practicality of his claim to the French inheritance in 1415 was extremely
low.

The summons, and with it the idea of the victor becoming heir to France,
was all for show. In reality, no prince would have countenanced putting a major

international quarrel to the uncertain outcome of a duel, nor could its outcome have been legally binding on Charles VI. The summons was a ploy which kept Henry in the diplomatic as well as military driving seat after the fall of Harfleur. Its sending was a deliberate insult to the French and specifically to the Dauphin. Henry anticipated that, should the French give battle, they would be led by the Dauphin. If he could be portrayed as afraid to meet Henry in single combat, then his credibility as military commander would be diminished in the eyes of Henry's own troops. Their confidence needed to be boosted at this point, since a march into hostile territory was imminent. There is evidence that Henry was faced with desertion of troops at this point. Both the *Liber Metricus* and Usk comment that many stole away in secret, much to the king's disgust.[64] Furthermore, there were some in Henry's army who were advising that the campaign should be abandoned. No reply was received after the eight days and nor did the herald or any other emissary return. The *Gesta* links this directly to the king's resolve to start out on his march. We can take this as strong evidence that the king publicised in his army the sending of the summons and the lack of a reply.

If it is true that de Gaucourt was sent with the summons, we see the same royal tactics at play. He would have to explain why he had been forced to surrender Harfleur, and the French court would be reminded of its own failure to respond to English attack. The English would thereby appear all the stronger. But whether de Gaucourt actually went to the French court at this point is uncertain. We have a statement made by him in a later dispute with Louis d'Estouteville.[65] In this, he does not mention that he was sent with Guienne Herald to the Dauphin, but he does confirm that Henry gave permission to himself and about 260 others to depart from the town on the grounds that 'many of us were extremely sick'. The condition was that they should appear before the king at Calais on the feast of St Martin, 11 November. This could be taken to confirm that Henry had already determined to march to Calais and that he anticipated being there by that date. The wording in the *Gesta* states, however, that de Gaucourt and his associates were to surrender at Calais to the king or to his lieutenant or specially appointed deputy. The Berry Herald states that they would only need to do this if the king was not brought to battle before he reached Calais, but there is no certainty that this was in the terms of their release.

Chroniclers are unanimous in their view that Henry decided to march straight from Harfleur to Calais. Yet in a letter sent to Bordeaux from the siege on 3 September, Jean Bordiu reported that he had heard that Henry did not intend to enter Harfleur after he had taken it but to stay in the field, adding that 'in a short while after the capture of the town, he intends to go to Montivilliers, and thence to Dieppe, afterwards to Rouen and then to Paris'.[66] If true — and we have no other indication of Henry's intentions at this point of the siege — then the king had changed his mind. It may be that Henry had always intended, once Harfleur was taken, to campaign through Upper Normandy to Calais, following the precedent of Edward III even to the point of bringing the French to battle within Ponthieu, part of the land given to the English in the Great Peace. Henry's route to the Somme could be taken as confirming this desire, but we know that when he arrived at Edward's crossing point at Blanchetaque, he considered the French to be there in strength and so changed direction. This suggests that he had not included a battle in his planned northward move. All the chroniclers suggest that he was aiming to get to Calais as quickly as possible. The *Gesta* speaks of eight days' supplies being allowed, which would only just be enough for the journey.

The idea that the march northwards was the result of his desire for battle is not credible. Had Henry wanted to engage with the French he would have moved towards Rouen, where he must have known the French were gathering. More likely, he wanted to draw the French away from the Seine valley. Harfleur was potentially vulnerable because no other places in the vicinity had been taken by the English to create a march. The Burgundian chroniclers claim that they had tried to do so, but been foiled by the French. Whether this was the case or not, Henry had undoubtedly left his only conquest exposed. This may also help to explain why he decided on a march overland, since this would permit him to leave some of the royal ships to defend Harfleur on the seaward side. Henry had clearly decided after the fall of Harfleur that he could not engage in further sieges. That of Harfleur had taken its toll, and winter was drawing on. Sieges created as much difficulty for the besieger as the besieged in terms of food supplies. Although he was now in a position to bring in victuals through Harfleur, there were too many mouths to feed and he could not allow the campaign to continue for much longer. Furthermore, the French were gathering at Rouen, which was by its nature a much more formidable challenge than Harfleur had been and therefore a target far too difficult to attempt. Bordiu had suggested in his letter to Bordeaux of 3 September that the king had a plan to take Dieppe. No effort was made to take the town on the march north. Since Henry left all his gunners in Harfleur, as well as the carpenters who made towers and defensive hoardings, we can assume that he also left his guns there. He would not have been in a position to lay siege to anywhere else. The overwhelming impression is therefore that Henry was making for Calais as quickly as possible.

Several English chronicles report that the king had discussions with his council over what to do. The Pseudo-Elmham outlines two options: a secure return to England by sea, or an overland march to Calais, where the army might be exposed to the French and to other dangers. This text, as also the *Gesta* and Titus Livius, suggests that the majority of Henry's advisers preferred the first option. Since one victory had been achieved, what was the point of running the risk of failure? It is interesting that Titus Livius, writing under the patronage of the Duke of Gloucester, should name Clarence as the spokesman of those who wanted to end the campaign straightaway. This was surely to emphasise the loyalty of Henry's youngest brother, who was injured at Agincourt while Clarence was invalided home. By the time Titus Livius wrote, Clarence and Henry V were both dead and therefore the truth of his possible libel could not be questioned. It seems likely, however, that there was considerable discussion about what the next move should be, and that Henry's own plans were not universally shared. It is significant here that the king had lost one of his closest confidants, Richard Courtenay, to death during the siege. His other close friend, the Earl of Arundel, was seriously ill and returned home on 28 September.[67] As in the preparations for invasion, however, it had to be the king's will that prevailed. For the chroniclers, writing with hindsight and full conviction of God's blessing on the victorious king, it offered an opportunity to emphasise his faith in divine intervention and also to link him to Judas Maccabeus, the frequently cited example of a warrior who triumphed against all odds. The author of the *Gesta* makes the link again when one of Henry's knights allegedly wishes for more men on the eve of battle.

The *Gesta* explains Henry's decision to march north in hindsight-influenced terms, with reference to 'the few defeating the many should God wish it'. In other words, the battle was preordained by God, whatever Henry might chose to do. Titus Livius and the Pseudo-Elmham give a more practical insight into the king's mind. If he fled, the French would say it was on account of fear and that he had thereby abandoned his rights. It is likely too that Henry was not certain he had done enough to impress his English subjects. If he went home by sea, he left Harfleur vulnerable and he could easily lose all he had gained and have nothing to show for the money and effort put into the campaign. Remember that Fusoris had been told that if Henry came home quickly without achieving anything for all of the expense that had been incurred, he would not be welcomed.[68] Better, then, a compromise. The English army would execute a quick march across French territory. This had the advantage of showing the French population that Henry was a force to be reckoned with. If the army moved quickly enough, it could get to Calais without risk of failure and loss of face. It would then be open to Henry to invade again. In this context, the comments of the Religieux, the only French chronicler to mention any debate in the English camp on what to do next, are important:

> …on the advice of his most important men, Henry did not want to trust to the dubious fate of military engagement with troops so unequal in number. So he decided to go to Calais and await there the spring which would be more suitable for military action.

In other words, Calais might provide winter quarters for the king and at least some of his men, much as Bordeaux had done for the Black Prince in 1355–56.[69]

There was another practical consideration. It was much easier and cheaper to take an army overland, where it could partially feed off the land, than it was to transport it by sea. To take his troops to France in the first place Henry had relied largely on hired ships from Holland and Zealand, which had now returned home.[70] If Henry had decided to take his whole army home by sea immediately after the siege, this would have required a new round of hiring and impressment on a large scale. It would be much easier to ship men home from Calais and Dover or Sandwich, since this was a shorter crossing with regularly available shipping. To take the sick to England from Harfleur required only the use of the royal ships and a few small merchant vessels, especially as the horses of those going home remained with the army in France. The Earl Marshal, for instance, was taken back to Portsmouth with twelve of his men-at-arms and forty-five archers, but the 138 men of his retinue who stayed on the campaign were assigned the horses of their sick companions, giving them a total of 537 horses.[71] The earl and his men were taken back on the *Nicholas of Hull* by an arrangement made with its master. Ships from Seaton, Dartmouth, Plymouth, Hartlepool, Boston, Colchester and Sandwich are also found transporting men to England at this point, but this was by hiring, not impressment.[72]

The beginning of Henry's march northwards coincided with the beginning of the second quarter. Having distributed his jewels at great future expense, since enough funds needed to be raised by 1 January 1417 to redeem them, Henry was not going to allow captains to default on the service for which they were contracted. This would have been to the detriment of his honour as king. Remember that his captains had entered into indentures for a whole year. Reinforcements were already being sought in England. On 5 October the Duke of Bedford had ordered the sheriffs of London to proclaim that 'all knights, esquires (*armigeri*) and archers (*valetti*) who wished to go to Normandy' should present themselves before the Bishop of Winchester to receive wages.[73] Later in the month there were efforts to recruit more troops in England, although this was subsequently cancelled.[74] The town accounts for Boulogne tell us that Clarence came to Calais on 12 October.[75] This was possibly *en route* to England, but it is also credible that Henry intended that those invalided home should rejoin the campaign later. The *congés* given under the royal signet to authorise their departure simply allowed their return to England; they did not terminate the contracts, although in practice this was what happened, since the campaign did end a short way into the second quarter of service. There is evidence in the Issue Rolls that in mid-October privy seal letters were sent to some of the lords invalided home to despatch their retinues to the king abroad as soon as possible, although this was later countermanded.[76]

At base, therefore, the reason for the march northwards was Henry's obsession and royal will. His intention was to move quickly to Calais, yet surely he cannot have been so naïve as to think that the French would not try to intercept him. While he was not battle-seeking but rather made every effort on the march to avoid engagement until he had no choice, he must surely have realised that he might be forced to fight. In this context, therefore, it is important to consider how large an army he still had at his disposal. The chronicle accounts suggest that one reason why his advisers had argued for an immediate return home was that the English army was, as the *Gesta* puts it, 'daily growing smaller'.

How many men had he lost? There is no doubt that 300 men-at-arms and 900 archers were put into garrison since the figures are noted in the records of the privy council.[77] Gunners, carpenters and masons recruited for the campaign were also detailed into Harfleur for its defence and rebuilding.[78] The *Gesta* suggests that 5,000 were invalided home but gives no figures for the dead or deserters. The Burgundian chroniclers place the mortality total at 2,000 and the number of those invalided home as 500 knights and esquires, in addition to those of lower rank. Appendix B tabulates the figures for the size of Henry's army as given by chronicles at various stages of the campaign. Not all writers distinguish between the different phases. But for the army as it left Harfleur, the lowest figure is that given in the *Gesta* and *Liber Metricus* of 900 men-at-arms and 5,000 archers. This has been accepted by historians as accurate. French sources cite higher figures for the army at all stages. We do not have to rely, however, on narrative sources, since there are financial records for the English army on which we can draw. Because Henry did not want to give pay to men who were no longer in a position to serve him, the post-campaign accounts give details of those who died at the siege or were invalided home. In addition, since Harfleur remained in English hands, the cost of those put into garrison could be transferred to another budget.[79]

Using these materials, what conclusions can we come to on the size of Henry's army as he set out on his march? We can immediately deduct the 1,200 detailed into garrison. It is interesting to see how this was managed. The post-campaign accounts show that 285 of those put into garrison were drawn from nineteen retinues. In ten cases, the captain entered the garrison with his whole company:[80] William, Lord Botreaux was also detailed into the garrison with the whole of his retinue of sixty men, but became ill and returned to Dover on 19 October, leaving his company in the garrison under the command of Sir Andrew Ecton (or Acton).[81] In the remainder, only part of the retinue was placed in Harfleur. Three retinues provided only one man, the Duke of York eight. Thirty-two of the 159 who had crossed with the Earl of Suffolk, who had himself died at the siege, were put into garrison. In the case of whole retinues it is easy to suggest the rationale. In the case of Suffolk's men, it may be that they were recovering from dysentery and were considered a risk to take on the march, but not so ill that they should go home.

A further insight can be gleaned from muster roll of the Harfleur garrison for the first quarter of 1416.[82] It records the names of 1,198 men, consisting of an earl, four barons, twenty-two knights, 273 men-at-arms and 898 archers. Several of those known to have been transferred into garrison in early October were still there.[83] It is likely that the retinues of the remaining peers (Dorset, Edward, Lord Hastings and William, Lord Clinton) had also been transferred in their entirety to the garrison before Henry began his march, but they do not have post-campaign accounts surviving.[84] The majority of those in the 1416 muster were therefore probably men who had served in Harfleur since its surrender. Others were men like John Fastolf, who had crossed in the Earl of Suffolk's retinue but had been invalided home, only to return to France to join the garrison and to be knighted by the time of the grant to him of the nearby lordship of Frileuse on 29 January 1416.[85] Fastolf's pattern of service reminds us again of the possibility that men invalided home were not necessarily out of the war thenceforward.

The post-campaign accounts reveal very few losses from deaths at the siege. Michael de la Pole, Earl of Suffolk died on 18 September. Two of his archers also died, and permission was given for two men-at-arms and four archers to accompany his body home for burial.[86] Sir John Southworth, one of the commanders of the archers from Lancashire, died on 27 September.[87] Two men-at-arms and thirteen archers in the retinue of Thomas, Earl of Arundel died between 24 September and 3 October.[88] Deaths are found in thirteen other retinues. In all, therefore, there is record of the demise of fifteen men-at-arms (counting peers and knights in this category), twenty-one archers and one member of the retinue of the sergeant tailor, William Tropenell.[89] Not all may have died from disease. Monstrelet refers to some soldiers being killed by French crossbows.

Many more men were invalided home, including four nobles, Clarence, the Earl Marshal, and the Earls of March and of Arundel. The latter returned to England on 28 September, and made his will at his castle of Arundel on 10 October, where he died three days later.[90] In addition to the post-campaign accounts, we have another source for those who returned home. Because Henry was extremely concerned about desertion after the fall of Harfleur, those allowed to go back to England had to have royal permission to do so. The administration of this was given to the chamberlain and steward of the household. Lists were drawn up which suggest that a mustering system was used, probably as men went on board the ships.[91] These lists add to the information in the accounts, but caution has to be exercised in using them as a source for calculating the size of the remaining army. Because of fears of desertion, the lists do not only record men-at-arms and archers but also servants and others going home with their masters. We cannot simply count all of the names in the lists, as has been done in the past.

In addition, we can see considerable discrepancies between the numbers on the sick list and in the post-campaign accounts. The best example is presented by the Earl of Arundel.[92] The sick list for his retinue names nineteen men-at-arms and sixty-eight archers as well as three minstrels. This appears to be a considerable loss out of the 100 men-at-arms and 300 archers with which he had departed. His post-campaign account, however, shows that the retinue that continued on the campaign was only six men-at-arms under strength. It had been possible to find replacements for two-thirds of the men-at-arms and all of the archers who had died or were being invalided home.

Above: 1 Monmouth Castle. The building in which it is believed that Henry V was born.

Left: 2 The coronation of Joan of Navarre (widow of Duke John IV of Brittany) as queen of England, shortly after her marriage to Henry IV on 7 March 1403. Joan was the mother of Arthur, Count of Richemont, who was captured at Agincourt.

3 The battle of Shrewsbury, 21 July 1403, from the *Pageant* of Richard Beauchamp, Earl of Warwick. This drawing dates from the end of the fifteenth century so the armour reflects that period rather than the time of the battle.

Clockwise from top left:

4 A representation of a charge made by Richard, Earl of Warwick (d.1439) against the forces of Owen Glendower in 1404.

5 Henry V as Prince of Wales, from the presentation copy of Hoccleve's *Regimen of Princes* (1412).

6 Henry V, from a series of roundels of British monarchs produced by Wedgewood in 1779.

Clockwise from top left:

7 A *gros* of Henry V, showing both the leopards of England and the *fleur de lis* of France.

8 A representation of the funeral effigy of Henry Beaufort, Bishop of Winchester and cardinal (d. 1447). Beaufort was the half-brother of Henry IV and was appointed chancellor at the accession of Henry V.

9 The coronation of Henry V on 9 April 1413, from a bas relief on his chantry chapel in Westminster Abbey.

Left: 10 A representation of a king, probably Henry V, at the opening of a parliament.

Below left: 11 Henry Chichele, previously Bishop of St David's, who became Archbishop of Canterbury in May 1414.

Below right: 12 Richard, Earl of Warwick, made captain of Calais in February 1414. The earl kneels in the presence of Henry V to receive from the chancellor, Bishop Beaufort, sealed letters of appointment.

Above: 13 A later representation of the Tower of London, where Henry met the Mayor and aldermen of London on 10 March 1415 to discuss the funding of his campaign to France.

Right: 14 Tomb effigy of Thomas, Duke of Clarence in Canterbury Cathedral. Clarence was Henry V's eldest brother and led an army to France in 1412 as well as providing the largest retinue in 1415. He was invalided home after the siege of Harfleur but served on later campaigns, meeting his death at the battle of Baugé.

Below: 15 Humphrey, Duke of Gloucester, the youngest brother of Henry V, who was the only one of his brothers present at the battle of Agincourt. Drawing by the herald Jacques le Boucq (d.1573) but possibly based on an earlier work of c.1425, when the duke was protector of England for the young Henry VI.

Left: 16 John, Duke of Bedford from his Book of Hours. The duke was the middle brother of Henry V and remained in England as keeper of the realm during the Agincourt campaign, but was later Regent of France during the minority of King Henry VI.

Below left: 17 Thomas Montague, Earl of Salisbury (d.1428), who served on the 1412 campaign as well as in 1415, and was also involved in negotiations with the French in 1414. He was killed by a gun wound at the siege of Orléans.

Below right: 18 Muster of troops under Sir Thomas Erpingham, taken on 13 July on 'the hethe of Southampton'. His name heads the list of esquires (men-at-arms). The archers are listed in two columns. He has also brought along four men-at-arms and twelve unnamed archers, in addition to those required by his indenture.

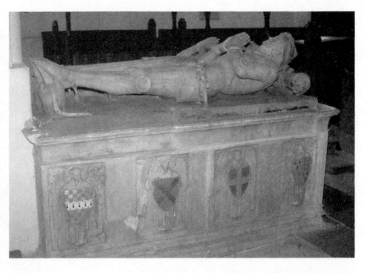

Left: 19 Retinue list presented with Sir Thomas's account after his death. This notes what had happened to each man on the campaign, indicating that most were present at the battle.

Above: 20 Tomb chest and effigy of Sir Edmund de Thorpe (d. 1418) at Ashwellthorpe (Norfolk). It is not known whether this knight served in 1415 but he was on the campaign of 1417. The effigy gives a good indication of the armour of the period of Agincourt.

Below: 21 Detail of the effigy of Sir Edmund de Thorpe, showing mail protection below the gorget and the Lancastrian 'SS' collar.

Right: 22 Effigy of Sir Thomas Erpingham from gateway of Norwich Cathedral. This effigy may once have been on or close to his tomb. Sir Thomas played an important command role at the battle.

Below left: 23 Michael de la Pole, Earl of Suffolk who died at the siege of Harfleur on 18 September 1415, from the effigy on his tomb in Wingfield, Suffolk.

Below right: 24 Fighting at sea, from the *Pageant* of Richard Beauchamp, Earl of Warwick. Although this was drawn in the late fifteenth century it provides a useful reminder of how men engaged on board ships. The French launched an abortive attack on English ships, besieging Harfleur shortly before the end of the siege.

25 Brass of John Peryent and wife at Diwell (Herts.). This was made shortly after the wife's death in April 1415 and therefore provides a good representation of armour of the period. Peryent served on the campaign with two other men-at-arms and nine archers, and was a royal esquire of Henry V as well as master of the horse to Queen Joan.

Right: 26 Brass of Sir Simon Felbrigg at Felbrigg (Norfolk). Sir Simon headed a retinue of twelve men-at-arms and thirty-six archers in 1415, and had been standard-bearer to Richard II. The brass was made after his wife's death in 1416 but the knight himself did not die until 1442. (The dating on the cover illustration is therefore the possible date of the brass).

Below: 27 Men-at-arms fighting in the mêlée, from a fifteenth-century manuscript. This gives useful indications of the various kinds of staff weapons in use.

28 Brass of Thomas, Lord Camoys and his wife Elizabeth (Trotton, West Sussex). Camoys (1350–1420) was commander of the rearguard at Agincourt. His wife was the widow of Henry Percy (Hotspur).

29 'The morning of the battle of Agincourt', one of a series on the battle by Sir John Gilbert (1817–97), who specialised in historical subjects.

30 Henry V giving a battle speech before the battle, as portrayed by Ernest Crofts (1847–1911), another artist who specialised in historical subjects. There is a suggestion in chronicles that the king spoke from horseback.

31 Artist's impression of the French cavalry attack against the archers at Agincourt.

32 In this painting, one of a series on the battle by Sir John Gilbert (1817–97), who specialised in historical subjects, the French herald Mountjoye is shown before the mounted King Henry while thanks are given by the English for the victory.

33 A similar representation of thanksgiving after the battle by Charles Blair Leighton (1823–55), who was a pioneer of early colour printing for illustrated books.

Left: 34 Charles VI with his court. The herald of Richard Beauchamp, Earl of Warwick kneels in front with a challenge from his master for a tourney between fifteen knights of France and England. The rubric notes the acceptance of the challenge by Sir Hugh Lawney (possibly Lannoy), Gerard d'Herbaumes and Colard de Fiennes. At Agincourt, Lannoy was taken prisoner, the other two were killed.

Below left: 35 The joust between Richard Beauchamp, Earl of Warwick and Gerard d'Herbaumes, 'the red knight'. The late-fifteenth-century rubric dates this to 6 January 1415.

Below right: 36 The joust between Richard Beauchamp, Earl of Warwick and Sir Hugh Lawney/ Lannoy, 'the white knight'. The herald in the centre holds examples of tournament saddles, which had a higher front to give extra protection.

Right: 37 The joust between Richard Beauchamp, Earl of Warwick and Colard de Fiennes, 'the black knight'.

Below: 38 The siege of Calais by Philip, Duke of Burgundy in 1436, from the *Pageant* of Richard Beauchamp, Earl of Warwick. This late-fifteenth-century view of the town is thought to be one of the earliest in existence.

Below: 39 A representation of Old St Paul's Cathedral, where thanks were given once news of the victory arrived in London on Tuesday 29 October.

Above: 40 Letter of Henry V in his own hand referring to the safekeeping of the Duke of Orléans and other prisoners captured at Agincourt, *c.*1419. The letter, written while the king was on his second Norman campaign, also asks that the marches of Scotland should be well defended.

Below left: 41 Charles, Duke of Orléans, as a prisoner in the Tower of London. The duke is shown three times. Note also old London Bridge in the background.

Below right: 42 This may be the betrothal of Henry V and Catherine of France in the cathedral of Troyes on 21 May, or their marriage at the church of St John in the city on 2 June. It is derived from an illuminated version of the chronicles of the Religieux of Saint-Denis.

Right: 43 Henry V's chantry chapel in Westminster Abbey from an engraving of around 1665. Work on the chapel started in the late 1430s in accordance with the king's will that he should be buried close to the shrine of Edward the Confessor.

Below: 44 Henry V's tomb in Westminster Abbey from an engraving made in 1665, based on a painting then in Whitehall Palace. The effigy of silver gilt finally disappeared in 1546.

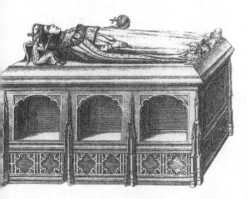

45 Early-twentieth-century photograph of the tomb chest of Henry V in Westminster Abbey, above which the chantry chapel was constructed.

Above left: 46 Detail of carving on one of the facades of Henry's chantry chapel in Westminster Abbey, showing saints, badges and coats of arms.

Above right: 47 Equestrian figures, probably of Henry V, on the king's chantry chapel in Westminster Abbey.

Below: 48 Tilting helm from the chantry chapel of Henry V in Westminster Abbey. Legend has it that it was worn by the king on the battlefield at Agincourt but this is very unlikely. It would have been deposited in the abbey as an achievement used at his funeral on 7 November 1422.

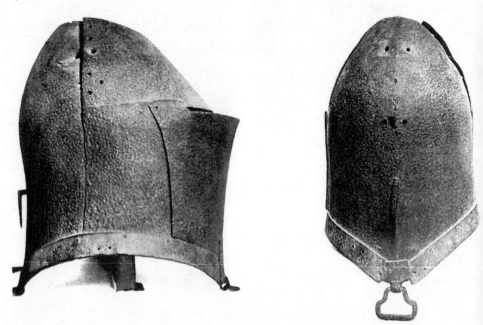

The retinue list presented with the post-campaign account gives the names of incoming as well as departing soldiers, as well as the dates between 24 September and 3 October on which the replacements were made. Either reinforcements had crossed or else extra soldiers had crossed in the first place in the hope of gaining employment.

This situation makes it difficult to know the real impact of disease at the siege, since we do not have post-campaign accounts for all of the retinues with members appearing on the sick lists. Simply counting the names of soldiers in the lists could therefore exaggerate the actual loss to the army size as a whole. The royal household and its support groups appear to have been particularly hard hit by disease. One of the lists of sick includes office-holders such as William Kynwolmersh, cofferer, and Master Lewis, the armourer, as well as eight of the sumpter men, two wheelwrights, six of the pavilioners, sixteen of the smiths (including Baldwin Smith of Aldgate in London), twenty-six of the masons and fifty-four of the labourers.[93] Many of those going home were therefore not front-line troops. The latter did incur losses. At least fifty of the Welsh archers and eleven of the Cheshire archers went home. Overall, around 1,330 soldiers can be shown to be returning home. These include at least 183 men-at-arms and 753 archers, with the remainder undifferentiated. Adding in the dead and those detailed to the Harfleur garrison, we come to a total of 2,568, without taking into account the fact of replacements. Since the army that left England contained a minimum of 11,248 men and most likely nearer 12,000, we can prove that Henry still had at least 8,680 soldiers with him on his march and at the battle. He probably had more since the departing army was larger and replacements were found for some of those invalided home. A working total of at least 9,000 is therefore credible.

It is important to note that the *Gesta* does not say that Henry's decision to march to Calais was occasioned by the loss of men, rather it was the other way round. Having resolved on the march, Henry caused those who were sick to be separated from those who were fit and well. This was a sensible military decision. He could not take sick men on his march since they could not be properly cared for, would delay progress, and might infect others. They were thus equally disadvantageous, whether Henry wanted to make a quick getaway or whether he intended further military action or might be forced to it by the French. It stood to reason that the sick could not be left in Harfleur, where resources were stretched and buildings unfit for habitation, and where there was danger of French attack. Henry made as many preparations as he could for the march. Soldiers who had lost their captains were reassigned at the king's command to other retinues.[94] Money and food was brought across to Harfleur in the days before the army departed, including peas, salted fish, barrelled eels and other preserved commodities.[95] There is also evidence of messages and instructions being carried to and fro across the Channel and to Calais. It was already known at Calais that the king was planning to march there, another indication that his intention was to take his army straight there. Foodstuffs, medicines and messages for the king were being sent from London to Calais from mid-October in anticipation of his arrival.[96]

It was believed at Calais that the French would try to engage him. The lieutenant there, William Bardolf, wrote to the Duke of Bedford in England on 7 October saying that 'several good friends' (a euphemism for spies) coming to the town from France and Flanders had told him that 'without doubt the king, our lord, will have battle with his enemy within fifteen days next coming at the very latest'.[97] Since Bardolf went on to speak of French preparations, his meaning was that they intended to fight Henry. Bardolf had already received orders from Bedford to 'make the most hard war that we can against the French... in order to prevent those on the frontier crossing or advancing near to where he now is in person'. These instructions reveal that the English plan, presumably drawn up at Henry's behest, was to deploy the Calais garrison to prevent troops from the northern frontiers from joining with the rest of the French army against Henry. This did not succeed. As the Religieux tells us, 300 men set out from Calais, 'not knowing the troubles that the king was experiencing', but were routed in their operation by Picard companies.[98] Tradition has it that these Calais troops came within a league of Blanchetaque before they were driven back. Whether Henry was aware of this is uncertain. What we do know is that he hoped to reach Calais in a week but it took almost three. His plan to return his army to England swiftly and cheaply overland misfired because of French counter-measures.

6

From Harfleur to the Crossing of the Somme, 8–19 October 1415

Henry's intention was to march directly from Harfleur to Calais. This would involve a journey of at least 230km (144 miles). The *Gesta's* belief of 100 miles is therefore a considerable underestimate. The chronicler adds that the army was ordered to take provisions for eight days. If Henry believed that he could reach Calais in that length of time, then he would need to cover 29km (18 miles) per day, a rate he never achieved at any stage of his march. If the *Gesta's* figures were based on the king's own expectations, then Henry began his march under a gross misconception. He was already exposing his army to food shortages even if he succeeded in marching by the direct coastal route. As it happened, his march to Calais lasted for twenty-two days. After the first seventeen days, his army arrived at Maisoncelle, where it prepared to give battle on the next day. By this stage, it had travelled somewhere between 378km and 402km, giving an average distance travelled each day of between 22.2km and 23.6km.

Historians have generally accepted the route and dating of the English march as given in the *Gesta*, on the grounds that its author was with the army throughout. Its level of detail, however, is not consistent, and there is a marked decline in its level of information as the march goes on.[1] Variations in the route are found in *Le Fèvre*, also with the English 'in all the business of this time', and in three Burgundian chronicles as a whole. By taking all the narrative sources together, adding in references from administrative records where possible, we can piece together the events as well as possible routes. This chapter follows Henry's march in chronological fashion until the crossing of the Somme. In the next chapter the second stage of the march is reconstructed and there is an evaluation of the English march as a whole. Appendix A gives details of distances of the various phases. What is often forgotten is that the French were also involved in considerable movement of troops in their effort to harass and intercept Henry.

Unfortunately, it is much more difficult to trace their routes, since no chronicler provides a detailed account, but we must attempt to look at the movements of both armies to understand the game of cat and mouse played out over these weeks in October 1415.

At the start the advantage lay with the English, since the French could not be wholly certain what route Henry would take, even though his final destination was already strongly suspected. On 6 October a messenger came from Abbeville to Boulogne to say that Henry had installed a garrison at Harfleur and now intended to march to Calais.[2] This suggests that the French already knew of his plans, even before he left Harfleur. The *Gesta* gives the departure date as Tuesday 8 October. This may have been deliberately chosen as the eve of the feast of St Denis, the patron saint of France. It was also timed to fit with the beginning of the second quarter of the army's service on 6–7 October.[3] As the army passed on their right Montivilliers, 4km north of Harfleur, there was a skirmish in which some Englishmen were killed or taken prisoner.[4] Henry had probably sent a detachment of his army to keep the French garrison busy while the main part of the army passed the place. By this stage the Montivilliers garrison housed several companies under Sir Louis de Lignières, Pierre Hotot and Colart de Villequier. The latter had twenty-five crossbowmen under his command.[5]

The English army moved on to the plateau to the west of the Lézarde, open country easily trodden. The next location mentioned by the *Gesta* and other English chronicles is Arques, reached on the fourth day of the march, Friday 11 October. The route is less certain. Des Ursins claimed that the king took his route towards Fécamp but passed beyond (*oultre*) the town.[6] Fécamp lay on the coast 29km north of Montivilliers and had already suffered damage from an English seaborne raid on 15 July 1415.[7] Since it was expected that the English would go there after Harfleur, many of the townspeople had left, but there was a French garrison within the abbey precinct under the command of David, Sire de Rambures, the master of the crossbowmen, although he may not have been there at this point. In mid-September a messenger sent from Boulogne found that he was not at Fécamp but Rouen.[8] Local tradition has it that Henry launched a bombardment on Fécamp but there is no indication of this in the sources, although the financial records of the army mention one man-at-arms and two archers as prisoners there.[9] The Burgundian chroniclers do not mention Fécamp but have Henry lodging at Fauville and thereabouts.[10] This lies 20km inland from Fécamp and 33km from Montivilliers. Most likely the main bulk of the army was sent across the easily traversed plateau of the *pays de Caux* via Fauville, an important market centre, with foragers and scouts fanning out towards the coast. The prisoners at Fécamp may have been captured on such a manoeuvre. The route from Fauville cannot be known for certain, although there is a clear cross-country route on today's map passing by Saint-Riquier, Doudeville, Saint-Laurent-en-Caux, Bacqueville-en-Caux, Anneville-sur-Scie and Tourville-sur-Arques, which would have offered easy passage across flat, open country with occasional gentle descents into river valleys. Had the army marched closer to the coast, its passage would have been rendered difficult by steep-sided inlets.

From Harfleur to Arques by the inland route is 88km. This journey took four days, giving an average of 22km per day – a credible pace for an army of this size. Arques lay on the River Béthune which flowed down to Dieppe. The French feared Henry might attack Dieppe and had installed troops there by this time.[11] Arques had a twelfth-century castle on the high ground to the south of the river, which commanded the valley and hence the crossing, but it was small and the town that lay beneath it was not fortified. The *Gesta* tells us that Henry drew up his 'battles and wings' in sight of the castle. Given that the land falls away very steeply to the north and west, it is very likely, and also consistent with a route from Fauville, that Henry approached it from the south. The defenders initially responded by firing their guns. The chronicler's comment that no injury was caused to the English is confirmed by the lack of any reference to losses in the post-campaign accounts. Here, as in similar locations, Henry aimed to avoid unnecessary engagement and delay and had no desire to capture the place. The castle occupied a strong position but was not in fully defensive condition.[12] The town itself was not walled, although the *Gesta* tells us that the inhabitants had blocked off access by means of large trees and other obstacles. Henry was able to negotiate free passage and provision of victuals, in return for his army not burning the town and its vicinity.

It is not surprising that Henry had chosen to make for Arques, since it offered an easy crossing of the Béthune. The route taken between Arques and Eu, his next recorded location, was probably closer to the coast along the route of the D925. The *Gesta* has Henry at Arques on 11 October and Eu on 12 October. Since they are 35km apart, this distance would have been hard to achieve within a day even with ten hours of daylight available for marching. Thus it is more likely that a large detachment was sent against Eu, with the main army moving more slowly to locations further upstream on the Bresle. Eu was walled town with a castle and an abbey containing a major shrine. Its population was *c*.1,000, although it had suffered some decay in the late fourteenth and early fifteenth century.[13] It was situated on a steep hill to the south of the river Bresle, thereby being, as Le Fèvre puts it, 'the last town in Normandy'. Once Henry had passed over the river he would be in the county of Ponthieu, which had belonged to his ancestors as kings of England and which he had included in his territorial claims before the invasion. Titus Livius states that when the English approached the town with their standards, the townsmen rushed out to attack them but were soon driven back, defending themselves with arrows and missiles. The Pseudo-Elmham speaks rather of a cavalry charge by the French. These chronicles and the *Gesta* speak of English casualties, although none are evidenced in the records of the army. The valour of one French soldier – Lancelot Pierre – is specially mentioned in English and French chronicles. He was struck with a lance, which pierced the armour protecting his stomach. Although mortally wounded, he managed to kill his English assailant. The inclusion of such personal deeds of arms is not uncommon in the chivalric tradition of chronicling. The writers also add that Pierre's death was much lamented by the Count of Eu, implying that his prowess was already well known. Indeed Fenin describes him as 'a valiant and much renowned man of war', who hailed from the Bourbonnais.

Henry had anticipated that Eu would be well-defended. While he had no intention of attempting to take it, he could not run the risk of leaving it un-challenged, since the French troops within in it would be in a position to attack his rear as he crossed the Bresle. As at Arques, however, the English were too great in strength overall for any long-term resistance to be offered. Again, therefore, the inhabitants negotiated a deal whereby they saved the vicinity from burning by providing victuals to the English. This was achieved on Sunday 13 October, the day after the engagement outside the town. That the English had taken some prisoners at this stage of the march is implied in the *Gesta*. The author follows his account of events at the town with report of discussions in the English army. The prisoners had divulged that the French were assembling in large number to give battle, perhaps as soon as 'the following Sunday or Monday at our crossing of the Somme'. It may be that the French had placed a larger garrison at Eu to delay Henry's advance. The *Gesta* notes that there were differing opinions within the English army on the likelihood of battle, although we must remember that these comments were made with the advantage of hindsight. Some claimed that because of animosity between the French princes and the Duke of Burgundy, the French would not want to move away from the interior of the country in case the duke took advantage of their absence. Others argued that the French could not bear the stain on their honour if they did not meet the challenge of the English, especially given the success of their enemy to date.

This is a useful moment to review what we know of French movements at this time. On 11 October a messenger from Montreuil brought news to Boulogne that Henry had now left Harfleur and was finally on his march, looking to cross the Somme at Blanchetaque. As a result of this information, constant watch was ordered to be kept on the high ground to the south of Boulogne (Mont Hulin and Mont Pelé) in case the English approached. The clerk of the Mayor was sent to Saint-Omer with an *ouvrier salpetrier* to procure ingredients for gunpowder. There is also evidence of further provision of artillery and the demolition of extra-mural properties in anticipation of a siege. Even while Henry had still been at Harfleur, there had been a fear that he might later threaten Boulogne, whose proximity to the English garrison at Calais made it doubly anxious. David, Sire de Rambures was captain of Boulogne as well as Fécamp. As we have seen, he was in Rouen by mid-September. After the surrender of Harfleur he detailed 500 of his troops as reinforcements for Boulogne under the command of the Sire de Longroy, who also held the captaincy of Ardres, on the edge of the Calais march, and who had served alongside Rambures in actions against the English of Calais in early August. Longroy was at Boulogne on 12 October, when he learned that the Duke of Clarence had come to Calais with a great number of men. He sent on this information to Constable d'Albret, then at Abbeville.[14] This last piece of information reveals that the constable had responded quickly to (or anticipated) Henry's march by moving from Rouen to Abbeville. His intention was to block Henry's attempt to cross the Somme, which was already expected to be at Blanchetaque.

Des Ursins suggests that Boucicaut, Clignet de Brabant and the bastard of Bourbon were ordered to ride out against the English and inflicted great damage upon them.[15] It is possible, although not proven, that Boucicaut's company was operating to the right of the English, aiming to limit English foraging and to delay Henry's advance so that the constable could secure the Somme crossing. If only part of the English force had been sent against Eu, the main army would have passed over the Bresle around Beauchamps. Belleval suggests that Boucicaut's company crossed the river a short distance upstream, at Soreng, and that a skirmish probably occurred near Buigny-les-Gamaches. This may have been with an English force operating on the right flank of the main army, much as Henry had sent a detachment to Eu on the left flank.[16] Such interactions would give the impression of planned tactical acts to delay Henry's approach to the Somme. The Count of Eu was certainly gathering troops in the first weeks of October. On 14 October, a receipt for pay was given by Pierre de Faiencourt for seven men-at-arms and eight mounted archers of the count although the location of their service is not known.[17]

In the meantime Henry's northwards march continued. The *Gesta* tells us that the English advanced near to Abbeville on Sunday 13 October with the intention of crossing the Somme on the next day, only to be told by their scouts that the French had broken all the bridges and causeways and also that 'a great part of the French army was on the opposite bank to obstruct our passage'. The text does not, however, give any precision on the route between the Bresle and the Somme or on where Henry intended to cross the river. On the first matter, few chronicles say anything at all. Basset says that Henry passed close to Saint-Valery, implying that he took the route along the then coast, along which the D940 now runs, but the Burgundian chroniclers claim that he went from Eu through Vimeu, suggestive of an inland route. There is no doubt, however, that his objective was Blanchetaque. This was a well-established crossing point, so called because those using it were guided by sight of an area of chalk on the higher ground to the north of the river. It lay between Noyelles to the west and Gouy and Port le Grand to the east, through an area that was tidal. According to Froissart, it was possible at low tide for men to cross twelve abreast in water that reached no higher than their knees.[18] This was, of course, the place where Edward III had crossed the Somme in 1346 before battle was given at Crécy, 18km to the north-north-east. This link to past glories is noted only by the Burgundian chroniclers, although Titus Livius, the Pseudo-Elmham and Basset name Blanchetaque as the intended crossing point. The omission of any mention of Blanchetaque in the *Gesta* is perplexing, but explained by the fact that if the ford had been Henry's initial intention, he soon changed his mind and drew his army to the south and east of Abbeville in order to seek an alternative crossing.

Waurin and Le Fèvre say that Henry came within two miles of the ford at Blanchetaque, with his vanguard 'spread out across the land'. This suggests that he was deploying part of his army in reconnaissance before deciding on his next move. These chroniclers tell us an extremely interesting story about the capture of a Gascon gentleman in the service of Charles d'Albret. When interrogated by the commander of the van (whose name, alas, is not given), the prisoner said that he had sallied out of Abbeville where his master the constable was based. He also disclosed 'after several interrogations' that the ford at Blanchetaque was well guarded by 6,000 men under the command of several great lords. Waurin names two of the commanders as Guichard Dauphin and Marshal Boucicaut. The Gascon was brought before Henry, where he repeated his story. As a result, all of the English companies were halted. The king held a council which, after two hours' deliberation, decided that another crossing should be chosen. The king therefore decided to move upstream to find another crossing point.

Providing a good example of the culture of blame that surrounded the battle in subsequent decades, Waurin and Le Fèvre curse the Gascon. Had Henry crossed at Blanchetaque, there would have been 'no sad and sorrowful day for the French at the battle of Agincourt', adding that many Frenchmen consider him 'a devil and not a man'. The chroniclers' comment is not based on the view that had Henry attempted a crossing, the French would have engaged and defeated him at that point. Rather, their argument is that the Gascon was lying. There was no large French force at Blanchetaque. So Henry would have crossed unchallenged and gone straight on to Calais. In this scenario, therefore, he would not have been intercepted at Agincourt and there would have been no disastrous battle for the French. Yet all of the evidence suggests that Henry believed from his military intelligence that the French *were* already in strength at Blanchetaque. As a result, he did not lead his army to the ford. This suggests considerable caution and anxiety on his part, an example of his periodic uncertainty and panic. He did not want to have an engagement with the French at this point. He knew that his army would place itself in a vulnerable position were it to be attacked while crossing. His scouts would have told him that the causeways were narrow and could only be crossed a few abreast. This would limit the use of mass arrow fire or make difficult the establishment of a defensive position. Transporting carts and horses across would also be time-consuming and increase the English vulnerability. Henry deemed that he could not take the risk. It was coming home to him that he had delayed his departure from Harfleur for too long. Although the two weeks after the surrender allowed him to reorganise his army and to see to the defences of his conquered town, it also allowed the French time to gather and to respond appropriately as soon as they knew he had begun to march northwards.

The records of the *chambre des comptes* reveal many companies in existence before the king and Dauphin arrived on 12 October, with a notable expansion in numbers between the surrender of Harfleur and the beginning of Henry's march. Their function was commonly stated to be 'for service against the English in the *pays de Caux*', and they were largely under the command of d'Albret, Alençon, Boucicaut, Marle,Vendôme, Rambures and Guichard Dauphin, Sire de Jaligny and grand master of the royal household. Some companies are also described as being in the command of Berry, although he did not arrive in person at Rouen until 12 October. These were, therefore, the troops and commanders who were operating against Henry and who blocked his passage at Blanchetaque, subsequently following his progress by moving along the north bank of the Somme. This ties in with chronicle evidence. Monstrelet places at Abbeville the constable, Alençon, Vendôme and Guichard Dauphin, Sire de Jaligny. He also adds in Richemont, Boucicaut and the admiral, the Sire de Dampierre. Des Ursins had Clignet de Brabant and the bastard of Bourbon with Boucicaut during Henry's march across the *pays de Caux*, thus making it possible that they too were at Abbeville with the marshal. Perceval de Cagny, chronicler of the Dukes of Alençon, credits his master alone with the foresight, while at Rouen, of 'knowing what had to be done', and 'by his diligence' managing to reach the town of Abbeville before the king of England could effect his crossing, thereby cutting off his route so that he had to go further upstream to find another.[19] The chronicler also has it that the duke had previously 'been with the king at Rouen'. Since the king did not arrive in Rouen until 12 October, this cannot be true. There are so many references in the records for the French army to Alençon's command of troops that it is certain he had already gone north of the Somme. Indeed, he appears to have been in charge of the attempts to intercept Henry at this stage.

The army records suggest that in the weeks before 8 October when the French were unsure of the direction in which Henry would move, Alençon was operating in Lower Normandy and d'Albret was sent northwards, thereby covering both possibilities. Joint operations between the constable and the Seneschal of Hainault (already at Amiens in August) are evidenced. Furthermore, the records of the Somme towns show that d'Albret drew on urban militias from Abbeville, Montreuil and Amiens in order to assist with the blocking of the crossing at Blanchetaque. Indeed, they were probably the people who staked the ford to facilitate its defence. For Amiens we have details of a meeting held in the town on 13 October, at which the inhabitants were told what provisions for the defence of the Somme d'Albret had already made. At first they were reluctant to send him reinforcements, since they feared that might leave their own town vulnerable, but they finally agreed to send a number of crossbowmen and *pavisiers*, as well as other materials which were transported by river to Abbeville. Large amounts of artillery were also moved to Abbeville.[20]

There is enough evidence to suggest, therefore, that the French had made considerable effort to move troops to Abbeville/Blanchetaque in anticipation of Henry's advance. This raises the question of what their intentions were. Remember too that immediately after the engagement at Eu, the *Gesta* tells of information gleaned from prisoners that French were assembling in large number to give battle, perhaps as soon as 'the following Sunday or Monday at our crossing of the Somme', in other words, on Sunday 13 or Monday 14 October. Although we know that Henry did not attempt a crossing, the French were not to know that he would make that choice. The French strategy was not to block his crossing and force him eastwards but rather to engage him at the Somme. The plan may have been to make his crossing of the river at Blanchetaque as difficult and time-consuming as possible, so that his troops would be in disarray when they reached the other side. What better place for the French to give battle than in Ponthieu, one of the hereditary possessions of the English and, even better, in a location close enough to Crécy to expunge the memory of that defeat?

A French battle plan for the 'Agincourt campaign' survives in the British Library.[21] (I shall call this henceforward the BL plan.) Phillpotts argued that it was drawn up sometime between 13 and 21 October. Given what we know of French troop movements, it is most likely that it reflects intended deployment for an engagement at or near Blanchetaque. The plan begins as follows: 'This is how it seems to the lord marshal and to the lords who are with him, by the command of the Duke of Alençon and of Richemont and the lord constable, subject to the correction of these lords, for the matter of the battle'. The battle plan also mentions the grand master of the royal household, Guichard Dauphin, and the Count of Vendôme. As we have seen, most of these men can be shown to have troops under their command by 8 October.

The role of Boucicaut remains shadowy, since no materials survive in the army records. But what of Richemont, for whom there is also no evidence of companies? He had been appointed by the Dauphin as his lieutenant on 10 April, having on the previous day received the captaincy of the Bastille in Paris.[22] He was still in Paris at the end of May, but departed in late June to besiege the town of Parthenay (Deux-Sèvres). This place was held by a Burgundian supporter, Jean II Larchevêque, whose lands had been declared confiscate on 6 May 1415. The king had granted them to the Dauphin on 14 May, and the latter granted them to Richemont on 23 May.[23] For the count, therefore, the siege of Parthenay was an operation to gain possession of what he now saw as his. When he received news from the king and Dauphin of events in Normandy, he abandoned the siege and led his troops northwards.[24] The Dauphin created him his lieutenant for the campaign, putting the men of his household at his disposal. Gruel has him moving to the Somme to join with the other lords who were gathering to fight the English. There is no evidence that Richemont ever joined the king and Dauphin at Rouen. It is more likely that he met with the Dauphin at Vernon earlier in October and then moved northwards with the Dauphin's troops, joining d'Albret, Alençon and the others at Abbeville. This is given extra credence by the presence of Jaligny, who was also a member of the Dauphin's household. Indeed, he had been governor of the Dauphinée for Louis and the latter's envoy to the Duke of Burgundy in late July of 1415. That he was an experienced and trusted military commander, like Richemont, is also shown by the fact that he commanded the vanguard at the siege of Bourges in 1412.

The chronicler Gruel also claims that Richemont had a good 500 knights and esquires from Brittany under his command. He gives eight of these by name, two of whom are also mentioned in the battle plan within the right wing of foot under the command of Richemont. These are the Sire de Combourg and Sire Bertrand de Montauban. The latter had been chamberlain of the Dukes of Brittany and Burgundy and more recently of the Dauphin. On 13 May 1413 he had been appointed as lieutenant of the Louvre. His connections with Richemont therefore came through the Dauphin's household. Combourg had served under the Count of Armagnac at the recovery of Saint-Cloud in October 1411. On 24 September 1415 he acknowledged receipt of pay for himself, seven knights bachelor, ten esquires and sixteen archers serving in Normandy.[25] Both Combourg and Montauban were killed at Agincourt, where Richemont was captured.

The movements of the two other lords mentioned by name in the battle plan, the Count of Eu and the Sire de Bosredon, are not certain. Louis de Bosredon was closely associated with the Duke of Berry, serving as captain of the latter's castle of Dourdan in 1411 in the king's war against the Armagnacs. In the summer of 1413 he and Clignet de Brabant had led forces to put down the Cabochiens.[26] By this time he was chamberlain of the Duke of Orléans. On 30 September the duke ordered his treasurer to pay Bosredon 400 *livres tournois* for the wages of troops he and Bouchard de Morny had procured for service against the English.[27] This makes it possible, therefore, that he had already come with some of the duke's troops to join the army. On 12 September, another of the duke's men, Aubert Fouquant, had been paid 200 *livres tournois* for the wages of troops raised against the English.[28] Charles d'Artois, Count of Eu, was the grandson of the Duke of Berry and hence a committed Armagnac, who had served in the king's army at the siege of Arras in the summer of 1414. Although only nineteen in 1415, Eu had shown evidence of prowess. At the siege of Arras in August 1414 he had participated in a feat of arms against Jean de Neufchâtel, Sire de Montaigu, the chamberlain of John the Fearless. His whereabouts in September 1415 are not known. Companies under his command appear by 14 October.[29] The French battle plan also mentions 'the master of the crossbowmen'. This was David de Rambures, who, as we have seen, was in Rouen by mid-September 1415 and had various companies of crossbowmen under his charge. He had been a member of the royal household since 1388 and from 1410 had been chamberlain of the Dauphin, although in 1413 he was suspected of pro-Burgundian leanings and had been briefly dismissed. He had already seen service under Boucicaut in Genoa in 1409.[30] His presence in the battle plan is all the more significant given that his seat of Rambures lay just north of the river Bresle in Vimeu, the territory that Henry would be passing through as he advanced towards Blanchetaque.

In general all of the commanders mentioned in the BL plan were mature and had much experience in military matters. It is not surprising, therefore, to see them entrusted with important roles in a prospective battle. Similarly, they are the kinds of commanders we would expect to find rallying promptly to the French cause. The BL plan envisaged two main battles. The first (the van) would be made up of the men of the constable on the right and the marshal on the left. The second battle would contain the Duke of Alençon, the Count of Eu and other lords. Richemont would command the wing of foot on the right (with Combourg and Montauban serving with him), and Vendôme and Guichart Dauphin that on the left. The archers were to be placed in front of each wing. A company of heavy horse to attack the archers would be under the command of Rambures. A further company of 200 men-at-arms and further horsemen under Bosredon would attack the English baggage. All would start to move once Rambures's company had set out to override the archers. If the English fought with only one battle, then the French battles also would combine. Archers and axe men were to be drawn from all retinues and placed together. None of the horsemen were professional cavalry but the *valets* of the company mounted on the best horses of their masters.

With only two battles and with ingenious ways of creating different kinds of attack, the BL plan reads as though the French were keen to maximise their forces, implying that they did not have many men at their disposal. But can we have a better idea of how many troops the French had raised by the time Henry approached Blanchetaque? The Gascon prisoner mentioned by Waurin and Le Fèvre claimed that there were about 6,000 warriors, although the chroniclers then say that his words were not true, since the French did not assemble until eight days later. Gruel notes that Richemont had 500 knights and esquires, a credible figure given that des Ursins suggests all lords were asked to provide this number by the king. We have evidence in documents pre-dating 8 October of intended contingents for some of the other lords: for Berry 1,000 men-at-arms and 500 archers, Vendôme 300 + 150, the Seneschal of Hainault 120 + 60.[31] The latter was based at Amiens in August. We have evidence in the pay records of around 200 companies by 8 October, although some lay within these lordly contingents. It is impossible to know for certain how many troops the French already had north of the Somme, but it was much more than an advance guard. It may indeed have already numbered 6,000.

We cannot prove that the battle plan was drawn up for a possible engagement with Henry at Blanchetaque. As we shall see later in this chapter, there is another significant point south of Péronne where battle might have been intended. But there is no doubt that the French had raised a sizeable army in the weeks following the surrender of Harfleur. While they had not been in a position to save the town, they were now capable of hounding Henry. They could not be sure that

Henry would shy away from crossing at Blanchetaque, therefore they had to be ready to engage him there. It is also possible, however, that the Gascon prisoner had been used as a means of subterfuge. The French may have considered themselves not to be strong enough in numbers to face Henry at this point, because they had not delayed him long enough to gather all their forces in the area. They therefore had already decided to drive him further inland to allow more time for troops to join them, perhaps to give battle south of Péronne. What better than to make Henry believe that they were already in enough strength, thereby scaring him into a march away from the coast which was most certainly not in his interests? Henry may also have reckoned that if the French *were* at the ford, then they could not also be in large numbers at crossings of the river to the east of Abbeville, thus making his passage possible in that location. There again, they could not be sure the subterfuge would work. Henry's scouts clearly saw some French troops guarding the ford. In the *Gesta*, it was this intelligence, rather than the confessions of a prisoner, which persuaded him to change direction.

The exact route Henry took to the south of Abbeville is not certain. The *Gesta* tells us only that he came close to the town on 13 October. The simple explanation would be that he approached from the south through Cambron and then kept to the high ground above the Somme, descending into the river valley towards Mareuil-Caubert, a place at which Waurin has him lodging. But there is another possibility. Intelligence about French defences at Blanchetaque could have reached Henry while he was still on the Bresle near Eu. In this scenario, he crossed the river between Incheville and Beauchamps and then headed away from the coast and to the east of Abbeville.[32] Monstrelet has him, once he hears of the French presence at Blanchetaque, altering his route by moving towards Airaines, 'burning and destroying the whole country, taking prisoners and acquiring great booty'. The significance of this comment is twofold. First it emphasises Henry's annoyance at not being able to achieve his initial plan of crossing the Somme. If it is true that he had ordered his army to carry victuals for only eight days, anticipating that it would take that length of time to reach Calais, then he would have realised as he changed direction on 13 October that these supplies would not be enough. Hence the raiding of the countryside through which he passed. The *Gesta* also comments, in a passage immediately following the failure to find a crossing on 14 October, that the English were running low on supplies. In the *pays de Caux* it had been possible to negotiate the provision of supplies from the towns. Henry does not seem to have tried this again until his arrival at Boves to the east of Amiens. Furthermore, as the *Gesta* notes, the enemy had been laying waste the countryside. According to de Cagny, this was effected by the passage of the constable as well as the Dukes of Bourbon and Bar and their troops as they moved from Rouen to Amiens, Corbie, Péronne and St-Quentin, at the orders of the Duke of Alençon.[33] Certainly the lack of food on the march was a feature reported back by soldiers after the campaign, furnishing Walsingham's comment that there was so little bread, men were forced to eat hazelnuts and dried meat instead, and to drink water for almost eighteen days (in place, no doubt, of beer and wine!)[34]

The second significance of Monstrelet's comment is that it suggests Henry took a route that skirted well south of Abbeville, keeping away from any possible French army based at or near the town. This path would fit with the comment of the *Chronique de Ruisseauville* that Henry had wanted to return to Calais 'by the frontier', but that since his passage was blocked he had to return 'through the vicinities of Amiens and Beauvais'. Airaines is on the road to Beauvais. The Religieux of Saint-Denis also suggest that since Henry could not cross the Somme where he wished, he had to retrace his steps:

> making a virtue out of a necessity the English advanced into the interior of the kingdom. Making their way through the dense woodlands of Gournay situated in the region of Beauvais, 22 leagues inland from the sea, they met with no obstruction and carried out actions as one might expect of an enemy. After about four days, although this is by no means exact, they turned towards the city of Amiens.

Timings make it unlikely that Henry could have journeyed very far inland to the south of Abbeville, but it is credible that victualling raids by his men were made into the hinterland as his army advanced eastwards. Most likely Henry kept the bulk of his army on the higher ground, well to the south of Abbeville. This was not only because of the marshy nature of the Somme valley but also military intelligence on the large French presence in Abbeville. In this scenario, Henry would have passed through the middle of Vimeu in the direction of Abbeville but then cut across country towards Airaines, in order to gain access to the Somme to the east of the town. Basset mentions that once Blanchetaque was impracticable, the English made for Pont-Sainte-Maxence. This is an error, since this town is on the Oise between Pontoise and Compiègne, but the chronicler may have meant Saint-Maxent, which lies midway between the Bresle valley and Airaines.

The *Gesta* suggests that Henry made reconnaissance of an unnamed crossing of the Somme on 14 October, but that his men found that the causeways were broken and the French were on the opposite bank. This location was likely Pont-Rémy, 8km upstream from Abbeville, since other chronicles suggest that the English had hopes of crossing here. Fenin has Henry choose Pont-Rémy in preference to Blanchetaque. Monstrelet has Henry lodging his army at Bailleul in Vimeu, 8km to the south-south-east of Abbeville, which is on a direct route northwards from Saint-Maxent. Waurin has him rather closer to Abbeville, at 'Mareuil, Pont-Rémy and other villages thereabouts', in order 'to obtain a crossing at a narrow part'. All three Burgundian writers suggest that Henry sent a detachment to gain control of the crossing at Pont-Rémy, although this is not mentioned in *Le Fèvre*, who was allegedly with the English army at this point. It

is possible that Basset's Pont-Sainte-Maxence is an error not for Saint-Maxent but
for Pont-Rémy, or else that the chronicler has conflated the two places into one.
He tells us that the enemy were in large numbers at this place, guarding the crossing, and that, as Henry thought he might have to give battle, he created several
knights, whom Basset names.[35] That some engagement at Pont-Rémy took place
is found in Monstrelet and Waurin. They claim that the English were repulsed by
the Sire de Wancourt, who was lord of the place, and his two sons, thanks to their
personal bravery and their effective and well-equipped troops. This fits with the
Gesta's comments that the English saw French troops on the opposite bank 'in
line of battle as if prepared to engage us there and then', although the chronicler
adds that the marshland made it impossible for either side to come close enough
for a fight. By 20 October, the Sire de Wancourt had joined the army under
Constable d'Albret with a knight and twelve esquires, and was serving under the
banner of the Seneschal of Hainault. He was captured at Agincourt.[36]

The route of Henry's army after this interaction is unclear. Chroniclers associated with the English army name no places until the army came close to Amiens.
Fenin has Henry moving towards Airaines after the failure to cross at Pont-Rémy.
Monstrelet moves the English eastwards along the river at Hangest-sur-Somme,
Waurin at Crouy, 'Neige' (unidentified but possibly La Mesge, south of Hangest)
and other villages near to Picquigny, although no attempt seems to have been
made to effect a crossing at any of these places. It is possible that not all of the
army had descended to the Somme valley but that the main part had remained
on the uplands at Airaines while reconnaissance was carried out for a crossing.
This would also explain the messages received at Boulogne on 17 October, from
both Montreuil and Abbeville, that the English army had 'gone up onto the hill
along the River Somme'.

The French had scored a considerable coup in preventing the easy passage
to Calais that Henry had anticipated when he left Harfleur. His gamble that a
crossing to the east of Abbeville might be possible was also misjudged. He presumably did not know that the north bank of the Somme above Pont-Rémy
rises very sharply and that, again, there was too much marshland to negotiate.
Therefore he was forced against his will to move further and further inland away
from his intended route, with all the problems that generated in terms of food
supplies and exhaustion. Once the French at Abbeville knew of Henry's eastward
route, they shadowed him by moving along the north bank of the Somme, first
at Pont-Rémy and then along the stretch towards Picquigny. A continued move
eastwards would bring Henry close to Amiens, a well-fortified city (although he
was presumably unaware that its militia had been detailed to Abbeville). As he
did not wish to engage and he could not be sure how many troops the French
could muster, he had to avoid coming too close to that city. The Gesta claims that
Amiens was passed on 15 October, at about a league to the left. Waurin says that
the English arranged themselves in battle in a plain before the city. This is not

found in any other source, but it is possible that Henry anticipated an attack from
the French. Constable d'Albret was certainly in Amiens by 16–17 October at the
latest, as were other important officials, as is evidenced by the gifts of wine that
the town made to them.[37]

Henry's exact route south of Amiens is not known, but it may have passed
through Pont-de-Metz, which lies to the south.[38] That the next English port-
of-call was Boves on the river Avre, 5km to the south-east of Amiens, suggests that
Henry did skirt quite far south of the city. The English presence at Boves, which
the *Gesta* dates to 16–17 October, excited a good deal of interest by chroniclers.
This may have been because the town on the river and the castle that overlooks
it belonged to the Count of Vaudémont, a supporter of the Duke of Burgundy.[39]
Its reaction to the English was therefore a test of allegiance. The count himself
was absent and serving with Boucicaut to the north of the river.[40] At Arques the
defenders had made some show of resistance by firing their guns. At Eu there
had been a sortie. At Boves only negotiations are recorded, although these aimed
at the same objective as at the earlier mentioned places, namely that the town
and its neighbourhood would be spared from burning in return for foodstuffs.
The Burgundian chroniclers claim that the English were very short of bread at
this point, so that Boves was required to provide in composition eight baskets of
bread, each to be carried by two men, suggesting that they were sizeable. This
was a useful point of refreshment, to which the local wine supplies noted in the
Gesta and the Burgundian chroniclers added a further benefit. Waurin also adds
the name of the captain of the fortress on the hill above the town, Sir Jean de
Matringueham, and says that he acquitted himself so well towards the English
that it stood him in good stead later.[41] This may have been related to their further
story that Henry delivered two very sick men from his army to the captain. They
each gave two horses for their ransom so the idea was that they should recuperate
and then leave freely.

The English crossed the Avre at Boves. Monstrelet suggests that the army kept
on the plateau around 6km south of the Somme, marching through Bayonvillers,
Harbonnières and Vauvillers. Waurin and Le Fèvre send them along a route slightly further south, with Waurin adding that Henry quartered at night in the large
village of Caix, which lies 4km to the south of Harbonnières. These places are
all close to each other. It is therefore entirely possible, given the size of the army,
that it bivouacked in all of these places before moving on towards Nesle in the
Vermandois. The *Gesta* recounts an engagement with the French near Corbie on
Thursday 17 October. Corbie lies on the north bank of the river and was well
fortified and garrisoned under the captaincy of Pierre de Lameth and Gauthier de
Caulincourt.[42] This engagement is recorded only in English chronicles, suggesting
that it was regarded as a moment of success worthy of record. A large-scale sortie
was launched from the town with, as Titus Livius puts it, 'a huge shout and an
impetuous rush as is the custom of the French'. The French were, however, driven

back by the English and at least two were taken prisoner. Capgrave has it that the enemy were put to flight during the sortie 'by the actions of the archers'.[43]

In the sixteenth century a story developed that 'in the fight against the French near to Corbie' Sir Hugh Stafford (known by the courtesy title of Lord Bourchier through his marriage to Elizabeth, heiress of John, Lord Bourchier) had been entrusted with the keeping of the standard of Guienne, but it was lost to the French and only recovered by the bravery of one of his men-at-arms, John Bromley. This was based on a supposed grant made by Stafford on 10 March 1417 of an annuity of £40 per annum to Bromley, the text of which was recorded in a heraldic visitation.[44] There is a problem with this, however, since the pay records of the campaign note that Sir Hugh Stafford and the whole of his retinue were placed in the garrison of Harfleur after the surrender. A list of his men survives, and there is no John Bromley to be found among them.[45] As the grant is only known through a sixteenth-century source, it seems that it was invented in order to enhance the pedigree of Bromley's descendents.

It was after this engagement that, according to the *Gesta*, a soldier was brought to Henry accused of stealing a pyx from a church. He was hanged in the next hamlet, 'where we spent the night'. This incident is found only in English texts. The Pseudo-Elmham includes a lengthy account of both the military engagement and the incident concerning the pyx, claiming that the miscreant was hanged on a tree near the very church that he had robbed. We shall consider the significance of this incident in the review of the march as a whole at the end of the next chapter.

No chronicler suggests that Henry was attempting to secure a crossing point at Corbie. The accounts of the incident suggest that it was the French who launched the attack. Since they were deploying cavalry, it is possible that the attack occurred not in the river valley near Corbie but near Villers-Bretonneux, on the higher ground above the Somme across which Henry was leading his army. The experience may have contributed to the order to prepare stakes which the *Gesta* places immediately after the account of the engagement. The author has it that information from French prisoners (presumably those captured in the engagement at Corbie although this is not made explicit) led to a rumour in the English army that 'the enemy command had assigned certain squadrons of cavalry many hundreds strong and mounted on barded horses, to break the formation and resistance of our archers when they engaged us in battle'. The king therefore ordered each of his archers to prepare a stake around six feet long, sharpened at both ends, so that these could be placed in front of them for protection against cavalry charge. Other chronicles imply that the order to prepare stakes occurred later. Waurin and Le Fèvre, for instance, place it after the French heralds issue a summons to Henry on 20 October.

If the *Gesta* is correct in its timing, then it suggests that while *en route* to Nesle, Henry thought that the French would give battle soon. Furthermore, the rumour about the intention to override the English archers is reminiscent of the BL plan, which has already been discussed. This is a useful moment, therefore, to consider French movements and possible plans in this stage of the march as Henry moved east of Amiens. Where did the French intend to give the battle that the prisoners had divulged? The army that had gathered at Abbeville had moved to the north of the Somme, paralleling Henry's eastwards move. The constable had reached Amiens by 16 October. The accepted view has been that a large French army came north from Rouen in the days following the king's arrival there on 12 October, reconnoitring at Amiens around 17–18 October. Bennett suggests that it cannot have left Rouen before 14–15 October, since otherwise 'it would have bumped into the English moving south at Amiens'.[46]

It is impossible, however, to detect the existence of this large French army. The Religieux tells us that Charles had arrived at Rouen 'towards the beginning of October' (a rather inexact expression), with more than 14,000 men 'commanded by the most illustrious leaders whose names deserve mention here, for they were mainly of royal blood and exceeded all others in authority'. He goes on to name the Dauphin, the Dukes of Berry, Orléans, Bourbon, Alençon, Bar and Brabant, the Counts of Nevers, Richemont and Vendôme and fifteen more besides. The chronicler does not, however, tell us how this putative army moved from Rouen to Agincourt. As we have seen, there is evidence that Alençon, Richemont and Vendôme were already north of the Somme. Orléans can be proven to have still been at Cléry close to Orléans on 17 October.[47] Brabant, Bar and Nevers never went to Rouen at all. Indeed, the most likely scenario is that the French army at Agincourt was made up of the army under Alençon and d'Albret which arrived at Abbeville in advance of Henry, plus the lords of the areas to the east and north of the Somme who came directly to the area in which the battle was appointed to be fought. The records of the army show that twenty-eight companies were paid on 12 October, the day the king and Dauphin arrived at Rouen, but for most this was simply pay for a further period of service under Alençon. From this date, however, the troops are described as being in the company of the duke and 'under the government of the Dauphin', the first time that the king's son is mentioned in the pay records as the overall commander. It is possible that some additional troops from Rouen joined the 'Somme army' at Corbie or at Péronne, such as those under Bourbon. The duke was at Rouen by 17 October and Péronne by 19 October and his companies first appear in pay from 17 October.

According to the Gesta, there had been rumours as early as 13 October, when the English were south of Abbeville, that a great French army was assembling at the head of the river sixty miles away, 'making ready to do battle with us with every sort of practice and stratagem of war and with engines and other subtle contrivances', and 'that they would not allow us to cross the river before them anywhere in between'. The distance would suggest the vicinity of Péronne which lies 100km (62.5 miles) from Blanchetaque. The French intention may therefore have been to continue to force Henry eastward to the bend of the Somme, south of Péronne, where there was flat open land which would offer a good battlefield. The BL plan may therefore have been drawn up for this occasion, and that is why it only includes those commanders known to have been operating already north of the Somme. It does not include Orléans, Bourbon, Brabant or any of the Picard lords who came in the days after Henry crossed the Somme on 19 October. A French intention to give battle south of Péronne also makes sense of the sortie from Corbie. This was not an unplanned excursion but rather a means of keeping him away from any possible crossing point in the stretch west of Péronne. To this end, troops had been gathered in Corbie. Evidence from the archives of Amiens shows that reinforcements had been sent there from the city,[48] and the chronicles of the Berry Herald, de Cagny, Waurin and Le Fèvre note that the constable, d'Albret, and other commanders passed through Corbie with their troops. It is an intriguing thought that the French commanders were at Corbie at the time of the sortie. They were likely at Péronne by 19 October, making a presence at Corbie around 17 October a real possibility. Furthermore, the Religieux speaks of successful sorties being made by Clignet de Brabant, Boucicaut and other captains against English foragers and other groups, even claiming that 'their prowess and memorable exploits would have won them eternal glory if they had been written down'. The Tournai chronicle also speaks of the French gathering troops in the area between Eclusier and Nesle to prevent Henry crossing, although it claims that the commanders were the Duke of Bourbon and Constable d'Albret.[49]

The sortie from Corbie also had the added advantage of testing Henry's response at this stage but it may have worked to his benefit. If the chronology of the *Gesta* is accurate, it gave him forewarning of the French intention to use cavalry against his archers. This does not mean that the BL plan itself fell into his possession. Its fate before it entered the collection of Sir Robert Cotton in the early seventeenth century is not known. There is certainly no proof that Henry captured it before the battle. Since Boucicaut was captured at Agincourt, it is possible that it was taken along with his effects at that point. But it is equally plausible that it came to England well after the event.

However, if Henry had gathered intelligence, as a result of the Corbie sortie or by any other means, that the French were gathering at Péronne, then it would explain his subsequent move southwards towards Nesle in the hope of avoiding their trap. The question that remains is how far east he thought he might have to travel in search of a crossing of the river. It was reported at Mons on 18 March that both English and French troops were moving towards Saint-Quentin.[50] The *Gesta* claims that their success in crossing where they did was considered to have shortened the march by eight days, which implies that a journey of perhaps four days further upriver – another sixty miles or so – was anticipated. Henry's decision to effect a crossing in the stretch of river between Péronne and Ham could be taken to imply that he was not aware of the French assembly at Péronne, since the northwards route to which he was then committed perforce had to pass close to that town. We could, of course, interpret Henry's decision to move eastwards as a desire, even from the outset, to seek out the French and give battle. In this scenario, Henry had deliberately chosen not to attempt to cross the Somme and to engage the French close to Abbeville because he wanted to meet the whole French army later. The *Gesta* does not support this interpretation, since the author tells us the English were dejected by the rumours of battle and that they were concerned that they would be easily overwhelmed at the head of the river, given their shortage of food. Of course, this chronicler, as all others, is writing with hindsight. No author could criticise Henry's march in the light of his later victory. But it is hard to believe that it was not a worrying time for the English army, especially as the outcome of the march was so unclear. If the army believed it was making for Calais, then it must have been disconcerting to be moving so obviously in the wrong direction.

If the stakes were prepared on or around 17 October, then Henry was expecting the French to launch an attack sooner rather than later. His moves from this point onwards are thus of considerable interest. According to the *Gesta* and the Burgundian chroniclers he next moved towards Nesle, where the townspeople were invited on 18 October to make the usual arrangements for avoiding their neighbourhood being put to the torch. But on this occasion, the inhabitants refused, hanging red banners on their walls as a symbol of their resistance. The king therefore ordered that the burning should be carried out on the next day. The *Liber Metricus* claims that Henry, 'out of anger', did set fire to the villages around Nesle that had refused his terms, but the *Gesta* never tells us whether the king carried out his threat, since the author moves on to tell us that news was brought that a possible crossing of the Somme had been located. Wylie suggests that the inhabitants had deliberately fed this information to the English 'in the hope of getting rid of the plunderers'.[51] Whatever the case, Henry now had the possibility of ending his luckless march along the south of the river. By the time he reached the crossing, he had already led his army on a march of around 270km, at a fairly constant pace of 25km a day. What has been overlooked by historians, however, is that the French had also moved their forces over considerable distances and at a similar pace. These were impressive troop movements on both sides.

7

From the Crossing of the Somme to the Eve of Battle, 19–24 October 1415

Both English and French chroniclers assign considerable importance to Henry's achievement in finding a crossing of the Somme. The *Gesta* records that on that night, Saturday 19 October, the English army were full of cheer at shortening their journey and at their hopes that the enemy 'would be disinclined to follow after us to do battle'. Exactly where the author meant by the 'head of the river' is uncertain, but it is clear that he was wrong both about the location of the French army and about its intentions. On the following day, French heralds brought him notification 'that they would do battle with him before he reached Calais'. Four days later, Henry found the French waiting for him at Agincourt. He therefore established his camp at Maisoncelle and prepared to give battle on the following morning. The six days between 19 and 24 October offer much of interest concerning Henry's movements and the plans of the French. The chapter will end by considering Henry's march from Harfleur to Maisoncelle as a whole.

Given the importance that chroniclers give to the crossing of the Somme, it is surprising that very few name the location, including the *Gesta*.[1] The usually accepted place is that named by Monstrelet as lying between Béthencourt and Voyennes. The argument is that the geographical features described by the eye-witness accounts, especially the *Gesta*, tally well with the landscape in this stretch of the Somme. The problem is that the Somme valley has changed considerably over the centuries, not least since the extensive gravel and peat extraction over many centuries and the construction of a major canal in the early nineteenth century. The descriptions would fit many locations. Three other chroniclers also place the crossing in roughly the same area. For de Cagny, it was effected between Péronne and Saint-Quentin. In the *Chronique de Ruisseauville*, it was at Doingt, which lies close to Péronne but is not actually on the Somme. In the *Chronique de Normandie*, Henry's crossing was made beyond Péronne, at night.

The significance of Henry's crossing is confirmed by the desire of chroniclers to ascribe blame. Burgundian writers blame the men of Saint-Quentin, whose responsibility it had been to stake and defend the ford. De Cagny claims that the Duke of Alençon had placed Saint-Quentin under the command of the *bailli* of the Vermandois and other royal officers of the area, with the plan that all of the crossings should be broken. It is implied that Alençon had given this order while these officials were with him at Péronne, suggesting, perhaps, that the English succeeded in crossing before they were able to return to execute their instructions. (Alençon's role fits with his command of the army sent north of the Somme, as elucidated in the previous chapter.) The *Chronique de Ruisseauville* displays pro-Burgundian sentiments, first by suggesting that it was the fault of Constable d'Albret, who himself 'stayed in the towns' and had given an order that no one should fight, and secondly by claiming that the Count of Nevers appeared with a very fine company of men in order to give battle but that the English made off. Nevers was the youngest brother of the Duke of Burgundy. Since the Berry Herald speaks of him 'recently arriving at Corbie', it is possible that as he moved there his company met with some English scouts after they had crossed the river. Waurin and Le Fèvre mention that the French, under d'Albret, had gone to Corbie and Péronne in an effort to guard all the crossings of the river. It was probably military intelligence that the French were gathering at Péronne that had led Henry to 'cut the corner' of the Somme where it passes through that town, by advancing towards Nesle and thence to the stretch of the river towards Ham. He may also have reckoned that the river would be more easily passable the further upstream he was able to go.

There are two chronicles, however, which give a very different location for the crossing, placing it on the stretch of river to the west of Péronne rather than to the south-east. These are the Berry Herald, who puts it between Corbie and Péronne, and Fenin, who defines this more closely as Eclusier (now Eclusier-Vaux). The first-named author adds that the English ability to cross was the fault of Frenchmen who had expected that the English would cross further upstream. These men had been lodged at the crossing but had left, and as they passed through other villages, they said that the English had already gone by, so causing those in the vicinity to evacuate their posts. His account continues with the English discovering the crossing place by accident. A party had come down to the river in search of food. From the top of a windmill they saw that the place was undefended, and on reaching it, found that it was full of meat, bread and wine which the French had left in their rush to depart. All of this was reported back to the king, and a crossing was effected.

A crossing to the west of Péronne might be easily dismissed were it not for several features. Fenin and the Berry Herald are independent commentators and generally offer a reliable account of events in 1415. In terms of landscape, Eclusier would fit the bill very well, although there is a very steep hill leading north out of the valley which might have proved a hard climb for a heavily equipped army. The city of Amiens had sent troops to defend the crossing at Eclusier.[2] Furthermore, a crossing to the west of Péronne would explain how Henry was able to bypass the main French army which was gathering in that town. Certainly the route that Fenin mentions after Eclusier makes sense as a route that eventually ended up at Agincourt. He has Henry moving from Eclusier to Miraumont, then to Foreceville, Acheux, Bonnières, Frévent and Blangy-sur-Ternoise. The account given by the Berry Herald is less detailed but mentions Henry moving off towards Beauquesne, so that he could reach Calais as soon as possible. This town also lies on a route that could imply a crossing west of Péronne. In both cases, Henry's march would have been shorter than that generated by a crossing of the river at Bethencourt/Voyennes, cutting 25–30km off the journey to Maisoncelle.

Given that the *Gesta* and other leading chroniclers do not name the location, it is not wholly impossible that a crossing was effected at Eclusier. But the claim in the *Gesta*, the *Liber Metricus*, *Waurin* and *Le Fèvre* that Henry passed by Nesle makes this problematic, since it would require the army to have doubled back on itself. Furthermore, the author of the *Gesta*, who was with the English army, claims that Péronne was passed on 21 October 'a short distance way on our left', which makes it necessary for the crossing to have been made to the south of the town. Le Fèvre locates the army after the crossing at Athies, a village that lies half-way between Péronne and the proposed crossing point between Bethencourt and Voyennes. Waurin and Monstrelet also have the English army quartering just to the east of Athies in Monchy-Lagache. If the crossing was effected to the west of Péronne then all of these references must be incorrect.

Most likely, therefore, the crossing was south of Péronne and can be dated securely to Saturday 19 October. The *Gesta* provides the most detailed account, couched in a way that stresses Henry's mastery of the situation. It begins by saying that news came to the king that there was a suitable crossing a league away. This implies that Henry was deploying scouts to find a crossing, although Titus Livius suggests that it was 'with the help of certain men of the region who had been taken captive by the army' that they came to a place where crossing could be effected. The Pseudo-Elmham tells a different tale in order to show how fortune had favoured the English. In his account, Englishmen were looking for a particular crossing but happened to notice another place which looked suitable, which, 'as prisoners from that country asserted, had never been known of before'. Henry's response, according to the *Gesta*, was to send further mounted patrols to the suggested place in order to examine its potential, in particular the depth and current of the water. We must assume that favourable reports came back, since Henry followed with the rest of the army. In order to reach the crossing point, the English had to pass through a marsh between the Somme and one of its tributaries, which the editors of the *Gesta* suggest was the river Ingon. The author makes the valid point that the English could have been very vulnerable while hemmed in between the two rivers, but that fortunately the enemy were not aware of this.

The crossing is described as consisting of two long but narrow causeways. The French had broken the causeways mid-stream in the hope of making them unusable, but it remained possible to cross in single file. Advance parties of men-at-arms and archers under Sir John Cornwall and Sir Gilbert Umfraville, the same men, we must note, as had been involved in the reconnaissance for the initial landing at the Chef de Caux, made their way across in order to establish a bridgehead.[3] This would serve to protect the English soldiers from potential French attack as they clambered from the water onto the northern bank of the river. But more importantly, a way was devised to allow the army to cross more quickly than if they had had to move in single file. The king ordered the breaches in the causeways to be filled up with faggots, straw and planks so that three men could ride abreast. In the accounts in *Waurin* and *Le Fèvre*, the English are credited with demolishing houses and taking away shutters, ladders and windows in order to make a bridge across the existing arches. This provides a rather different impression, although it is one which the Religieux also pursues. Here the English advance guard find the bridge across the Somme so broken that they throw themselves in fury on the villages round about and put them to the torch. Then they gather together all the workmen and carpenters and order them to build a new bridge with trees from the nearby woods so that they can cross.

French accounts therefore provide a much more *Brut*al account of English actions. In the *Gesta*, it is all much more gentlemanly, since local inhabitants are totally missing. Henry's mastery of the situation is also exemplified by his orders that the baggage should be sent across one causeway while the soldiers cross by the other. He apparently positioned himself with trusted lieutenants at the entrance to both causeways to prevent congestion and crushing, since no doubt the troops would be anxious to cross as quickly as they could. According to Waurin and Le Fèvre, the foot archers were sent over first, to act as defence as the rest of the army crossed. Once a large enough number had gained the other bank, one of the standards was planted. Then the whole of the vanguard crossed, and the horses were led over the makeshift bridge. After this, the main force and the rear guard followed.

These accounts give a vivid impression of how much organisation was needed to effect a crossing. With the numbers involved, it would have taken several hours. The *Gesta* claims that it began at 1 p.m. and was not fully completed until an hour before night. It would have been dark by around 5 p.m. at this time of year. Waurin and Le Fèvre begin the crossing at 8 a.m. but also let it proceed until nightfall. The time-consuming effort helps us to understand why Henry had been reluctant to effect a crossing where any French resistance was likely to be present, since troops in transit were vulnerable, at least until a decent number had been established on the northern bank. The *Gesta* tells us that some French cavalry did appear shortly after the crossing was commenced, and were joined by other companies which had been stationed in villages nearby. They sent outriders to see if they might still drive the English back and the English sent small mounted patrols against them. By such means they kept the French away from the causeways and prevented them combining forces to attack during the early stages of the crossing. Once enough English had reached the northern bank, the French companies realised that they were outnumbered, and so withdrew. They had been taken by surprise by the English crossing, although this was not unexpected, given the length of river to guard and the difficulties of communications. We can suggest that in an effort to patrol all possible crossings they had diffused their forces too greatly and could not regroup quickly. A potential strength had thus been rendered a weakness.

The crossing of the Somme is portrayed as a significant English victory in the *Gesta* and several other texts. After over a week of helplessness and perhaps increasing panic – as witnessed by the provision of the stakes – they had outwitted the French. The *Gesta* tells us of the cheerful night that followed, in the belief that the crossing had cut eight days of what might otherwise have been their journey. It is unwise to use this figure to try to calculate how far the English thought they might have had to penetrate upstream. The author of the *Gesta* seems to have had a particular liking for the notion of eight days. That was the period for which he claims Henry had ordered victuals to be prepared as the army left Harfleur, on the assumption that that was how long it would take to reach Calais. Thus the figure may be symbolic rather than real. The *Gesta* also claims that the English were heartened by the thought that if a French army was gathering in strength further upstream, it might now 'be disinclined to follow after us to do battle'. In fact, the opposite was the case. Once the English were across the Somme, the French had to act swiftly. They had reckoned on the English being delayed and weakened further, thereby giving themselves more time to gather their troops. Time was no longer on their side.

On the day the English crossed the Somme, 19 October, the French, according to the Brabant chronicler Dynter, held a council in Péronne. Those present were the Duke of Bourbon, the Duke of Alençon, the Count of Richemont, the Count of Eu and the Count of Vendôme, the *maître d'hôtel* of the king (Guichard Dauphin), Constable d'Albret, Marshal Boucicaut, the Seneschal of Hainault and the Lords of Waurin and Rons. Letters sent by this group were received by the Duke of Brabant at Louvain on 21 October. These requested the duke to set out in person, since the French intended to give battle in the following week.[4] This dating suggests that the French had already determined to give battle even before they knew that the English had managed to cross the Somme, but their decision must have been influenced by the fact that Henry had escaped their grasp by moving southwards towards Nesle. They knew that at some point he would be able to cross the river, since the passage would be easier the further he moved upstream. Therefore, there was now every reason to try to draw in lords from the northern lands, such as the Duke of Brabant.

According to the *Gesta* it was on the very next day, Sunday 20 October, that French heralds came to Henry with notice that battle would be given before the English reached Calais, although they did not assign a day or a place. Several important questions are raised by this incident. The first is exactly where the English were at this point. The *Gesta* is not helpful in terms of geography. In fact, the chronicler gives very little detail on Henry's march between the crossing of the Somme and the eve of battle. He describes the English as spending the night of 19 October just to the north of the river, in villages which had previously served as bases for the French companies who had threatened to prevent their crossing. No movement is noted for 20 October, the day on which the author claims that the French heralds came to Henry. The march then continued on 21 October, with the implication that on that day the English passed the 'walled town of Péronne… a short distance away to our left'.[5] The chronicler speculates that the French cavalry that came out of the town were intended as a decoy to entice the English within range of enemy shot, but adds that once the English cavalry advanced against them, they returned to the town. Other chronicles provide possible clarification of the English location. Le Fèvre places the army at Athies on the night after the crossing of the Somme. Waurin and Monstrelet place the English slightly further to the east, at Monchy-Lagache. These are the last places noted before the sending of the heralds. If the chronology given in the *Gesta* is correct then we must assume that the heralds came to Henry as he lay south of Péronne.

The second issue is by whom the French heralds were sent. English chronicles name the Dukes of Orléans and Bourbon, with the Burgundian writers adding Constable d'Albret. Titus Livius has a larger group in whose name the heralds came: the Dukes of Orléans, Brabant, Bourbon, Bar, Burgundy and Alençon, as well as the constable, the Count of Nevers and the Archbishop of Sens. In other French accounts, Orléans is not mentioned. The Berry Herald comments that 'the constable, the duke of Bourbon, the duke of Bar and the count of Nevers who had just arrived at Corbie were furious when they learned that the English had crossed the river', and that they therefore sent heralds to Henry. Two of these names overlap with the list provided by Dynter for the council held at Péronne on 19 October. Given that Henry was in the vicinity of Péronne when the heralds came, the easiest explanation is that it was the lords assembled there who determined that battle would be given and sent the heralds to Henry.

Two difficulties arise from this, however. The first is the meeting of a council at Rouen on 20 October, noted in Monstrelet. The chronicler claims that those present with the king and Dauphin were the Duke of Anjou, the Dukes of Berry and Brittany, the Count of Ponthieu, youngest son of Charles VI, along with thirty-five or so royal councillors. Thirty of these men decided that Henry should be brought to battle, but the other five counselled that 'it would be better, in their opinion, that they should not fight on the day which had been appointed'. The majority held sway and the king immediately sent letters to the constable and others to assemble as soon as possible with all the force they could, in order to fight Henry and his army. The chronicler then has it that a nationwide *semonce des nobles* was issued for men to hurry to join the constable, 'wherever he might be found'. Waurin and Le Fèvre also say that the king and his council decided that battle should be given and mention that the decision was soon known 'in many places in the kingdom as beyond', but they give no date for the council meeting. Des Ursins does not explicitly speak of the meeting but notes that an order had been given in Rouen to give battle in a particular manner. We shall return to the intended deployments in the next chapter.

It is feasible that a meeting was held in Rouen on 20 October. The Duke of Berry entered Rouen on the same day as Charles (12 October).[6] At that point, Louis II, Duke of Anjou, was still at Orléans, but he had reached Rouen by 20 October, although his son-in-law, Charles, Count of Ponthieu remained south of the Loire.[7] The Duke of Bourbon arrived in the Norman capital by 17 October,[8] but as we have seen, there are suggestions that he was at Péronne by 19 October. It is possible that the dating of the Rouen meeting is incorrect, and that it occurred before the date that Monstrelet suggests. In this interpretation, therefore, Bourbon brought word of its decision and its suggested battle deployment to Péronne. At that place had gathered not only the lords who had been with the army operating north of Somme, such as the constable, the marshal, Alençon, Vendôme and Richemont, but also lords from the north-east such as Nevers and Bar. Heralds were sent to Henry either as a direct result of the decision taken at Rouen or after further discussion by the lords at Péronne.

The second issue is the whereabouts of the Duke of Orléans. A reliable source places him in Orléans on 17 October.[9] This makes it difficult for him to have been present in Péronne with the other lords. As will be noted, French chroniclers never include him in that group, nor does Monstrelet give his presence at the council at Rouen, although it would have been feasible for him to have moved from Orléans to Rouen between 17 and 20 October. There is a likelihood that he came north late in the day, and only arrived at Agincourt on the day of the battle. How, then, does this square with his name being linked to the sending of heralds? A solution is that it had already been decided at Rouen and communicated to Péronne that the king, the Dauphin and the Duke of Berry would not be present at the proposed battle, but that Orléans would be. Monstrelet follows his account of the council on 20 October with the comment that 'even the duke of Guienne had a great desire to go', implying that a decision had already been taken that he should not. In the Berry Herald, the Duke of Berry argues that the king should not be present, since, influenced by recollection of his father's capture at Poitiers, it was 'better to lose just the battle than both king and battle'. Charles VI, the Herald adds, would willingly have gone because he was a 'brave, strong and powerful knight'.

At some point, it must have been decided that the king and Dauphin were not to be present at any battle. The Duke of Berry was too old. The Duke of Orléans was therefore the next closest member of the royal family, and hence it was appropriate that the heralds' summons to Henry should be issued in his name, alongside that of Bourbon (who had been present at the council at Rouen) and Constable d'Albret (the leading military commander). It will be remembered, however, that initially the council had advised against the service of both Burgundy and Orléans in person. As a result, notice now had to be sent to Orléans so that he might come north to join the rest of the army, countermanding a possible earlier order that he should not serve in person. The solution proposed here is based on an assumption that there was co-ordination between the lords at Péronne and the court at Rouen. It is possible, of course, that there was no co-ordination, and that each was pursuing its own plans. This is implied by the Berry Herald. In his account, once the constable, Bourbon, Bar and Nevers at Corbie discovered that Henry had crossed the Somme, they sent heralds to Henry summoning him to battle on Thursday 24 October at Aubigny in Artois. When news reached Rouen, the Duke of Berry was, as we have seen, 'much annoyed that the lords had accepted to give battle' and refused to let the king join them. This would fit with Dynter's comment that the letters sent from Péronne to the Duke of Brabant on 19 October said that the king and Dauphin intended to be present in person. At this stage, the lords gathered at Corbie/Péronne thought that would be the case, but later received news from Rouen that it would not be so.

Once the heralds had come to Henry he continued his march. The *Gesta* gives no indication of locations until the river Ternoise was reached on 24 October. Le Fèvre has Henry pass Doingt, to the south-east of Péronne, and then move on to Miraumont, a location also noted in Fenin. Miraumont lay on the river Ancre, 10km away, just to the west of Bapaume.[10] This must have been on the night of Tuesday 21 October. On the following day, Le Fèvre has Henry making his way towards Ancre (now Albert) and lodging in Forceville, with his men billeted in villages round about. Fenin, Monstrelet and Waurin add the village of Acheux as one of the places the English were quartered. There is no evidence that Henry passed through Ancre itself but his route would have necessitated a crossing of the river Ancre at some point.

Le Fèvre's proposed route raises an important question. From Miraumont, Henry could have marched north-north-west towards Lucheux and Calais. Why did he turn instead westwards towards Acheux and Forceville? This might seem a trivial point, were it not for the Berry Herald's account of the heralds' challenge to Henry to give battle at Aubigny in Artois. Henry accepted the challenge, 'promising to come to the field and fight on that day (24 October) without default'. Aubigny lies 18km to the west of Arras, on the road to Saint-Pol-en-Ternoise. It was in an area traversed by the French royal army in the summer of 1414, and would have been a convenient meeting point for the troops coming from Péronne, Picardy, the Marne-Meuse area and the Burgundian and Brabantine lands to the north and east. In contrast to the area to the south of Arras, characterised by the ridges fought over in the First World War, the terrain was more open and flat. More significantly for the present discussion, Aubigny lies almost due north of Miraumont.

It can be suggested, therefore, that once Henry had been made aware by the heralds of the location of battle, he made his way from the vicinity of Péronne towards Aubigny. But then he changed his mind and turned westwards towards Acheux, which he reached by the night of Tuesday 22 October. The Berry Herald's account comments that Henry did not keep the promise he had made to the French heralds: 'In fact, he did the very opposite because he passed by a place called Beauquesne so that he should reach Calais as soon as possible'. Beauquesne lies directly to the west of Acheux. Although not giving any details on the intended location, the *Chronique de Normandie* also claims that the two armies had agreed, by their heralds, to give battle on Thursday 24 October, but that the English had not kept to their convenant, 'but held on their way more to the left than in their direct course'. French plans to give battle at Aubigny thus had to be changed. The Religieux includes the following comment:

> ...suddenly, at the order of some leaders whose names I do not know, the French were ordered to change their position and to move off to establish themselves elsewhere. They obeyed, but not without regret for they foresaw that this manoeuvre was to the benefit of the enemy.

We cannot be certain that the chronicler is referring to the change from Aubigny to Agincourt, but it is important to bear this possibility in mind, especially when considering in the next chapter that the French had not been able to assemble their entire strength by the time the engagement began. That they were now planning to fight on Friday 25 October is stated in a letter sent by the *bailli* of Hainault to the town of Mons, which arrived there on 23 October.[11]

There is no doubt that Henry anticipated battle after the visit of the heralds. The *Gesta* tells us that he even made ready to give battle on the morrow (i.e. 21 October). On that day, a mile or so beyond Péronne, the English found the roads were churned up by the French army, 'as if it had crossed ahead of us many thousand strong'. Although we cannot pinpoint this location precisely, it would fit well with the French moving from Péronne towards Aubigny. The *Gesta* continues that this made Henry and many others fear that battle was imminent, and that prayers were offered that God might 'turn away from us the violence of the French'. This sense of panic is found in several other works. The *Liber Metricus* has it that 'the English sought camp and their hearts were quaking with fear'. In *Waurin* and *Le Fèvre* also, the interaction with the heralds is followed by mention that since the king knew the French wished to give battle, he put on his own armour and ordered his troops to do likewise, additionally commanding that his archers should thenceforward be provided with a stake. 'And so he rode on each day up to the battle'. The implication is that the English made ready for battle but that they did not seek it.

This is also the impression given in Henry's response to the French heralds. The account in the *Gesta* and *Liber Metricus* is very perfunctory, saying simply that the heralds brought a message that the French would do battle with him before he reached Calais. No time or place was assigned. There is no mention of Henry's response, although the texts go on to say that he accepted the summons as divine will and made ready to do battle, trusting in God's will and the justice of his cause. The account in Titus Livius and the Pseudo-Elmham is essentially the same but Henry is attributed with a response to the heralds. When he is asked what route he intends to take, he replies 'straight to Calais', before going on to say that he had no intention of seeking out the enemy, nor was the speed of his march determined by fear of them: 'However we urge them not to impede our way nor should they seek a great shedding of Christian blood'. In *Waurin* and *Le Fèvre*, the heralds are given a longer oration. They begin by saying that the French wished to help him achieve his desire, 'for they knew well that, even from the moment he left his own kingdom, his desire was to give battle to the French'. Thus, 'if he wished to appoint a day and a place to fight against them, they would be pleased to have him do so'. They suggested that the details should be decided by representatives of each side, so that neither should have an unfair advantage. Henry initially sends the heralds off without a reply but subsequently despatches two of his own heralds to the French lords with his answer. This was that ever since he had left Harfleur his aim was to return to the kingdom of England. As a result, he had not stayed in any fortified town or fortress: 'Thus, if the three princes of France wanted to fight with him, there was no need to appoint a time or place because they could find him any day they liked in open country and without hindrance'. As in the English narratives, therefore, there is no indication in these Burgundian texts that Henry was seeking battle. Only the Berry Herald, therefore, suggests that Henry agreed to a pre-arranged battle.

As with so many incidents of the campaign, we cannot be sure of what really happened. All of the narratives were written in hindsight. Although the *Gesta* and *Liber Metricus* were composed closest to the event, both pursue a line consistent with Henry's own propaganda that the French were the aggressors and that Henry had only been forced into taking arms by their refusal to give him what was rightly his. The accounts of Waurin and Le Fèvre were compiled several decades later when the long-term impact of Agincourt was apparent. Both men were present at the battle and saw many men of their own areas killed. Remember that, earlier in their narrative, they cursed the Gascon who gave false information when Henry first approached the Somme at its western extremity. Had Henry crossed at Blanchetaque, they claim, there would have been 'no sad and sorrowful day for the French at the battle of Agincourt'. It is not surprising, therefore, that they should emphasise that

Right: 49 Effigy of Henry IV from his tomb in Canterbury Cathedral.

Below: 50 Battlefield Church, near Shrewsbury. This has its origins in the chantry founded in 1409 by Henry IV at the site of his victory of 1403.

51 View of the field of the battle of Shrewsbury from the tower of Battlefield Church.

Left: 52 The garter stall plate of Sir Thomas Erpingham at St George's Windsor.

53 Archer's headgear as worn by a re-enactor, Paul Hitchin.

Above: 54 Modern
reproductions of
equipment of a
medieval archer.

Right: 55 An artist's
impression of a
mounted archer on
the 1415 campaign.

56 English banners. Left to right: Sir Thomas Erpingham (present at Agincourt); John Fastolf (invalided home from Harfleur but was later knighted and joined the garrison of the town); Henry, Lord Scrope (who indented to serve on the campaign but was executed for his failure to reveal the 'Southampton plot' to the king).

57 Portchester Castle. Henry resided here in late July and early August before embarkation for France in 1415. It was while here that he learned of the 'Southampton plot' to depose and kill him on the day he had assigned for departure – 1 August.

58 View of Portsmouth harbour from the keep of Porchester Castle. The king set sail on 7 August 1415.

59 The outer wall of the Bargate at Southampton which defended the northern entrance to the town. The gate dates back to the late twelfth century but was strengthened in the fourteenth century.

60 A late-fifteenth- or early-sixteenth-century gun now in the Royal Armouries. Guns of this style of manufacture, made of abutting iron staves held together by a series of hoops, may already have been in existence in 1415.

61 A mid-fifteenth-century breech-loading hand gun now in the Musée des Beaux Arts at Rouen.

Right, above: 62 Cliffs at Chef de Caux, just north of the lighthouse at Cap de la Hève. It would have been extremely difficult to land an army in this vicinity.

Right: 63 Sainte-Adresse, west of Le Havre. It is likely that Henry landed his army in the lee of the hill on which the lighthouse at Cap de la Hève can be seen.

Below: 64 This view seawards from the priory of Graville shows the hill and valley along which Henry probably moved his army towards Harfleur.

65 The church of the abbey of Graville to the west of Harfleur. According to the Burgundian chronicles, Henry lodged at the priory during the siege.

66 Domestic range at the abbey of Graville where Henry may have lodged.

67 This graffiti of the defences of Harfleur, found in the church of St Martin, dates from the sixteenth century but gives an impression of the walls and gates, although with some artistic licence.

68 View of the river Lézarde and St Martin's church in Harfleur.

69 The Porte de Rouen, Harfleur. Much of what survives is of sixteenth-century construction.

70 Remnants of walls on the eastern side of Harfleur, the site of Clarence's siege camp.

71 Ditches at Harfleur on the northern side of the town, to the east of the site of the Porte de Montivilliers.

Right, above: 72 The fishmongers *Poissonerie 104,* so called in memory of the 104 men whose ancestors had been driven out in 1415 but who recaptured the town for the French on 25 November 1435.

Right: 73 Arundel castle (West Sussex), where Thomas, Earl of Arundel died on 13 October 1415 after being invalided home from the siege of Harfleur.

Below: 74 The typical landscape of *pays de Caux* around Fauville. This was terrain that the English army could cross easily and relatively quickly.

75 View towards the castle of Arques. Henry and his army came here on 11 October.

76 The keep of the castle of Arques.

77 View northwards across the river Béthune from the castle of Arques.

78 View towards the church and town of Eu from the river Bresle, showing clearly its hilltop site. Henry's troops engaged with the French who launched a sortie out of the town on 12 October.

Above: 79 The collegiate church at Eu containing the shrine of St Lawrence O'Toole, the Archbishop of Armagh, who died in the town in 1180. The church was built in the twelth and thirteenth centuries but the apse was remodelled in the late fifteenth century.

Left: 80 View from the defences of Eu northwards across the river Bresle.

Left, below: 81 The likely site of the ford at Blanchetaque where Edward III had crossed the Somme in 1346. Henry received intelligence that the French had guarded the ford and decided not to attempt a crossing here.

82 A view inland across the Somme close to Blanchetaque, which emphasises the extent of the river valley. This would have been marshland in 1415 and therefore difficult for a large army to traverse in safety.

83 The market square at Abbeville, rebuilt after damage in the Second World War. This was where the French army had gathered in order to intercept Henry's attempts to cross the Somme.

84 The village of Pont Rémy on the Somme just to the east of Abbeville, where the English also investigated the possibility of a crossing of the river.

85 The church at Airaines, a place to which at least part of Henry's army probably came during the march. Edward III's army had also passed through the village in 1346.

86 View of the castle of Boves. Henry and his army were present in the village on the other side of the castle on 16 October.

Right: 87 The church at Corbie. From this town, on the
north bank of the Somme, the French launched a sortie
against Henry's army on 17 October.

Right: 88 The village of
Harbonnières where part of
Henry's army lodged around
17–18 October.

Below: 89 The area around
Eclusier-Vaux, now a
landscape similar to the
Norfolk Broads because of
centuries of peat extraction.
Some chroniclers suggest that
Henry crossed the Somme
here and then moved directly
north towards Albert (Ancre).

90 Bethencourt on the Somme, one of the likely crossing places for Henry and his army on 19 October.

91 Voyennes on the Somme, another possible crossing place on 19 October.

92 The town of Péronne, where the French army had gathered around 19 October and to the south of which they may have hoped to engage Henry and his army.

93 The castle of Péronne, likely location of the meeting of French lords on 19 October.

Left, above: 94 The village of Athies, where Henry's army may have lodged after crossing the Somme.

Left: 95 Typical landscape north of Somme, in the area to the south of Albert (Ancre) through which Henry's army passed.

Below: 96 The castle at Lucheux, a place through which the English may have passed on their march.

Above: 97 A view from the high ground to the north of Frévent towards the valley of the river Ternoise. Directly north of here lies Agincourt.

Right: 98 The church at Blangy-sur-Ternoise.

99 The river Ternoise at Blangy, where Henry's army crossed on 24 October.

100 A view from the road northwards from Blangy towards the village of Maisoncelle.

101 Banners of the French royal family. Left to right, top row: Charles VI; John, Duke of Alençon (killed at Agincourt); John, Duke of Bourbon (taken prisoner); Anthony, Duke of Brabant (killed); John, Duke of Burgundy (not present). Bottom row: the Dauphin Louis (not present); Charles of Artois, Count of Eu (taken prisoner); Philip, Count of Nevers (killed); Charles, Duke of Orléans (taken prisoner).

Above: 102 General view from Maisoncelle towards the field, showing the variety of levels which made visibility problematic.

Right: 103 View from Maisoncelle towards the possible location of the initial position taken up by the English.

104 View from the west towards the first French position at Azincourt. The water tower is close to the village of Ruisseauville. The woodlands are those between Tramecourt and Ruisseauville.

105 View eastwards from the field towards Tramecourt showing how the land falls away on that side of the field.

106 View eastwards from the village of Azincourt towards the battlefield, showing how the land falls away on this side of the field as on the Tramecourt side.

107 The woodlands on the Tramecourt side of the field. Henry sent a group of 200 archers towards the rear of the French lines on this side.

108 Ground conditions around the location of the second English position. The church at Agincourt can be seen on the left, with the buildings at La Gacogne on the right.

109 View across the field from the second English position to the likely location of the French position.

110 An artist's impression of Sir Thomas Erpingham wearing plate armour and a surcoat.

Left: 111 The centre of the field near La Gacogne. It is likely that the main engagement between the men-at-arms of each army occurred in this vicinity.

Below: 112 An English archer preparing a stake in accordance with the king's command. The *Gesta Henrici Quinti* suggests that the king issued the order to make the stakes after the sortie from Corbie, in response to rumours of French intentions to override the archers in any engagement. He wears the typical light armour of the archers – a padded jaquet and bascinet.

Above: 113 Two archers at full draw. The figure on the left wears a kettle hat and padded jacket and has his hose loosened for ease of movement. The man on the right wears a bascinet, and upper body defence of small plates. Some may have worn brigandines where metal plates were riveted inside a leather or canvas jacket.

Right: 114 A close-up of ground conditions close to La Gacogne, showing the ruts easily created in rainy seasons.

115 A well-equipped bowman, wearing a mail shirt beneath his jacquet and a bascinet on his head. To create a 'storm' effect against oncoming cavalry and men-at-arms, the archers fired their arrow into the air.

116 The battle as portrayed in a later fifteenth-century manuscript celebrating the achievements of Charles VII in driving the English out of Normandy and Gascony in the early 1450s. Note the act of killing on the far left, by a swift dagger thrust to the neck, and the tying of the hands of the prisoners in the foreground. The armour does not represent that of 1415.

Right: 117 English battle banners of St George and of the Trinity.

Right, below: 118 Banners of the English royal family. Left to right, top row: Henry V; Thomas Beaufort, Earl of Dorset (captain of Harfleur); John, Duke of Bedford (keeper of England in 1415); Richard, Earl of Cambridge (executed for his role in the Southampton plot). Bottom row: Thomas, Duke of Clarence (invalided home from Harfleur); Humphrey, Duke of Gloucester (present at Agincourt); Edward, Duke of York (killed at Agincourt).

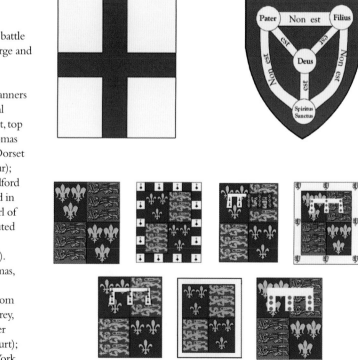

119 The battle as portrayed in a mid-fifteenth-century illuminated version of Thomas Walsingham's *St Albans Chronicle*. The landscape is fanciful. Note the trumpeters in the background. Such men would have been used to sound signals during the battle.

120 The *Calvaire* close to La Gacogne which is believed to mark the site of the French grave pits. The existing monument was erected after the Franco-Prussian War of 1869–70.

121 Henry V at the battle of Agincourt. Several English choniclers mention Henry's bravery in the midst of the battle; *Liber Metricus* (an early English chonicle) claims that his crown was broken off his helmet by an axe-wielding Frenchman. Other than the French cavalry advance against the archers, the battle was fought on foot, including by Henry himself.

122 The farm that occupies the site of the castle at Agincourt. There are some cellars dating back to the fifteenth century but no remains above ground.

123 The *Centre Historique* at Azincourt, designed by Eric Revet and Bertrand Klein, was officially opened on 1 July 2001. The front resembles a series of longbows with arrows ready to fly.

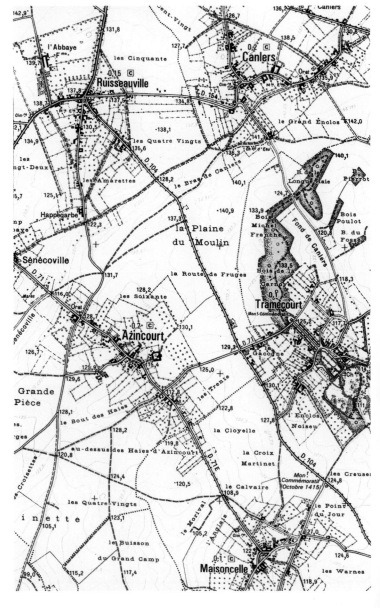

124 Map of the field of Agincourt.

the battle could have been avoided. As we shall see, they are at pains in their narrative of the fight to stress Burgundian bravery, thereby implying Armagnac folly. As for the Berry Herald, he too was writing several decades later and was closely connected with Charles VII. It is therefore possible that he portrayed Henry as a coward who reneged upon a promise. By contrast, he claims that Charles VI would have willingly gone to the battle 'because he was a brave, strong and powerful knight', but that he was prevented from doing so by the Duke of Berry.

Since all accounts suggest that it was the French who sought battle, there is no reason to doubt that this was not the case. As for Henry, the route he took across Picardy would suggest that he was trying to escape from the French clutches even if he had initially agreed to fight. The onus was now on the French to force him to stop in another location. On Wednesday 23 October he set out from Acheux, crossing the river Authie at Thièvre and passing between Doullens on his left and Lucheux on his right. Doullens was a walled town. Lucheux had a fortified gate in addition to a strong castle owned by the Count of Saint-Pol. The army was kept away from these places, however, as it had been from other fortified centres since the crossing of the Somme. The night of 23 October was spent at Bonnières-le-Scallon, with the vanguard under the Duke of York lodged at Frévent on the river Canche.[12] Bonnières lies on the hillside that descends towards Frévent. This was a suitable place to camp, since it offered extensive open countryside overlooking the town. That Henry sent York with the vanguard to secure the crossing over the Canche indicates that he wanted to ensure that the forward march north of the river could be undertaken without delay on the next morning. The securing of the crossing was a difficult manoeuvre because the bridge was broken and the French had patrols in the area who put up resistance.[13]

On the morning of Thursday 24 October the English crossed the river and continued in a fairly straight direction toward the Ternoise. Titus Livius and the Pseudo-Elmham say that York was sent to reconnoitre with part of the vanguard. The use of a larger force than usual for this purpose reminds us that Henry expected the French to be hoping to engage him on this day. News was brought back to him that the French were indeed assembling in large numbers. At this stage, however, they were still on the move and it may have been evident to English reconnaissance exactly where they were intending to gather. The English response was to cross the Ternoise as quickly as possible. The watercourse looks narrow and easily passable today, but the extent of the low-lying area between the village of Blangy and the hill leading towards Maisoncelle suggests that there was in the past a very extensive area of march. As at the crossing of the Somme, the army was potentially vulnerable as it made its way across narrow causeways. There was certainly fighting on this day, since English archers are recorded in the financial records as having been taken prisoner.[14] Once across the river, the English began to climb the hill to the north, only to find the French assembling in large numbers. The march was over. Preparations for battle began.

By this time, Henry had led his army over a distance of between 378km and 402km.[15] We have discussed the route taken, but there are general comments we can make on the march as a whole which can shed further light on his intentions. The first is that he made no attempt to capture any places *en route*. Since he had left his artillery in Harfleur, he was not in a position to try to do so, nor did he wish to. He wanted to move on as quickly as possible. To that end he avoided major fortified centres. His response to the French heralds sent to him on 20 October was that he had not stopped in any walled town or fortress. That was true, since at Boves he had lodged in the town not the castle, with whose defenders, as at Eu and Arques, he had negotiated the passage of his army.

The march was not devoid of military action, however. Some was at the initiative of the French. At Arques, the castle garrison launched some volleys from their guns to prevent Henry's army coming too close. At Eu and Corbie the French launched sorties against the English, and at the crossing of the Canche there was also an effort to trap the English and force a fight. This does not mean, however, that Henry was not prepared for action. At Arques we are told that the king drew up his battles and wings in full view of the castle. On 24 October he similarly drew up his army in a state of preparedness. Chroniclers also suggest that in general he had his army proceed in full armour from 20 October onwards, the day on which the heralds had brought notice of French intention to give battle.

On other occasions he deployed parts of his army for specific functions, for instance, testing possible crossings of the Somme; ascertaining the location of French troops, and finding billeting sites for overnight bivouacs. The scouts sent out on spying activities were likely in small parties mounted on the best horses and operating as unobtrusively as possible. Those looking for food supplies and lodgings, known as the herbergers, needed to be in large enough groups to impress the local population with which they interacted, but had a less dangerous military task, since peasants were in no position to offer serious resistance. The cavalry companies sent out against the French who threatened to disrupt the crossing of the Somme would have needed to be well-mounted, well-armed and well-drilled men-at-arms. On occasion, the impression given by chronicles is that larger companies of mixed troops were deployed for military action. This was what happened in resisting the sorties at Eu and Corbie, where the use of archers is noted. Larger companies were also sent ahead to secure the bridge over the Canche at Frévent and the bridge over the Ternoise at Blangy. Mounted companies were constantly used to patrol and protect the flanks of the army as it marched and also to launch small-scale raids into the hinterland. Although we have much less to go on, the French were using companies in a similar variety of functions. On several occasions, we hear of French mounted patrols coming out of fortified centres to observe the English, but with no intention of engaging.

Military actions on the march are revealed by references in the financial records of the English army. At least one man was killed and three taken prisoner on

8 October in an engagement with the garrison of Montivilliers.[16] There were some losses in the area of Fécamp.[17] English soldiers were captured on 21[18] and 23 October,[19] but the largest losses were on the day before the battle, when seven of the Lancashire archers were taken prisoner.[20] On the face of it, English losses were small. The problem is, however, that decisions taken on accounting after the campaign removed the need to record events on the march, since all those who served for the second quarter up to and including the battle were to be paid for the whole period, irrespective of their fate. A similar difficulty surrounds the capture of French prisoners and booty. This is suggested in the chronicles, but there is no evidence of such gains in the post-campaign reports. Either a blind eye was turned to them, they were redeemed for food during the march, or they were of too little value to fall within the rules on the crown and captains creaming off their share.

The chronicles offer a few insights into the possible organisation of the army on the march. Several comment on the division into three battles from the leaving of Harfleur. Titus Livius also suggests that there were two wings in addition to the battles, a reflection, perhaps, of the parties used to protect the flanks. According to Waurin, the vanguard was led by Sir John Cornwall and the 'Earl of Kent'. Since there was no peer of this title, the person meant is most likely Sir Gilbert Umfraville, Earl of Kyme. At the initial landing and on other occasions during the campaign, Cornwall and Umfraville are found operating together. The centre battle was commanded by the king, along with the Duke of Gloucester, the Earl of Huntingdon, Lord Roos and others. The rearguard was led by the Duke of York and the Earl of Oxford. Whether these commands continued for the whole march is uncertain, since York is referred to towards the end of the manoeuvre by Waurin and Monstrelet as leading the vanguard, a command he was also to hold at the battle. This would fit with random comments that it was York who sent out reconnaissance parties, and that they reported back to him, as, for instance, in the approach to Blangy and Agincourt. York also received the heralds before they were admitted to the king's presence. There are also suggestions that he was constable and marshal of the army. Putting all of this together, we can suggest that he was in practice the commander of the march.

At the Canche, the vanguard was lodged in Frévent with the king at Bonnières, and troops distributed between eight to nine villages in the vicinity. The assumption must be that they were still organised by retinues, although since some had been disrupted by some of their number being invalided home and others being detailed into garrison, it must be assumed that there had been some redistribution and amalgamation. The distribution of soldiers or of retinues between the three battles cannot be known, nor how it relates to deployment at the siege or the battle. Likewise we cannot be certain whether most of the army was mounted on the march. The evidence of the Duke of York's muster roll for the second quarter – the only muster known to survive of those taken on the march – indicates that most archers had one mount but men-at-arms more.[21] This is borne out for other retinues by the shipping accounts for the return from Calais to England. There were therefore thousands of horses with the army. In some retinues at least, the horses of those invalided home had been kept for use of those still on campaign.[22] By far the easiest way of moving horses was for them to be ridden at a gentle pace. There were ample numbers of soldiers and servants to make this possible. The distance covered each day would permit the use of one horse without the need to change mount. But the speed is also compatible with some men moving on foot. We know that material was carried on sumpter horses and also in carts. Although the heavy artillery and siege engines had not been taken on the march, there was a very large quantity of arrows and victuals to transport, as well as all of the tents and domestic equipment. For the king alone there were all the trappings of royalty, crowns, seals and devotional items.[23] Titus Livius suggests, however, that there had been an effort on leaving Harfleur to limit the amount of unnecessary baggage. Again the suggestion is that Henry wanted to ensure his army moved as quickly as possible and unhindered.

Furthermore, he engaged in very few formal interactions with the local population. At Eu, Arques and Boves there was negotiation so that the army might pass unmolested and so that it would not, in its turn, cause damage. In coming to these agreements, Henry's aim was to avoid delay but also to gain food to supplement the rations that the army had brought with it from Harfleur. As the Religieux puts it: 'I know by accurate information that the English were so pressed by lack of food that instead of ransoming the inhabitants of the towns and country for money, they asked them for victuals'. In the face of such a large English army, the population had little choice but to give them supplies. Even fortified places in the *pays de Caux* were, as Titus Livius and the Pseudo-Elmham put it, 'struck by fear'. Only when the army arrived at Nesle did the local people refuse such terms, leading to Henry's order that the hamlets should be set on fire and totally destroyed on the next day. The *Gesta* ducks the issue of whether this actually happened, since he follows mention of the order by news that a possible crossing of the Somme had been found. After the crossing of the river, no chronicle mentions any negotiations with the local population at all. The implication is that, once over the river, Henry was keener than ever to move his army as quickly as possible and so avoided negotiating supplies, since these might cause delays. Thus his army became extremely short of rations by the time of the battle, and also at their arrival at Calais.

A further point rises out of this. If negotiation for food was limited, did Henry's army simply pillage its way through Normandy and Picardy? The *Gesta* provides no references at all to such behaviour. It is possible that its author deliberately omitted mention of it, since he wished to portray Henry as a truly Christian king who displayed concern for his French subjects as much as his English. He may betray a different reality in the passage where, as Henry approaches the Somme, he records debate on when the French will give battle. Some of Henry's advisers, he tells us, considered that the French could not bear the dishonour of not engaging, since Henry had 'entered their land, remained there for so long, besieged and taken a town, and, at length, with so small a following and so reduced an army, laid waste their country for such a long distance'.[24] While other English accounts also remain silent on acts of pillage and violence towards the local population, French chronicles provide a less flattering account of Henry's actions.

Thomas Basin, who was at the time of Henry's invasion a three-year-old living at Caudebec, 40km upstream of Harfleur, wrote fifty years later that Henry ravaged everything on his route across the *pays de Caux*. This line is also followed in the Bourgeois of Paris, which follows the surrender with the comment 'and all the countryside was devastated and pillaged'. Waurin too has it that after leaving Harfleur, the king of England 'journeyed in the midst of his troops through the lands of Normandy destroying all before him', although this is not found in this context in *Monstrelet* and *Le Fèvre*. Monstrelet does speak of English pillaging after the failure to cross the Somme at its western end, which forced Henry to move towards Airaines, 'burning and destroying the whole country, taking prisoners and acquiring great booty'. Des Ursins likewise speaks of Henry taking his way towards Gournay and Amiens (this is the same stage of the march as in Monstrelet's observation), 'committing countless evil deeds, burning, killing people, capturing and abducting children'. At the crossing of the Somme, Le Fèvre and Waurin also suggest that the English demolished houses and took away ladders, shutters and windows in order to construct a bridge. The Religieux adds that they were so annoyed to find the bridge broken that 'they threw themselves with fury on the villages round about and put them to the torch'.

The behaviour of English soldiers, however, was subject to disciplinary ordinances. The *Gesta* mentions that Henry issued some ordinances before siege was laid to Harfleur giving the standard protection from attack to churches and to women. It notes further clauses as the army began its march, including the king's command that 'no man should burn and lay waste or take anything save only food and what was necessary for the march, or capture any rebels save only those offering resistance'.[25] The text does not say, of course, that the English soldiers were banned from taking food, but indicates that Henry was trying to prevent excessive pillaging. In addition, the English chroniclers tell us that Henry put to death a soldier who had stolen a pyx from a church near Corbie. There is ample indication, therefore, that Henry was keen on the maintenance of discipline. The set of ordinances that he issued in 1419 is well known, but we have another undated set which may belong to the 1415 campaign.[26]

From the text, we can see that they were publicised by being cried throughout the host. Copies were also given to the captains, who were charged to ensure that their men were fully informed of them. Punishment was enforced centrally by the constable and marshal, who had rights to fine and arrest. The ordinances required the soldiers to wear the cross of St George and laid down protocols concerning prisoners and gains of war. One of their main aims was to prevent disputes within the body of soldiers, to ensure military readiness in the keeping of watch while also limiting opportunities for independent military action and for desertion. All men leaving the host had to have a ticket ('billet') to do so under the king's signet, which was the method used to authorise the invalidings home from Harfleur.

Several of the clauses regulated interactions with civilians. Only the herbergers of the retinue were allowed to ride out before the banner, and their allocations had to be accepted and obeyed. This ensured that only a small number of soldiers dealt with civilians. There were further controls on pillaging from those who were within the king's obedience. This would have prevented actions once towns had negotiated the provision of victuals in return for freedom from attack. Overall, therefore, just as Henry set high store by his own rights as king, so he did by the obligations towards those he considered his subjects, in this case the French. This is well-evidenced in his second Norman campaign, but we are seeing clear signs of it in the march of 1415.[27] This is revealed in an incident recounted in the Burgundian chroniclers, who note that Henry 'always observed proper and honourable practices'. They illustrate this with the general observation that when he wanted to send scouts before towns and castles, he had them take off their cote-armour when they set out, putting it back on again at their return. They then add a specific incident in which the king had left Bonnières and was heading for Blangy. The herbergers had found a village in which he could lodge, but he did not realise this and went on beyond it. When told, he said that he could not return to the village because he had his cote-armour on. So he moved on to where his vanguard was lodging and moved his vanguard further forward. The point here was that he was in armour and this was inappropriate for dealings with civilians. He wished to make clear that they were not his enemy but his people. This was also the impression that he wanted his scouts and herbergers to make in non-military operations.

Henry also realised that discipline was important for military effectiveness. While at Boves, the soldiers went to look for wine to fill their bottles, much to the annoyance of the king. When he was asked why, 'he replied that he was not troubled by the idea of bottles but that the problem was that many would fill their stomachs as well as their bottles, and that was worried him'. The presence of the king assisted considerably in the maintenance of discipline. It is important to remember that the king on the march would have been a remote figure for all save his household and leading commanders. Separate accommodation was always arranged for him and the courtly rituals of eating and devotion would have continued. The army, like contemporary society as a whole, set great store by hierarchy and deference. The ordinances were premised on the threat of punishment. In this context, the execution of the soldier who stole the pyx is highly significant, both as an incident and as an expression of Henry's style of command, which related closely to his concept of kingship as a whole. The Gesta uses it to stress the king's own devotion to the Almighty above all other concerns. After all, the king was having one of his own soldiers killed. Comparison is drawn with the action of Phineas, who did not hesitate to slay a fellow-Israelite, Zimri, so that 'the fierce anger of the Lord' might be turned away from Israel.[28] The evils of the worship of 'false idols' and of the deadly sin of greed are further exemplified by having the thief steal a pyx made of copper in the belief that it was made of gold. Titus Livius has the king order his army to halt until the religious sacrilege has been expiated and the vessel returned to the church. He also has those who committed the theft (implying more than one malefactor) led out through the whole army to be hanged. The Pseudo-Elmham has only one thief, but provides a very colourful account of his being dragged through the army and hanged very near the church from which the pyx was taken.

Whether the king's presence assisted morale is impossible to know. If it was the case that the soldiers considered their objective to be Calais, then there was surely increasing consternation as the march continued. But the chronicles do not allow us to penetrate into the minds of the soldiers at this point. The victory at Agincourt removed any need to narrate their earlier anxieties or Henry's uncertainties as he led his men across northern France. This was not the first time, of course, that an English army had pursued a long-distance march in France nor that a French army had set about chasing it. The famous marches of Edward III across northern France in 1346, culminating in Crécy, and of his son from the Atlantic almost to the Mediterranean and back in 1355, and towards the Loire in 1356, leading to the battle of Poitiers, are well known, but there are a myriad of other medium and long-distance actions throughout the fourteenth-century phase of the war. More recently, the Duke of Clarence had led his men from a landing in the Cotentin all the way to Blois and thence to Bordeaux. These actions tend to be classified as 'chevauchées', mounted raids through French territory undertaken to loot and pillage, and to undermine the morale and the authority of the enemy, rather than to capture towns and fortifications. Rogers has argued that this style of campaigning was also intended to draw the French to battle.[29] Henry's campaign appears to include much less of the deliberate looting, devastation and pillaging of these other campaigns.[30] Recent research on Edward III's march through Normandy in 1346 emphasises how 'an army on the march could be vulnerable, especially when raiding parties were widely dispersed and pillaging was pursued carelessly', and that while Edward allowed such activity, he tried to ensure that it was regulated by military and disciplinary needs. For instance, destruction for its own sake was only allowed after the foragers had carried out their task of finding supplies.[31] Some of Edward's methods were similar to those of Henry, but it is important to note that in general the latter moved his men more quickly than either Edward III did in 1346 or his son in 1355–56, and he did not, like them, have long stops in one particular place. So little time was allowed for pillaging that it is unlikely much could have occurred. Furthermore, Henry avoided places with rich pickings and

conducted a march through areas with relatively small villages. Even if food supplies were negotiated or taken, the quantity cannot have been great. Although
victuals had been carried from Harfleur, there seems little doubt that his army
would have been suffering from lack of food by the time it reached Maisoncelle.

It is easily forgotten that the French also engaged in long marches during the
1415 campaign. The problem is that chroniclers tell us much less both on the
routes taken and on more general matters. English writers, after all, would be
totally ignorant about French manoeuvres. No chronicler was with the French
army on the march. We have pay records for several companies during the period
of Henry's march. These will be discussed more fully in the following chapter, since they may have contributed to the force which the French assembled
at Agincourt. Their nature does not make it possible, however, to see how the
French army was organised and grouped in its own movements.

Where chroniclers do comment, they are critical of the behaviour of French
troops. The Religieux mentions the *semonce des nobles* issued on 28 August, noting
that it forbade troops from billeting on the local population more than a night
in any one place. Since we have the full text of the order, we also know that it
banned any pillaging and damage to the people of the areas they passed through.[32]
The chronicler claims that those recruited ignored this completely, although his
comments on the motley origins of the troops are not wholly true:

> The soldiers who were in the service of princes and who were for the most part
> foreigners, illegitimate and of insignificant origins, exiles and outlaws, keener
> on pillage than accustomed to military discipline, paid no regard to the orders
> to the king and made the inhabitants of the kingdom suffer even more than
> was usual. With a rapacity hitherto unheard of, they forced them to sell their
> carts, their beasts of burden and their own homes. They took off anything they
> could carry and forcibly removed the animals, even the horses who were used
> for agricultural work. In short, they committed more crimes than the enemy
> himself save for murder and arson.

Des Ursins also reports that the French garrison at Fécamp caused damage to the
town and to the abbey, telling us that their horses were billeted even near the high
altar and the soldiers broke into the chests of valuables which the townspeople had
placed in the abbey for safekeeping.[33] The *Chronique de Ruisseauville* adds to this picture of indiscipline with a comment that the women ejected from Harfleur, although
protected by Henry's ordinance that they should leave unharmed, were robbed and
raped by the French once they were a good way from the town. The same chronicler
comments that in the campaign along the Somme, French troops also 'did nothing
save robbing and pillaging towns, monasteries and abbeys and violating women'.

The overall impression is that the English were better disciplined. To some
degree, this resulted from the nature of the march. Henry wanted to keep up a

good pace and therefore there was no time for gratuitous acts of violence. While the English had brought supplies from England, the French army was inevitably a drain on local food resources and would expect to be billeted on a population already burdened by high tax demands of the crown. Although victuals were supposed to be paid for, army wages were irregular. There were particular difficulties if troops were based for long periods in the one area. This was very much the case for those troops that had gathered in the Rouen area while the siege of Harfleur was underway. The inhabitants of Daubeuf, just to the west of Louviers, complained in late October that they had had to give grain and hay to support soldiers for over two months.[34] The abbey of Bec also complained that the army 'stayed there continually devastating and destroying the whole region from the month of August right through to the battle'.[35] There was also a military consideration. The Pseudo-Elmham and Titus Livius suggest that once the French discovered what route the English were taking from Harfleur, they immediately sent out troops to denude the area of victuals for men and horses, to make the enemy short of food. This tactic had been used during the siege itself when the hinterland found itself at the mercy of both English and French companies. Local populations, therefore, hated the passage of troops even of their own supposed defenders. It is significant that in the order sent out on 20 September to raise troops in the *bailliage* of Amiens, those who refused to serve could be punished not only by arrest and seizure of their goods but also by having *mengeurs* billeted within their houses at their own expense.[36]

Chronicles suggest that the English did billet on some occasions in villages, but generally they would have slept in tents or in the open. The French would have billeted more frequently within dwellings but would also have found it necessary to pitch camp on some occasions. Thus they too would suffer from the inclement weather conditions of which chroniclers speak. In the *Chronique de Ruisseauville*, for instance, reference is made to 'filthy, wet and windy weather', and Walsingham also speaks of cold nights. Rainy conditions before the battle are also suggested in several texts. Many of the French who found themselves at Agincourt on 24 October were likely to be just as exhausted and demoralised as the English. Even if commanders on both sides were speaking reassuringly and inspirationally, the soldiers of both sides would have experienced trepidation. Battles were by their very nature uncertain events.

8

The Armies Assemble,
24–25 October 1415

On 24 October, the English army crossed the Ternoise at Blangy.[1] The *Gesta* tells us that as they reached the top of the hill on the other side, they saw 'emerging from higher up the valley about half a mile away from us the grim looking ranks of the French'. According to Monstrelet, Henry's scouts operating ahead of the main army reported that the French were 'coming from all directions in great companies of men to lodge at *Ruisseauville* and Agincourt so that they could get in front of the English to fight them on the next day'. In response to their own intelligence that the English were now in the area south of Maisoncelle, the French began to take up a hostile position across the broad field, facing the English as they approached. With French patrols much in evidence and troops continuing to arrive, it was impossible for Henry to have moved his army away from danger. Such an act would also have been dishonourable. His response was to draw his own men into battle formation, since he anticipated that the French intended to give battle that day. According to the Berry Herald, Thursday 24 October was indeed the day that the French had assigned for the battle.

This chronicler tells us, however, that the place the French had chosen was Aubigny in Artois not Agincourt, and that Henry, having accepted the challenge, had not kept his promise but had moved in the opposite direction. If this was true, the French had needed to decide upon another location at which to engage. The Religieux supports the notion that there had been a change of plan:

> …suddenly, at the order of some leaders whose names I do not know, the French were ordered to change their position and to move off to establish themselves elsewhere. They obeyed, but not without regret for they foresaw that this manoeuvre was to the benefit of the enemy.

Unfortunately, in terms of French movements beyond Péronne we have very little to go on. The French are described in Monstrelet as moving towards Saint-Pol, before reaching *Ruisseauville* and Agincourt. He mistakenly places Saint-Pol on the river Aunun. What his account probably means is that the French moved northwards along the left bank of the Ternoise before crossing the river at Anvin. From there they would have proceeded via Crépy and Tramecourt towards *Ruisseauville*. The small valley over which the author of the *Gesta* saw them may therefore have been that in which Tramecourt lay, and along which the 'fond de Caniers', an unmetalled road, still runs today. Moving to the east of the English, they had managed to get ahead and to block Henry's path.

Saint-Pol also lay on the river Scarpe, 20km directly west of Aubigny. It is possible, therefore, that the French army, or at least some of it, had initially assembled at Aubigny before moving westwards to intercept the English at Agincourt. Although many of the leading commanders had gathered with their men at Péronne, Monstrelet also speaks of the French being at Bapaume when the English were at Monchy-Lagache. In addition, according to Dynter, the Duke of Brabant responded to the letters from Péronne that he received on 21 October by ordering his troops to join him at Cambrai. The latter lay 50km south-south-east of Aubigny via a direct route through Arras. If the battle site had already been decided at this point as Agincourt, an assembly point further north might have been expected for Brabant's company. On 25 October the duke was, according to Dynter, at Lens-en-Artois. This was only 18km north-east of Aubigny but 48km distant from Agincourt. Could it be that Duke Anthony had expected battle to be given at Aubigny? Dynter reports that he later discovered that the Count of Nevers had sent letters to the duke on 22 October, encouraging him to rush to fight in the battle, and that other letters had been sent about the English movements. Dynter laments that the duke did not read all of these, since, had he done so, he would have not tried to move so quickly on 25 October in order to reach Agincourt. He arrived late at the battle, made an impromptu coat of arms out of the flag of one of his trumpeters, and was killed. It may be, therefore, that news of the intended location of the battle, or of a change of location, had been slow in circulating. This explains why other French troops arrived late or not at all, a point to which we shall return.

Whether or not Agincourt was a second choice for the engagement or not, we do not know when it was decided upon or by whom. The Burgundian chroniclers simply tell us that the constable planted the royal banner 'in the field they had chosen in the county of Saint-Pol in the territory of Agincourt'. Waleran of Luxembourg, Count of Saint-Pol, died on 10 April 1415. His first wife was Margaret Holland, half-sister of Richard II. Their daughter, Jeanne, was married to Duke Anthony of Brabant. Waleran had committed himself to hostile acts against Henry IV in the early years of the century. He became constable of France when d'Albret joined the League of Gien in 1411, but lost the office when John the Fearless was declared a traitor in 1413. In the war against the Armagnacs in

1412 he had campaigned jointly with Boucicaut. This link may be significant in the choice of the battlefield. It also possible that the marshal knew it through campaigns in the area against the Burgundians in 1414. There were also lords from the region present at the battle, who may have influenced the decision. Jacques de Heilly, for instance, had been captain of Beauquesne near Doullens in 1408.[2]

The area between Agincourt and *Ruisseauville* offered a large open site which was relatively flat in an area that was otherwise undulating, especially to its immediate north. More significant, perhaps, was its geographical position. For the French it was imperative to intercept Henry before he came too close to Calais. Although the Religieux tell us that the Picards had managed to thwart the southward sorties of a three-hundred-strong company from Calais, there was always the danger that, if the engagement took place near the English march where there were comparable flat areas, garrison troops from the various English garrisons could, if alerted in time, enter into the fray as reinforcements, and, even worse, attack the French from the rear. Furthermore, the French may have reckoned that if they fought and won at Agincourt, they were close enough to proceed immediately to attacking Calais. Such a manoeuvre would be double revenge for Edward III's victory at Crécy in 1346.

Henry expected battle to be given as soon as he arrived at the field that the French had selected. A fascinating aspect of the Agincourt narratives is the space they give to the events of Thursday 24 October. We are thereby provided with an insight into a 'phoney battle', but certain problems arise as a result. As we shall see, some of the events that have been taken to characterise Agincourt are ascribed by the most reliable chroniclers to 24 rather than 25 October. Since the English prepared for battle twice, chroniclers also show themselves to be confusing the two occasions. This affects our reading not only of the events of 24 October but also of 25 October.

The *Gesta* tells us that Henry lost no time in drawing up his army into 'battles and wings as if they were to go immediately into action'. Titus Livius adds that he distributed to each leader the order and place for the proposed conduct of the battle, with the Pseudo-Elmham adding that he chose the position for his army 'with the advice of experienced soldiers'. All these English texts note that arrangements were made for the soldiers to make confession, as was customary before engagement. This is also seen in the Burgundian chroniclers, who comment 'you could have seen the English thinking that battle was to be given that Thursday paying their devotions, all kneeling with their hands towards heaven asking God to keep them in his protection'. Le Fèvre adds that 'this was true as I was with them'. The English chroniclers and the Religieux imply that Henry made an oration. The longest version is provided in the Pseudo-Elmham, especially in relation to the king's emphasis that God was on his side. In one version of the *Brut* chronicle, Henry bade his men be of good cheer: 'for they should have a fair day and a gracious victory and the better of their enemies'. He added that he would rather die that day than be taken by enemy, 'for he would never put the realm of England to ransom for his person'. This chronicle continues with the Duke of York asking for and being granted command of vanguard. The king then ordered each man to provide himself with a stake, although in another version of the *Brut* chronicle heavily influenced by later Yorkist propaganda, it was the Duke of York who made this instruction.

Although the *Gesta* is less explicit about the king's oration, this chronicle, as also the *Liber Metricus*, gives as part of the preparations on 24 October the story that Sir Walter Hungerford expressed to the king a wish that he might have had, in addition to those present, 'ten thousand of the best archers in England who would have been only too glad to be there'. The king rebutted him with his belief that God, 'with these His humble few', would be able to overcome 'the arrogance of the French'. This has become one of the legends of Agincourt, largely because of Shakespeare's use of the incident. Whether it actually occurred is impossible to know. Hungerford was certainly present at the battle and was closely connected with the king, being one of the executors of his will and steward-elect of the household. The supposed royal reply is closely modelled, however, on biblical precedent, with a direct link being drawn to divine support for Judas Maccabeus. It may be, therefore, that the author of the *Gesta* embellished an off-the-cuff remark by one of Henry's captains into an opportunity to show Henry's complete faith in divine intervention. The incident must be seen in the light of hindsight. The English won in emphatic fashion. It was not surprising that they should consider that God had been on their side, nor that this was because of divine approval for Henry's kingship.

Henry was astute enough not to be taken by surprise. Thus he kept his men in their battle array until night started to fall and it was clear that there would be no combat that day. It is not wholly certain to what extent the French had drawn up their lines. According to the Burgundian writers, the French, who could see the English, 'also thought that they would fight that Thursday and so stopped and put themselves into formation, putting on their armour, unfurling banners and dubbing many knights'. No action seems to have taken place. According to the *Gesta*, the French simply took measure of the small size of the English and then withdrew 'to a field at the far side of a certain wood which was close at hand to our left between us and them, where lay our road towards Calais'. This prompted Henry to move his army, since he feared that the French plan was to circle around the wood to make a surprise attack or even to circle around the more distant woodlands of the area so that they could surround the English on every side. So the chroniclers observe that he moved his own lines, 'ensuring that they always faced the enemy'.

It is impossible to plot positions on the map since we do not know where either side established themselves. At sunset, which was around 4.40 p.m., Henry stood his army down and had it pitch camp for the night. The *Gesta* notes that the king himself took up quarters in a nearby hamlet, where there were a few

houses as well as gardens and orchards in which to billet. Titus Livius says that
a little house was found for him. The place is not identified in English texts, but
Le Fèvre and Waurin have Henry moving his army to lodge at Maisoncelle. With
night descending, the French also established their camp. All accounts suggest
that the two camps were quite close. In Titus Livius, 250 paces is cited. In the
Gesta, no measurement is given but the camps were near enough to be in earshot.
This point is also made by Le Fèvre and Waurin, with a distance of a quarter of a
league mentioned. Monstrelet expresses the gap as three bowshots, Fenin as four.
A bowshot can be taken to be around 150 metres.

The Gesta tells us that the French lit fires and established heavily manned
watches across fields and roads in case the English tried to make off under cover
of darkness. No French account confirms this. It is possible, therefore, that it was
included to denigrate the French, by emphasising that Henry had no intention to flee. In this context, we have to exercise caution over stories that the
French were so sure of victory that they cast dice that night for the king and his
nobles. It is unlikely that the English had spies so close to the French tents that
they could report this level of detail. The remark most likely reflects talk in the
English army as a means of encouraging a spirit of resistance. This was the kind
of tale deliberately circulated to fan English hatred of the French in anticipation
of armed engagement on the morrow. This is very much how the story is told
in Walsingham. He has it that the French had published abroad that they would
spare no one save for the king and certain named lords; the rest would be killed
or else have their limbs mutilated: 'Because of this our men were much excited to
rage and took heart, encouraging one another against the event'.[3] The vernacular
chronicles develop this to include the notion that the French not only gambled
for the king and his lords but also 'bid for an archer a blanc of their money for
they intended to have them as their own'. These are good stories, but they cannot
be taken as evidence of what was happening in the French camp.

English texts emphasise that Henry ordered complete silence in his camp. The
truth of this is proved by the detailed account which the Gesta gives of the pen-
alties for transgression. These were graded according to status: the men-at-arms,
here described as 'gentlemen' (generosi) were to lose their horse and equipment,
while anyone of the status of valettus or below would have their right ear cut
off. Archers were sometimes called valetti, although the term was also used for
servants. This reminds us of the strong social division between the two military
ranks, even though some archers would be young men who later in their careers
became men-at-arms. Le Fèvre and Waurin also remark that 'as for the English,
never did anyone make such little noise. It was hard to hear them speak to each
other since they spoke so low'.

Why did Henry want silence in his camp?[4] The principal answer is to be found
in the Pseudo-Elmham. Henry there orders his men to refrain from making their
customary noise and clamour, 'in case the enemy might thereby devise some

means of annoying them'. Henry feared that the French might mount a surprise attack during the night. Therefore he wanted his men to be on their guard. It was imperative to ensure that any necessary commands and trumpet summons would be heard and responded to quickly. Indeed, Monstrelet suggests that during the night the Duke of Orléans ordered Richemont to take his men 'almost right up to where the English had camped'. The English allegedly put themselves in formation outside the limits of their camp and both sides began to fire on each other, but then the French returned to their billets and nothing else happened during the night. The exact truth of this incident is uncertain, although we might have expected some activities to be carried out even at night, so that each side could gauge the strength of the other. The Pseudo-Elmham, which drew on information from Walter Hungerford, has it that the king decided that an acquaintance with the place where the battle would be fought on the next day would be useful. As a result, he sent some knights by moonlight to examine the field. According to the chronicler, this did indeed give him information, 'the better to help him array his forces'. The moon would have been in its last quarter on this date so that visibility would not have been easy, but it is tempting to believe that all commanders would, where possible, try to reconnoitre in advance the field of battle. Otherwise how did Henry choose the position for his troops on the next day?

There are other reasons why the king should require silence in his camp. It encouraged prayerfulness, and it is likely that confessions continued to be heard through the night in preparation for the conflict of the next day, since men would not want to die unshriven. Silence also kept bodies rested and minds focused, and discouraged panic talk. Opportunity was also taken to make preparations. Le Fèvre and Waurin have the archers renewing their strings and the men-at-arms getting their 'aiguillets' ready. This probably means the extra protective pieces of armour which would be worn specifically in hand-to-hand combat on foot. It is also possible that Henry intended the silence of his camp to disconcert the French, even to prompt them into fearing that he might launch a night attack on them.[5] This impression would have been encouraged if, as Monstrelet suggests, the English sounded their trumpets and other instruments during the night 'so much that the earth round echoed to their sounds'. The *Liber Metricus* has it that the silence of the camp made them think that Henry was intending to flee, and that they therefore rode out over the fields to investigate.

What of the French camp? Not surprisingly there is little comment in English texts, save for the *Gesta*'s claim that he could hear men calling out for their servants and friends because they were so much separated 'in so great a host'. The Burgundian chroniclers also say that there was so much noise from pages and servants that the English could hear it, but they add that the French had hardly any musical instruments to cheer them up. Their accounts provide detail on how, after the army had been stood down from its lines, the French camp was established in the field between Agincourt and Tramecourt where the battle was fought the next day, although it is difficult to assign a location on today's map. Monstrelet has the lords bivouacking in the field near their banners, but the lower ranks lodged in villages nearby, an interesting contrast with the tendency of the English to place the king in a building. Banners and pennons were furled, armour taken off, mules and trucks unpacked, bonfires lit. The herbergers were sent into villages to find straw and litter to sleep on and to put underfoot. This was necessary, the authors claim, because the ground had been so churned up by the trampling of horses. In the account of the Religieux, the ground was in this condition because it had been newly worked over and torrents of rain had flooded it and turned it into a quagmire'. It was therefore hard to sleep. The Burgundian chroniclers say that it rained all night. This is not found in the *Gesta* but it is mentioned in the *Liber Metricus* and by Capgrave. The impact of folkloric traditions is seen in the Burgundian comment that the French horses were quiet that night – an omen of what was to happen on the next day. The comment on musical instruments may be intended to be further indication of this, although it may also suggest lack of organisation and co-ordination.

English writers credit the French with choosing not to give battle on Thursday 24 October, while having it that Henry was ready to engage. In the *Gesta* the French watch the English and then take to their camp when they realise that no battle is going to happen. The Pseudo-Elmham develops this in order to extol further the virtues of his own side: 'The enemy noted the keen expectation of such a small army and its worthy preparations, and gathering themselves for a night's rest, refused to enter the contest of harsh battle on that day.' An even more bellicose tone is found in Hardyng: 'On Thursday the king suddenly moved his army by riding in full array towards them'. The Burgundian writers imply that both sides thought battle might be given but are neutral in assigning responsibility to either side for the fact that it was not. Neither they nor any English accounts mention any negotiations between the two sides on the Thursday, but this is a theme in some French texts. As a result, these texts suggest that it was the English who were responsible for not wanting to fight on that day.

The Berry Herald suggests that the English sought a truce until the next day, which was agreed. In the account of the Religieux, the English also sent representatives to the French, after Henry had held a council with the principal leaders of his army about what should be done. Their initial reaction was that they should fight, and as a result the churchmen with them were ordered to start their prayers. Yet when they saw just how many French they were up against, they decided to open talks and to offer to give up what they had conquered in return for being allowed to leave the country unharmed. Des Ursins also claims that the English made these approaches, specifically mentioning that they would surrender Harfleur and restore their prisoners without giving ransom, 'or to come to a final peace and deliver hostages as guarantees'. Waurin and Le Fèvre have it that Henry gave all the prisoners who were with his army licence to leave in return for their promise that they would surrender to him if he won the day, 'if they still lived'. It was not common practice for those already taken prisoner to be allowed to join their side to fight. Therefore, this story is unlikely to be true.

Two problems arise with the accounts of negotiations in the Religieux and Des Ursins. The first is that it is impossible to be certain that they belong to the Thursday rather than the Friday. As we shall see in the next chapter, several chroniclers have it that there were talks on the Friday morning. While the Religieux emphatically says that the approaches were made on 24 October, Des Ursins could be read as meaning the day of the battle. The second problem relates to the blame culture that developed after the battle. The purpose of inclusion of this story in both chronicles is to show the folly of the French in rejecting English approaches for peace. As the Religieux puts it, 'the annals of earlier reigns [Poitiers is mentioned in particular] ought to have served as lesson for the lords of France that the rejection of such reasonable conditions had often been cause for repentance… But having too much confidence in their forces and guided by the poor advice of some of their company they rebutted all proposals for peace and made reply to the king of England that they would give battle on the next day'. Des Ursins is more expansive, claiming that the French did debate the English approaches. Some advised they should let the English pass without giving battle, since it was always a dangerous event. Others said the French were well armed and strong, while the English were foolish and poorly armed, with the *jacques* of their archers in tatters. They were away from home, 'and would sooner sell themselves than be defeated'. Some disagreed, mentioning particularly that disaster could easily befall if the English archers engaged the French men-at-arms, who were heavily armed and could easily get out of breath. Harfleur would be easy to recover, they claimed. But if they decided to fight then they should employ the communes who would be useful. These views were apparently those of d'Albret and Boucicaut, and of others with experience in arms. The Dukes of Bourbon, Alençon and others wanted to fight. Since the English had already shown how panic-stricken they were in making the approach for negotiations, they would be easily defeated and they would not need the help of the communes. They accused those who did not want to fight of cowardice. As a result, it was decided to give battle. This passage is full of the wisdom of hindsight. It is impossible to know whether a debate of this kind on the eve of battle or whether any English approaches were made.

The passage is more significant, perhaps, for what it suggests about who was present. The implication is that d'Albret, Boucicaut, Bourbon and Alençon were already at the field. At the beginning of the passage, however, the chronicler says: 'they had already diligently sent to seek the duke of Orléans, the duke of Brabant, the count of Nevers, and others'. The suggestion is therefore that not all of the French lords and their troops had arrived on Thursday 24 October. This was why the French did not give battle on that day. This takes us to the heart of the matter concerning the French at Agincourt. What size did they intend their army to be, and who was to be in command?

They had certainly planned for an engagement with the English. We have already discussed the BL plan devised for the army, which the French had deployed to bring Henry to battle near the Somme.[6] It contained two battles, a van containing the men of d'Albret and Boucicaut and a main battle with the men of Alençon, Eu and other lords. If the English formed only one battle, then these two French battles were to be joined together. There were also to be two wings of foot, under Richemont on the right and Guichard Dauphin on the left. In front of these wings would be placed the archers. There would also be a thousand-strong cavalry under de Rambures to attack the English arches and a smaller mounted group of 200 under de Bosredon to attack the baggage. Subsequently another plan was drawn up at Rouen. This is to be found within the chronicle of des Ursins.[7] Since it names the Duke of Orléans as leader of the main battle, and hence, by implication, commander of the army as a whole, it must post-date the decision that the king and Dauphin would not engage but that the duke would, overturning a possible previous decision that Orléans, like Burgundy, should not serve in person. It may therefore be the result of a meeting at Rouen which Monstrelet dates to 20 October, although it is unlikely that Orléans was in the Norman capital at this point.[8] The decision may therefore have been taken in his absence.

The Rouen plan, as we shall call it, was for a larger army which included a greater range of nobility. Three battles were envisaged. The van would include the Duke of Bourbon, Boucicaut and Guichard Dauphin. In the main battle would be Orléans, Alençon, d'Albret and the Duke of Brittany. In the rearguard would be the Duke of Bar, the Count of Nevers, the Count of Charolais, and Ferry (Count of Vaudémont), brother of the Duke of Lorraine. The wings would be led by Richemont and Tanneguy du Chastel, the *prévôt* of Paris. The cavalry intended to break the archers would be under the admiral (either Clignet de Brabant or the Sire de Dampierre) and the Seneschal of Hainault (Jean, Sire de Ligne). Of those mentioned, Brittany, Charolais and Tanneguy du Chastel were not present at the battle.

The Duke of Brittany had been present in Rouen on 20 October, yet by 25 October he was only at Amiens, and had returned to Rouen by 3 November. We cannot know for certain whether he had deliberately delayed his advance so that he would not be present at the planned engagement, thereby saving the dilemma he faced as a result of his treaty with Henry V. Des Ursins claims that he did not wish to be present if the Duke of Burgundy was not going to be there. It may be, however, that his non-arrival was simply the result of poor intelligence as to where the battle would take place. This interpretation would gain extra credibility if the initial intention had been to give battle at Aubigny. Whatever the reason for his absence, it was certainly an important element in the subsequent culture of blame. There were some Bretons present at the battle, however, within the retinue of Richemont. Gruel gives several names, including his standard-bearer, the Sire de Buisson.

For the Count of Charolais, we have a lengthy explanation for his absence in the Burgundian chronicles. They claim that as d'Albret moved towards Artois, he sent the Sire de Mongaugier to the count at Arras, to tell him of the decision that had been reached to fight the English and to request him on behalf of the king and the constable to be present. Charolais was keen to be there but his father, Duke John of Burgundy, told his son's governors that he should not be allowed to go into battle. To that end, they took the count to the castle of Aire near Ghent, to which d'Albret again sent messengers, including Mountjoye Herald. The count was kept ignorant of what was happening and of when the engagement was to take place, although some of his household managed to leave secretly in order to fight. When the count discovered that his father had forbidden him to go he 'took to his chamber in floods of tears'.[9] But is this story true? By the time the chroniclers were writing, Charolais was Duke Philip the Good of Burgundy. He probably felt the need to have a way of exculpating himself for his absence from the battle, especially in the light of his alliance with the English, from shortly after he became duke in 1419 until his reconciliation with Charles VII in 1435. Le Fèvre ends his version of the story with the following observation: 'I have heard tell that the count, even when he achieved the age of 67 [which was in 1463] was still annoyed that he had not had the good fortune to be at the battle, irrespective of whether he might have survived or been killed at it'. By the time these narratives were written, his father was long dead and therefore it was convenient to place the blame at his door. According to the text of Duke John's letters found in the chronicle of Des Ursins, his father had earlier told Charles VI that he would allow his son to take the field with as large a company as possible.[10] This makes it possible that the explanation of Charolais's absence is true and that the duke had changed his mind, or else had always been unwilling for his son to be present. Duke John knew well the horrors of battle, since he had been at Nicopolis in 1396, where he was captured and only released two years later. He may have wished not to risk the life of his only son, who was only nineteen at the time of Agincourt. As for Duke John's own absence, the king and Dauphin had requested him in letters sent out on 31 August not to be present. Although there are signs that the duke was preparing to set out with troops, there is no evidence that this original order was ever countermanded. The duke's absence was therefore not necessarily of his own choosing but was the result of continuing mistrust of him at the royal court. As for Charolais, the Bourgeois of Paris noted that on 20 October the French lords heard that the English were moving through Picardy, 'and my lord of Charolais was pressing so hard upon them'. Since this account was not written until the 1440s, by a pro-Burgundian commentator, this could again be simply flattery of the then Duke Philip. If it is true, then it is also possible that the count had set out but was countermanded by his father, or else had changed his own mind.

None the less, there were many of the duke's supporters at Agincourt. This is revealed by the names of the dead. At least twenty-two leading captains of the

Burgundian group were killed, including Jean, Sire de Croy and de Renty, one of the duke's favourites.[11] The duke's two brothers, the Duke of Brabant and the Count of Nevers, were killed. It cannot be said, therefore, that the army was 'Armagnac' in composition. Many of the duke's allies in Picardy and in the lands adjacent to his own were present at the battle. The Count of Nevers is given a larger role by some chroniclers, thereby betraying their Burgundian sympathies. The *Chronique de Ruisseauville*, for instance, claims that he rode against the English shortly after they crossed the Somme, but they drove him off. Whether he had joined with the main army before 24 October is not clear. Monstrelet claims that Boucicaut knighted him and other lords on the eve of battle, but as he was already in his mid-twenties, it would seem unlikely that he had not yet been dubbed. The chronicler adds later that Orléans was similarly dubbed on the eve of battle. The truth of this is also uncertain, although knightings before engagements were a common French practice. Richemont had been knighted before the assault on Soissons in 1414.[12] No English dubbings are evidenced before the battle.

On 21 October Nevers's son was baptised at Clamécy, which lay close to Vézelay. The baby's grandfather, the Duke of Burgundy, was present, and probably also his father. It is possible, therefore, that the count only arrived on 24 October. This may explain the comment in the Berry Herald that when d'Albret and the others discussed English offers on the eve of battle they had 'already diligently sent to seek' Nevers, as well as Orléans and Brabant. According to Dynter, Anthony, Duke of Brabant was still at Lens on the morning of the battle and had 48km to travel. He came as quickly as he could and arrived during the battle, but many of his troops were following more slowly and hence did not reach Agincourt. According to Waurin and Le Fèvre, he did not even have all of his equipment, so took a banner from one of his trumpeters and made a hole in it to use as his surcoat.

Another person mentioned in the Rouen plan who was not present at the battle was Tanneguy du Chastel. The likely explanation of his absence was the need to ensure that Paris was well defended, since it was feared that the Duke of Burgundy might take advantage of the absence of the king and Dauphin to move to the capital. There is no evidence that any troops from Paris were present at the battle. Chroniclers also comment on some further absences and late arrivals. Although it had been decided at Rouen that Louis, Duke of Anjou would not serve in person, probably because he was suffering from a bladder disease, there is a suggestion in the *Chronique de Normandie* that he had despatched a company of men, and that they had reached Amiens by Thursday 24 October. They set out on the following day, but did not arrive until it was all over. This is also found in Monstrelet, who says that the Sire de Longny came with 600 men of the duke during the battle. When about a league away, he met with several wounded French who told him what was happening. As a result he did not proceed any further.

We can be certain, therefore, that the French had not managed to assemble as large an army as they had intended. Furthermore the army was still assembling as the time of battle drew near. As we shall see in the following chapter, there are indications that the French tried to delay the start on Friday 25 October because they hoped that more men might arrive in time. This is not just significant in terms of numbers but also of command. The Rouen plan suggests that Orléans was to be commander-in-chief. He would be the senior member of the royal family at the battle. Yet he probably did not arrive until 24 October. The Berry Herald has him arriving on the morning of 25 October. This chronicler comments that 'all morning, barons, knights, and esquires arrived from all parts to assist the French'. Even if the majority had arrived on the previous day, it is extremely important to remember that the French army was made up of various groups of troops which had come together for the occasion of battle. The army that had followed Henry along the Somme had been together for several weeks, but it was now joined by many other companies at the last minute, coming in response to messages sent out.

This situation would have been disruptive and hardly conducive to the co-ordination of command in the crucial lead up to the battle. It is also a major contrast with the English position, since Henry's army had been together for the whole march and so had a stronger sense of unity of purpose and mutual trust. This was very important in establishing discipline in a battle situation. In contrast, the French were lacking in knowledge of each other and a feeling of cohesion. Furthermore, since d'Albret, Boucicaut and the other lords had previously devised a plan of engagement, as witnessed by the BL plan, there would have been confusion between the 'old' and 'new' plans, a situation exacerbated by the fact that not all of those intended to play their part in the battle had turned up to fight. Anxiety levels would have been high. There could also have been annoyance and anger on the part of the seasoned commanders. They had done so well in hounding the English progress, yet now found themselves subject to changes of plan and the command of a royal duke who had played no role in the campaign at all until this point. The differences of opinion reported by des Ursins and implied by the Religieux need to be seen in this context.

Two further questions remain about the French. The first is what formation they chose to adopt; the second how large their army was. The fullest and clearest description is given by the Berry Herald.[13] Although this is a late chronicle, it is to be expected that a herald would have an interest in the commands assigned to specific individuals. His account makes for particularly interesting reading when compared with the battle plans, and includes intriguing figures. He suggests that the French drew up only two battles. The van contained the marshal and constable with 3,000 men-at-arms, Bourbon with 1,200, and Orléans with 600, commanded on his behalf by the Sire de Gaules. This gives a total size for the French vanguard of 4,800. The main battle comprised the Duke of Bar with 600 men, the Count of Nevers with 1,200, the Count of Eu with 300, the Count of Marle with 400, the

Count of Vaudémont, brother of the Duke of Lorraine, with 300, and the Count of Roucy and Braine with 200, as well as the Duke of Brabant, who brought few men, and the barons of Hainault who put themselves under his banner. The main battle therefore totalled at least 3,000. On the right wing was Richemont, with the Vicomte de Bellière and the Lord of Combourg, with 600 men-at-arms. On the left wing was the Count of Vendôme, Guichard Dauphin (described as the grand master of the royal household), the Lords of Ivry, Hacqueville, Aumont and La Roche Guyon, as well as the household officers of the king, together totalling 600 men-at-arms. There is a later reference to a group of horsemen led by Clignet de Brabant and others which was ordered to strike against the enemy. The total number was therefore 9,000, plus the smaller groups for which numbers are not given. Remember that at the end of August, a royal order had indicated the king's intention of raising an army of 6,000 men-at-arms and 3,000 archers.[14] The figure given by Berry Herald appears identical, although it must be borne in mind that he does not distinguish between the kinds of troops.

What is noticeable in his account is that the vanguard was over one-and-a-half times as large as the main battle. It would seem that Orléans and d'Albret had placed themselves in the vanguard, while the Rouen plan had put them in the main battle. This 'front loading', as it were, of the French army tallies with comments in chronicles that everyone rushed to be in the front. The French deliberately created a very large vanguard because they considered they could smash the very small number of English men-at-arms with ease. The main battle included many of those who had been placed in the rearguard in the Rouen plan. The Count of Marle (whose seat lay to the north of Laon) was Robert de Bar, nephew of the duke. The seat of the Count of Roucy and Braine lay just to the south of Laon, and Vaudémont took his title from a place of that name south of Nancy. The duchy of Bar itself lay just to the west of Nancy.[15] This main battle was therefore largely made up of men from the area of the Marne and Meuse, in addition to the Count of Nevers, brother of Duke John of Burgundy. That only two battles were formed may have been the result of the non-arrival of those who had been expected to be present. Since du Chastel did not come, command of the left wing at the battle was given to the Count of Vendôme.

In des Ursins's second account of the battle, he also has the French forming only two battles. He does not name any commanders but says that the lords wanted to be in the 'first battle', which totalled 5,000 men 'who never wielded a blow'. His 'second battle' is described as containing 3,000, excluding the *gros valets*, archers and crossbowmen. There was also a cavalry company to break the archers, which was intended to be 400-strong. The numbers are very close to those given by the Berry Herald. The *Gesta* and the *Liber Metricus* also say that the French formed two battles. In the *Gesta* the vanguard was made up of the nobles and the pick of the men, all armed with spears. The author makes the ridiculous suggestion that it was 'thirty times more than all of our men put together'. On each flank there were squadrons of cavalry to break the archers. The rearguard was mounted, giving the chronicler the opportunity to remark that they looked as though they were 'more ready to flee than to tarry'.[16] Only the wings of cavalry are mentioned by Titus Livius and the Pseudo-Elmham, although both also comment that the French line was so wide in extent that the field was not able to hold the whole force, and that it was thirty-one deep, a figure chosen for effect and to give a false impression of accuracy. Since it is close to the *Gesta*'s figure of thirty-fold, it may derive from a popular notion circulating after the battle.

The remaining French chroniclers, however, speak of the French drawing up three battles – 'l'avant garde' (vanguard), 'la bataille' (main battle), and 'l'arrière garde' (rearguard), as they are named in Fenin and the *Chronique de Ruisseauville*. The Religieux speaks of the vanguard as comprising 5,000 men, commanded by the Count of Vendôme and Guichard Dauphin. The last-named is also placed in the van by the Burgundian chroniclers, who also put there the constable and marshal, the Dukes of Orléans and Bourbon, the Counts of Eu and Richemont, the Sire de Rambures and the Sire de Dampierre. The Burgundian chroniclers place in the main battle the Dukes of Bar and Alençon and the Counts of Nevers, Vaudémont, Blâmont, Salm, Grandpré and Roucy, a list that has many similarities with that given by the Berry Herald. They give the commanders of the rearguard as the Counts of Marle (whom Berry places in the main battle), Dammartin and Fauquembergues, and the Sire de Longroy. They also place Vendôme and the officers of the king on one wing, with 1,600 men, and Clignet de Brabant and Louis de Bosredon, with 800 mounted men, on the other, to attack the English archers. The Religieux assign this task to 1,000 of the best troops and add as leader the Sire de Gaules, whom des Ursins has commanding the troops of the Duke of Orléans in the van. In *Ruisseauville*, the Sire de Gaucourt is named alongside Clignet de Brabant. Dynter names only Clignet, giving him 1,200 men.

The Burgundian chroniclers do not give figures for the main battle or the rearguard but they do for the van, which they claim contained 8,000 men-at-arms, knights and esquires, 4,000 archers and 1,500 crossbowmen, giving a total of 13,500. There is mention in the account of the Religieux of an intention that 4,000 of the best crossbowmen should march in front, but the chronicler tells us that these troops were given permission to depart by the lords of the army on the pretext that they had no need of their help. Dynter gives a slightly different version of this. He speaks of the French putting the archers, crossbowmen and infantry in the rear, not wanting their aid, since they wished to capture the king of England by hand-to-hand fighting. This takes us back to the fact that the vanguard had been increased in size and noble presence. The Religieux speaks of the leaders each claiming for themselves the honour of leading the van. Fenin also claims that the majority of nobles and the flower of the army were put into the vanguard.

There is therefore confusion and discrepancy among the chronicles on the number of battles, and between the wings and the groups intended to break the

English archers. Some consistent features emerge, however. One is that cavalry was assigned to this last purpose. We shall discuss this action in more detail in the next chapter. The second consistency is that the vanguard was the largest battle and that it included many of the leading nobles. The plan was to create as large a van as possible so that the English men-at-arms would be completely overwhelmed by the weight of the first French attack. The vanguard as deployed on the day probably absorbed the two wings under Vendôme and Richemont. It is this that explains the observation of Titus Livius and Pseudo-Elmham that the French formation was too broad for the field. It is also possible that the French battles were not one directly behind the other, as historians have tended to assume, but were obliquely positioned, so that they stretched across the field as well as containing many rows of men.

The third consistency is the lack of participation of archers and crossbowmen. Only the Religieux account hazards a number, and also explains why they did not fight. The initial intention had been to raise 3,000 archers alongside 6,000 men-at-arms. Pay records for the army indicate that some retinues contained archers as well as men-at-arms. The *semonce des nobles* called on men to bring along archers and crossbowmen as well as men-at-arms. Yet where were all of these archers at the battle? A solution is provided by the Burgundian chroniclers, who suggest a mixed composition of men-at-arms, archers and crossbowmen for the van and main battle, although no clarification is given of the order in which each group was intended to proceed. Was it that the bowmen were required to fight as general infantry rather than as archers? This would increase further the weight of the French vanguard in their plan to overwhelm the English men-at-arms, but it presupposes the French bowmen had full armour and were integrated within the 'chevalerie' of the men-at-arms and their leaders. To know whether this is a credible interpretation requires more work to be done on archers in France in this period. Other possibilities are that the numbers of archers had not been raised as intended. Charles V had made efforts in the 1360s and '70s to build up a force of longbowmen and crossbowmen from the towns, but there are some signs that the lack of war from the late 1380s had caused decay in French archery. Certainly many of the units in the pay records for 1415 contain men-at-arms only. In 1416 the French recruited 550 crossbowmen from Genoa, but there had been no move to provide foreign troops in the previous year, although some Spanish names are to be found in companies of crossbowmen in the pay records.[17] Other possibilities are that the *gens de trait* were used in earlier stages of the campaign but released before the battle (as the Religieux implies), or that they were at the battle but held back in a rearguard and never deployed. In the *Gesta* there is an indication that the French did use crossbow fire. A further possibility is that the *gens de trait* were used but that chroniclers simply do not mention them. After all, they had plenty of other disasters to report. They also tended to pursue a blame culture which singled out the French nobles, knights, esquires and others of gentle status who fought as men-at-arms, collectively called the 'chevalerie', for the shame of the defeat.

The problem of the *gens de trait* makes it particularly difficult to know how many soldiers the French had at the battle. Appendix B shows the great variety of figures cited in chronicles. The most obvious feature is that English sources accredit the French with much larger numbers than do their own chroniclers. The English estimates, stretching from 60,000 to as high as 160,000, are completely impossible. France was not able to raise armies of this size until several centuries later. It is not surprising that the English should exaggerate French numbers and minimise their own, since this made Henry's victory seem all the greater. The Burgundian chroniclers also give a high total number of 50,000, although the figures for the constituent elements of vanguard, wings etc. are lower. These writers were also keen to heighten the sense of defeat, since it was the fault of a government that was largely Armagnac-controlled. The figures given in other French chronicles are more circumspect. The lowest, 10,000, is found in the Berry Herald and in Gruel's *Chronique de Richemont*. In both cases, the English army is said to be larger, although only marginally so. Figures for those killed and taken prisoner at the battle are not very useful in helping us to gauge total army size. As we shall see in Chapter 10, fewer than 700 in total can be identified by name and chroniclers' estimates are as unreliable for casualties as they are for the army size as a whole.

Can we ascertain more reliable figures from the pay records? At the end of August, the intention was to raise an army of 6,000 men-at-arms and 3,000 archers.[18] As in England, this would be made up of companies of various sizes under individual lords. Each company would itself be made up of smaller groups under knights and esquires. For three lords, we have firm evidence of the size and composition of the company intended to be under their command. The Count of Vendôme was paid for 300 *escuiers* (men-at-arms) and 150 *gens de trait*, the Duke of Berry for 1,000 + 500, and the Sire de Ligne for 120 + 60.[19] For the other lords known to have companies in September and October, such as d'Albret and Alençon, we have details of some of their constituent groups but not of the total number of troops. However, it is unlikely that any would have had as many men as were expected of the Duke of Berry. As in Henry V's army, the largest retinues in the French army would have been held by the members of the royal family, with those of highest status having the largest retinues. Des Ursins tells us that both Burgundy and Orléans were asked to provide 500 men-at-arms. The letter of Duke John dated 24 September mentions a royal request for 500 men-at-arms and 300 archers.[20] This may imply that Orléans had been asked to provide the same number of archers. Gruel speaks of 500 men under Richemont.

What is uncertain, however, is whether these contingents fell within the 9,000-strong army. In the case of Richemont and all others, such as d'Albret, Alençon etc, known to be in active service with the army tracking Henry's progress along the Somme, we can suggest that they did. Richemont was leading not only his own men but also troops from the Dauphin's household. The Dauphin had requested troops from the town of Mantes but we do not know how many were provided.[21] Although the Count of Marle can be shown to have companies under his command from early October, the other lords from the Marne and Meuse area, such as Roucy, Braine and Bar, joined the army only after it moved away from the Somme. This also applies to the Duke of Bourbon, whose companies appear from 12 October when he joined the king and Dauphin at Rouen. Even if we consider Burgundy's numbers as outside the 9,000-strong army, a problem arises over whether the troops brought by his brothers, the Count of Nevers and the Duke of Brabant, lay within the contingent requested of Duke John or whether they were separate. For Brabant we have some information derived from the archives of towns and from the duke's *recette générale*.[22] The exact size of his company remains elusive but the financial records reveal that 219 horses were used in the expedition, which implies that the duke's men-at-arms cannot have exceeded this number. They were mainly men of his household, although troops were also requested from Louvain, Brussels and Anvers (Antwerp). The latter may have sent fifty-seven men, presumably mainly archers and crossbowmen, although there is evidence of a reluctance to raise troops. The town companies were ordered to assemble at Cambrai, to which the duke's vassals and officials elsewhere in his duchy were to send their men. How many arrived at the battle in time is uncertain. Only thirty-seven men under the duke can be identified by name, and the Burgundian chroniclers suggest that the majority of his men did not travel as quickly as he did and therefore did not participate in the battle.

Although muster rolls show that men-at-arms served as individuals, some would have been accompanied at their own expense by *gros varlets*, military servants who had limited defensive and offensive equipment and who could be given some function in combat, as the BL plan indicates. There were some urban militias, although these contingents were rarely more than fifty-strong. We know that some companies were summoned from the towns of the north. Contamine mentions four places in this context.[23] The first is Senlis, although we have no idea of how many men, if any, were sent.[24] The same is true of Saint-Omer.[25] Amiens is known to have provided thirty crossbowmen (*arbalétriers*) and twenty-five shield-men (*pavesiers*).[26] Tournai paid for two months' service its customary company of fifty *arbalétriers* and twenty *pavesiers*, led by Ernoul le Muisit, who had also commanded the urban militia in 1412, but it is possible that these men were guarding the king at Rouen rather than serving at the battle.[27]

It could be argued that the army must have contained at least 6,000 men-at-arms and 3,000 *gens de trait*, since those were the numbers planned for in terms of pay, but we have no guarantee that they were achieved or that all of the companies in evidence in September and early October were still in service at the time of the battle. We can assume that we should add additional numbers for soldiers brought by Orléans, Bourbon, Nevers, Brabant and others from the northern and eastern areas, who joined the army late in the day. These cannot have numbered more than 2,500, to which we need to add about 500 or so who responded within Picardy to the second issue of the *semonce* of 20 September. The presence of local men is evidenced by deaths in the battle. All in all, this suggests a total around 12,000, with at least two-thirds of its strength being men-at-arms.

This may seem a small figure but it is not incompatible with what we know of French armies in this period. Although armies of 15-16,000 men were raised in the 1380s, these had been drawn from the whole kingdom. In 1415 there was very little recruitment south of the Loire save for the companies of Bourbon and Orléans.[28] In June 1414 the king had hoped to raise an army of 10,000 men-at-arms and 4,500 *gens de trait* for war against Burgundy, but there is no firm evidence that this was achieved.[29] Furthermore, in 1415 some troops were kept to protect the king in Rouen and to ensure the defence of Paris. The military resources available to the French in 1415 were limited. It is possible that Burgundy could have been called upon to make a larger contribution, had there not been so much mistrust towards him. In the summer of 1414 he had probably raised 2,250 troops for the defence of his lands.[30] The army at Agincourt would also have been larger if Brittany had arrived in time, although Basin's figure of 10,000 troops under his command is not credible.

For the English army we have much firmer evidence of size. As we saw, the army had been reduced by 2,568 men as a result of the siege. Not all of the losses can be differentiated between men-at-arms and archers, but if we simply divide the number equally we can suggest that there were at least 1,593 men-at-arms and 7,139 archers at the battle, a total of 8,732 men. This is a minimum figure, taking the army size at its lowest possibility at departure. If the higher Cheshire figures are used, then the relevant figures are 1,643 men-at-arms and 7,632 archers, a total of 9,275 men.

The English army, at a few hundred either side of 9,000 men, was not small by contemporary standards. What made it distinctive, and what made it very different from its French counterpart, was its composition. It had a relatively small number of men-at-arms but high numbers of archers. In terms of proportions, men-at-arms made up less than one quarter of the whole force. This had been the case from the very outset of the campaign. If Henry had considered the possibility of battle with the French right from the start, then he would already have needed to think how best to deploy an army of this kind. It is likely that both of the armies that fought at Shrewsbury in 1403 had a large proportion of archers. Although only sixteen on that occasion, he would have gained some insight into deployment in battle situation. This was not the case, however, for the men appointed, according to the *Gesta*, to lead the van and rearguard at Agincourt: Edward, Duke of York (b. *c.* 1373) and Thomas, Lord Camoys (b. *c.* 1350).[31] Neither had been at Shrewsbury. Indeed, relatively few of the English army at Agincourt would have experienced a battle situation already. There would have been some who had fought alongside, and even against, Henry in 1403, and perhaps even a handful who had been present at Nicopolis. Battles were rare occurrences, so that Henry's experience already marked him out, both within his own army and among all of the warriors assembled at Agincourt.

The men he chose as his commanders at the battle had other qualities to recommend them. Camoys had served in an expedition to France in 1380, but there is no evidence he served in Wales or France under Henry IV. No other command is known for him during the expedition. The reason he was chosen was his age. Camoys, at sixty-five, was one of the oldest men at the battle, older even than Sir Thomas Erpingham, who was seven years his junior. The latter was assigned a command role in giving the signal to advance. These men were chosen by Henry because their advanced age gave them natural authority over other captains and, more importantly, over the soldiers as a whole. Henry's troops would have been filled with trepidation at the prospect of battle. Old men would be able to re-assure and keep discipline in equal measure. On the assumption that the rearguard was set further back and would engage last, this was particularly important, since the line would need to hold steady while it saw its comrades engage. The choice of the Duke of York was based on his proximity to the king. He was the king's second cousin, and the most senior royal present after the king and his youngest brother, Humphrey, Duke of Gloucester. The latter could not be given command as he had as yet no military activity under his belt. Clarence had been invalided home, although the king probably would have intended him to have a major command role, as he had done at the siege. York was the most experienced senior commander present at the battle, having served in Guienne, Wales and France, the last as recently as 1412. His involvement in command is seen at every stage of the campaign.

Although certain choices were open to Henry, deployment for battle was for-malised to a very great degree. The formation of three battles, van, centre or main, and rearguard, was commonplace. In Titus Livius and the Pseudo-Elmham, the king is placed in command of the middle battle (*acies media*), which was located in the field directly opposite the battle of the enemy. To the right was the vanguard (*acies prima*) and also the right wing (*ala dextra*), and on the left the rearguard (*acies postrema*) and the left wing (*ala sinistra*). These writers also claim that the three battles (*acies*) were very close together and nearly joined. No mention is made of the position of the archers. The *Gesta* says that Henry formed one battle (*bellum unum*) because of his lack of numbers, placing his vanguard (*aciem anteriorem*) as a wing on the right and his rearguard (*aciem posteriorem*) as a wing on the left. The chronicler adds that he positioned groups of archers in between each battle ('et intermisset cuneos sagittariorum cuilibet aciei').

The difficulty is knowing what all of these terms mean. The Latin vocabulary does not translate easily. The deployment in Titus Livius and the Pseudo-Elmham could indicate that there were three battles of men-at-arms, but positioned close together across the field, and that the archers were on the wings to the far right and left. We must remember, however, that no indication of the types of troops in the battles and wings is given by these two writers. All their formations could be made up of both men-at-arms and archers. After all, the retinues that made up the army were, save for the special archer companies, made up of both kinds of troops. The problem is knowing whether the administrative structure of the army also determined its deployment at battles or other engagements. Did retinues fight together, or were the different kinds of troops separated from each other? Or was there a middle way, where some mixed retinues were kept together and others separated by type of soldier?

A second issue is how the troops arrayed across the field. We would expect the van to be in front of the middle battle and the rearguard positioned slightly further back. This staggered deployment had certainly been used by the English at Crécy. In no chronicle account of Agincourt, however, is this clarified, and commentators have tended to draw the English position as a straight line. This may be a valid conclusion. It works particularly well if we think that the three battles contained only men-at-arms. Because Henry had relatively few such troops, it would be sensible to form a close and reasonably continuous line across the field, perhaps around four deep (a figure suggested later in Titus Livius). This would not prevent the line being oblique so that the right end of it was set forward and the left slightly further back. If men are placed in one straight line, it is more difficult to recover when that line is broken. If some troops are set forward and some back, the enemy who have broken through one group have then to engage with another.

The real difficulty comes over the positioning of the archers. The implication of the *Gesta* is that the archers were in groups between the main battle and its wings of van and rearguard. It has been suggested that they were arrayed in triangular-shaped formations with the apex towards the enemy. The relevant phrase can be interpreted as meaning, however, that each battle had archers within it.[32] Logic suggests that whichever interpretation is accepted, the archers have to be in front of the men-at-arms. There are similarities here with Monstrelet's description of the English deployment. Here Henry drew up his battle ('fist ordonner sa bataille'), putting the archers in the front and then the men-at-arms ('mettant les archers au front devant et puis les hommes d'armes'). Monstrelet then adds that Henry made two wings of men-at-arms and archers with similar arrangements ('et puis fist ainsi comme deux eles de gens d'armes and d'archers'). Monstrelet's wording could be taken as meaning that the archers either stood in lines in front of the men-at-arms or that they were grouped into units in a forward position. In these interpretations, the army is protected by forward-placed outworks of archers behind stakes. This would tally with the little that there is in the account of the Religieux on the English position. In the speech which the author assigns to Henry, he has the king say that 'our 12,000 archers will range themselves in a circle around us to sustain as best they can the shock of the enemy'.

An alternative view is that the archers were placed solely on the flanks. Waurin and Le Fèvre have it that Henry created only one battle, into which he placed all of his men-at-arms, putting his archers on their flanks. The original Latin text of Dynter has Henry placing his archers on one side and his men-at-arms on the other, but in the early French translation of this chronicle the archers are placed in front on the wings. This is also implied in Walsingham. Although the latter does not describe the English formation, he claims that in Henry's order to advance, 'he made the archers go first from the right and also from the left'. Historians have warmed to the idea of the archers being on the flanks because it prevents both them and their stakes getting in the way of the men-at-arms as they move forward. It also helps to explain the funnelling effect on the French advance, since archers firing from the sides would keep the French in close and restricted formation as they moved towards the English line.

The intended use of stakes is the only indication of any proposed deployment on the part of Henry that we are given during the march. According to the *Gesta*, after the engagement at Corbie the king ordered the archers to prepare a stake six feet long. He further commanded 'that whenever the French army drew near to do battle and to break their ranks by columns of horse, all the archers were to drive in their stakes in front of them in line abreast'. The stake was to be driven in dia-gonally, so that one end pointed up towards the enemy at waist height. The remainder of the order, although awkwardly expressed by the chronicler, gives an indication of the intended positioning of the archers. Some of them, we are told, were to drive in their stakes 'further back and in between', implying that there was a complex formation of stakes and not simply one line behind which the archers were to stand. Assuming that all of the archers had a stake, then this would create a formidable barrier to the enemy cavalry. Henry already anticipated that the latter would attempt a charge against his archers but hoped that the stakes would cause the horses to retreat or to become impaled, thereby throwing their rider. Safe behind their dense barrier, the archers could cause further damage by their arrow fire.

The *Gesta* tells us that the king's order had arisen from 'information divulged by some prisoners', which had led to the rumour circulating in the army that the French had assigned groups of cavalry to ride against the archers in battle. The BL plan confirms that this was part of the French tactics. The implication is that until the engagement at Corbie, Henry had not considered that his archers might be vulnerable. This is surely further indication that he had begun his march wishing to avoid battle. That said, once he knew of French intentions he had several days to think further and discuss with his leading captains how the archers and men-at-arms might best be deployed. He would have been able to anticipate that his men-at-arms would be severely outnumbered and that therefore the arrow power of the archers would be crucial in damaging the French before they could engage.

Henry did not invent the idea of the stakes. They seem first to have been used by the Ottomans at Nicopolis to protect their foot archers. The havoc they wrought on the crusader cavalry was mentioned in the *Livre des fais* of Boucicaut, based on his own experience of the battle, and, as noted earlier, it is possible that there were a few veterans of Nicopolis in the English army.[33] Where Henry deserves credit is in putting to good effect the lie of the land at Agincourt. In this respect he was fortunate that the French did not give battle on 24 October, and that he had ample opportunity to have reconnaissance of the field. The field was narrow but falling away quite steeply. This enabled him to disguise the weight of his archers by 'hiding' them, not only behind stakes but also on the inclines, which would have had some cover of scrub and trees but not enough to block their fire. It would have been extremely difficult for the French to see exactly how many archers the English had. This can be seen even today. As one walks from the French position towards the English, it is difficult to have full view laterally across the field. At the likely seat of battle on the road across from La Gacogne to Agincourt, visibility is particularly affected by the way the ground falls away on the flanks. Such limitations on view, especially when wearing visors, led the French to underestimate the threat the archers posed. In particular, the cavalry may have misconstrued how many there were to override, and also had the difficulty of riding into woodland. According to the Burgundian chroniclers, Henry also sent a group of archers to a meadow near Tramecourt, close to the French vanguard, where they hid until it was time to shoot: 'The purpose of this was that when the French marched forward the 200 archers could fire on them from the side'. This would certainly have been disconcerting and would have had the effect of forcing the French away from the flanks to the right, towards the English centre.

Henry therefore used subterfuge to protect his archers from cavalry attack, and to entice the French into thinking his men-at-arms would be an easy target. The French needed little encouragement, since they had already seen when the armies were arrayed on 24 October how few men-at-arms he had. Yet they seem to have been ignorant of the likely effectiveness of his massed archers in keeping them at bay, despite presumably also seeing the strength of his archers on 24 October. What is notable here is that no chronicle account mentions Henry ordering his archers to array behind their stakes on that day. It is possible, therefore, that when he drew up his lines on that day, in some haste as he thought the French were already planning an attack, they did not deploy in the same way as they did at the battle. Perhaps the stakes were still piled on carts. The French may therefore not have known about the stakes in advance and were therefore lulled into a further false sense of security. By the same token, Henry may have been lucky that the French did not decide to give battle on 24 October but chose instead to wait for as many men-at-arms as they could muster.

It is possible that all of the archers were placed behind stakes on the flanks at the battle. However, there are two reasons why it is unlikely that was the only place Henry put them. The first is their sheer number – well over 7,000. It would have been extremely difficult to divide this number between each flank and still allow enough space to fire. The second reservation is the wording of the *Gesta*, which can imply a positioning *between* the battles. This cannot be wholly dismissed, since the author was clearly trying very hard to describe something distinctive. As we have seen, several other writers imply that the archers were in front of the men-at-arms. My conclusion is therefore that Henry positioned most of his archers on the flanks but that there were also smaller groups placed between and in front of the men-at-arms. In the case of those archers on the flanks, their formation would extend for some distance down each side of the field. This would expose the advancing French men-at-arms to a long barrage of lateral fire. The archers at the front could add to the effect by bursts of forward fire and then move out of the way when the advance came too close. How this deployment operated in practice will be discussed in the next chapter.

The French outnumbered the English at Agincourt, but not hugely so. The French may only have been one-third as large again as the English – c.12,000 against c.9,000. The real contrast between the armies was their composition. Knowledge that the English had a small number of men-at-arms heartened the French even though they had not managed to assemble as large an army as they had hoped. It led to their placing more troops than originally intended in the vanguard. They anticipated winning the day with a huge first clash. Ignorance, or a lack of understanding, of the strength of the English archers made them under-estimate the danger that the latter posed. They may not have expected the archers to be behind stakes. From the English perspective, the large proportion of French men-at-arms, packed into a huge vanguard, made the army look so much bigger than their own. Even if the French had only a few thousand more troops than the English, in the confined field of Agincourt the difference would have appeared greater. It is extremely difficult to gauge numbers accurately on sight. In addition, it is possible that the French did not deploy their archers and crossbowmen, and that both they and other troops, perhaps in a rearguard, did not engage in the battle. After the victory, English chroniclers deliberately exaggerated numbers out of all proportion in order to make Henry's victory seem even greater. In no way could the French army have numbered anything like the figures they suggest. This was indeed the triumph of the few against the many – the few English men-at-arms against their many French counterparts – made possible by the faceless majority of Henry's archers.

9

The Fight, 25 October 1415

Reconstructing the battle is no easy matter. In simplest terms, both armies were drawn up in the morning some distance apart but remained in their initial positions for a few hours. Henry then decided to order his army to move forward. When the French saw the English were advancing, they too began to come forward. As they did so, they were faced by an arrow barrage. The French tried but failed in cavalry charges against the English archers on the flanks. The hand-to-hand fighting was fierce, but the French men-at-arms were too closely packed to be effective. They fell and others piled on top of them, becoming easy victims of English assault. During the battle, an attack was launched on the English baggage. After a lull, Henry thought that the French were regrouping and ordered the prisoners to be killed.

This seems straightforward enough but at every turn we experience difficulties. Chronicle accounts vary considerably in points of detail and in the chronology of events.[1] There is obvious conflation and confusion between the preliminary stage which did not lead to conflict and the final advance which did. This is not unexpected, since both stages could have witnessed standard preparations for battle, such as the setting of deployments and the performance of prayers and orations. Furthermore, the events placed by some chroniclers on the eve of battle are placed by others on the day itself. This is not surprising, since Henry believed that the French intended to bring him to battle on 24 October. As we saw in the previous chapter, he kept his men in their battle lines for some time on that day too.

Many of our difficulties derive from the nature of the chronicles on which we are dependent. Although the author of the *Gesta* was present, he was at his own admission 'then sitting on a horse among the baggage at the rear of the battle'. We shall see later that there is some confusion over how close the baggage had been drawn up. His position on horseback would help to some degree in viewing what was going on ahead. Indeed, it is interesting that he should choose to tell us how he was positioned, as if to give his account more credibility. Even so, most of the fighting would have been several hundred yards away and the author could not have seen anything in detail. Oddly, if he was with the baggage, his account of the French pillaging of it is very perfunctory. In many ways, his account of the battle is vague and bland, and at every turn he emphasises divine intervention, since the purpose of his work was to emphasise God's support for Henry and the English. It is not easy to use his account to unpick Henry's battle plan, and impossible to gain much from it about French actions. The accounts of the other eyewitnesses, Waurin and Le Fèvre, are more satisfactory in points of military detail and the movements of the French but they provide a good example of how difficult it is to deal with events that happened simultaneously. As a result their accounts are episodic and give an artificial sense of constant progression from one unconnected event to the next. The battle is likely to have lasted for several hours but there would not have been incessant or continuous fighting. All chroniclers tend to describe basic movements but not the many regroupings and lulls in fighting that must have occurred. Add to this the retrospective and politicised reflection that is intrinsic to all chronicle writings, and that colours in particular the treatment of the role of individuals in the conflict, and we can see how problematic it is, if not impossible, to reconstruct exactly what happened at Agincourt on that fateful day. All we can do is suggest possible scenarios. In doing so, we may be already creating artificial phases, but this is necessary in order to be able to reconstruct and analyse in any meaningful way.

Let us look first at what we might call the preliminaries – what happened before the fight began. Sunrise on Friday 25 October at Agincourt would have been around 6.40 a.m. Both armies prepared for an early start, since they could not afford to do otherwise. English chroniclers are most fulsome on this, since it was part of their admiration of Henry as a Christian prince and of his own emphasis that the victory was achieved by divine intervention. In this respect, then, what the chroniclers tell us about Henry's preparations for battle is coloured by the fact that he won so emphatically. Space is therefore given to the religious observances that the king heard before making ready for the field. Waurin and Le Fèvre (the latter an eyewitness to events in the English camp) tell us that Henry heard three masses, already in armour save for his helmet. He then put on his helmet, which had 'a very rich crown of gold encircling it like an imperial crown' and mounted a small grey horse, without his spurs, without having the trumpets sound. He then drew up his lines and made a battle speech.

These preparations are embellished in the vernacular tradition of the *Brut* chronicle in order to create a more inclusive environment uniting Henry and his army. Henry, drawing up his battle line when morning came, asked what time it was. 'Prime', came the reply, thereby allowing the king to comment that this was a propitious time (implicitly for fighting), since England would be at prayer at that very moment. In winter, the service of Prime would be held between 7 a.m. and 8 a.m. The *Brut* chronicle continues with Henry's oration, encouraging his troops to acquit themselves like men and to fight for the right of England, and invoking both God and St George to their aid. The king's speech urges his kneeling soldiers: 'in remembrance that God died on the cross for us, let every man make a cross in the earth and kiss it as a token that we would rather die on this soil than flee'. In embellishing the story, the French king (not, of course, present at the battle) is made to ask what the English were doing, to be told by a French knight that they were showing their intention to die there rather than flee.

There is some confusion in accounts, however, of what happened next. In the *Brut* tradition, the king's speech is followed immediately by an order to 'Advance banners!' This is an example of conflation between the events of first thing and what happened before the actual English advance later. What the *Brut* chronicle tells us about the soldiers making the sign of the cross surely belongs to the advance rather than to the early morning deployment, unless it happened twice. There are suggestions in other accounts that there was considerable delay before the actual opening of the conflict. Henry drew up his troops in battle position within the first hours of daylight. This echoed the action he had taken on the previous day. It was for the French to attack, since they were the party blocking the English passage to Calais and who had forced Henry to stop his march. Since Henry was in the position of defender, it was important to establish as strong a position as he could, with the archers, and in some accounts the whole army, protected by stakes. He could not be sure at what time the French would attack, but he had to be ready for them. Furthermore, in terms of morale, there was little to be gained by allowing his men to kick their heels in camp. Better to put them into defensive formation and focus their minds on the purpose of the day. As the Pseudo-Elmham remarks, Henry knew that the winter day would be short and he did not want to show the enemy any sign of fear, so he made sure that he came into the field early 'at the first show of dawn'. There would come a time, however, where he realised he could not keep his men inactive any longer. There was a danger that they would go off the boil, so to speak, by standing in the lines, worried yet doing nothing. But we can be certain that any advance would have been preceded by rituals aimed at raising their confidence and their rage for battle. We shall return to this point in a moment.

French religious preparations would have mirrored those of the English. The fact that no chronicler tells us of devotions is perhaps because of French defeat but also because the best-informed writers were secular. The account by the Religieux is highly judgmental in tone and loses no opportunity to emphasise folly at every turn. There is also a lack of certainty on when the French formed into battle order. Although the *Gesta* suggests that they drew up their lines early in the day, French writers suggest that this occurred later. The *Chronique de Richemont*, for instance, claims that it was about the time of Tierce or later. This monastic service was commonly held between 9 a.m. and 10 a.m. in winter. The Burgundian chroniclers also suggest that the French had drawn up their lines by between 9 a.m. and 10 a.m. In their accounts, mention is also made of the soldiers taking food and drink and exchanging embraces as signs of friendship and of unity, setting aside the dissensions of the past. It is notable that only Burgundian chroniclers mention this gesture.

Since the French were the aggressors, the battle would only commence when they were ready to do so. The impression is that they saw no need for urgency. This was because troops were still arriving. The Berry Herald claims that the Duke of Orléans did not arrive until the morning of 25 October, adding that 'all morning, barons, knights, and esquires arrived from all parts to assist'. The French were also delaying in the hope that, by so doing, the Dukes of Brabant and Brittany might arrive in time to participate. According to Dynter, Duke Anthony of Brabant was at mass that morning when he received news that the English were to be fought by midday. He immediately set out for Agincourt. It was also known that the Duke of Brittany was coming northwards. He may only have reached Amiens on 25 October but the French waited for as long as possible, in the hope that he or at least some of his men might arrive in time. Men of the Duke of Anjou may also have been expected. Monstrelet tells us that the Sire de Longny arrived with 600 men of the duke during the battle, meeting several wounded French when he was still about a league away from the field. As a result he did not continue to the battle.

As a delaying tactic, the French initiated negotiations. These are mentioned in Titus Livius and in enough independent French accounts to make it likely that some occurred, although as we saw, some chroniclers place them on 24 October rather than 25 October. It was not uncommon for attempts at mediation to be undertaken before battles. They were not serious attempts to avoid conflict but were rather an element in the justification process. The Berry Herald claims that Guichard Dauphin and the Sire de Heilly were sent to parley with Henry, who allegedly made offers to withdraw. The chronicler adds that no one knows what these offers were save for the Duke of Orléans, since all of the others involved were killed in the battle. Titus Livius also notes the coming of de Heilly, but in connection with a slur on his honour that he had not kept the terms of his release from his imprisonment in England several years earlier. This was a useful story of French dishonour but had its root in a real incident. Waurin and Le Fèvre are uncertain about which side requested discussions, but say that Henry sent some of his most trusted men to meet and talk with the French. In their account, the parley took place in the area between the battle lines. The French allegedly offered that if Henry would renounce his title 'king of France' and surrender Harfleur, they would allow him to have what he held in Guienne 'and what he held by ancient conquest in Picardy', which we can take to mean Calais and its march. In response, Henry's representatives demanded the duchy of Guienne and five appurtenant cities, as well as Ponthieu and a marriage to Catherine with a dowry of 800,000 écus. (These were close to his last demands in the spring of 1415.) If these terms were met he would renounce his French title and surrender Harfleur. Neither side would accept the offers, so the representatives went back to their own armies to prepare for battle. For Basin, it was Henry who offered to surrender Calais and to pay a large sum of money to return home without his men suffering any harm, but the French rejected his offers and the English were forced to give battle. In this short passage, Basin was able both to imply that Henry was panicstricken and that it was French arrogance that led to the disaster of Agincourt.

Whether negotiations occurred or not, there was a delay. According to Monstrelet, when the English saw that the French were not advancing they started to eat and drink, the implication being that they had not done so before drawing up their lines after dawn. They also sent out some of their scouts to the back of the village of Agincourt, but found no French soldiers there. The scouts burned a barn and a house (implicitly at Agincourt) belonging to the priory of St George of Hesdin. It was probably around the same time that Henry sent a company of 200 archers out on his right flank. According to the Burgundian chroniclers, they managed to position themselves with stealth in a meadow near Tramecourt, close to the rearguard of the French. In other words, Henry had sent out reconnaissance on both sides of the field to find out what the French were up to, and also to check that they were not preparing their own movements to skirt round his flanks and attack from the rear. That the French were also sending out scouts to view the English position is claimed in the *Gesta*. Their presence is also noted by Titus Livius and the Pseudo-Elmham, although they have the French knights forced to return to their own side at a gallop, in the face of arrow shot ordered by the king.

When, then, did the battle actually begin? As we have seen, the *Brut* chronicle places Henry's advance close to the hour of Prime. An early start time of 'after eight o'clock in the morning' is also given in one of the accounts of des Ursins. He has the French lowering their heads in order to avoid having the sun in their eyes in the face of English fire. This seems rather fanciful, since it is unlikely that the sun's position would have caused this difficulty at such an early hour. More likely this notion was lifted from accounts of Crécy. English accounts suggest that the French had by their delay used up 'much, or at least a great part, of the day', and that this finally prompted Henry to seize the initiative and launch an advance. How much of the day had gone is difficult to tell. As we have seen, the Burgundian writers have the French drawing up their lines between 9 a.m. and 10 a.m. The account of the Religieux, however, gives the same hour as the time at which Clignet de Brabant and others were ordered to begin the cavalry attack against the English archers. The *Chronique de Ruisseauville* names 10 a.m. as the moment at which the English uttered a great shout and began their advance. These times do not, on the face of it, tally with the idea that a great part of the day had passed, but from the perspective of men who had been waiting in position since between 7 a.m. and 8 a.m., the wait would have seemed long.

Overall, it is unlikely that actual battle began before 10 a.m. The French attempt to delay had failed. They were therefore faced with an English attack before the extra troops had arrived. In addition, they had only recently drawn up their lines to accommodate other late arrivals. A degree of confusion, or at least a lack of co-ordination, prevailed in their ranks, despite the battle plans that had been laid in advance. Although we must beware of hindsight, there may indeed have been at this point, as Monstrelet suggests, 'some wiser ones amongst them who were worried about fighting the English in open battle'. Both sides were full of trepidation at this point, since the outcome of a battle was never a foregone conclusion.

Where exactly were the armies at the point Henry began his advance? Walsingham gives the distance between them at the outset as 1,000 paces, which we can take to mean about 1,000 metres. Given the debate on how far the longbow could reach, it is interesting to note that the Pseudo-Elmham gives the distance as three bowshots, perhaps 450-500 metres. Locating the armies on the ground is impossible, however. The *Gesta* comments that after his religious observances Henry made ready for the field, 'which was at no great distance from his quarters'. This does not mean that the English position was established at Maisoncelle. If that were the case, it makes no sense of Henry's later order to bring the baggage up to his rear. Furthermore, if the English could see the French lines from their first position, which the *Gesta* and several other writers suggest, then their lines had to be well forward of Maisoncelle, otherwise the French would be hidden by the slope between Maisoncelle and the road between Agincourt and Tramecourt. The land falls away on either side of the field between the current D71 E and D104, and woodland probably came closer up to those routes in the period. Therefore, given the descriptions we have of Henry's position, it is likely that he drew his lines at least midway between Maisoncelle and Agincourt and probably nearer to the latter.

From my reading of the field, the most likely position for his front line is on a rough alignment with the church and château of Tramecourt, in the area described on the map as La Cloyelle. In this area the terrain is flatter and most resembles that described by Walsingham – 'a field newly sown with wheat, where it was extremely difficult to stand or to advance because of the roughness as well as the softness of the ground'. Towards Maisoncelle, the ground is more inclined and better drained. Furthermore, the field name is probably linked with *clouer* – 'to glue to the spot'. Since Henry intended to adopt a defensive position, he would have chosen this in order to make French approach to him as difficult as possible. The ground also had to be soft enough to drive in stakes with ease. Opportunity had been taken on the previous evening to carry out reconnaissance into the terrain and lie of the land. That said, since he himself chose to move first, he was laying his own army open to the same terrain.

This suggested first English position also fits well with the distances between his lines and those of the French. Measuring 1,000 metres northwards places

their front line in the area on the map called Les Soixante, with their companies occupying the highest ground of the area above the 130-metre contour. This
also places them between *Ruisseauville* and Agincourt, which fits with chronicle descriptions. Finally, tree cover came closer in on both the Agincourt and
Tramecourt sides. This, combined with the lie of the land, created a funnel effect.
The French were positioned at the mouth of the funnel with Henry at the narrower end. If his assumption was that the French would attack him then he had
adopted an ideal defensive position. His flanks were protected by the trees and by
the way the land fell away on both sides. His archers were protected by stakes, and,
as I have suggested earlier, may also have been partly hidden in the trees. To attack
him, the French would have to concentrate their troops within a lateral front
which became narrower as they advanced.

It was, however, Henry who made the first forward move. The question must
therefore be how far forward he and the French moved before the armies met
and engaged. Before we consider this we need to look at why Henry chose to
advance, having established a strong defensive position. The answer is because
the French showed no signs of attacking. The fullest account of Henry's decision
is found in Titus Livius and the Pseudo-Elmham, both chroniclers who drew
on information from commanders present. Since it was obvious that the French
were showing no signs of wishing to make the first move, Henry consulted with
his most experienced officers on whether he should 'advance with his troops
in the order in which they stood'. Their advice was that he should, because the
English army would only become weaker the longer it stood still, given its lack of
food and the exertions it had already undergone. The enemy, on the other hand,
were on their own soil and could easily be supplied. Delay permitted them to
'gather fresh and increased strength by virtue of new troops arriving'. How much
military intelligence Henry had on the arrival or anticipated arrival of reinforcements cannot be known, but this narrative fits precisely with what we suspect of
the French reasons for delay. In addition, if the English had deployed early in the
morning in anticipation of attack and had taken little sustenance, they would be
increasingly weakened and distracted. Action was needed.

THE ENGLISH ATTACK

Henry was taking a risk in making the first move. His awareness of this is represented by the fact that before ordering the advance, he commanded that the
baggage be brought up to the rear from its existing position at the overnight
encampment. The *Gesta*'s interpretation is that this was to protect the baggage,
by not leaving it exposed at a distance from the army, but there are other possible
reasons for Henry's order. The first is that he wanted to use the baggage train as a
form of rear defence. It has already been suggested that he feared a French flanking move around the back of his army. The drawing up of wagons would help to

protect his rear. Secondly, should his army be faced with defeat and the need to retreat, it would be sensible to have the baggage and horses as close as possible, so that there could be a speedy evacuation. This tactic was likely used by Edward III at Crécy. In reality, however, the baggage had not been fully brought up to the rear by the time the English advance began. This is admitted by the author of the *Gesta*, who comments that as a result pillagers were able to fall upon 'the tail end' of the baggage, where the king's valuables were to be found. We shall return to this when we consider the attack on the baggage in more detail.

Henry's order to advance was accompanied by various rituals. There is some confusion in the chronicles about whether Henry made an oration at the initial deployment, at the order to advance, or on both occasions. What precisely he said cannot be known for certain. Chronicles do put words into his mouth, although the *Gesta* cites only his speech on Thursday 24 October. In reality, any oration that the king made could not have been heard other than by those close to him, since there was no means of amplification available, although he would have delivered it from horseback in order to be seen and heard. His words would be to the commanders, who then fed them back to their troops. In this context, it is revealing that a number of chronicles mention that the king went around the columns on horseback encouraging the leaders. This would be a sensible move, both at initial deployment and at the actual advance. In order to make its communication time-efficient, the speech cannot have been as long as some chroniclers (and Shakespeare) suggest, but it probably included reminders of the rightness of the English cause, divine support and the king's own determination to fight to the death. Since soldiers were advancing to their potential mortal end, they would have spent time in prayer, kneeling on the ground and taking a small piece of earth in their mouth, as in the *Brut* text discussed earlier. There would also have been invocations of saints, especially of St George, Edward the Confessor, the Virgin and the Trinity. The priests are described in the *Liber Metricus* as leading these invocations. Chanting or singing in an ecclesiastical manner would have been a good way of transmitting the sound of these highly important preparations for an event that could lead to death.

Banners were then raised. This was a sign to both one's own troops and to the enemy that conflict was to begin, since the raising of banners was a formal declaration of hostile intent. In the actual advance, men followed the banners forward. This helped to keep men in formation, and suggests that the men-at-arms of the retinues were together as they advanced. But how precisely did the English troops know when to begin to move? The army numbered thousands and was divided into different groups. Cries of 'Advance banners' would carry, much as a modern sergeant-major operates, but to start this off there was a visual signal. This was the throwing in the air of a baton by Sir Thomas Erpingham, one of the king's oldest and most experienced commanders. It has sometimes been suggested that his signal was for the archers to attack, but the wording of the relevant passage, which occurs only in the Burgundian chroniclers, indicates that Sir Thomas was on horseback in front of the army as a whole at the point he threw the baton into the air. He also shouted a word which is recorded as 'Nestroque' in Waurin and 'Nescieque' in Monstrelet. Le Fèvre, who was with the English army, does not mention the word. Waurin adds that this was the signal for attack. What Erpingham shouted was therefore likely 'now strike'.[2] This gave warning that the advance was to begin. The Burgundian texts tell us that Sir Thomas then dismounted and put himself in the king's battle with his banner in front of him.

The cry 'Advance banners' then echoed around, and the English started to move forward with a great shout. This was another standard way of communicating the moment of advance within the army and to the enemy. Trumpets were also used at this point and as the advance got underway. (They were also probably used to order regroupings, although we have no examples of this in the narratives.) Several accounts suggest that this cry amazed or disquieted the French. The implication is therefore that the French were taken by surprise by the English decision to attack. Their assumption was that the English were in a defensive position and that it was therefore to themselves that the first move would fall. Instead, they found themselves obliged to respond, and they too began to advance. The chronicles do not give us any details on how this was commanded. In the *Gesta*, both armies advance towards each other 'over roughly the same distance, the flanks of both battle-lines extending into woodlands on both sides of the armies'. In Titus Livius, within twenty paces of the village of Agincourt, the English come up to the enemy and fall upon them. This would place the actual engagement around and to the north of the road that crosses the battlefield between Agincourt and Tramecourt.

According to the Burgundian texts, the English advance made a brief stop preceded by another great cry. This was said to be so that men could catch their breath, but it is also linked to the beginning of action by the 200 archers in the meadow. In other words, these archers were under command to start shooting on the French flanks shortly after the English advance began, as a way of goading the French into moving forward while also distracting them by sideways firing. The chroniclers then switch to commenting on the English army as a whole: 'straightway the English approached the French, first the archers... began with all their might to shoot volleys of arrows against the French for as long as they could pull the bow'. An important feature of the English advance was therefore the use of arrow shot against the French as they also began to move forward.

This is found in almost all accounts of the battle and is its distinguishing feature. What I am suggesting, however, is that the forward move of the men-at-arms was deliberately accompanied by arrow barrages. The difference between the opposing armies was not so significant in numerical terms as in type of combatant. As we have seen, the English had a very large proportion of archers compared with men-at-arms. Archers could not easily defend themselves in hand-to hand-fighting with fully armoured men-at-arms with spears, swords and other bladed weapons, maces etc. They could, however, cause substantial damage to these men-at-arms at a distance, all the more so because the archers were in such large numbers themselves. We shall turn in a moment to Henry's provision for protecting the archers and to the failure of French attempts to undermine their effectiveness by launching a cavalry charge against them, but first let us consider further how the use of arrow fire related to the advance.

As many accounts explain, the French men-at-arms moved forward through a storm of arrows which disrupted their formation. The *Gesta* notes that the French had begun their advance in line abreast, but that before they reached the English they divided into three columns, for two reasons: first, fear of the arrows which pierced the sides and visors of their helmets and, secondly, their own plan to break through the strongest points of the English line and reach the banners. Both would have the same effect – forcing the French to bunch up and to run the risk of colliding with each other. The *Gesta* adds that the archers kept up their firing into the enemy's flanks without pause until their arrows were used up. Henry's opening tactic was therefore to use the archers for as long as possible against the advancing French, in order to disrupt their attack on his men-at-arms. This was sensible, given that his army contained a low proportion of men-at-arms. What better than to damage the French as much as possible before they were able to engage in hand-to-hand fighting? The archers were therefore used like artillery in later centuries, to weaken the enemy at a distance so that their hand-to-hand onslaught would be diminished. Their value lay in two distinctive features. First, they were flexible and could easily change position or turn their bodies to fire from another angle in response to the French advance. Secondly, they could keep up a barrage. This was not simply because longbows were easy to reload and the best archers could fire fifteen a minute. It was also because over 7,000 men were firing simultaneously. In this scenario, there was no need for archers to be sharpshooters able to hit targets with consummate accuracy. It was the weight and continuous nature of their fire that had the necessary effect. This made it extremely difficult for the French to keep up the momentum of a foot charge. By the time the French engaged with the English men-at-arms they were wearied and wounded. We cannot imagine what it was like to try to walk forward under such a barrage. Men could not be trained for this situation. It was therefore a totally novel and exceptionally frightening situation. Furthermore, the archers were firing not only head-on but also from the flanks. The lie of the land already meant that the French were advancing into an ever-decreasing lateral front. The arrow fire from the flanks contributed further to this funnelling effect. We shall explore this problem further when we look at the mêlée, but first we must see why the French were not able to sustain effective counter-measures against the English. They tried three: a cavalry charge against the archers, the use of crossbow fire, and an attack on the baggage.

FRENCH COUNTER-MEASURES

The BL plan intended that a company of heavy horse 'of good men up to the number of 1,000 men-at-arms at least' [*hommes darmes*] should be drawn from all the retinues and placed under the command of David, Sire de Rambures, the master of the crossbowmen.[3] It was to hold itself on the left, a little way behind the second French battle. Its role was to attack the English archers and do the utmost to break them. Once it moved off, the battles and wings were also to begin their advance. Since it was mounted, it would reach the English lines well before these foot companies came close. Its function therefore paralleled the use of archers by the English, being intended to weaken the English in such a way as to benefit the main battles of men-at-arms. If the archers were prevented from firing, then the French foot advance would not be undermined, and could therefore do its worst once it engaged with the English men-at-arms. Given that Henry had a disproportionate number of archers, the plan was very sensible, since it would increase the vulnerability of his men-at-arms. The assumption must be that it had been drawn up in the knowledge of the distribution of troops that Henry had. This had presumably been discovered by spying at the siege and during the march. Since the army marched in armour, it would be obvious to observers that they had few fully armed men-at-arms. The intention of mounting a cavalry charge is also found in the plan of battle given in des Ursins's second account, although the wording does not specifically mention the archers: 'And the cavalry, intended to break the battle [*bataille*] of the English, were the admiral [Clignet de Brabant] and the seneschal of Hainault'. In des Ursins's first account, however, the intention is more explicit: 'it was ordered that there would be cavalry to charge the English archers in order to disrupt their arrow fire'. This cavalry would comprise Gaulvet, Sire de la Ferté-Hubert in Soulogne, Clignet de Brabant and Louis de Boisbourdon [Bosredon].

All chroniclers tell us that a cavalry charge against the archers was indeed attempted. In terms of chronology, it appears to have been launched, as the BL plan had intended, as the French prepared to move off, or, in the words of the *Gesta*, 'when the enemy were nearly ready to attack'. Descriptions also suggest that the cavalry had been divided into two, forming up on both flanks of the French army 'like two sharp horns', as Titus Livius puts it, and attacking the archers on both sides of the English army. Chronicles also are at one in emphasising the extremely damaging effect of the arrow fire of the English archers against the cavalry. Horses wore some protection around their head, chest, shoulders and rump, but had many exposed areas. It is also dubious whether it was possible to train horses to cope with a barrage of arrow fire, since it was difficult to simulate this in peacetime on the scale it would be experienced in warfare. Archers, on the other hand, would have practised not only against stationary targets but also moving ones, such as birds. In the battle, the ability to hit a target was at its most important in the response to the cavalry charge. Hence, it is interesting that the

Brut chronicle follows mention of the attempt by the cavalry to override the archers with the comment that 'archers were shooting that day for a wager', implying
that targets were being chosen. The impact of arrow fire was therefore to cause
the cavalry to stumble, scatter and wheel around. Those who fell hindered those
who came after. Those who turned continued to be subject to a barrage of arrow
fire. Worse still, they ran into the advancing men-at-arms on foot, 'spreading ter-
ror and confusion amongst their companions'. In the *Chronique de Ruisseauville*,
the out-of-control cavalry causes the French vanguard to break up and scatter,
thereby allowing the English men-at-arms to penetrate through to the battles
behind. We have here another way in which the archers assisted the men-at-arms
to fulfil their function.

The stakes are also seen as significant in some texts. The *Gesta*, for instance,
notes that many of the cavalry were stopped by the stakes driven into the ground.
Waurin and Le Fèvre put it rather that the stakes made the horses fall over, which
made it possible for the archers to make an easy kill. The stakes thus served their
purpose in protecting the English archers, and had caused damage to the French
cavalry. Henry's precaution had paid off. It is interesting, however, that the stakes
are mentioned in relatively few accounts. Their presence and location is also
somewhat problematic. The *Gesta* says that when the king drew up his lines in
the early morning, he had the archers drive their stakes in front of them, 'as previously arranged in case of a cavalry charge', but the author does not make it
clear what happened when the advance was ordered. Various possibilities present
themselves.[4]

First, it is possible that the archers on the flanks remained stationary behind
their stakes while the rest of the English army moved forward. This possibility
would fit well with the idea, implied in the *Gesta*'s awkward description of the
position of the archers within the army as a whole, that there were some archers
in between the men-at-arms as well as others on the flank. In this scenario, those
'in between' did not have stakes and so moved forward, firing on the advancing
French foot. The second group on the flanks stayed put behind their stakes, and
in the woodland on either side of the field. Note that this author has the French
cavalry which was not struck down or driven back by the archers managing to
pass into this woodland, thereby confirming its presence.

Secondly, it could be that the archers, whatever their position, uprooted their
stakes at the order to advance and then replanted them further forward. Carrying
the stake would have prevented use of the bow, but as the distance advanced was
not great, the duration of their incapacity would have been limited. But how easy
would it have been to place a stake in the ground so that it stayed in position? If
the stakes pointed towards the enemy, then the archers would have had to turn
their backs to the enemy to hammer them in. Would there have been time to do
this before the French cavalry advanced? Astute chroniclers demonstrate that they
are aware of the problem of the stakes. Thus Titus Livius has the archers take up

their stakes when they move towards the enemy. In his account, however, he has it that all of the English had initially fixed stakes in the ground as a shield against the advancing cavalry. The Pseudo-Elmham says rather that the archers left behind their stakes at the advance. Yet if the *Gesta* is correct in stating that stakes were used to lay into the French men-at-arms later in the mêlée, then the assumption must be that they were easily retrievable.

English writers portray the cavalry charge as a failure, and there is no doubt that it was, since it did not succeed in its purpose of limiting English arrow fire. None report, however, that the French had found it impossible to launch the kind of charge they had hoped. They would not know of the apparent difficulties in the French camp. Indeed, there is a problem in knowing whether the French really had failed to mount the charge as planned or whether this was a story invented later as part of the blame culture that developed. French chronicles vary in their versions of the event. The Religieux has it that between 9 a.m. and 10 a.m. Clignet de Brabant, Louis de Bosredon and the Sire de Gaules were charged to go with 1,000 crack men-at-arms, with the best mounts, to disperse the English archers, but the first volley of arrows caused them to flee, leaving their leaders stranded with only a few brave men. Dynter's account is similar, although he gives the number as 1,200 and the leader as Clignet de Brabant, claiming that because of the resistance of the archers he went on instead to rob the English camp. The *Chronique de Normandie* also gives the English arrow power as the cause of failure but gives the number of cavalry appointed to the task as 300.

Other chroniclers suggest that the French had not managed to find enough men for the charge. In the *Chronique de Ruisseauville*, Clignet de Brabant, the Sire de Gaucourt and several others had been ordered to come with a large number of good quality men, but only a few came. Des Ursins's second account claims that when they wanted to find the 400 horsemen they had ordered the day before to break the battle line of the English, they could find only forty. The longest explanation of this kind is found in the Burgundian chroniclers, but again there is variation between the writers. In Monstrelet, Clignet de Brabant's company was intended to number 800 but only 120 turned up. For Le Fèvre and Waurin, the appointed number was 1,000 to 1,200, with half intended to attack on the Agincourt side and half on the Tramecourt side, but only 800 could be found when it came to the time to attack. Waurin later says that there were only 120 under de Brabant. All three mention the bravery of Sir Guillaume de Saveuse, who advanced on the Agincourt side with 300 men and rushed ahead with his two-man escort. Oddly, it is claimed by Waurin and Le Fèvre that all returned save for Saveuse and his two companions. What we are seeing here is a deliberate attack on Clignet de Brabant and the other Armagnac supporters who were appointed to carry out the cavalry charge. Louis de Bosredon and the Sire de Gaucourt were closely associated with the Duke of Orléans. No reason was given for the alleged inability to find the full number of men, but its association with

the Armagnac group placed the blame firmly at their door, with an implication of
bad command and cowardice. This is why the supposed bravery of de Saveuse, a
Picard lord of Burgundian allegiance, was cited in contrast.[5]

If the full number of men was not found, it was more likely because the
French army was not as large as had been anticipated. Furthermore, given the
large number of archers that Henry had at the battle, even 500 cavalry on each
side would have found it difficult to override the archers while at the same time
being subject to intense arrow fire. But the French did mount an attack as part
of their advance. Titus Livius and the Pseudo-Elmham also suggest that *saxivora*
(stone-throwing weapons) were used on the French flanks to disperse the English
as they came to fight. This is not mentioned in any other source and may be a
confusion with the apparent use of crossbow fire after the cavalry advance. This is
mentioned in the *Gesta*. Just before he has the French men-at-arms begin their
advance, he comments that 'the enemy crossbows which were at the back of the
men-at-arms and on the flanks, after a first but over hasty volley by which they
did injury to very few, withdrew for fear of our bows'.

As we have seen, French retinues were sometimes made up of both men-
at-arms and archers, and there were also companies of crossbowmen alone. The
BL plan does not mention crossbowmen (it places the master of the crossbowmen in charge of the cavalry charge) unless they are included in the expression
'*gens de trait*', who were all to be placed on the flanks in front of the two wings
of foot. Chronicles suggest that both archers and crossbowmen were present at
the battle. In Monstrelet, 4,000 archers and 1,500 crossbowmen were placed in
the vanguard with 8,000 men-at-arms, although these figures are probably too
high, based on the evidence of ratios in documented retinues. Des Ursins places
the archers and crossbowmen in the second battle. Yet only in the *Gesta* is there a
definite reference to their use. Des Ursins has it that 'when they came to attack,
the archers and crossbowmen of our men never fired arrow or bolt'. This line is
also pursued in *Waurin* and *Le Fèvre*: 'they had plenty of archers and crossbowmen
but nobody wanted to let them fire. The reason for this was that the site was so
narrow that there was only enough room for the men-at-arms.' Dynter echoes
this line, claiming that the French put their archers, crossbowmen and infantry in
the rear, not wanting their aid, and intending in their great pride to defeat and
capture the English king and all his men by dint of their swords and hand-to-
hand fighting, for there were ten French nobles against one English. This is very
similar to the account by the Religieux:

> …four thousand of their best crossbowmen who ought to have marched in the
> front and begun the attack were not found to be at their post and it seems that
> they had been given permission to depart by the lords of the army on the pre-
> text that they had no need of their help.

It is important to note that only in this last account do we have the notion that such troops had actually departed. In reality, this cannot have happened on the day itself. This suggestion was simply a further element in the blame culture. More credible, however, is the idea that the French archers and crossbowmen were behind the men-at-arms (as the *Gesta* tells us). This is exactly where we should expect them, since they would not have been fully armed in plate and therefore could not have gone in front, both because of the danger of the arrows and their unsuitability for hand-to-hand engagement with fully-armed English men-at-arms. Their use as an advance force had failed at Crécy precisely because of this vulnerability. That said, it is not wholly clear how the French proposed to use their bowmen. The *Gesta*'s comment suggests that they may have intended their fire, aimed from the flanks and over the heads of the first lines, to follow up the cavalry charge and hence to 'soften' the English men-at-arms before the engagement. But English arrow fire drove them back and no opportunity came for them to participate. As we shall see later, they were probably not the only French troops who did not engage once it was clear that the vanguard had been completely overwhelmed.

There is no doubt, therefore, that the French had tried to cause damage to the English before their men-at-arms arrived at the English lines to engage. There was an attempt to undermine the archers and probably another to use their own artillery to open the fight at a distance. When the French reflected upon the battle, they sought to ascribe blame for these failures. In reality, the problem was intrinsic to their military system and not unique to Agincourt. Because the French were able to raise large numbers of men-at-arms, they did not deploy other kinds of troops in the same numbers. Crossbowmen tended to be concentrated in garrisons. French urban militias comprised small groups of crossbowmen and there is little evidence that many were called upon for service. This was because they were untrained in mass combat and also because there were fears of leaving towns undefended. Longbowmen were in small number and no match for their English equivalents in terms of mass fire. The French had placed too much hope in the cavalry charge to knock out the English archers, but there were too many archers for this to be feasible. At base, the reason for the failure of French countermeasures was English arrow power. The large proportion of archers in the English army was a strength not a weakness.

One French counter-measure did succeed, however. That was the attack on the baggage. In the BL plan of battle, a company of 200 mounted men-at-arms, fortified by half of the *varles* mounted on the best horses of their masters, was to attack behind the battle of the English against the servants and baggage. The text adds: 'and at the rear of the battle of the English'. Their principal aim was not to take booty but to distract the English and to make them fear an attack on their rear. It was carried out 'whilst the battle was raging', but we cannot be certain that it was actually launched at the same time as the cavalry charge. On the evidence of Fenin and the Burgundian chroniclers, it was led by Isambart d'Azincourt, Robert de Bourneville and Riflart de Clamace, local men of relatively low status. Their company was made up of *varles* boosted by the local peasantry. The *Chronique de Ruisseauville* suggests that the attack on the baggage was carried out by the men of Hesdin, and des Ursins claims that it was to Hesdin that the loot was taken.

It would appear, therefore, that the French had not been able to spare a large number of men-at-arms for the attack on the baggage. While local men would have knowledge of the terrain to enable them to skirt round the English lines, it reduced the attack to an act of plunder which focused on the king's treasure and bedding. The latter included a ceremonial sword as well as a crown. Walsingham adds that the taking of the crown enabled the French to pretend that Henry had been captured. This was undoubtedly one of the stories that circulated in England after the battle. The vernacular tradition represented by the *Brut* chronicle takes the tale further, saying that the crown was taken off to Paris, where the inhabitants were told that Henry had been defeated: all too soon, the city learned from returning wounded soldiers that the outcome of the battle was the very opposite. Problems of timing make this no more than a good story, but it was one which improved in the telling. In the *Chronique de Ruisseauville*, two crowns were supposedly taken, one the crown with which Henry intended to have himself crowned in Reims, as well as a 'sword of King Arthur so valuable that no one knew what to do with it'. Monstrelet has it that de Bourneville and d'Azincourt later gave the sword to the Count of Charolais. These writers were trying to salvage some act of French success from what was otherwise a narrative of failure.

The *Gesta* suggests that the attack was on the tail end of the baggage which had not yet been brought up to the rear of the army. For once there is a suggestion of blame in the English camp, since the author blames the negligence of royal servants. Since he also comments that the king ordered his advance 'once he thought that almost all his baggage had reached his rear', it would seem that the move of the baggage was not as close to completion as Henry had reckoned. In that respect he had made a mistake which could have been costly. That this was an issue is also suggested by the Pseudo-Elmham's concern to tell us that the king had left very few men to guard the baggage because he thought that the enemy would be more interested in fighting than plundering, a skilful way of denigrating the French rather than ascribing any blame to Henry.[6] As it turned out, the attack was less damaging than it might have been. It was not a raid on the whole English camp, as it is often portrayed. The target was the king's possessions.[7] The horses taken were pack horses only, as noted by the Burgundian writers. Certainly the financial records of the campaign reveal large numbers of the riding horses being shipped back to England. Furthermore, no chronicle account speaks of English casualties. More significantly in terms of tactics as a whole, there was no French attempt to attack the English from the rear with trained soldiers. For English chroniclers, including the author of the *Gesta* who was, at his own admission, sitting on a horse at the back of the baggage, the attack was by pillagers and thieves, not French troops. The French could not spare men for this task.

As with other elements of French failure, blame was subsequently apportioned. In Dynter's chronicle, the Armagnac, Clignet de Brabant, who rapidly became one of the Burgundian's favourite scapegoats, was targeted. Since he had failed in the cavalry charge which he had commanded, he went off to the English camp 'to rob it'. In other words, he did not join his comrades in the mêlée but chose rather a soft target as a plunderer rather than a true knight. Fenin and Monstrelet both claim that Henry's order to kill the prisoners arose when the king heard of the raid on the baggage.[8] Giving us a further example of the blame culture that developed, Monstrelet adds that as a result de Bourneville and d'Azincourt were arrested by Duke John of Burgundy, even though they had presented his son with the valuable sword. It is very unlikely that the killing of the prisoners was occasioned by the attack on the baggage. Since the author of the *Gesta* was with the baggage, he would surely have drawn a link, but he does not do so. Titus Livius, informed by the Duke of Gloucester, tells us that Henry did not know of the attack on the baggage until he returned to Maisoncelle on the evening of the battle (implying that the baggage had not been brought up to the rear of the army at all!). For Henry, therefore, the pillaging was a personal inconvenience but nothing more, since it had no effect on the outcome of the battle and was compensated for by the overwhelming nature of the victory.

THE MÊLÉE

Given the level of interest in the archers, the mêlée tends to be under-emphasised in studies of the battle. But in terms of duration and bloodiness, it was the most important part. Agincourt was hard fought. Since the French had more men-at-arms, their English counterparts were potentially at a severe disadvantage. As we have seen, however, Henry's ploy was to protect his own men-at-arms for as long as possible, while at the same time weakening the oncoming French men-at-arms. To this end, some archers were probably placed in front between the English battles. They fired on the advancing French, but ceased their fire shortly before the armies engaged. Once the French were close, the archers would have fallen back. Since the French had failed in their counter-measures against the English archers, the latter faced no danger, either while the French advance was being made or when the men-at-arms of both sides engaged. They were too lightly armed to engage in hand-to-hand fighting with men-at-arms in a mêlée. So they had to withdraw before the French came too close. This was not difficult, since they were very lightly armed. The description in the Burgundian chroniclers of their hose being loose around their knees is nothing to do with the lingering effects of dysentery but with their ease of movement. To the same

end they are described as bare-headed and bare-footed. Their nimbleness was a
further element in their flexibility.

It would therefore have been easy for any archers who had been in front of
the men-at-arms to regroup on the flanks with their fellow archers, perhaps even
behind the stakes. It is certain that the archers would not have stood idly by while
the mêlée was underway. They would have launched barrages of arrows against
subsequent French advances. Indeed, once the vanguard had engaged, the archers
could again move in from the flanks towards the centre and fire against the front
of the French main battle as it advanced. This is a very important point to bear in
mind. The archers' power was not used simply against the first French advance but
against subsequent advances too. This was another reason why the French failure
to knock out the archers by the cavalry charge and counter-artillery damaged the
whole of their attack, not simply the first advance. The chronicles do not emphasise this point, since they do not give a blow-by-blow account of the battle but
rather its main outline. Repetitive actions are excluded. This makes it difficult for
us to track the advances of the various French battles and the stages of the mêlée
but, as with the use of arrow fire, there would have been peaks and troughs.

It is not wholly clear whether the English men-at-arms continued to move
slowly forwards behind the protection of the arrows. If they did do so, their
momentum would give them extra force against the advancing French. It is also
possible that their advance and their position across the field was slightly oblique,
with the vanguard under York on the English right (and hence the Tramecourt
side) positioned forward and Camoys on the left (Agincourt side) set back.
Although English accounts of the formation suggest that the English battles
were close together laterally, the *Gesta* comments that the French divided into
columns to make for the centre of each English battle where the standards were.
This suggests that the three English battles were distinct. York was killed. His
post-campaign account shows that ninety of his men were also killed at the battle, almost a quarter of his original retinue of 400, although unfortunately it
does not distinguish between men-at-arms and archers.[9] Even so, this evidence
suggests that the English right bore the brunt of the French advance. It is
impossible to know where other lords were positioned, since no obvious pattern
can be detected. Michael de la Pole junior was the only person recorded as killed
in his retinue. In Huntingdon's retinue one man-at-arms and four archers were
killed. Sir Richard Kyghley was also killed, along with four of his archers.[10]

According to the Religieux account, the young hotheads on the French side
had predicted that the English would be struck with fear by the approach of
the French multitude. That they were not was the result of the damage that the
English arrows had already caused to the French. In addition, the French advance
had been further disrupted by the retreating cavalry. The state of the ground had
also caused them difficulties. All of the terrain was heavy and wet. According
to the Religieux, torrents of rain had made it into a quagmire. As a result, the

French sank deeply into the ground, causing them further exhaustion before they reached the English. But we have to explain why, if the mud was a problem for the French, it was not so for the English. Just as the *Chronique Anonyme* notes that the French were traversing newly worked land which was difficult to cross, so too Walsingham tells us that Henry led his men into a field newly sown with wheat, where it was difficult to stand or advance because of the roughness and softness of the ground. There would have been no perceptible difference in the weight of armour between the two sets of men-at-arms. Three answers present themselves. The first is that the ground the French crossed was further churned up by the horses retreating from the cavalry charge, and perhaps also by the effects of the charge itself. As anyone walking a bridle path in wet weather knows, the ruts caused by horses can make it difficult to have a firm footing. Secondly, the English had advanced, but only a short distance, twenty paces according to Titus Livius. Although the *Gesta* remarks that both armies moved about the same distance, it is likely that the French advance covered a longer distance. Thirdly, there were many more French men-at-arms packed into their first battle. Sheer weight of numbers made the position worse, especially for those following later. English arrow fire forced them to lower their heads and had the funnelling effect already mentioned. This was exacerbated by the likelihood that they were rushing to engage as quickly as they could, since they saw the English men-at-arms were far less numerous than themselves. As a result, the French became too tightly packed, which would further contribute to churning up the ground. Several chroniclers comment that the vanguard became so tightly packed that men could not raise their weapons. Their armour therefore felt heavier than it was.

By the time they reached the English they were exhausted. Some were wounded by arrows. Even if these did not pierce vulnerable points, the effect of an arrow barrage would have been to create severe bruising. Some may already have fallen in the advance. Furthermore, they had shortened their lances in anticipation of closing in easily on the English. Shorter lances were easier to control and had a greater thrusting impact, but as the English lances were longer they were able to push over the French before the latter were close enough to retaliate with their own lance. As a result many French in the first advance fell. The English also probably aimed at wounding men in the groin and legs to make them fall over. Ghillebert de Lannoy tells us that he received wounds to the leg as well as to the head.[11] The *Gesta* particularly emphasises how those killed at the outset had fallen at the front, and that others piled up on top of them. These included not only men mortally wounded but also others ('the living' as the chronicler calls them) who simply fell in the crush.

As the French main battle had been ordered to follow in close to the van, the pile-up became even greater. With these 'great heaps of dead', noted in the early chronicles on both sides, it was extremely difficult for the subsequent ranks of French soldiers to get anywhere near their enemy. Thus very few English were

wounded and even fewer killed. The French, on the other hand, were disorientated
by having to negotiate around their fallen comrades and so were easy pickings
for lances, axes and maces. As Walsingham puts it, 'the French stood immobilised
whilst our men wrenched axes from their hands and felled them in the same way
as if they were cattle'. The problem for the French was that their momentum was
entirely forwards. They could not turn round to retreat, rest and regroup. Not only
was there no space to do this, but they would be crushed by the next wave of their
comrades. If they moved towards the flanks they would run into the archers.

Several chroniclers note that the archers had joined in this stage of the mêlée.
Once the French men-at-arms had lost their weapons and were on the ground
in piles, it was safe enough for archers to play their further role. They were able
to enter the fray from the sides, encircling the French who had already been
pushed closer and closer together and towards the middle. Le Fèvre and Waurin
note that when the English archers saw the break-up of the French vanguard
they came out from behind their stakes, throwing down their bows and taking up
other weapons. The *Gesta* also comments on their entry into the fray once their
arrows were used up. Taking all of the chronicles together, the range of weapons
they deployed is as follows: swords, hatchets, axes, spear heads, falcon beaks, mallets (which implies war hammers as well as the instruments used to hammer in
the stakes) and stakes. Some of these are clearly the archers' own armaments, but
it is likely that they picked up the close-combat weapons dropped by the French
men-at-arms as they fell. It would be easy, while the French were concentrating
on engagement with the English men-at-arms, to attack individual Frenchmen
from the side or behind, dealing a sharp blow to the helmet and knocking them to
the ground and then briskly moving away out of danger. The use of lead mallets,
perhaps those used for driving in the stakes, is noted by the Religieux, although
not explicitly assigned to the archers. Furthermore, the lightly clad archers could
easily penetrate the piles of French to stab men in the groin, neck or, through the
visor, the eyes. Wounds to the head and neck were considered by chroniclers a
particular characteristic of the battle. In addition, as Le Fèvre and Waurin tell us,
the archers struck wherever they saw breaks in the French line. This opened up
gaps, into which the English men-at-arms were able to penetrate. Rushing forward, they attacked the French main battle. The English were now clearly on the
offensive. Both English and French chroniclers mention specifically that when
the attack on the main battle began, it was the king who followed up by marching in with all his men-at-arms in great strength. His personal involvement at this
stage is suggestive of his belief that the French were about to be routed.

THE END OF THE BATTLE AND THE KILLING OF THE PRISONERS

When was this? The *Chronique de Ruisseauville* claims that the battle lasted only
half an hour. It is impossible, given the weight of numbers in the French van and

main battle, as well as the need to fit in the cavalry charge, that it could have been over so quickly. The *Gesta* says that the French vanguard had been run through after two to three hours. Three hours is also a figure mentioned by Titus Livius. In his account, 'no one who came into the combat during the three hours did so without slaying or being slain'. The Religieux claims that he had heard it from a reliable source that 'each side fought until midday'. If we assume that the English advance began around 10 a.m., these writers suggest that there was intensive fighting until between midday and 1 p.m. We have another possible indicator of timing. If Dynter is correct that the Duke of Brabant was at Lens in the early morning but managed to arrive at the battle before it ended, then he cannot have arrived much before 1 p.m., since he surely needed at least six hours to travel the 48km between Lens and Agincourt. In the narratives of the Burgundian chroniclers, the duke's arrival is placed immediately following the penetration of the English into the French main battle. He had arrived hastily with only a few men, rushing ahead of his main contingent and of his equipment. Seizing a banner from one of his trumpeters, he made a hole in the middle of it and used it as his surcoat. According to Le Fèvre, no sooner had the duke dismounted than he was immediately killed by the English.

Dynter comments that after the duke's arrival 'the battle did not last much longer for the French'. Several chronicles suggest that, with the vanguard annihilated, the French troops coming in behind decided to withdraw. This is made very clear by the Religieux. In this account, 'unexpected defeat put fear into the two lines of the army which remained. Instead of marching to the aid of their companions, they fled since they had not one to lead them'. Since the leading French nobles had placed themselves predominately in the vanguard, and the vanguard was disproportionately large, this is a credible scenario, repeated also by Pierre Fenin. The *Chronique de Ruisseauville* also comments on the many who fled, 'being not even noble enough to engage with the English compared with those who had been defeated'. The Burgundian writers pursue the same line. In their account, however, the English engage fully with the French main battle, continuing to kill and take prisoners. Seeing the first two battles doing so badly, the rearguard, mounted, take to flight, save for some of their leaders. According to the second account of Des Ursins, the English deployed a further form of attack once the vanguard had been defeated. This was a group of mounted troops which sallied out from a wood, attacking the French from the rear: 'The English horsemen made so great and amazing a cry that they scared all of our men, so much so that our second battle took to flight'. Since this is not found in any other source, and may be a confusion with Henry's later use of cavalry against the French who threatened to regroup, we cannot be certain of the truth of it. Even so, English sources also suggest that the French withdrew and there was a cessation in the fighting. The *Gesta*, for instance, claims that with the vanguard riddled through and the rest put to flight, the English began to pull the heaps of French apart and

ce separate the living from the dead, intending to hold them to ransom. This is
confirmed in Titus Livius and the Pseudo-Elmham.

Two important points arise from this. The first is that not all of the French army
engaged in the battle. This makes discussion of its size immaterial, since however
large it was, not all of it was used against the English. In the blame culture that
surrounded the battle, there is accusation of cowardice and flight. Those who
thought about regrouping 'took flight to save their own lives', as the Burgundian
writers put it. In Alain Chartier's 'Livres de Quatre Dames', the most wretched
lady is the one whose husband fled from the battle as a coward. This would be
easy to dismiss, were it not for the evidence given above for a cessation in the
fight. The second point relates to the killing of the prisoners. Henry's order did
not arise within the main period of battle on which we have concentrated so far.
Rather there was a lull during which Henry and his army believed that they had
won the day. They therefore began to search among the heaps of French casualties
for potential prisoners, and also presumably for their own dead. We cannot know
how long this lull was, but it was enough for the English to begin to relax from
the ardour they had previously faced. Since Henry was subsequently to order his
men to kill their prisoners, there must also have been enough time for the prisoners to have been demarcated and collected together.

It is easy to see how those lying on the ground wounded, or pinned under
the bodies of their dead comrades, could now be taken prisoner. Richemont
is described by Gruel as being pulled from under the dead, 'a little wounded'.
Ghillebert de Lannoy tells us that he too, wounded in the knee and in the
head, was lying on the ground with the dead, but when they were pulled apart
(*despouiller*) he was taken prisoner. With the battle over, such men had no choice
but to give their surrender. We must imagine that they would be disarmed and
their helmets removed, and that they were then taken to collecting points. An
illustration on the cover from the *Vigiles de Charles VII* portrays prisoners with
their hands tied in front of them, but whether this was standard practice is uncertain. Interestingly, the prisoners are portrayed fully armed, helmets and all. In the
case of Ghillebert de Lannoy he tells us that he was taken off to a house nearby,
with ten to twelve other prisoners who were all, like him, wounded (*impotens*). [12]

The collecting of prisoners at the end of a battle is straightforward, but what
we do not know is how and whether prisoners were also taken *during* the battle. Monstrelet's account of the fate of the Duke of Alençon implies that it was
theoretically feasible. The duke, allegedly responsible for killing the Duke of York,
then began to threaten the king, knocking Henry so fiercely on the head that a
fleuron of his crown was broken off. The king's bodyguard (a unique reference to
the existence of such a group) immediately surrounded the duke:

> The latter, seeing that he could not escape death, lifted his hand to the king of
> England and said 'I am the duke of Alençon and surrender myself to you'. But

just as the king was ready to take his oath, the duke was quickly killed by the bodyguard.

If a warrior accepted a surrender offered, what then happened? It was surely impossible for the captor to busy himself with disarming his prisoner and leading him to a collecting point, since this would have taken him out of the fight. It is difficult to believe that at the height of the mêlée the conventions of war were so mutually respected as to render inviolate anyone escorting a prisoner. How then did it work? Was the prisoner simply expected to move to the sidelines and become a non-combatant, obliged on his honour to acknowledge his prisoner status at the end of the stage of the battle? Was he obliged to disarm himself? It may be that certain soldiers were earmarked in advance as keepers of prisoners. It would not have been necessary to use front-line troops. Men with minor wounds, pages or other servants would have sufficed. Indeed, youngsters would gain useful experience of fighting conditions through such involvement. But were they obliged to carry out of the mêlée men who were wounded and had surrendered? (The same question can also be applied to English troops wounded during the battle. Was there a field station to which they took themselves, or to which comrades, servants and pages took them? This would be feasible if, as suggested, fighting was not continuous but carried out in phases.)

The case of Alençon may suggest that at Agincourt surrenders were not accepted during the battle. This runs counter to the account of the *Gesta*, however, where in the mêlée the French were so seized with fear that 'some of them, even their more nobly born, had surrendered themselves more than ten times that day'. The author goes on to comment, however, that 'no one had time to take them prisoner but all, without distinction of person, were put to death by those who had laid them low or by others as soon as they were struck down'. The passage is awkward, since if men were killed as they surrendered, how was it possible to surrender ten times? But it could be taken to mean that those who surrendered simply stopped fighting for a while, but then started again. It might also mean that even if they had surrendered to one Englishman, this was not apparent to others, and hence they could be taken prisoner repetitively. Clauses in disciplinary ordinances for armies, as well as ransom disputes, indicate that soldiers could be unscrupulous in claiming for themselves prisoners who had first been taken by someone else, but in the heat of battle it is easy to see how confusions arose. In the post-campaign accounts, there is one example of a prisoner, the Sire de Corps, being taken jointly by soldiers in different retinues: William Callowe, a man-at-arms in the retinue of Sir Robert Babthorpe, and William Kempton, a man-at-arms in the retinue of Sir William Phelip.[13]

Whatever the mechanics of prisoner-taking were, there is no doubt that many met their end as a result of the king's order to kill the prisoners. But why did this order arise? The most common scenario found in the chronicles is that the

English thought that the French were regrouping. This is the line pursued in the *Gesta*. As the English soldiers look through the heaps of French vanguard for prisoners, a cry goes up that the enemy rearguard are re-establishing their position in order to attack. Does this imply that the rearguard had already attacked once, or that they had not as yet been involved in the fight? This is an important point, to which we shall return later. But to continue with the *Gesta*'s account. As a response to the believed threat:

> regardless of distinction of person, the prisoners, except for the Dukes of Orléans and Bourbon and certain other illustrious men in the king's battle and a very few others were killed by the swords either of their captors or others following after lest they should involve us in utter disaster in the fighting that would ensue.

This wording is very interesting, all the more so as this is probably the earliest written account of the event. There is no mention of a royal order. The killing occurs, as it were, spontaneously. This was a deliberate obfuscation of Henry's role, in order to avoid any implication that he had acted in a murderous and unchivalrous fashion. Remember that the purpose of the *Gesta* was likely to extol to a European audience at the Council of Constance the king's virtues as a Christian prince. The *Liber Metricus* provides an identical account, which likewise places the killing in the passive voice ('the English killed the French they had taken prisoner for the sake of protecting their rear') and omits any mention of the king. This work was also written for a clerical audience.

Interestingly, Thomas Walsingham does not mention the killing of the prisoners at all. We can speculate that this was for the same reason – to preserve Henry's reputation intact – but we cannot discount the possibility that the killing was deemed to be of little significance and interest at the time. After all, Walsingham had not found it necessary to spare us comments on Henry IV's brutality in handling the Welsh. Several other later English accounts do not mention the killing of the prisoners at Agincourt. These include John Capgrave and John Hardyng, in his first version. In the second version, however, Hardyng includes the following: 'The field he had and held it all that night, But then came word of a new host of enemies, For which they slew all prisoners down right, save dukes and earls in fell and cruel wise'. Although the specific responsibility of Henry is once again omitted, the last phrase and the inclusion of the incident at all fits with the anti-Lancastrian revision of his work under Yorkist rule. The quotation also demonstrates the dangers of versification, since the search for a rhyme makes Hardyng imply that the killing took place well into the night.

All of the English accounts that mention the killing explain it, like the *Gesta*, on the grounds of a new French threat. Titus Livius echoes the idea of the *Gesta* that the vanguard had already been defeated, with the author adding 'and victory achieved'. The king then prepares to fight 'another army of the enemy no less than the first'. But the English were exhausted and were afraid that because they held so many prisoners – as many as their own number, the author opines – they might have to give battle not only against the enemy but also against the prisoners. As a result, they put many to death, including many rich and noble men. There is an attempt here to provide a more expansive explanation of the English decision, a sign that the author thought an excuse was needed. Note the additional emphasis on English exhaustion and on the alleged large number of prisoners. As in the *Gesta*, there is some irony in the fact that earlier the author has told us that when the battle against the vanguard was at its height 'no one was captured; many were killed'. Indeed, according to Titus Livius, the English had been keen to kill, as it seemed that 'there was no hope of safety except in victory'. But later, 'once the French had yielded to death and the certain victory was apparent, the English spared the French and captured them, including many princes, lords and nobles'. There is no mention in this work of soldiers searching through piles of dead but there is the same impression of the phases of battle, peppered with reference to English magnanimity, and by implication, French cowardice. Note once again the omission of any direct mention of Henry in the killing. Titus Livius does go on to say, however, that the king sent heralds to the new French army asking whether they intended to fight or to withdraw, 'informing them that if they did not withdraw of if they came to battle, all of the prisoners and any of them who might be captured would be killed by the sword with no mercy'. This allows an emphasis on Henry's firmness, although we can also adduce his level of anxiety and uncertainty, as well as a further implication of French cowardice, since 'they, fearing the English and fearing for themselves' choose to depart 'with great sadness at their shame'.

The account in the Pseudo-Elmham is essentially the same, but speaks more explicitly of the fear that if any new battle occurred 'the men they had taken would rush upon them in the fight'. There are two further differences. The first is that during the battle a vast multitude is said to be killed, but princes and magnates, we are told, are led off as captives. The second is the notion that Henry was about to direct his own troops to assist his own vanguard when he saw a large group of French preparing for battle, against whom he had to march. (This fits with the suggestion that York's battle bore the brunt of the fighting. The author of the Pseudo-Elmham did draw information from Walter Hungerford, who had been present at the battle.) We are then told that 'after a while' all of the king's battles, front and rear and each wing, were victorious. The implication is again of several phases of the conflict, and also that the English thought they had already won. The various versions of the *Brut* chronicle follow this same line of approach. In one account, the number of slain is given before mention of news that a new battle of French had drawn up. Here, however, it is explicitly the king who gives the order that every man should kill the prisoners he had taken. Since this vested the killing in individuals, it does not require the prisoners to have been collected together. No heralds are sent to the French, but Henry draws up his battle line ready to fight. When the French see that 'our men were killing their prisoners', they withdraw and disband the army. The implication is that the French were near enough to see what was going on. Another version, however, denies that the French had gathered a new army. Rather it was a great crowd of women and others who came to the field in order to see which side had been defeated. When the English spotted them standing on a hill next to the field where the battle had been (note again the impression that the battle was effectively over), a rumour went round that this was a new French army. In due course, news came to Henry that there was another French army in array and ready to march on him. So he gave the order that each man kill his prisoners. Once this had been done, Henry ordered his army to make ready to fight, but when the French saw that the English had killed the prisoners, they withdrew. What we see here is evidence of various oral testimonies reaching the ears of the chroniclers.

This version of the *Brut* chronicle, compiled in 1478–79, is one of only two English accounts to give any judgment on the killing of the prisoners. It was, the author writes, 'a mighty loss to England and a cause of great sorrow to the French'. The chronicle of Peter Basset (*c.*1459) concludes his account of the killing with the remark 'and that was the reason why so many nobles were killed'. Basset is the only English chronicler to name Sir Guillaume de Thibouville, Sire of La Rivière-Thibouville, as the man who rallied '20,000 men of war and more under a white banner to give battle'. In Basset, the king had it cried throughout the host that every man should kill his prisoners, implying, by placing the adjective 'victorious' before the king's name, that the battle was already deemed to be won.

All English accounts that mention the killing of the prisoners agree, therefore, that it arose from a belief that the French were intending to restart a battle that the English thought that they had already won. All also give a strong suggestion that this French regrouping and English response occurred some time after the first phases of the battle. Do French accounts pursue the same line? On the whole they do, but there are some interesting differences in emphasis. The Religieux chronicle, probably the earliest account, suggests that the force that Henry thought was intending to attack him was a large group of warriors on the flank of the vanguard who were in reality making for the rear in order to leave the field. In other words, they were cowards. The chronicler gives Henry the responsibility for ordering the killing of the prisoners but also for eventually 'seeing with his own eyes' that the French were fleeing and not intending to fight. The overriding feeling, therefore, is that the French were themselves responsible for the deaths of the prisoners.

This view, and with it an accompanying desire to apportion blame, is found in several other texts, although no other implies that the supposed new army was really a group of cowards. In both the *Chronique de Ruisseauville* and Dynter, Clignet de Brabant is named as the person responsible for gathering together men-at-arms to launch a new assault. *Ruisseauville* tells us that the killing led to great cries in both the English and French camps, 'because of the good prisoners held'. But, more significantly, it implies that the Count of Nevers (son of the Duke of Burgundy) was one of the prisoners put to death. In other words, an Armagnac who survived the battle is deemed responsible for the deaths of Burgundian heroes. This theme is also pursued in Dynter, who has Clignet returning not to fight but to pillage. He is more explicit in telling us that 'as a result, many princes and noblemen who were still alive as prisoners were killed'. One of these was the Duke of Brabant, brother of Duke John of Burgundy. Dynter concludes that Brabant met his death in this way because he was wounded in the face and neck, which would not have happened had he been wearing a helmet. (This suggests that prisoners would have had their helmets removed as a sign of their capture.) Dynter adds that other prisoners had seen the duke captured but had not spoken to him, in the hope that he might be put to a low ransom, on the grounds that the English would not recognise him for who he was. Remember that Brabant had apparently arrived at the battle late and was wearing an improvised coat drawn from the flag of one of his trumpeters.

Dynter concludes his lengthy exposition by commenting that the duke's body was found a long way from where the battle had been fought. This is an overt reference to the prisoners being taken to a collecting point, but it also fortifies the argument that the battle was already deemed to be over well before the killing of the prisoners was ordered. Both points are borne out by the reminiscence of Ghillebert de Lannoy. He had been lying on the ground with the dead but was pulled out and taken prisoner. After a while he was taken to a house nearby, with ten or twelve other prisoners: 'There, when the duke of Brabant made his attack [*rencharge*] there was a cry that each man should kill his prisoners. To do this more quickly they set the house on fire, but I was able to drag myself out.' He was taken prisoner again when the English came back and sold to Sir John Cornwall.[14] The mention of Brabant's attack as the cause of the order casts some doubt on the claim that the duke himself met his end in the killing of the prisoners, unless we consider it unlikely that Lannoy, inside the house, would have known who was leading the new French attack. Des Ursins also has it that peers such as Nevers, Alençon and Brabant met their end in the killing of the prisoners, but in his account it was rumour that the Duke of Brittany was coming with a large company that caused the French to rally, 'which was a bad thing for most of the English killed their prisoners'. This may reveal an anti-Breton stance. For the *Chronique de Normandie*, it was rather the people of the king of Sicily (i.e. Duke Louis of Anjou) whose arrival prompted English fears of a new attack. Uniquely, this writer claims that the order to kill the prisoners specifically excluded men of noble rank.

Several French accounts, including the Berry Herald, Basin and the *Chronique de Richemont*, make no mention of the killing of the prisoners at all. But lengthy accounts are found in other texts of Burgundian affiliation. Those of Le Fèvre and Waurin have been seized upon by English historians because of their story that English soldiers refused to kill their prisoners as they had hoped to become rich. Henry's response was allegedly to appoint a gentleman with 200 archers to carry out the order. The assumption has been that archers were men of lesser rank who had fewer sensibilities and no prisoners of their own. Evidence from the post-campaign accounts would suggest that the latter point was certainly not the case. We cannot be certain that the story is true, since it is only found in these highly interdependent works. Although Le Fèvre was with the English army, we might have expected the story to find its way into an English source. More useful is the rest of the explanation provided by these authors. They also suggest that the English were already victorious; when they saw the French could no longer resist, they started to take prisoners, 'hoping all to become rich'. Once captured, the prisoners had their helmets removed. But then many of the rearguard, in which were French, Bretons, Gascons, Poitevins and others (Waurin specifically mentions the central division) *who had previously been put to flight*, began to regroup. Since they had with them a large number of standards and gave the appearance of marching forward in battle order, Henry responded by ordering each man to kill his prisoner. The esquire and his archers carried out the order in cold blood. Here the authors echo Dynter, with the cutting of heads and faces mentioned as the way the killing was effected. A quick knife to the neck was all it took. The *Chronique de Ruisseauville* also notes that any found on the field the next day, whether living or dead, and whether French or English, were cut in the face. Waurin and Le Fèvre continue their account by telling us that when the company of French saw that the English were ready to take them on and fight, they took to flight. The mounted managed to get away but many of the infantry were killed. These are the only accounts that suggest that Henry did launch an attack at this stage. As with other accounts, Waurin and Le Fèvre are keen to apportion blame. For them it was 'the wretched company of French' who had caused the death of the noble knights. Again, therefore, this is probably a Burgundian complaint against Armagnac traitors.

Monstrelet's account also speaks of Henry's fear that the French were planning a new attack. Everywhere he looked they seemed to be regrouping. The order in this work is directly linked to a fear that in an attack the prisoners might help their compatriots. The way Monstrelet orders his text shifts the blame to Robert de Bourneville and Isambard d'Azincourt, who had previously launched an attack on the baggage. This is made more explicit by Fenin. In his account there is no mention of a French regrouping or of English misunderstanding. The killing of the prisoners is the direct result of the attack on the baggage by Bourneville and d'Azincourt, and for this they were later punished by Duke John of Burgundy.

Again therefore, the Burgundians emerge as heroes. The killing of the prisoners is therefore a distinctive and important element of the battle, and one which we shall return to again in the final section of this book.

BRAVERY OR COWARDICE?

In a defeat on the scale of Agincourt, it is not surprising to find a desire among chroniclers of both sides to emphasise French cowardice and folly. In some cases, some of which we have already noted, this extended to identifying particular individuals to blame. By contrast, English bravery, skill and strength of command was given pride of place in English accounts. These themes are worthy of further consideration in the context of how Agincourt was actually fought. Medieval battles, as their modern counterparts, were fought by massed troops. As a result, engagement is largely anonymous. This is indubitably the case with the use of artillery, including arrow fire. Even if some archers were particularly talented in hitting their target, this would be difficult to detect within the battle situation. When it came to hand-to-hand fighting, however, there was opportunity for acts of valour and achievement to be noted, but chroniclers were dependent upon reports fed to them after the event. There is a further complication, and that is their tendency to be interested only in the deeds of those of the highest social rank. We can gain a brief glimpse of personal successes through the post-campaign accounts, which record the capture of prisoners by the rank and file. For instance, it was Ralph Fowne, a man-at-arms in the retinue of Sir Ralph Shirley, who captured the Duke of Bourbon, but neither in his case or any other can we flesh this out with further detail.

The majority of chronicles mention no individual acts at all. This may have been due to a lack of information but it was also related to the purpose of the writer. It is noticeable that the *Gesta* includes no deeds of arms, not even any performed by the king. The explanation is simple: for this writer, the victory was God's. A popular tradition of the king's own bravery did emerge quite soon, however. For Walsingham, for instance, the king fought 'not so much as a king but as a knight, yet performing the duties of both'. The chronicler credits Henry with flinging himself against the enemy, showing an example to his men and scattering the enemy with his axe. The *Liber Metricus*, another early text, gives two specific examples of Henry's personal valour. The first is that the crown of the king was broken off his helmet by an axe-wielding Frenchman. This found its way into the vernacular tradition, since some of the versions of the *Brut* chronicle note that a piece of his crown was broken off and afterwards brought to him. All of the *Brut* chronicles have Henry fully involved in the fighting 'with his own hands'. This line is also found in Titus Livius and the Pseudo-Elmham and in the poetic commemorations of the battle, such as the 'Agincourt Carol'.

The second example given in the *Liber Metricus* is that the king stood over his brother, Humphrey, Duke of Gloucester, in order to protect him when he had been wounded and was lying on the ground. This is also found in Titus Livius and the Pseudo-Elmham but with some interesting variation between the two. While Titus Livius is at pains to tell us that Gloucester (who was after all his patron) had himself fought bravely and had fallen with his feet towards the enemy – making it clear that he was facing up to the French attack and not retreating – the Pseudo-Elmham says rather that the duke was pushing forward too vigorously on his horse into the conflict. This last reference takes us back to the possibility that the leading commanders of the English, including the king, were on horseback for all or part of the battle. It would have been a convenient means of visiting the various parts of the conflict and of inspiring the troops to fight.

Few French chronicles give any mention of Henry's personal involvement. Gruel, in his *Chronique de Richemont*, includes the story about the king standing over his brother, although it erroneously names Clarence rather than Gloucester. In this text, it was while in this position that Henry received a blow to his crown which forced him to his knees. In Monstrelet, however, it is the Duke of Alençon who breaks the crown with an axe blow, while the king is making efforts to come to the rescue of the Duke of York, whom Alençon had previously engaged. In *Waurin* and *Le Fèvre*, the fleuron is struck off by the axe of one of an eighteen-strong company drawn from the retinue of the Sire de Croy, which had made it their particular aim to attack the king. The *Chronique de Richemont* includes a further unique reference to two other men being dressed like the king in the battle, both of whom were killed. It is possible that it was deployed at Agincourt, as it may have been at Shrewsbury in 1403, and is another example of Henry's use of guile.

Although chronicles written under the Yorkist kings credit the Duke of York with the idea of the stakes, neither they nor any other chronicle include any specific deeds of arms by the duke during the engagement. Only in the ballad tradition do other peers gain mention. In the poem on the battle included in the BL Cleopatra CIV chronicle, the bravery of the king and Gloucester is emphasised, although without reference to the story of the king protecting his brother.[15] York, Huntingdon, Suffolk, Sir Richard Kyghley, Sir William Bourchier and Sir Thomas Erpingham are all given by name with poetic reflection on their role. Another ballad of the 1440s mentions Gloucester, Huntingdon, Oxford and the 'young Earl of Devon'. This presumably means Sir Edward Courtenay, the eldest son of the blind earl, who was on the campaign but who died before his father, rather than his younger brother, who succeeded to the title but did not serve in 1415.

What of references in chronicles to individual prowess on the part of the French? We might have expected Gruel to have emphasised the valour of the Count of Richemont but this is not the case. Indeed, none of those taken prisoner is mentioned in connection with any deeds of arms. The Religieux' account expresses sadness that his commanders of the van, the Count of Vendôme and Guichard Dauphin, both equally renowned for their prudence as well as their valour and fidelity, were forced to retreat in the face of the English archers after they had lost many of their best men. While this author seeks to explain their actions in a sympathetic manner, he is less flattering about the Duke of Alençon. Until then, the author opines, the duke had held a good reputation for wisdom, but 'carried away by a foolish passion and an overwhelming desire to fight, he left the main body of the army over which he had the command and threw himself boldly into the middle of the mêlée'. Other writers provide a rather more positive interpretation. In the *Chronique de Normandie*, Alençon is portrayed as mounting his horse and trying to rally the French. When he realised that he could not, 'he returned to the fight and performed marvellous deeds of arms before he fell'. Des Ursins also mentions report that Alençon 'did wonders with his body'. Monstrelet provides a fuller account of the duke's doings. In this version Alençon had penetrated with the aid of his troops the whole English battle, right through to the king himself. In this he had already overcome and killed the Duke of York. The king tried to come to York's defence and was hit on the helmet by Alençon's axe. The king's bodyguard rallied to protect their sovereign and surrounded the duke, who gave his name and expressed his willingness to surrender. The king would have accepted his oath but his bodyguard struck him down. It is surprising that Perceval de Cagny, chronicler of the Dukes of Alençon, does not include any of this story nor any other remark on the duke's supposed bravery at the battle.

Likewise, although Dynter's chronicle on the Dukes of Brabant provides a narrative of Duke Edward's determination to reach the battle and to enter the fray, the author does not use the opportunity to extol the duke's prowess. He simply describes him as 'throwing himself into the battle'. Indeed, he earlier laments that the duke did not read all of the letters sent to him about English movements, since had he done so he might not have tried to move so quickly. As with Alençon, therefore, rashness is emphasised rather than valour. The Religieux is even more scathing. In his interpretation, Brabant was 'a young prince who was well loved and in whom one had placed great hopes for the well being of the kingdom'. As we saw, he had been an important mediator between his brother of Burgundy and the crown in the period of civil war. But in the battle, the Religieux account speaks of him abandoning 'the command of troops placed under him in order to distinguish himself by some act of prowess, and had therefore going off to join the leading barons who had flocked to the front in their rash and imprudent haste'. Although several other chronicles mention Brabant's late arrival and desire to fight, nowhere is he applauded for his valour. Indeed, in some cases, including the autobiographical account of Ghillebert de Lannoy, his action is cited as a reason for Henry's order to kill the prisoners.

References to individual valour in the French army are therefore sparse. The Religieux account speaks of the Archbishop of Sens dealing blows on the enemy to the right and left, for which he paid with his life for his 'bold effort'. The Seneschal of Hainault is also mentioned by this author although, as with Alençon and Dynter, the emphasis is on his past valour and exploits rather than on his bravery in the battle. Des Ursins cites the *bailli* of Boulogne as carrying out great deeds in the battle, for which he was recognised as a worthy man by the English. Waurin and Le Fèvre applaud the bravery of the eighteen members of the company of the Sire de Croy, led by Lauvelet de Masinguehem and Gaviot de Bournoville, who tried to attack Henry in person. This displays a local bias in favour of the Picard soldiers, but despite telling us that all eighteen were hacked to pieces, neither of the two named men appears in the chroniclers' lists of dead. More telling is their concluding comment that 'if everyone had behaved in this fashion on the side of the French, it is credible that the English would have fared much worse'. Once again, therefore, we are faced with the blame culture that came to surround the battle. Not surprisingly, no English writer mentions French feats of arms. Rather the emphasis is on how their pride and arrogance had led to their destruction. In reality, those French who did engage fought as bravely as they could. These included Burgundians as well as Armagnacs. The question remains, however, as to whether all who were present at the battle did engage. Once the vanguard was annihilated, there is a strong suspicion that those who had not yet joined the fight declined to do so. When some decided to do so after a lull, Henry's order to kill the prisoners persuaded them too to withdraw. The day was his.

The Aftermath,
26 October–16 November 1415

A s night fell on Saturday 25 October, how different stood the world for the English and French compared with twenty-four hours earlier.[1] The English army, although exhausted and lamenting their own losses, had won the day. The bodies of their dead littered the ground. Clearing-up operations could begin. Unfortunately, just as it is difficult to assign preparatory events with certainty to the Thursday afternoon or the Friday morning, so too it is not easy to know the distribution of activities between the late afternoon of the battle and the morning of the next day. It is interesting to review this subject, however, since the immediate aftermath of medieval battles is not an area that has been given much thought. In this chapter we shall try to reconstruct what happened between the end of the battle and the return of Henry to England around 16 November. This will be interspersed with detailed considerations of the French and English dead, and of the French who were taken prisoner.

How did everyone know the battle had ended? The *Gesta* and the Religieux suggest that it was simply by the French abandoning the field to the English by flight, although it is not possible to ascertain precise movements as they dispersed. In three accounts, heralds feature in 'formal closures'. In Titus Livius and the Pseudo-Elmham, Henry sent his heralds 'to the French of the new army', which seemed to be threatening attack and whose appearance had occasioned the order to kill the prisoners. The heralds asked whether they would come to fight, in which case the rest of the prisoners as well as they themselves would be put to the sword, or whether they would withdraw. The chronicler has them departing, with great sadness at their shame. The more famous use of heralds is in Monstrelet's account. After the French had 'departed in flight to many different locations', Henry summoned the king-of-arms of the French, Mountjoye, and other French and English heralds. The conversation began with Henry claiming that the killing was not his fault but divine intervention to punish the sins of the French. The king then asked to whom victory should be accorded, himself or the king of France, which seems to be an extremely contrived remark to which Mountjoye made the obvious answer. Then the king asked the name of the castle nearby and, on being told it was Agincourt, uttered the famous opinion that 'since all battles ought to take their name from the nearest fortress, village or town where they happened, this battle from henceforward and for ever more will be called the battle of Agincourt'. The king's comment is also found in *Waurin* and *Le Fèvre* but without reference to heralds: it is the French princes who tell him the name. The omission of reference to the heralds in these accounts is significant, since Le Fèvre is thought to have been with the English heralds and was later himself King-of-Arms of Duke Philip of Burgundy's order of the Golden Fleece. If this incident had occurred, then we would surely have expected to find it in *Le Fèvre* and hence also in *Waurin*, since their accounts of the battle are extremely close.

Since there is no other contemporary example of the principles of battle-naming, we cannot know whether the story was invented or whether it followed practices common by the time the Burgundian chroniclers compiled their works. When the victory was announced in London on 29 October and in parliament on 4 November, it was given no name, a situation that continued into the parliaments of 1416. When news arrived in Bordeaux on 23 November 1415, it was described as 'the victory of Picardy' (*la victoria de Piquardia*). It is difficult to know when it became commonly known in England as 'Agincourt', since we cannot date precisely writings such as the couplet found in Adam of Usk which attributed the victory at Harfleur to St Maurice, and that of Agincourt to St Crispin and Crispianus, and in the 'Agincourt Carol'. The 'field of Agincourt' is mentioned in an entry in the ledger book of the city of Salisbury, which may be derived from a newsletter, and it was certainly the description used in the *Liber Metricus* and the *Gesta*. The impression is, therefore, that it developed as the popular name for the battle and was taken up as the official term later in the reign, much as the brothers Crispin overtook Henry's own association of the victory with St John of Beverley. In France, it became the immediate name, as can be seen from its inclusion in a royal letter dated 29 October.[2]

There is no doubt that Henry ordered the English to return to Maisoncelle, where they had lodged on the eve of battle and where presumably English tents were still *in situ*, even if some of the baggage train, containing the royal treasures, had been brought up behind the lines for the battle. According to Titus Livius and the Pseudo-Elmham, Henry held a feast that night, where he was served by his French noble prisoners. If true, this provides a contrast with the victory at Poitiers, where the Black Prince waited upon the captured John II. No English source makes further comment on the events of the night of battle. The Religieux claims that Henry called his army together after the victory and gave them an oration.

This thanked them for risking their lives and encouraged them to remember the day as proof of the justice of his cause. He urged his men to thank God that English losses were so few, declaring himself horrified that so much blood had been spilled, a contrast with Monstrelet's comment. It is an attractive thought that Henry gave a post-battle oration connected, as the Religieux also implies, with an opportunity for his men to pay their last respects to the dead, but only one source – and a French non-eyewitness at that – mentions the event. While the *Gesta* waxes lyrical on the theme of 'not to us, oh Lord, but to You', and also of how the English were moved by the sight of the heaps of slain and by rejoicing and amazement that so few English had died, there is no suggestion of formal religious ceremonial.

Nor does the *Gesta* mention that as night fell the English searched through the heaps of the fallen, but this is found in other eyewitness accounts. The aim was to retrieve English dead and wounded as well as to find Frenchmen who were still alive and to strip armour from the enemy dead. Le Fèvre and Waurin tell us that archers carried off to their lodgings across their horses both their dead companions and armour booty. When night fell and Henry was told about the armour taken to their billets, he had it proclaimed throughout the camp that no one should take more than he needed for his own use, ordering that what was surplus to requirements should be put into a house or barn and burned. The burning of military equipment as well as of English dead in a barn is also mentioned in Dynter, although placed on Saturday 26 October. It may indeed have continued into the next day. The implication is that English soldiers had limitations placed on booty. Monstrelet takes this further by suggesting that when the French came to the field on the Saturday after the English army had left, they found a great amount of armour still there. He also remarks that the English did not take away 'much gold and silver, clothing or hauberks or other things of value', but that it was rather the local peasantry who stripped the bodies of their remaining clothing and shoes, thereby leaving them naked.

The sources are contradictory on the issue of booty-taking. Le Fèvre and Waurin later suggest that the English soldiers sold their gear as well as prisoners at Calais in order to buy food, which may be taken to read that they had booty to sell but refrained from selling it! In the *Gesta*, however, French bodies are described as being stripped by English pillagers, and there it is also claimed that the French in their flight abandoned their wagons, 'many of these loaded with provisions and missiles, spears and bows'. Yet there is no evidence in the post-campaign accounts of war gains derived from booty taken at the battle. The indentures required that in gains of prisoners, booty, money, gold, silver and jewels worth more than 10 marks (£6 13s 4d), the captain would be entitled to a share of a third and the crown to a third of a third. A suspicious mind might think that it was simply a case of soldiers not disclosing their gains, but in the close-knit and generally well-disciplined camp it would have been difficult for gains to be kept secret. There are two further interpretations. First, that Henry allowed gains of value to be kept by their taker. This would be most unlikely given his emphasis on royal rights and his shortage of funds. Secondly, that soldiers took gains, but of low value and principally of military equipment. Battles were not the best place for finding booty other than this. Much better a captured town for coffers of money, plate and jewels. The records of Amiens inform us that the town sent men to recover from the battlefield war material that belonged to it and that the *bailli* had requisitioned. They found none save for two large cannons, two small but damaged *pavises* (large wooden shields) and parts of tents.[3] Unfortunately no date is given for this visit to the field, but the implication is threefold – that the surviving French had left hastily, that the field bore the scars of battle for some time afterwards, and that war gear was removed, whether by the English or local scavengers.

It is also worth noting that Le Fèvre and Waurin explain the king's order by his belief that the English were not yet out of danger from the French. The *Chronique Anonyme* adds that Henry wanted to move swiftly to Calais because he feared that those who had fled or survived the battle might reassemble to fight with him again. Perhaps Henry had gleaned military intelligence that the Duke of Brittany was at Amiens and that other 'latecomers' were nearby. His fear would also fit with the suggestion in the previous chapter that some of the French at the battle left the field without entering into combat, and were therefore still in a condition to fight should they choose to do so. Into this context we must also place a remark made by Le Fèvre and Waurin that 'if the battle had been on the Saturday there would have been an even greater number [of banners present] since on all sides men were flooding in as if they were going to a festival of jousting, joust or to a tournament'.

Neither in chronicles nor in the post-campaign financial accounts is there any mention of the capture of French horses by the English. Monstrelet claims that three-quarters of the English army were on foot in the subsequent journey to Calais, implying a shortage of horses. As we saw, chroniclers suggest that horses were plundered from the English camp during the battle, therefore we might have expected evidence of attempts to recoup their losses, but there is none. The post-campaign accounts that detail the cost of shipping horses and men back to England certainly indicate that there were still substantial numbers of horses with the army. Monstrelet's comment is not wholly reliable and is not found in the eyewitness accounts of Le Fèvre and Waurin. Interestingly too, there is no mention of the capture of banners. Certainly none of the accounts of Henry's entry to London suggest that he paraded the French banners, although they do mention the presence of prisoners. Either none were taken or, more likely, this was not considered a relevant symbolic act in this period. I have often been asked why the English did not capture the *oriflamme*, that symbol of French resistance which Charles VI had taken from Saintt-Denis on 10 September 1415 and entrusted to Guillaume Martel, Sire de Bacqueville. The latter was killed at the battle, but there is no comment in any text that the banner was taken as a result. The king was not present in person at the battle, so neither was the *oriflamme*. Since it was taken from St Denis on later occasions, such as for the proposed relief of Rouen in November 1418, it must have been returned there.

Henry's caution, as suggested through his possible ban on the keeping of booty, is mirrored by his initial reluctance to let the French recover their dead, another sign that he feared their regathering. In the *Chronique de Ruisseauville*, there is a claim that representatives of the defeated (perhaps the heralds) came at the end of the day to 'the king of France' (the context makes clear, however, that Henry is meant) to ask whether they might see to their duty: 'that is, they might go amongst the dead to see which lords were dead and which were not'. The king replied that because of the late hour they could not go that day but on the next. The chronicle goes on to tell us that Henry had 500 well-armed men sent out to search among the dead and to remove their coats of arms, no doubt as an aid to identification so that the heralds could compile lists of dead, the implication being that the French were kept away despite their request. The chronicler adds that those charged with carrying out this task were armed with small axes, with which they cut both the dead and the living in the face, and that they took off much armour. Le Fèvre and Waurin also suggest that some searching by the English was carried out on the Friday, but in their narrative it continues into the Saturday. On that day, they claim, any Frenchman found alive in the searching of the field was either taken prisoner or killed.

Whenever it occurred, this was effectively a second 'killing of the prisoners'. In theory, all who surrendered should have been ransomed or released. Yet men were apparently killed. Presumably this was because many were not 'of name' and therefore not appropriate for ransom. Others may have been so wounded that they were unlikely to survive long enough to be ransomed. The implication is that such men were not left alive but were put out of their misery by a quick thrust of a dagger to the face or neck. This raises a question of whether medieval society had a concept of 'mercy-killing', or whether these acts were seen as simply a finishing-off of the business of the day before. Many French would have been seriously wounded and hence unable to leave the field, but the nature of their wounds would not necessarily have led to a quick death. Gruel tells us that Richemont was pulled out from under the dead 'a little wounded, being recognised by his coat of arms even though it was all bloody'. Most likely this searching was done as soon as possible after the battle, since the English would have been keen to ensure that no valuable prizes escaped them.

By the same token, it was to be expected that the French would try to recover their dead as soon as possible. Monstrelet has it that some French came during the night and dragged bodies to a woodland area close to the field where they had them buried. There is no suggestion in any account that Henry posted guards on the battlefield during the night. The *Chronique de Ruisseauville* suggests that some of the defeated had hidden after the battle in hedges and bushes, but were discovered by local men from the Ternois and Boulognais who then killed them and stripped them of their money, armour and horses. Particularly vulnerable here it seems were the *gros varlets* (military servants of the men-at-arms), pages and servants, unless they had the protection of soldiers. Even if the English did not attack what was left of the French camp, the servants of the dead and wounded would have been in a vulnerable position, not knowing what to do, with their masters dead or missing. While they might have wished to find their master's body, they would have waited until it seemed safe to do so, hence, perhaps, Monstrelet's comment on the night-time activities to retrieve bodies. If the *Chronique de Ruisseauville* is to be believed, then the French death toll was boosted by the actions of what were effectively local gangs, out for rich pickings and also perhaps for revenge on any connected with the shameful defeat.

Arrangements were made for disposal of the English dead. According to the *Brut* chronicle, the only bodies taken back to England were those of the Duke of York and the Earl of Suffolk.[4] The *Liber Metricus* claims that Henry washed the body of York for burial himself. This may have been an act of personal respect for a close relative and comrade-in-arms, but the bodies were boiled on the Friday night so that the bones could be put into barrels and taken back to England. This procedure is mentioned in *Waurin* and *Le Fèvre*, although they mistakenly refer to Oxford instead of Suffolk (the former survived the battle). Boiling stripped the flesh from the bones and was a means of preserving bodies more appropriate for armies on the move than embalming. Evidence suggests that it was customary for armies to carry a large cauldron for this purpose.[5] It is unclear whether any other English bodies were brought back for burial. Although there is tomb chest for Roger Vaughan in the church at Bredwardine (Heref.) we can never be sure that such monuments actually house bodies. The texts give no indication of where the remaining English were buried. Dynter comments that on the Saturday, the bodies of the English slain, save for those of the leading lords which were taken to England, were placed into a barn along with military equipment and burned. Whether this is the same barn-burning as referred to by Le Fèvre and Waurin is unclear.

The burning of bodies may seem an unusual gesture but it was a speedy way of disposal which avoided danger of disease. Furthermore, as the English intended to move on quickly, it would have taken less time to dispose of cremated remains. We have no idea as to where these were buried, nor whether there was a need to consecrate ground for the purpose. The Religieux ends Henry's supposed post-battle oration with the king's expression of compassion 'for all the deaths and especially those of his comrades in arms'. The chronicler then goes on to say that 'he had them pay their last respects and ordered that they should be buried so that they would not remain exposed to the weather and that they would not be devoured by wild animals or birds of prey'. This may represent some kind of office for the dead. English accounts are silent on this and on the details of disposal of the bodies. It might be considered surprising that the *Gesta* says nothing other than to note the king's order, 'out of consideration for his men', that they should spend the night of the battle where they had spent the previous night, and to tell us that on the Saturday morning Henry resumed the march to Calais, 'past that mound of pity and blood where had fallen the might of the French'. In the next sentence the king arrives in Calais. Once the victory was secured, and God's support for Henry made manifest, the author did not consider it relevant to his purpose to include mundane details about the clearing-up activities.

Several French chronicles have Henry commenting on the high mortality rate, either in the aftermath of the battle or in conversation with his noble prisoners *en route* to Calais. In both circumstances, his emphasis is that God has brought this disaster on the French because of their sins. Des Ursins includes a lengthy tirade when the king entertains his prisoners to dinner (here given as the Sunday), which blames marital infidelity as well as sacrilege and robbery of the whole population. A watered-down version of them, considerably more flattering towards Henry, is found in *Waurin* and *Le Fèvre*. Even if the latter was still in the king's company after the battle, it is unlikely that he heard any such conversations first hand. More likely these stories were developed as part of the blame culture in France, but they may have a root in Henry's arrogance which, ironically perhaps, derived from his religiosity and 'humility' in ascribing the victory to God.

Where English chronicles mention the French dead, their purpose is to praise Henry. One version of the *Brut* chronicle has Henry returning to the battlefield 'to see what dead there were, both French and English, or if any were wounded that might be assisted'. In the *Liber Metricus*, though not in the *Gesta*, Henry revisits the field on the Saturday, 'with a great show of pious compassion'. It is only in French accounts that any detail is given to the question of burial, and there is a variety of comment, dependent upon the political inclinations of the writer. The Religieux, for instance, omits any mention of the idea that the English killed those they decided not worth ransoming: 'the English put to ransom all the others, even those who were lying on the ground amongst the dead and who were still breathing and giving signs of life'. This writer later tells us that the king showed his willingness that the French dead should be buried honourably. To this end, in response to the requests of the captured French princes, he agreed that the Bishop of Thérouanne should bless 'the unhallowed place' so that it might serve as a cemetery.

Monstrelet gives a fuller, and as we shall see, contradictory narrative on how the pits were consecrated.[6] In his account, the French came back to the field on Saturday once Henry had left it. They carried out a further search through the bodies to find their masters, so that they might be taken off for burial in their own lands. Any found alive were taken to local towns and hospitals, where some subsequently died. According to Dynter, Engilbert d'Enghien was found three days after the battle and was taken to Saint-Pol, but did not long survive. Over the next five days, the bodies of the Dukes of Brabant, Bar and Alençon, the Counts of Nevers, Blâmont and Vaudémont, and of the Sires de Fauquembergues and Dampierre were found, washed and taken off for burial. Monstrelet adds that 'all who could be recognised were taken up and carried away to be buried in the churches of their lords'. Des Ursins notes that servants who had come in search of bodies found most of them unrecognisable. This was due in part to the laceration of faces by the English, both in the killing of the prisoners and of the wounded in the aftermath of the battle. We noted in the previous chapter Dynter's comments on how the dead Duke of Brabant was found to have been wounded only in the face and neck, having been seen taken alive in the battle. The bodies would soon start to decompose and become carrion, since they had been stripped of their clothing either by the English or local pillagers. Monstrelet mentions a search lasting till the next Wednesday. Dynter comments that it was not until two days after the battle that the duke's naked body was found by his servants, 'a long way from the battle site and from where his men had been'.

Monstrelet continues his account of the burials with a note that Dampierre was buried at (Vieil) Hesdin in the church of the Franciscans. A later manuscript places him in the church of Auchy-les-Hesdin with twenty-eight others who fell at the battle, of whom sixteen were buried in the church and twelve in the cemetery.[7] Another tradition has it that Dampierre was laid in the church of his manor of Rollancourt on the Ternoise, a short distance downstream from Blangy.[8] D'Albret was buried at the Franciscans of Vieil Hesdin, with thirteen others. The leading peers were carried further: the Archbishop of Sens to his cathedral, along with his nephew, Charles de Montagu, Lord of Marcoussis; the Count of Nevers to the Cistercian monastery of Elan, near Mézières in the Ardennes; the Count of Roucy to the abbey church of Braine-Sur-Vesle; the Duke of Alençon was transported to the abbey church of Saint-Martin at Sées (although his entrails were buried at the same location as d'Albret); the Duke of Bar to Bar-le-Duc, where he was buried on 6 November in his castle chapel. The body of his brother John was never recovered. Even men of lesser rank were sometimes taken home. Guillaume de Longueil, captain of Dieppe, and his son were buried at the church of St Jacques in the town.[9] Dynter tells us that the body of the Duke of Brabant was taken to Saint-Pol where it was put into a lead coffin with spices and aromatic herbs. On the vigil of All Saints (31 October, although Dynter gives the day as a Tuesday, which would make it 29 October) it was taken to Tournai, where it was escorted by the bishop and chapter. On 1 November (which Dynter wrongly gives as the Wednesday), it was then taken to Hal, where it rested overnight at the church of St Mary, being transported to the church of St Gaule at Brussels on 2 November. The duke was then taken to Fure on 3 November and buried, after a requiem mass in the church of St John, alongside his first wife.

According to Dynter it was the duke's confessor, Brother Hector, and his chamber servants who sought out the Brabant's body at the battlefield. Monstrelet claims, however, that Philip, Count of Charolais, son of the Duke of Burgundy, was responsible for having the bodies of his uncles of Brabant and Nevers sought out, and for seeing to the burial of the French in general, commissioning the Abbot of *Ruisseauville* and the *bailli* of Aire for this task.[10] The chronicler goes on to say that they had an area of twenty-five square feet marked out, within which three trenches were dug 'each as wide as two men'. Into these pits were placed, 'according to an account kept', 5,800 men, namely those who had not been taken for burial elsewhere. The burial land was blessed by the Bishop of Guines (more likely the Bishop of Aegina *in partibus*) at the command of Louis de Luxembourg, Bishop of Thérouanne, and thorny branches placed across it so that animals could not get in to defile or eat the bodies.

The involvement of the Bishop of Thérouanne is, as we have noted, also mentioned by the Religieux, but there it was Henry who gave permission for the consecration. We cannot be wholly confident about either account. As elsewhere in his account of the campaign, the Religieux saw fit to emphasise Henry's good lordship in contrast to that of the French. In reality, it is unlikely that Henry would have had time before he left Agincourt to have given permission for the consecration of the ground, nor would it have been his responsibility to do so, either at that point or as he waited at Calais for his return to England. Monstrelet, writing in the 1440s, was as equally keen to flatter Philip, erstwhile Count of Charolais, who was by then Duke of Burgundy. All three of the Burgundian chroniclers have it that Philip was keen to serve at the battle but his father prevented him, by having him kept in the castle of Aire. Suspiciously, that is the very place from which hailed the *bailli* supposedly involved in the burials. There is, however, no reason for the Count of Charolais to have authority in the matter. More likely, the burials were effected by ecclesiastical intervention. Agincourt lay within the diocese of Thérouanne; thus the involvement of the bishop is credible. The *Chronique de Ruisseauville* also comments that the ground was blessed by the bishop of Thérouanne accompanied by the Abbot of Blangy.[11] It speaks of five grave pits, each containing 1,200 men and topped with a cross of wood. The digging of pits is credible since there was no church at Agincourt until the sixteenth century. The traditionally assigned location is where a Calvaire was placed in later centuries close to the crossroads, but without further archaeological work that must remain only an assumption, albeit one that has become firmly held by all those interested in the battle. All in all, therefore, it is difficult to know with certainty what happened to the French dead and when, since the accounts of the burials are so politicised.

All chronicles give high figures for the French dead (see Appendix C). John Hardyng provides us with both the lowest figure in his second verse account

(1,508) and the highest in his prose account (100,000). In general, English writers give higher figures than their French counterparts. They exaggerated numbers for effect in order to glorify the victory, just as they did the size of the French army to start with. Even so, all chroniclers chose to give the impression that mortality in the battle was considerable. In other words, this was one of the most, perhaps the most, significant characteristics of the battle, and was a widespread opinion in England, France and elsewhere.

Hardyng precedes his figure of 100,000 by saying that this was 'according to the reckoning of the heralds'. Their role is mentioned in several other chronicles. In some cases there is express reference to their compiling a written list. This could only have been done systematically by surveying the bodies and recognising the coats of arms. We have an immediate difficulty, therefore, since only those of the armorial-bearing classes would be recorded. While in theory the heralds could draw up a list, all that could happen for the other ranks was to estimate numbers. There was no need to count them. At the time there would have been a lot less interest than we now have in knowing the level of total mortality at the battle. No one would have counted as the bodies of rank and file were buried. The total figures put forward in chronicles are therefore not to be taken as accurate but were included for effect. By 100,000 Hardyng meant a very large number, but in reality it is not easy to assess the numbers of dead lying on the ground in heaps after a battle or to assess with accuracy numbers in a massed army seen from a distance.

A further issue arises even for those who could be recognised by their armorial bearings. If some of the bodies had been stripped on the night of the battle and subsequently, it would not have been possible to recognise even all of the dead of rank. As we have seen, several texts tell us how difficult it was for servants to find their dead masters. The longest lists of specific names are to be found in the Burgundian chroniclers, in an entry in the Salisbury ledger book (75) and in one of the versions of the *London Chronicles* (97, although with some garbled). These were presumably based on heralds' information. In addition, some chronicles add in names based on local knowledge. Dynter, for instance, mentions by name some associated with the Duke of Brabant; Gruel some of the Bretons fighting under Richemont. Town records also note deaths of office holders. It was indeed the case that many *baillis* and others were killed. Almost immediately Charles VI was bombarded with requests from men who wished to acquire the newly available and often lucrative posts.

It was not certain at the time, however, who had died at the battle. This is revealed by confusion over office-holding and by disputes over land which arose in the case of those 'missing believed dead'. In this context, it is significant that Alain Chartier includes this category in his poem lamenting the battle, the 'Livre des Quatre Dames'. His first woman has been widowed; the second's husband is a prisoner in England; the third does not know the fate of her husband. The fourth has the ignominy of her husband still living, since he fled in cowardice from the battle. It therefore took several years for Agincourt deaths to come to light, and there is a possibility that the battle was used as a convenience in property disputes.

Given all of these difficulties, it is not surprising that family and local traditions should spring up that so-and-so was killed at the battle. When Belleval drew up his list of named Agincourt dead, he included not only those named in the chronicles but also those given in the standard French genealogical and antiquarian works. Their reliability cannot be wholly trusted, since as in England there was kudos to be gained in later centuries from having an ancestor who died at Agincourt. By such means, Belleval created a list of 388 named dead. Ten more names can be added from Dynter, a text he did not use, and a handful from other sources, such as the town records of Amiens which reveal the death of the town captain, Louis de Brimeu.[12] What is striking is that many of the dead came from Picardy, Normandy and from other areas of northern France. There were a good number of local office holders among them, but relatively few, it seems, from the royal household.[13] There were several from the Burgundian group, especially among the peers and the retinue of the Duke of Brabant. This was politically significant. While the leading Armagnacs, Orléans and Bourbon, were captured, the martyrs to the French cause were largely lords from the eastern and northern frontiers, including two brothers of the Duke of Burgundy and the Duke of Bar. This is a point to which we shall return in the concluding section, since it had an impact on French politics thenceforward. Furthermore, there is no doubt that the high number of deaths of the gentry of Picardy and Normandy contributed to the difficulties of mounting effective resistance during Henry's second invasion of 1417–19.

There are also examples of more than one death in a family. David de Rambures, for instance, was killed as well as three of his sons. We can suggest from this that such men were fighting in the same part of the French formation, which leads to a more general conclusion that the 'esquires' of the various French retinues were kept together in the French army's main battles. That men of rank were killed also confirms the chroniclers' accounts that the French vanguard was packed with those of high status. We will never know for certain how many of the rank and file were killed. Many of the high figures must be placed within the context of chroniclers' exaggeration of the size of the French army in the first place. For instance, the *Brut* chronicle gives a high figure of 12,000 dead, but also an impossibly large French army at 120,000. Nor should we take this as representing 10 per cent, since medieval chroniclers did not think in this statistical fashion. Overall, there is no consistency in proportionality.

There is a further interesting phenomenon. While French writers tend to give rounded figures, English writers' often cite a random number, such Usk's 8,523. It is likely that this was a device deliberately employed to give an impression of exactitude. There is a wide variety even in texts written close to each other. This suggests that they were making the figures up or relying on hearsay rather than on any official statements issued by the government. The entry in the Salisbury ledger book may reveal such a statement. It gives seventy-five by name and adds '4,000 knights and esquires without counting the rest'. Perhaps this was therefore the figure being circulated in England, since it is reasonably close to the '4-5,000 other gentlemen' noted in the *Gesta*. We must conclude, however, that neither the French nor the English knew how many had died at Agincourt and that we cannot be any more certain today. Further research, especially in French local records, would throw up a few more names, but given the lack of formal demographic records for the period, we could never be able to ascertain the exact number killed. Excavation of death pits, if such could be found and investigated, might inform us on the nature of injuries but could not assist in the counting. Unfortunately too, we cannot distinguish between those who met their deaths in the battle or in the killing of the prisoners or in post-battle activity.

A feature of chronicles, and one which may have encouraged them to exaggerate the numbers of French dead, was the apparent contrast with English mortalities. While the former are given in thousands, the latter are numbered in tens or hundreds at most, and very few named individuals are given beyond York and Suffolk. English chroniclers give particularly low figures, ranging from thirteen in the *Gesta* to 102 in the Pseudo-Elmham and the Latin *Brut*. These last two sources, along with Titus Livius, which gives a hundred dead, are out on a limb compared with the rest of English texts where totals in the thirties predominate. French sources rarely mention the English dead at all, but where they do, the figures are in excess of those provided by English commentators.

We saw the careful way in which the dead and sick of Harfleur were recorded so that the crown might avoid paying for the service of men who were no longer in a position to render it. We might therefore have expected the same precision over deaths at Agincourt, yet few are noted in such sources. The totals found to date are fourteen archers killed at the battle, with a further three dying at Calais from wounds. Only three men-at-arms are recorded: Sir Richard Kyghley, who had his own retinue as well as charge of one of the contingents of Lancashire archers; Henry Strete in Huntingdon's retinue; and John Aungers in Erpingham's, who died at Calais.[14] Ninety men died in York's company, but we do not know the distribution between archers and men-at-arms.[15] Chronicle sources also mention Davy Gam. The fact that there was no systematic recording of the English dead in the financial records could be taken as confirmation that numbers of deaths were low. However, there is a further complication – the decision taken by Henry in March 1417 when the settlement of accounts for the campaign was debated. When faced with the question whether 'those accounting for men killed at the battle of Agincourt should have allowed to them for the whole of the second quarter or only to the day of their death', the king's decision was that 'they should be allowed as the others who are still living'.[16] In other words, indentees were not to suffer deductions for the days between 25 October and the end of the campaign, which was taken to be 16 November, although, for all companies save those of the royal household, it was subsequently extended to 23 November to allow for the time taken in shipping men home.

The decision not to make deductions for the Agincourt dead may have been for administrative ease, especially in the light of the extremely complicated calculations arising out of the siege of Harfleur, although the wording of the question implies that some records had been kept of the Agincourt dead. It could also act as further confirmation that English losses were low and therefore it was not worth worrying about, in terms of financial loss to the crown, if captains received money for a few dead men for a couple of weeks. Or was Henry deliberately obfuscating the level of English deaths in order to make the victory seem all the greater? At the time he made his decision, he was planning another major expedition to France. It would have been an encouraging gesture to allow payment for the Agincourt dead as if they had lived to see the victory, and a useful way of reminding the military classes of past triumphs when hoping to attract them towards a new bout of service. Furthermore, from the time of the battle onwards, the government emphasised how few English had died compared with the French. The opening sermon of the November 1415 parliament stated that 'all of the French were defeated, taken or killed, without great loss to the English'.[17] This situation surely confirmed God's support for the king and his people. It is not surprising, therefore, that the *Gesta* should give an exceptionally low figure in order to demonstrate this. As with the French, however, it remains unknown how many English died but we can be certain that it was many fewer. The significance of this will be returned to in the concluding section.

After revisiting the field on Saturday 26 October, Henry ordered his army to march on to Calais. The arrival at the town is dated in the *Gesta* and other English sources to Tuesday 29 October. Titus Livius and the Pseudo-Elmham place him at the castle of Guines overnight before he made ceremonial entry to Calais; Waurin and Le Fèvre imply not only that he stayed there for several days before entering Calais but also that he lodged there on other occasions before his return to England. These Burgundian chroniclers do not give an exact date for his entry to Calais, although it must have been before 1 November, since they have him celebrating the feast of All Saints in the town.

The route taken from Agincourt to Guines must be speculative. Since Ardres was in the hands of the Burgundians (indeed, Henry considered the feasibility of attempting its conquest while he was at Calais) the English would have taken a north-north-east direction after reaching Fauquembergues. The most direct route crossed the Bléquin at Nielles and the Hem at Licques, then traversed what was to become the Field of the Cloth of Gold. That field would have offered easy camping for the army while the king, his leading nobles and the major French prisoners lodged in Guines. The king entered Calais from the west across the Nieulay bridge.[18] The distance from Agincourt to Calais by this, the most direct route, is 64km. Assuming the journey took from Saturday to Tuesday, an equivalent of three whole days of marching, this gives an average of 21.3km per day. If the night of Monday 28 October was spent at or near Guines, the march to Calais on the following day would be only 12km. That would leave two-and-a-half days to traverse 52km, at an average of 20.8km per day. Overall, the speed of march appears marginally slower than the march from Harfleur.

We can dispute Monstrelet's comment that three-quarters of the English army were on foot, but not his suggestion that they 'were exhausted not just because of the battle but also because of hunger and other discomforts'. The English had been short of supplies before the battle and the victory had not eased that problem. No chronicle mentions the taking of victuals from the defeated army or from neighbouring villages. Some men, both soldiers and prisoners, would have been wounded, thus causing a further burden. The army probably moved in close formation to avoid the danger of ambushes on the flank. The records of Boulogne indicate that members of its garrison did carry out sorties, probably to ascertain whether Henry intended to make a move against their town, since this was greatly feared once news of his victory had arrived there on 26 October, and that they attacked some stragglers of the English army, taking a few prisoner. Le Fèvre (who may still have been with the army, although we cannot be sure of this) tells us that Henry always had his French prisoners placed between the vanguard and the main body of the army (batailles).

Chroniclers emphasise the welcome that Henry received in Calais. In the account of Le Fèvre and Waurin, he was received by the captain and by the inhabitants, who came out almost to Guines to meet him, accompanied by priests and clerks with crosses and banners of the town's churches and all singing the Te Deum. Once in Calais, the population greeted him with cries of 'Welcome, our sovereign lord', the children adding their own shouts of 'Noel'.[19] For Henry's soldiers the welcome may not have been so warm. The same chroniclers suggest that although the king stopped off at Guines, the majority of the army moved straight to Calais, hoping to enter the town to find refreshment and rest, 'of which they had great need for most of them had spent eight to ten days without eating bread and having of other victuals only the little they could find'. The people of Calais, however, would not let them enter because they wanted to protect their own food supply. Only some of the English lords were admitted. This story is not found in any English chronicle, but is entirely credible. The victualling of Calais was difficult even at the best of times, but the influx of thousands of soldiers would have taken it to breaking point. The royal household had supplies brought across for its consumption, but these would not have been distributed widely.[20] Furthermore, the town was not extensive enough to lodge all of the English army.

The Burgundian chroniclers suggest that once the king at Guines knew what privations his soldiers were suffering, he made provision as soon as he could for

shipping to transport them to England. The indentures obliged him to provide
return shipping but, as at the outset of the expedition, he was reluctant to impress
merchant ships. Shipping was assigned to the king's retinue,[21] but other captains
had to wait their turn and pay the shipowners directly, being empowered to claim
back from the crown 2s per head for their troops and 2s per horse. Whether this
was the actual expense borne by the captain or whether the latter made a profit
or loss is not known. It took many days for the troops to be shipped back. As a
consequence, for administrative ease and to avoid inequalities in length of service,
it was decided in March 1417 that captains should be allowed in their accounts
wages for eight days after the shipping had been assigned. All retinues were therefore paid up to 23 November. The post-campaign accounts provide useful detail
on the transport arrangements. As in the original crossing, retinues were kept
together where possible. In some cases we can see on which ships they crossed.
The majority were taken to Dover or Sandwich, but some went to Portsmouth
and Southampton. Not only are numbers of men given but also horses. In the
case of the Earl of Oxford, numbers of pages are also uniquely given. The earl
returned with twelve horses; his thirty-nine men-at-arms, all save four with
their own page, had seventy-seven horses between them. Of eighty-four archers,
thirty-seven returned with horses; the rest without.[22]

According to Waurin and Le Fèvre, Henry departed from Calais on
11 November. His arrival at Dover is given as 16 November in the *Gesta*, Titus
Livius and the Pseudo-Elmham. It does not appear, therefore, that the king had
rushed to return to England, despite the fact that parliament was due to open
on 4 November. Several reasons can be suggested for this. The first is that he
was waiting for the arrival at Calais of Raoul de Gaucourt and the other hostages from Harfleur, who were under obligation to come to Calais at Martinmas,
11 November.[23] The second interpretation is that he delayed until all of his army
had crossed to England. A third possibility is that he was considering remaining
in France in order to pursue further military endeavours. Only Titus Livius and
the Pseudo-Elmham mention this. The latter gives the longer account, claiming
that the king consulted with his 'people' on whether an attempt should be made
to take Ardres and other fortresses in the march of Calais. Opinion was against
this. In the wording of the Pseudo-Elmham, 'a decision was made that victories
so miraculous, given to the king by divine providence and without serious difficulty for himself and his army, should suffice for his honour for the present'.
Besides, there would be, they envisaged, by the will of fate, future times suitable
for the fulfilment of his desire. Interestingly, in Titus Livius, where Ardres is not
specifically mentioned, the king's alternative to continuing the campaign is that
the army should go back home to recover for a few months. Given the scale of
victory, it would not be surprising if the king was already contemplating another
invasion even at this point. At the opening of the parliament on 4 November,
the chancellor spoke of how well the 'propitious, honourable and profitable

expedition' of the king had begun, and that therefore there needed to be discussion and support, 'such as will be suitable for the accomplishment and continuation of the expedition'. The commons responded by agreeing to advance the second payment of the lay subsidy from 2 February to 13 December. The army was not kept in existence, however, despite the fact that technically it had indented for twelve months and had only served for four.

The progress of the king to London is not noted in the *Gesta* but is detailed in the *Brut* chronicle, since it included urban entries of interest to this style of vernacular chronicling. After Dover Henry went to Barham Down, where he was met by the representatives of the Cinque Ports, who presented him with a golden nef. This also allowed insertion of a story in praise of the English people that the Duke of Orléans thought the 10,000 fully armed men assembled by the Cinque Ports were a new army. Henry then rode on to Canterbury, where the townsmen and clergy met him and took him to the cathedral. There he made an offering at Becket's shrine. He then journeyed via Eltham Palace to London. Neither in the progress from Dover to London nor during the entry to London on 23 November is there any suggestion that he was accompanied by large numbers of his victorious army. The *Gesta* explicitly mentions that in the London entry the king did not have 'an imposing escort of impressively large retinue', but rather only ' a few of the most trusted members of his household in attendance, there following him, under a guard of knights, the dukes counts, and marshal, his prisoners'. The army had ceased to exist as soon as it left Calais. Alas, we have no materials that tell of the movements of individuals or retinues after the troops landed back in England.

As for the French, the situation is the same. News of the defeat was taken to the king and Dauphin at Rouen. The Religieux includes a lengthy discussion of this, with the supposed response to the king's desire to know how many dead there were. Interestingly, the number given is 4,000 as in the Salisbury ledger book. It does seem, therefore, that this may have been the figure in circulation in the period following the battle. On 29 November the king and his son returned to Paris. Meanwhile, there was one group of men for whom the aftermath of the battle persisted in a very distinctive way – the French prisoners. Chroniclers emphasise these for the same reason as the dead – they included some men of very high status. The majority name most or all of the 'big six' – the Dukes of Orléans and Bourbon, the Counts of Eu, Vendôme and Richemont, and Marshal Boucicaut. All six offered potential income in terms of ransom, but their value to Henry was more than monetary. Their capture remained a living symbol of French defeat for many years to come. This, fanned also by a fascination in the dealings of fate, encouraged chroniclers to include stories about them in the aftermath of the battle. First we have them serving the king at a banquet on the night of 25 October. The Pseudo-Elmham embellished the incident by reminding us that those were the self-same princes who in the morning believed that they would take Henry prisoner. This leads to a moralising on fate: 'for such is the change of fortune wrought by the right hand of Him on high'. Le Fèvre and Waurin provide another story, to much the same end, about the march to Calais. At a rest point, the king sent wine and bread to the Duke of Orléans, but he would not eat. When the king asked him why, the duke replied that he was keeping a fast. This provides a vehicle for another royal speech claiming that the victory had been brought about by the desire of the Almighty to punish the French for the excesses, sins and wicked vices that reigned in their kingdom. The implication is twofold: that the duke was fasting because he knew the truth of Henry's interpretation, and that, had he and the other lords shown more humility before the battle, then things might have transpired differently.

Given their status, Orléans and his fellow prisoners would have been treated well after the battle while being guarded carefully. The story in Le Fèvre and Waurin ends with the observation that 'they continued to ride in fine order as they had always done save that after the battle they no longer wore their cote armour as they had done before'. In other words, they were not allowed to be in defensive gear. Whether the prisoners were allowed to carry bladed weapons, very much a mark of status, is not indicated. Presumably after their capture they were not allowed to return to the French camp to collect their belongings. Des Ursins tells us that Henry gave them all a damask robe for the banquet, which he claims took place on the Sunday. If true, the king must have had surplus clothing in his royal baggage! It is interesting to note that Ghillebert de Lannoy, on his release from captivity in England, had to be given twenty nobles by his 'master', Sir John Cornwall, in order to buy a suit of armour.[24] That the prisoners were kept under close guard is implied by the remark in Le Fèvre and Waurin that on the march from Agincourt to Calais Henry 'always had his French prisoners placed between the vanguard and the main body of the army' (batailles). In addition, it is likely that they were allowed to keep only a few of their body servants. Gruel tells us that when Richemont went to England, there remained only one servant with him, Jennin Catuit. From the night of the battle onwards, the leading prisoners would have been lodged close to the king and his inner circle. This was, again, to ensure their safekeeping, but was also an acknowledgment of their status. Similarly, they were housed with Henry at the castle of Guines before formal entry was made into Calais, and may have mainly been kept at Guines until they were taken across to England with the king.

Chroniclers tell us of a few more Frenchmen taken to England as prisoners, such as Raoul de Gaucourt and his fellow defenders of Harfleur, who kept their bond to surrender at Calais on 11 November. It is not clear how and when they heard of Henry's victory. The assumption must be that they had gone to Rouen after the surrender of Harfleur. Ghillebert de Lannoy tells us that he was taken from Calais to England, where he was kept until a ransom of 1,200 écus and a horse was agreed. As with the dead, however, the chronicles display shortcomings in terms of providing a total number for prisoners. As Appendix C demonstrates, many chroniclers give the 'big six', along with a vague phrase about others. Only two textual traditions give larger numbers. Walsingham gives a total of 'up to 700, as it is said', with one version of the *Brut* chronicle suggesting 800. If the entry in the Salisbury ledger book is based on a newsletter, then it publicised only the six lords, adding 'and other gentlemen'. This could be deliberate government obfuscation because the killing of the prisoners had lowered the potential number, but this may be too modern a gloss. English writers did not see the victory as significant for the *number* of prisoners taken but simply for the status of the leading captives. As we shall see, there is evidence in administrative records of other prisoners put to ransom.

Several French chroniclers give higher figures for prisoners, as they do for the dead. Their purpose was to emphasise the scale of disaster that Agincourt was for their country, and to this end, exaggeration is to be expected. The highest number (2,200) is given in the *Chronique de Ruisseauville*. The numbers in the Religieux (1,400, with four named), *Monstrelet* (1,500) and *Le Fèvre* and *Waurin* (1,600) are close enough to suggest a common report, and it may be significant that the number reported to the Council of Constance was also 1,500.[25] In addition, all of these chroniclers emphasise that the captives were 'men of name' or, as otherwise expressed, 'knights and esquires'. Fourteen men are named by all three of the Burgundian chroniclers, with a total of eighteen different people mentioned by them altogether. Their emphasis is generally on men of the Artois/Picardy area. Two families are represented both by father and son. Other chronicles also add to the main prisoners' names, based on their regional interest. Gruel thereby names four Bretons in Richemont's company. Dynter gives five names from the Duke of Brabant's retinue, one of whom is named as 'of Brussels'. Des Ursins names two prisoners coincidentally. In his first version, he mentions the *bailli* of Boulogne, 'who at his caution delivered great resistance', reflecting some incident of which we are now ignorant. He claims that his second version of the battle was reported to him by someone called Tromagon, the king's yeoman of the chamber, who was taken prisoner and had come in search of his ransom, which had been set at 200 francs. The implication here is that Tromagon had been taken to England but had been allowed to return to raise his ransom, since Des Ursins adds that the Duke of Orléans stood pledge for him in this.[26]

Belleval identified fifty-one French prisoners, based on his search through chronicles and other sources. He found eight of these in the English governmental records printed in Rymer's *Foedera*. These included the local lord, Guillaume d'Azincourt. Belleval derived nine names from later antiquarian sources. As with the dead, this indicates local and family traditions rather than certainty that the individuals were captured at the battle. We can in fact trace larger numbers of prisoners through the English royal records. The indentures required any French prisoner of royal status or vice-regal command to be handed over to the king in return for compensation to the captor. In addition, the captains of retinues were entitled to one third of the war gains of their men, from which the crown creamed off a third of a third, in addition to a third of the gains made by the captain himself. Furthermore, the disciplinary ordinances laid down strict controls on soldiers' claims to prisoners, since it was all too easy for counter-claims to be put forward as a result of confusion in the heat of battle. As a result, there would have been recording of prisoners in a way that was not necessary for the dead. The Pseudo-Elmham tells us that at Calais 'the king ordered the names of all the prisoners to be presented to him so that at least he might know about them'. No list is known to survive, but prisoners can be traced through a variety of documentary sources.

From the account of Sir Ralph Rocheford, captain of Hammes, another fortress within the Calais march, we can see that eleven prisoners were lodged there, from the date the king returned to England until they were shipped over to the Fleet prison in mid-February 1417, by which time two had died.[27] There is also information in the post-campaign accounts, because of the royal rights to shares in ransoms. The account for Sir Ralph Shirley, for instance, records that the Duke of Bourbon had been taken by one of his men-at-arms, Ralph Fowne, esquire. As the indenture clause required, Fowne had handed over his prisoner, but we do not know what compensation he received. In the same source, Boucicaut is recorded as captured by William Wolf, esquire, within the retinue of the late Earl of Arundel. There are ten entries falling within the rules on sharing of war gains. In four of these the entry is for an unspecified number of prisoners, but the remaining six entries give three prisoners by name and a further five as 'French'. There is also some information given on the level of ransoms. For the Sire de Corps, who had been captured jointly by William Callowe, a man-at-arms in the retinue of Sir Robert Babthorpe, and William Kempton, a man-at-arms in the retinue of Sir William Phelip, the total ransom was £356 13s 4d. For Edrad de Droyle, captured by Robert Sadler, an archer in the retinue of Sir Thomas Chaworth, it was £58 13s 4d. In both cases the captains took one third of this price, with the crown taking a ninth.[28] Where an entry concerns a number of prisoners together, it is not possible to ascertain the ransom for each individual. There are other sources at our disposal, however, both for the names of prisoners and for ransom values. Those taken to England needed to find some way of raising their ransom. To that end, either they or their servants were given safe conducts to travel to France. These are recorded in the French (or Treaty) rolls.[29] Entries continue for several years after the battle. This raises a problem where a name first appears in later years, for we cannot be too sure that these were all Agincourt prisoners, as opposed to men taken on later campaigns. The comings and goings of the servants of the leading prisoners are noticeable, as also the release on parole of such as Gaucourt.

This reminds us of a major problem with ransoms – the time and effort needed to collect them. This affected the crown since the indenture terms entitled it to a share of the profit. In order to ensure that men rendered to the crown its dues, bonds were entered into, obliging the money to be handed over at a particular date. A number of these bonds still survive, naming around 100 prisoners. These shed interesting light on the ransom system.[30] They begin from the middle of December 1415 onwards, suggesting that it was at that point that the king became anxious about guaranteeing his share, but continue well into the following year. They set a deadline for payment between four and six months in the future. Some of those entering into bonds were men of the army. For instance, Henry, Lord Fitzhugh, entered into obligation to pay £27 to the king for the royal share for seven prisoners. In some cases the bonds were entered into by two men. These may reflect joint responsibility for capture, as we saw also in the post-campaign accounts. We cannot be wholly certain, however, that the prisoners had been taken by the soldier entering into the bond. It was common for captors to sell on prisoners, in order to achieve an immediate gain and to avoid the burden of maintaining the prisoner and the uncertainty that a ransom would ever be raised. Soldiers did buy prisoners from each other, but other men, such as Calais and London merchants, were also keen to make such purchases. For these 'ransom brokers' there was a good degree of speculation. Some are known to have purchased the rights to several prisoners, thereby spreading the risk, since the collection of a ransom was not necessarily easy.

The fact that the bonds obliged payment to the treasurer of Calais suggests that many prisoners were not brought to England but kept at Calais. Based on the French mainland, the Calais merchants were in a better position than most to pursue and collect ransoms. Some of the French may have managed to raise funds at Calais by sales of equipment and valuables or by borrowing from moneylenders. It was common for a prisoner to be released on surety, or after making a down payment on the full sum. He could then return home to raise funds. Men were on their honour to render payment to their captor or to the broker who had bought the right to their ransom. Even so, we cannot be certain that ransoms were collected in full, or even at all. Sir Roland Lenthale, for instance, entered into a bond for two prisoners on 10 February 1416, but when his post-campaign account was drawn up in the early 1420s no war gains were included.[31] This suggests that he never raised the ransoms, or that the royal share was settled and therefore was omitted from the final accounting procedure. There were also later disputes about ransom shares. Two soldiers who had taken prisoners at the battle, John Craven and Simon Irby, petitioned the Chancery later that William Bucton had wrongfully taken the prisoners from them and put them to ransom without giving them or the king their rightful shares.[32] The ransom brokerage system operated as soon as the army arrived at Calais, and to the disadvantage of the rank and file. Relevant here is a comment in *Waurin* and *Le Fèvre* that many English soldiers had to sell their equipment and their prisoners to the townsmen of Calais so that they could get money. Since all they were really interested in was to have bread to eat and to return to England, they were apparently prepared to set ransoms at a lower level, 'giving what was worth 10 nobles for four'. The sale and release of prisoners at Calais is another reason why numbers of prisoners taken to England may have been low, and hence another reason why English chroniclers do not record the battle as generating a notably high number of prisoners.

From all of the sources available, I have been able to name 282 prisoners so far. Historians tend to have an over-rosy view of ransom income as an incentive for military service. Only the post-campaign accounts can be used to prove the actual receipt of money from ransoms. In these, very few men made a handsome windfall. The archer Robert Sadler gained £32 11s 10 ½d, even after the crown and his captain had taken their share. Given a wage of 6d per day as an archer, this was equivalent to four whole years of service. Even more fortunate were William Callowe and William Kempton, who gained £99 each for their capture of the Sire de Corps. But arguably the real winners here were their captains, Babthorpe and Phelip, who pocketed £59 each as their perquisite, without having had the effort of taking the prisoners in the first place. This reminds us of how hierarchical the military system was. Exploitation of royal rights had also brought useful income to the crown at a time of financial pressure. More significant for Henry, however, was the capture of the French princes and commanders. At his entry to London on 23 November, they walked after the king and his leading nobles.[33] This was not a victory parade for the army as a whole but a manifestation that Henry had proved himself as king and warrior.

Epilogue:
Battle or Murder?

Surprisingly, Agincourt has not been seen as one of the decisive battles of the western world, but it should be. The events of Friday 25 October transformed the position of Henry V within his own kingdom and as a claimant to rights in France. Henry had invaded France in 1415 as the son of a usurper and with his own title insecure. There was even a plot to kill him on the very day he had chosen for embarkation. Had he failed in France, his future in England would have been precarious. But he did not fail. He returned as God's chosen king and warrior. He had proved himself. Now no one could challenge his title or his obsession with France. The English people entered one of the most heavily taxed periods in their entire history, as well as one of the most militarily demanding. Armies were sent to France almost every year between 1416 and 1444.

Victory at Agincourt inaugurated a remarkable set of triumphs. It immediately prompted diplomatic approaches from other European rulers, confirming Henry's new-found importance on the European stage. Most significant of all was the visit of the Emperor Sigismund, which culminated in admission to the Order of the Garter in May 1416 and an alliance three months later. The *Gesta* remarks that both men were 'as eager as blood brothers for one another's successes'.[1] Meanwhile, on the other side of the Channel, the inhabitants of northern France, having already borne the brunt of losses at Agincourt, lived in fear of the next attack. Henry intended to invade in the summer of 1416 but the army raised was diverted, to save Harfleur from French naval threat. Victory was gained by the Duke of Bedford at the battle of the Seine on 15 August, the day the imperial alliance was sealed. The fact that it was also the feast of the Assumption provided further evidence of Henry's God-given kingship. Even more remarkable was Henry's systematic conquest of Normandy, launched on 1 August 1417 with an army close to the size of that of 1415. Now calling himself Duke of Normandy as well as king of France, Henry conquered all of the duchy by the spring of 1419 and began to threaten Paris. French attempts to unite against the English threat failed. On 10 September the Duke of Burgundy was assassinated. Through the hole in Duke John's skull, as a friar graphically told Francis I in 1521, the English entered France.[2] The Burgundians, now led by Duke Philip, finally came to an open alliance with Henry. In the treaty of Troyes in May 1420, the English king was accepted by Charles VI as heir to the throne of France, thereby disinherit-ing the entire French royal family. Within less than five years of his first invasion, therefore, Henry V was poised to achieve what Edward III and all subsequent kings of England had claimed – the crown of France itself.

Shakespeare's *Henry V* moves us straight from Agincourt to the negotiations at Troyes. While much happened in the meantime, the direct link is justified. The memory of Agincourt was so deeply ingrained on French consciousness that they were never prepared to meet Henry in battle again, and hence were unable to offer resistance to his conquest of Normandy. Henry also exploited his hold-ing of the French prisoners, initially using them to put pressure on Charles VI to restore the terms of the Great Peace, and after Troyes to persuade them to accept his inheritance of France, which Bourbon and Richemont agreed to do.[3] While Agincourt had placed Henry's star in the ascendant, that of Charles VI and his family was in free fall. The battle had briefly united the French by the need to act against a common enemy, but the defeat threatened to reopen all the old divisions. In the midst of this came the premature death of Dauphin Louis in December. Huge efforts had to be put into the defence of Paris against the threats of the Duke of Burgundy, until the latter agreed to disband his army in March 1416.[4] Even then, all of the earlier mistrust continued, fanned by Henry's meeting with the duke at Calais in October. Although there is no firm evidence that they became allies, Henry's conquest of Normandy facilitated John's seizure of the capital and the king in May 1418. By this time another Dauphin, John, had died, and the last son of Charles VI, Dauphin Charles, was forced to flee south with the support of the Armagnac party. Full civil war erupted and led to Duke John's murder – revenge not only for his assassination of Duke Louis of Orléans in 1407 but also for his perceived treason over the intervening years.

The disaster of Agincourt had worked to Duke John's advantage. Given his absence from the battle, this may seem a strange outcome. What we must remem-ber is how much the Armagnac party had been sullied by the defeat. Burgundians at the battle, including the duke's two brothers and many of his trusted men, had died, martyrs to the French cause. Although Armagnacs had also been killed, their most prominent leaders, themselves royal princes, had been captured. In contrast to the Burgundian heroes, they had not fought to the death but had submitted to the ignominy of surrender. Their living presence in England, and their apparent willingness to work for Henry's interests, was a constant reminder of their failure. Given that Duke John had been discouraged or even banned from participation in the battle, it was all the easier for him to assign blame to the Armagnacs. On 25 April 1417 he issued a manifesto at Hesdin, charging them with, among other things, 'deliberately permitting Henry to invade France and to win the battle of Agincourt'.[5] Each side blamed the other for the disaster. Even though the failure in battle was not directly the result of divisions within France, the French turned on themselves because of the defeat.

The culture of blame was exceptionally politicised, but the feeling of humiliation was ubiquitous. As the Religieux puts it, there was grief at the loss of so many men and the waste of so much public money, 'but most galling of all was the thought that the defeat would make France feeble and the laughing stock of other countries'. Past triumphs had made the glory of France so brilliant: 'you, o shame, have tarnished this brilliance by your ill considered rushing forward, your disorder and your ignominious flight'. The exact date that this was written is not certain, but historians agree that the Religieux chronicle is the earliest French chronicle account of Agincourt. The three explanations put forward can all be sustained by an analysis of the battle. Too many men had been in the vanguard. They were already too packed but were made more so by the effect of the English arrows. When they reached the English line they could not raise their arms to fight. They fell on top of each other and those coming behind them could do little to save themselves from the same fate. Those in the rear formations did not participate in the battle but fled the field when they realised that their comrades had been mown down.

In this scenario, it was the French who lost the battle rather than the English who won it. They had been over-confident when they saw how few men-at-arms the English had and rushed to be in the front, since they hoped to win glory. It is not surprising that they should have been buoyed up by the fact they had hounded Henry for over two weeks and had finally brought him to battle at a place and time of their choosing. Yet research has revealed that there were intrinsic weaknesses even before the French began to fight. Henry had succeeded in crossing the Somme despite their best efforts, forcing them to act quickly to ensure that a large army could be assembled in the right location and at the right time. This was impossible to achieve. The situation may not have been helped by a change of intended location for the battle from Aubigny to Agincourt. Soldiers arrived in dribs and drabs over 24 and 25 October. Several never got there at all. As a result the army was smaller than it should have been, and only a few thousand in excess of the English. That in itself was less serious than the lack of time for adequate discussion on tactics. The man to whom command fell because of his royal seniority, the Duke of Orléans, arrived late, imposing his will on the more seasoned military men. Other lords arrived with their retinues and had to be fitted in at the last minute. There were conflicting plans, and input from Rouen by men who knew little of the reality of the situation that had developed. No one seems to have known what to do with the archers and crossbowmen. The numbers put into the cavalry charge were inadequate for the vast quantity of archers they were intending to override. And it had been raining.

We can analyse French weaknesses with the advantage of hindsight. Henry was not so well-informed. As he assembled his army, he was a desperate man. He had failed to avoid battle, and had perhaps even behaved unchivalrously if it is true that he defaulted on his promise to engage at Aubigny. He had failed to lead his army to Calais in safety. The result was a need to fight to the death, and his tactics at Agincourt must be seen in that context. He and his men had to kill since otherwise they would be killed. Battles were never aimed at taking prisoners. Henry maximised the resources at his disposal by using his archers *en masse*, firing thousands of arrows in volleys. Once the French cavalry attack failed because of the effectiveness of arrows against horses, the archers remained immune to any counter-measures, hidden behind their stakes and by the lie of the land. Their incessant bombardment was exceptionally frightening. The French men-at-arms had no training for the situation and no means of retaliation. They had no choice but to keep marching through it. Even if arrows did not pierce armour, the volleys would have caused severe bruising and confusion. The natural response, especially to flanking fire, is to move inwards towards the protection of the centre of one's own division. By the time they reached the English lines they could not fight as effectively as they should have been able to. Knocked to the ground, they were easy targets for the English men-at-arms and for the non-armoured archers. Most were killed when already helpless, and not through hand-to-hand combat. Others were wounded, but pinned to the ground by those who had fallen on top of them.

The battle came to an end because the French could not do anything to redress this situation. The arrows kept coming against their advances, and the heaps of comrades made it impossible for them to engage. They gave up and their attacks ended. The English believed they had won, and began to search through the piles for those who were still alive, since they were now their prisoners. Any found would have expected to survive, as they had surrendered and the fight had come to an end. Agincourt would have been renowned for its large number of prisoners as well as its one-sided intensity, and the French shame would have been no less. The French death rate, however, was boosted by Henry's order to kill the prisoners. It is this act that makes the battle truly distinctive. To this point, there were similarities with other engagements in which archers had contributed to the demise of men-at-arms.[6] No other medieval battle is known to have included the deliberate killing of a large number of men whom both sides believed would be ransomed. As a result, Agincourt displays very high mortality rates even for the nobility and gentry. Chronicle figures for the dead are much higher than those for Poitiers (*c.*2,500) and Crécy (2-4,000).[7] Some prisoners were kept alive at Agincourt, although the panic was enough to kill some who would have raised large ransoms. It also seems likely that the killing was ordered to stop before all were destroyed. Others were found alive on the field on the evening or day after the battle, although those considered to be mortally wounded were put out of their misery. It is therefore what happened after, as well as during, the first phase which gave the battle its great discrepancy between the numbers of dead on each side. Some of the French were murdered rather than being killed in battle.

The key to understanding Henry's bloody action is that he believed that he had already won. Time had passed since the fighting had stopped, certainly long enough for prisoners to have been taken from the field and gathered together. The king then thought that the French were regrouping. It is not surprising that he should consider this possible. Enough of the French army had chosen not to engage in the first phase and others were still arriving. They were themselves confused as to what they should do. Honour would dictate that they should mount an attack. This they prepared to do. Henry panicked. His soldiers had already started to relax, to remove their armour and put down their weapons. They were busying themselves with their own dead and wounded, and with the French prisoners. The king had to make a quick decision to save his own men. He feared that the prisoners might form a rearguard action if their comrades attacked. They had to be killed so that they could not be in a position to kill. He must surely have announced his action by sending heralds to the French who were threatening to attack. How else would they have known what was happening, other than by the cries and screams of those being murdered, either by stabbing or by being burned alive in a barn? Henry therefore deliberately used an act of savagery to put pressure on the remaining French to withdraw. No commander could risk the lives of his own men. A man with such a drive to succeed could not allow the possibility that he might lose – especially not after he thought he had won.

By the standards of the time Henry did not follow chivalric conventions, but his act was militarily necessary. This explains why he was not criticised in the chronicles of the period. However, the treatment of the incident in our earliest commentary, the *Gesta*, where the king's role is obfuscated, suggests that there was a fear that Henry might be deemed culpable for killing men who had surrendered, especially as it was in anticipation of an attack which never came. While the *Gesta* was not written to exculpate him in the eyes of the Church for this act alone, it was composed to reveal an overriding theme, that the victory was God's will and that Henry was God's chosen warrior. This was the line that Henry himself encouraged. He was personally overwhelmed by such a clear manifestation of divine support. The campaign had proved arduous and had not gone according to plan. He had faced the prospect of personal failure and the destruction of his army. Yet the result was the complete reverse. His prayers were answered. His steadfastness, his willingness to kill in God's name, had been rewarded. The French were not simply defeated, they were annihilated. God had used him to reveal their stubbornness and rebellion against Himself as well as against Henry's own claims. A further fillip to the king's pious response was the coincidence of the victory with the feast of translation of a saint to whom he was already devoted – St John of Beverley. The shrine expressed oil as the battle raged, as it had when Bolingbroke landed at Ravenscar in 1399 on the way to becoming king.

The impact of Agincourt on a man who had already survived one battle in 1403 despite a serious injury from an arrow, and who had been transformed upon taking up the mantle of kingship, is not to be dismissed as medieval 'spin'. Henry now truly believed he was God's anointed. It was not surprising that this should urge him to further invasions and heighten his ambition. Furthermore, he associated his victories strongly with his role as English king. The special commemoration of the feasts of St John of Beverley ordered by Archbishop Chichele in 1416 mentioned the 'gracious victory granted by the mercy of God to the English on the feast of the translation of the saint to the praise of the divine name and to the honour of the kingdom of England'.[8] The final pageant of the royal 'advent' to London on 23 November 1415 symbolised Henry entering the city of Paradise as the humble subject of the King of Heaven, as well as his entering the earthly city as the proud sovereign of his people.[9] Agincourt was a formative moment in Henry's own life as well as in his kingship. The psychological impact was all the greater given his precarious position as he set sail and the relatively short time he had been on the throne.[10]

Would that we could know what Agincourt meant to others in Henry's army, but we can imagine a similar effect. A battle was a frightening yet exhilarating event. There was no other experience like it, no other occasion when medieval man was brought face-to-face with death in a focused and collective manner. Henry's army would have shared his belief in divine intervention since this was fundamental to contemporary religious faith. As men entered battle they did so shriven and with remembrance of their mortality, as symbolised by the kissing of the earth. By that means it was possible to kill their enemy, since they could be confident they died in a state of grace. In our more secular world we have become enamoured of the story of English archers inventing the V-sign, to show their enemy after the battle that threats to capture them and remove their shooting fingers were empty and worthless. Such threats do occur within chronicle accounts of Henry's battle oration, intended to stir his men to the level of rage needed to sustain them in action.[11] If Henry's archers did make any sign after their victory – no fifteenth-century text says that they did and I have been unable to discover who first suggested the notion – it would have had a strong religious connotation. If the story contains any truth, then the V-sign is the surely the reverse of the customary Christian sign of blessing. The French were indeed cursed. For them, Agincourt was 'the wretched day', a day of shame and grief from which it took decades to recover.[12]

Notes

INTRODUCTION

1   *Memorials of London and London Life in the xiiith, xivth and xvth centuries*, ed. H.T. Riley (London, 1878), 620-2.

2   This was recorded in the guild account, *Archives Communales d'Abbeville CC* 204, a document that was destroyed in 1940. Cited in J. Godard, 'Quelques précisions sur la campagne d'Azincourt tirées des archives municipales d'Amiens', *Bulletin trimestre de la Société des Antiquaires de Picardie* (1971), 134.

3   English-held Bordeaux heard of it by 23 November; Venice by 1 December (*Sources*, 194, 263).

4   In chapters 2 and 4 of *Sources*, I discuss interpretations from the sixteenth century to the present. I have consciously avoided using sixteenth-century histories in this present work, since these were very much the product of their own time. Only the *First English Life* of Henry V of 1513 has a link back to the period of the battle itself. Although it is derived from the chronicles of Monstrelet and Titus Livius Forojuliensis, it also drew on reminiscences from James Butler, Earl of Ormond (1392–1452), although how these were transmitted to the author is not clear (*Sources*, 204).

5   For the stage of the campaign between the leaving of Harfleur and the return to England, all of the chronicle texts mentioned are translated, and their authors fully discussed, in *Sources*, Chapter 1. To avoid excessive footnoting, the relevant page ranges from this work are given at the outset of each set of chapter notes. For the siege and other periods, I will refer to the published versions of the chronicles, again giving page ranges at the outset.

6   Furthermore, the man who he claims was his master on the campaign, Sir Robert Umfraville, was one of the defenders of the Scottish march at the time and did not serve in France (E28/31: letters written by Umfraville at Berwick on 3 August 1415). No John Hardyng has so far been found serving on the campaign. Hardyng added a Latin prose account to his second version. This is generally very close to the *Gesta*.

7   For the latter's own reminiscence on the battle, see *Oeuvres de Ghillebert de Lannoy, voyageur, diplomate et moralist. Recueillies et publiées par Charles Poitvin* (Louvain, 1878), 49-50.

8   C. Given-Wilson, *Chronicles. The Writing of History in Medieval England* (London, 2004), 2.

9   See the examples in *The Wars of Edward III. Sources and Interpretations*, edited and introduced by C.J. Rogers (Woodbridge, 1999).

10   For England these are housed in The National Archives at Kew. For France they are to be found in the Bibliothèque Nationale and Archives Nationales in Paris, as well as in various Archives Départementales and in the British Library. See *Sources*, Chapter 5, for an overview.

CHAPTER I. HENRY V'S INHERITANCE: ENGLAND AND FRANCE, 1399–1413

1   *Sources*, 125-6 (*Chronique de Ruisseauville*).

2   For varying historical opinions see *The Wars of Edward III. Sources and Interpretations*, edited and introduced by C.J. Rogers (Woodbridge, 1999).

3   There is debate about whether he was born in 1387 or 1386 (C.T. Allmand, *Henry V* (London, 1992), 7-8.

4   All Souls College, Oxford, MS 182, folio 197b, printed in H.G. Richardson and G.O. Sayles, 'Parliamentary documents from formularies', *Bulletin of the Institute of Historical Research*, 11 (1933–4), 157.

5   A.L. Brown, 'The English Campaign in Scotland, 1400', *British Government and Administration. Studies presented to S.B. Chrimes*, ed. H. Hearder and H.R. Loyn (Cardiff, 1974), 40-54.

6   Brown, 'English campaign', 46, n. 22.

7   R. Griffiths, 'Prince Henry, Wales and the Royal Exchequer, 1400–13', *Bulletin of the Board of Celtic Studies*, 32 (1985), 202-13; *idem*, 'Prince Henry's war: armies, garrisons and supply during the Glyndŵr rising', *Bulletin of the Board of Celtic Studies*, 34 (1987), 165-73.

8   *PPC*, ii, 62-3.

9   C.J. Phillpotts, 'The fate of the truce of Paris 1396–1415', *Journal of Medieval History*, 24 (1998), 68, from *Choix de pieces inédites relatives du règne de Charles VI*, ed. L. Douet-d'Arcq (SHF, Paris, 1863–4), i, 189-90.

10   *Rotuli parliamentorum*, iii, 454.

11   E101/69/2/308; *PPC*, i, 117.

12   *CP*, XII, 899-905. Also useful is the *New Oxford Dictionary of National Biography* for many of the men mentioned in this and subsequent chapters.

13   Wylie, *Henry IV*, i, 293, ii, 61.

14   *Welsh Records in Paris*, ed. T. Matthews (Carmarthen, 1910), 25-31.

15   E31/8/135 section 4, cited in Phillpotts, 'Fate', 72.

16   *Johannis de Trokelowe et Henrici de Blaneford monachorum S. Albani necnon quorundam anonymorum, Chronica et Annales*, ed. H.T. Riley (Rolls Series London, 1866), 401-2.

17   Phillpotts, 'Fate', 74.

18   For discussion of events in France I must acknowledge my debt to R.C. Famiglietti, *Royal Intrigue. Crisis at the court of Charles VI 1392–1420* (New York, 1986) and to R. Vaughan, *John the Fearless* (London, 1973).

19   Intriguingly, in the marriage contract 'the king transferred to Louis "all the rights, actions quarrels and demands" he had or could have versus Henry IV and others because of Isabelle's first marriage' (Famiglietti, 36). While this concerned the 200,000 francs of dowry not repaid when she was returned to France, it gave Orléans a very direct interest in relations with England .

20   Lille, AD Nord B 546 no. 15,082 and 15082 bis, cited in Famiglietti, 60.

21   *Monstrelet*, i, 397-400.

22   For references see Phillpotts, 'Fate', 74.

23   Wylie, *Henry IV*, iv, 32.

24   *Rotuli parliamentorum*, iii, 632. For a full discussion of this period see G. Harriss, *Cardinal Beaufort. A Study of Lancastrian Ascendancy and Decline* (Oxford, 1988), Chapter 3.

25   Phillpotts, 'Fate', 76. For the period of the prince's captaincy of Calais see J.L. Kirby, 'Calais sous les anglais, 1399-1413', *Revue du Nord*, 37 (1955), 27-9.

26   BL Additional Charter 7926. For full discussion see F. Lehoux, *Jean de France, duc de Berri. Sa vie. Son action politique*, 4 vols (Paris, 1968), iii, 168 sq.

27   His first wife, Isabella, daughter of Charles VI, had died in childbirth in 1409.

28   J.A. Tuck, 'Henry IV and Europe: a dynasty's search for recognition', *The McFarlane Legacy. Studies in Late Medieval Politics*, ed. R.H. Britnell and A.J. Pollard (Stroud, 1995), 107-25; G.A. Knowlson, *Jean V, duc de Bretagne, et l'Angleterre (1399–1442)* (Cambridge/Rennes, 1964).

29   *Religieux*, iv, 318.

30   *Monstrelet*, ii, 92.

31   For the campaign see Vaughan, *John the Fearless*, 90-3.

32 *Ordonnances*, ix, 635.

33 *PPC*, ii, 19-24.

34 Vaughan, *John the Fearless*, 92.

35 *CCR 1409–13*, 166.

36 Harriss, *Cardinal Beaufort*, 57.

37 C76/95 m.22.

38 *Monstrelet*, ii, 202.

39 Religieux, iv, 476, 526; *Monstrelet*, ii, 189.

40 Wylie, *Henry IV*, iv, 57, 62; *Monstrelet*, ii, 189, 203-4.

41 D. Lalande, *Jean II le Meingre dit Boucicaut (1366–1421)* (Geneva, 1988).

42 Famiglietti, 102-3.

43 Wylie, *Henry IV*, i, 63.

44 Wylie, *Henry IV*, i, 64.

45 *Foedera*, IV, ii, 12-14.

46 For the campaign, with full references to indentures, events and outcome, see J.D. Milner, 'The English Enterprise in France 1412–13', *Trade, Devotion and Governance. Papers in Later Medieval History*, ed. D.J. Clayton, R.G. Davies and P. McNiven (Gloucester, 1994), 80-101.

47 Religieux, iv, 630.

48 E404/27/394; *CCR 1409–13*, 339. See *PPC*, ii, 33-4 for the prince's intention of going on the campaign.

49 *St Alban's Chronicle 1406–1420*, ed. V.H. Galbraith (Oxford, 1937), 65-7.

50 Wylie, *Henry IV*, iv, 74, n. 1.

51 *Monstrelet*, ii, 266-7,

52 Religieux, iv, 674.

53 Famiglietti, 107-10.

54 Plancher, iii, CCLXXVII.

55 Famiglietti, 262, n. 211, with Clarence's comment in *Lettres des rois, reines et autres personages des cours de France et d'Angleterre*, ed. J.J. Champollion-Figéac (Paris, 1847), ii, 331-2.

56 Douet-d'Arcq, *Choix*, i, 359.

57 Religieux, iv, 732-3.

58 Wylie, *Henry V*, i, 116-8, 129.

59 J. Poquet de Haut Jussé, 'Une renaissance littéraire au cour d'Henry V', *Revue historique*, 224 (1960), 329-38.

60 R.R. Davies, *The Revolt of Owain Glyndŵr* (Oxford, 1995), 124; *St Albans' Chronicle*, 22-7.

61 P. McNiven, 'Prince Henry and the English political crisis of 1412', *History*, 65 (1980), 1-16, and 'The problem of Henry IV's health, 1405–13', *English Historical Review*, 100 (1985), 747-72.

62 *PPC*, ii, 34-40.

CHAPTER 2. HENRY V AND THE REOPENING OF WAR, MARCH 1413–AUGUST 1415

1 Allmand, *Henry V*, 65; T.A. Sandquist, 'The holy oil of St Thomas of Canterbury', *Essays in Medieval History presented to Bertie Wilkinson*, ed. T.A. Sandquist and M.R. Powicke (Toronto, 1969), 330-44.

2 Fusoris, 243.

3 *Gesta*, 2-3.

4 E. Powell, *Kingship, Law and Society. Criminal Justice in the Reign of Henry V* (Oxford, 1989).

5 *Foedera*, IV, ii, 57. G.A. Knowlson, *Jean V, duc de Bretagne, et l'Angleterre (1399–1442)* (Cambridge/Rennes, 1964), 83-8.

6 Thomas Hoccleve, *Works, iii. The Regement of Princes, AD 1411–12*, ed. F.J. Furnivall (Early English Text Society, 1897), 192-6: C. Tyerman, *England and the Crusades 1095–1588* (Chicago and London, 1988), 303, 341-2. For his invocation of Deuteronomy 20: 10-12, both before and during the expedition, see *Gesta*, xxx, 34-7, 49, 155.

7 Religieux, iv, 770.

8   *PPC*, ii, 125.

9   For discussions on the various military commitments in late July 1413 see *PPC*, ii, 125-31. On
     Burgundian aid to the Scots, Plancher, iii, 373.

10   These were members of the 1412 army who had chosen to stay in service. They mustered at
     Bordeaux on 1 August (BL Cotton Caligula D5 folio 1). For the campaign see Wylie, *Henry V*, i,
     134-9.

11   Cited in Wylie, *Henry V*, i, 136, n. 1.

12   C61/114, m. 1. E101/186/2 records the order of Dorset to pay clerks for copying the truce and
     a herald for proclaiming it, with further payments to the *trompettes* and others who went around
     the garrisons proclaiming it.

13   Phillpotts, 'Fate', 77.

14   *Foedera*, IV, ii, 40-41

15   Wylie, *Henry V*, i, 149.

16   *Foedera*, IV, ii, 48

17   *Foedera*, IV, ii, 53.

18   *Foedera*, IV, ii, 50, 53, 62, 69, 72.

19   Phillpotts, 'Fate', 78.

20   *Foedera*, IV, ii, 66-7.

21   Religieux, v, 158-61.

22   Des Ursins, 490, 496.

23   *Monstrelet*, ii, 403; *Le Fèvre*, i, 118. Both speak of the Duke of York and the Earl of Rutland, con-
     fusing the same man under two names. Waurin (ii, 163) does not include this story but has York
     in command in Guienne, adding that at his return to England several councils were held and it
     was decided to send troops to Calais to reopen the war.

24   *Ordonnances*, x, 70-141.

25   *A Parisian Journal 1405–1449*, ed. J. Shirley (Oxford, 1968), 72.

26   AN Xia 1479 folios 254v-55v (register of the *conseil du Parlement*). Vaughan, *John the Fearless*, 100-1,
     plays down the role of the Cabochien revolt in John's fall from power, seeing it rather as an
     Armagnac coup with the support of the king, then in good health, and the Dauphin.

27   Religieux, v, 136.

28   *Monstrelet*, ii, 409.

29   Famiglietti, 138.

30   *Ordonnances*, x, 192-5; *Monstrelet*, ii, 442-57.

31   Famiglietti, 142.

32   Religieux, v, 286.

33   BN pièces originales 7171 Chaumont (134).

34   BN manuscrit français 25709/711, cited in P. Contamine, *Guerre, état et société à la fin du moyen âge.
     Étude sur les armées des rois de France 1337–1494* (Paris/The Hague, 1972), 223.

35   *Monstrelet*, ii, 465.

36   *Monstrelet*, iii, 7-8. Des Ursins has Henry claim in the speech to his troops before Agincourt that
     'he had not come as mortal enemy, for he had not consented to burning, ravaging, violating
     nor raping girls and women, as they had done at Soissons' (*Sources*, 134). Thomas Basin reports
     the common belief that the French defeat in 1415 had been divinely inflicted on the French
     because 'of their acts of impiety and their cruelty which they had committed in great numbers
     and to such a great degree by their sacking of that city and their plundering of the saints shrines'
     (*Sources*, 191). For De Bournonville, one of whose crossbowmen had allegedly killed Bourbon's
     illegitimate brother during the siege, see Vaughan, *John the Fearless*, 146-7.

37   F. Lehoux, *Jean de France, duc de Berri. Sa vie. Son action politique*, 4 vols (Paris, 1968), iii, 356 n. 1.

38   *Foedera*, IV, ii, 77.

39   *Foedera*, IV, ii, 79-80.

40   *Foedera*, IV, ii, 99:

41   E30/1531; Vaughan, *John the Fearless*, 206-7.

42   See below, 102.

43   Dijon, Archives Départementales du Cote d'Or B11926, printed in O. Cartellieri, 'Zum Frieden
     von Arras (1414–5). Beiträge zur Geschichte der Herzöge von Burgund', *Sitzungsberichte der*

Heidelberger Akademie der Wissenchaften (1913), 9, Abh. no. II.

44   *Brut*, ii, 552.

45   *Foedera*, IV, ii, 84.

46   *Foedera*, IV, ii, 106.

47   E101/321/15, 21.

48   *Monstrelet*, iii, 28.

49   Vaughan, *John the Fearless*, 199.

50   Famiglietti, 151; Vaughan, *John the Fearless*, 200-2.

51   *Rotuli parliamentorum*, iv, 34.

52   *Rotuli parliamentorum*, iv, 35. The clergy had also given a double tax grant at the Canterbury convocation in October.

53   *PPC*, ii, 140-2, 150-1.

54   *Foedera*, IV, ii, 96-8, 105.

55   *Monstrelet*, iii, 46-7.

56   Famiglietti, 154-8.

57   *Archives Municipales de Bordeaux, vol. 4. Registres de la Jurade: délibérations de 1414 à 1416 et de 1420 à 1422* (Bordeaux, 1883), 125. Henry had written to them on 23 January saying that he hoped that he would soon be in ease and comfort as a result of the restitution of his inheritance so long unjustly withheld by the French. This letter was not read at Bordeaux until 10 April: *Jurade*, 138.

58   That men like Courtenay were active in the collection of intelligence is suggested by the testimony in the trial of Jean Fusoris.

59   E403/619, m.12; *PPC*, ii, 150-1, 155-8.

60   Allmand, *Henry V*, 71-2; F. Taylor, 'The Chronicle of John Streeche for the reign of Henry V (1414-1422)', *Bulletin of the John Rylands Library*, 16 (1932), 150; Wylie, *Henry V*, i, 425 for discussion of dating, although he favours October 1414.

61   The Countess of Kent allegedly told an Italian before the second embassy arrived in Paris that the king would be prepared to do fealty if peace came about (Fusoris, 199).

62   *Ordonnances*, x, 219-21.

63   Fusoris, 152.

64   *Foedera*, IV, ii, 104, E403/619 m.14.

65   *PPC*, ii, 167.

66   E101/406/29, E403/621 m.7.

67   E30/1597.

68   Lille, AD Nord B935 no. 15281, cited in Famiglietti, 160.

69   *Religieux*, v, 498-505. A further letter was sent on 15 April (507-11).

70   Wylie, *Henry V*, 486-92.

71   *Monstrelet*, iii, 72-5; Religieux, v, 513-25.

72   Fusoris, 137-287.

73   *CCR 1413-19*, 215.

74   Fusoris, 247-9.

75   In the decisions reached about post-campaign accounts in March 1417, it was deemed that the start of the campaign should be taken as 8 July rather than 1 July (*Sources*, 448).

76   *CPR 1413-16*, 344.

77   *Foedera*, IV, ii, 136-7.

78   *Foedera*, IV, ii, 137.

79   Religieux, v, 527-31; Des Ursins, 505-6 (which also includes the full text of Charles's reply dated 24 August). Monstrelet dates Henry's letter to 5 August.

80   *Foedera*, IV, ii, 141.

81   T.B. Pugh, *Henry V and the Southampton Plot* (Southampton Record Society, 1988), with the confessions in Appendix 2.

82   *Gesta*, 18-19.

83   Religieux, v, 522-5. Public pronouncements, for instance to the city of London, also gave this as Henry's aim (*Memorials of London and London Life in the xiiith, xivth and xvth centuries*, ed. H.T. Riley [London, 1868], 603-5).

84   *Gesta*, 16-17. One of these copies still survives (E30/1695). The reference to rebels fits fully with

Henry's invocation of the laws of Deuteronomy.

85   *Gesta*, 16-17.
86   *Rotuli parliamentorum*, iv, 62. For fuller discussion of the focus on Normandy and Harfleur see A. Curry, 'Lancastrian Normandy: the jewel in the crown?', in *England and Normandy in the Middle Ages*, ed. D. Bates and A. Curry (London, 1994), 235-52.
87   Wylie, *Henry V*, i, 457.
88   *Gesta*, 16-17.
89   E403/621.
90   M. Bennett, *Agincourt 1415. Triumph against the odds* (London, 1991), 6;Vale, *English Gascony*, 71-4.
91   *Sources*, 445. For further discussion of Henry's plans after the fall of Harfleur, see Chapter 5.
92   *CCR 1413-19*, 214.
93   *Foedera*, IV, ii, 143.

CHAPTER 3. THE RAISING OF HENRY V'S ARMY, APRIL—AUGUST 1415

1   For an explanation of the system see J. Sherborne, 'Indentured retinues and English expeditions to France, 1369-80', *English Historical Review*, 79 (1964), 718-46; A. Curry, 'English armies in the fifteenth century', in *Arms, Armies and Fortifications in the Hundred Years War*, ed. A. Curry and M. Hughes (Woodbridge, 1994), 39-68. Also useful for in-depth discussion of two expeditions (1387 and 1388) is A.R. Bell, *War and the Soldier in the Fourteenth Century* (Woodbridge, 2004), Chapter 2.
2   For fuller discussion, see *Sources*, 409-414. For the campaign, musters are classified in the National Archives at E101/45-7; indentures in E101/69; Warrants for Issue in E404/31; Issue Rolls in E403/619-21. The conclusions drawn in this chapter are based on a detailed study of these records.
3   D. Hay, 'The division of spoils of war in fourteenth century England', *Transactions of the Royal Historical Society*, fifth series, 4 (1954), 91-109.
4   E101/45/5, listing payments to 210 indentees on 6 June.
5   These are also found in E101/45-47. There is also a set of enrolled accounts for fifty-nine of the leading captains in E358/6, and some enrolments on the Foreign Accounts (E364).
6   *PPC*, ii, 140-2.
7   This and the following point are revealed in a document of 16 April 1415 which recites earlier events (*PPC*, ii, 151).
8   *PPC*, ii, 145-8.
9   *Rotuli parliamentorum*, iv, 52. This remained a cause of anxiety even on the eve of departure. On 5 July Sir Gilbert Talbot was given power to negotiate with Glendower if he could be found (*Foedera*, IV, ii, 587).
10   The Earl of Arundel was sent to Wales in April to carry out the musters (E403/621 m.4).
11   No provision is mentioned for South Wales (*PPC*, ii, 172-80). The wartime garrison for the whole Calais march comprised 229 men-at-arms, 244 mounted archers, 254 foot men-at-arms, 303 foot archers, and 60 crossbowmen, plus a few scouts and gunners (J. Kirby, 'The financing of Calais under Henry V, *Bulletin of the Institute of Historical Research*, 23 [1950], 166).
12   *PPC*, ii, 168.
13   Fusoris, 247-9.
14   *Foedera*, IV, ii, 583; E403/619 m.15.
15   The treasurer's estimate exists in *PPC*, ii, 172-80 and gives further details on expected expenditure on routine military commitments, such as at Calais, Ireland, Wales and the Marches against Scotland.
16   *Memorials of London and London Life in the xiiith, xivth and xvth centuries*, ed. H.T. Riley (London, 1868), 603-5.
17   *Foedera*, IV, ii, 141, dated 1 August. The Calais staplers were also approached for a loan of £10,000 (E28/31/2).
18   *PPC*, ii, 154.
19   E403/621 m.3, 4 (under 26 April, 18 May). Unfortunately there is a gap in the record between 20 May and 2 September.

20 *PPC*, ii, 155-158.

21 A. Ayton, *Knights and Warhorses. Military Service and the English Aristocracy under Edward III* (Woodbridge, 1994), Chapter 4.

22 For instance, Sir Thomas Grey of Heton sealed his indenture on 4 June: *Foedera*, IV ii, 126. In his confession he told the king that as he went homeward 'when I had made my retinue with you', he met with the Earl of Cambridge at Conisbrough on 17 June. T.B. Pugh, *Henry V and the Southampton Plot* (Southampton Record Series, 1988), 161.

23 The majority of payments were accounted by the Exchequer on 6 June (E101/45/5) but some men received money before this date. Sir Thomas Erpingham, for instance, was paid on 18 May (E101/47/20 m.3).

24 E403/621 m.2.

25 The *Gesta*, 17, claims that, even at embarkation, Henry 'concealed from all save his closest councillors the destination of the ships'

26 Wylie, *Henry V*, i, 457.

27 *Foedera*, IV, ii, 125. For further conciliar discussion on redemption, see *PPC*, ii, 167.

28 *PPC*, ii, 166-7 (order of justiciar of Chester, 26 May). Several men, including the king, made wills before the expedition.

29 E101/69/7/509; E28/31/3.

30 E28/31/3.

31 Based on BL Sloane 4600, Nicolas 373-9, gives twenty-five names for whom records do not appear to survive.

32 Brown, 'English army', noted 212 different contingents, with sizes ranging from one archer to 1,200 under the Earl of Westmorland. Half of the companies number fewer than ten men. Since the campaign was not overseas, indentures were not issued.

33 E28/31/84.

34 Hals: E404/31/406 (with a clerk and two archers in his company); E28/31/55. Bordiu, E404/31/402 (with two archers); *Gesta*, xix. His letter to Bordeaux from the siege is translated in *Sources*, 445-6.

35 E101/695/35.

36 E101/69/7/514, 515; E101/45/5 m.9.

37 He also indented to serve with ten men-at-arms and thirty archers (*House of Commons*, iii, 243-6).

38 *CPR 1413-16*, 346.

39 *Foedera*, IV, ii, 109.

40 *PPC*, ii, 171.

41 A. Curry, 'Sir Thomas Erpingham', *Agincourt 1415*, ed. A Curry (Stroud, 2000), 53-77.

42 SC6/776/4 m.3d-4d; E403/624 m.3, E403/629 m.12.

43 Nicolas, 385.

44 E101/46/35 (the account of the sheriff, Sir Robert Urswyk, which details all of the companies).

45 E101/46/20, giving details of numbers raised in each commote.

46 DL7/1/25 document E.

47 C47/2/49, documents 9-10 (dated 1 April 1418); for the rebels, Powell, *Kingship, Law and Society*, 232-40.

48 A. Ayton, 'The English army at Crécy', in A. Ayton and P. Preston, *The Battle of Crécy, 1346* (Woodbridge, 2005), 181-6.

49 *CPR 1413–16*, 407-9.

50 E101/69/4/403.

51 E101/69/4/421 (indenture, Michael de la Pole jnr); E101/46/24 (retinue list of the earl presented with the post-campaign account). BL Sloane 4600 notes William as indenting with 20 + 60, however.

52 His son, Sir John Grey of Ruthin, served with sixty men (E101/47/17).

53 *CP*, VI 128. Robert Twyford had already been retained by the king for the expedition but petitioned and was granted that he might stay in the company of Grey for the safekeeping of the March (E28/31, under 10 May; *PPC*, ii, 165).

54 *PPC*, ii, 178

55   E28/31/77; E404/31/315.

56   E404/31/423. There are a few other possible foreign contingents which need further identifica-
     tion.

57   S. Walker, 'Janico Dartasso: chivalry, nationality and the man-at-arms', *History*, 84 (1999), 31-51.
     He was probably detailed, along with his son, into the garrison of Harfleur. P. Bonenfant, *Du meu-
     tre de Montereau au traité de Troyes* (Brussels, 1958), index, Robessart. Sir John Robessert indented
     with twenty-four men (E404/30/257), Lewis with four (E101/69/3/366). For the muster of Sir
     John at Southampton Heath, see E101/44/30, roll 2. A similar conclusion applies to Hartung van
     Clux, who indented with twelve men (E404/31/221).

58   Carr, 'Welshmen and the Hundred Years War', 36.

59   This and what follows is derived from the evidence of Clarence's muster, E101/45/4.

60   The other knights were Sir Edward Burnel (33), Sir John Colville (65), Sir John Heron (35), Sir
     William Bowes (34), Sir John Goddard (42), Sir William Bowet (33), Sir William Cromwell (21),
     Sir Philip Branche (10).

61   *House of Commons*, iv, 460.

62   Based on the muster roll, E101/45/13. That it was common for peers to have their own archer
     companies is also shown in the musters for the Duke of York, where eighty-seven are noted
     under his direct command. Many were his servants, being described as 'of the chamber', 'of the
     pantry', 'sumperterman' etc. (E101/45/2, 45/19).

63   E404/31/170 (warrant for issue; no indenture survives); E101/47/38 (retinue list); Nicolas,
     337-8. For discussion of the latter, which is commonly called the Agincourt roll, see *Sources*,
     407-8. The receiver-general's account for 1414-5 is held at Berkeley Castle but can be viewed
     at Gloucestershire Record Office as microfilm 12. For fuller discussion see A. Curry, 'Personal
     links and the nature of the English war retinue: a case study of John Mowbray, earl marshal,
     and the campaign of 1415', *La table ronde de Glasgow*, ed. E. Anceau, V. Gazeau and F.J. Ruggiu
     (Publications de la Sorbonne, Paris, forthcoming, 2005).

64   A. Curry, 'Isolated or Integrated? The English soldier in Lancastrian Normandy', in *Courts and
     Regions in Medieval Europe*, ed. S. Rees Jones, R. Marks and A.J. Minnis (York/Woodbridge,
     2000), 200.

65   Nicolas, 344.

66   No knight of this name served on the campaign, although a John Barre is found in the retinue of
     the Earl of Arundel (E101/47/1).

67   Powell, *Kingship, Law and Society*, 234; E101/47/1 (post-campaign retinue list for the Earl of
     Arundel).

68   More work is needed on this, drawing on unpublished estate records, but for evidence of tenants
     serving Arundel's father, see Bell, *War and the Soldier*, 117-24.

69   E101/69/7/508 (Salisbury); E101/69/7, nos. 488-505 and C47/2/49/7. An example is given in
     Sources, 439-40.

70   This last term tends to be found, however, in the post-campaign accounts, which were often
     compiled several years after 1415.

71   It is hoped that now a full transcription of the muster rolls has been undertaken this may be
     made easier.

72   *Sources*, 160.

73   Bell, *War and the Soldier*, 10.

74   The distinction between foot and mounted archers in Nicolas, 373-386, is not to be trusted,
     since the indentures and warrants are often inconsistent.

75   C76/98. There is a calendar for the reign as a whole in the *Annual Report of the Deputy Keeper of
     the Public Records*, 44 (1883).

76   E101/47/6 (Bourchier); E101/46/36 (Oxford).

77   A statute of 1439 limiting what a captain could deduct suggests that this could be opportunity
     for abuse (*Rotuli parliamentorum*, v, 32).

78   *Rotuli parliamentorum*, iv, 505. See also *Sources*, 413.

79   E101/40710. This list also indicates that the transfer from wages of the household to wages of war
     began on 12 July.

80   *PPC*, ii, 168.

81   CCR 1413–19, 214; Foedera, IV, ii, 123.

82   CCR 1413–19, 217-8; Foedera, IV, ii, 123.

83   Foedera, IV, ii, 138.

84   PPC, iv, 126.

85   E101/45/4 (Clarence); 45/13 (Gloucester); 46/36 (Oxford); 45/18 (Huntingdon etc); 44/30 (Erpingham, Horton etc.).

86   CCR 1413–19, 223.

87   Wiltshire County Record Office, G23/1/1 folio 54v. Harrington had received pay for his company at Winwick (Cheshire) on 27 June (E101/46/35).

88   Jaquet Selby, for instance, was to bring three horses, his two archers one each (E101/69/7/488).

89   E101/47/38; E358/6 m.6.

90   E101/45/2.

91   The Navy of the Lancastrian Kings. Accounts and Inventories of William Soper, Keeper of the King's Ships 1422–1427, ed. S. Rose (Navy Records Society, 1982), 34-5.

92   Foedera, IV, ii, 109-10, 118; E403/621 m.2-4.

93   CPR 1413–16, 344.

94   See below 114.

95   For a previous attempt to calculate, based on some, but not all, of the manuscript evidence, see M.R. Powicke, 'Lancastrian captains', Essays in Medieval History presented to Bertie Wilkinson, ed. T.A. Sandquist and M.R. Powicke (Toronto, 1969), 371-82.

96   Erpingham had four men-at-arms and twelve archers thus described (E101/44/30, doc. 2).

97   Sources, 449.

98   E101/48/2.

99   Ayton, 'The English army at Crécy', 189, and his 'English armies in the fourteenth century', 28.

100   In 1406 he defeated a French knight in the fait d'armes during negotiations at Leulinghem (CPR 1405–8, 161). With all known soldiers now entered onto a computer database, it will be possible to undertake systematic comparison with the campaigns in Wales, France and Scotland under Henry IV, as well as tracing service before 1399 and also forwards into the English occupation of Normandy.

CHAPTER 4. THE SIEGE OF HARFLEUR, 13 AUGUST–22 SEPTEMBER 1415

1   AD Nord B935 no. 15281, cited in Famiglietti, 160.

2   AN Xia 8602, folios 301-2v; AN J369B no. 22.

3   BN manuscrit français 25709/722 (order by the bailli of Caux to the vicomtes of the bailliage to make proclamation). It is possible that the bailli of Rouen had been sent an order to this effect as early as 19 April (AN K59/12, but with problems over dating).

4   BN Clairambault 54/4113.

5   C. de Vic and J. Vaissète, Histoire générale de Languedoc, 16 vols (Toulouse, 1872–1905), ix, 1028.

6   Although no official record is known, des Ursins (506-7) notes that 'it was ordered and appointed by the king's council that the constable should have in this war the same power as the king to make arrangements, issue orders and countermands as he saw fit, demolish fortresses and castles if need be'.

7   P. Contamine, Guerre, état et société. Étude sur les armées des rois de France 1337–1494 (Paris/The Hague, 1972), 208.

8   The details of companies derive from surviving records of the French chambre des comptes now found in various collections in the Bibliothèque Nationale. Most are from the Collection Clairambault and the Pièces Originales, for which chronological indexes on microfiche are available. Since the evidence is derived from a very large number of document references, it is not possible here to cite each separately but key references will be given. For repairs in the vicomté of Coutances see BN manuscrit français 25709/724 (order of 3 August).

9   BN manuscrit français 25709/697/

10   Deseille, 415. This is a very useful study based on the account of receipts and expenses of the town of Boulogne, AN KK280.

11   To save excessive referencing the relevant sections of the main English chronicles are: *Gesta*, 20–55;
      Hardyng, 374–5, 389–90; Walsingham, 89–93; Titus Livius, 8–11; Pseudo-Elmham, 36–49. For the
      French there is no eyewitness account but there are extended treatments in Religieux, 532–45; *Le
      Fèvre*, i, 224–31, *Monstrelet*, ii, 82–6, Waurin, 180–5, Des Ursins, 506–9, Berry Herald, 64–5.

12   Fusoris, 251.

13   *French rolls*, 577. E101/46/24 (service under Earl of Suffolk); E101/47/39 (garrison of Harfleur).
      Guy de Malet was at Agincourt.

14   E101/47/20. Both were subsequently invalided home from Harfleur so did not serve at the battle.

15   John Holland was not earl at this point, since the title was only restored to him in March 1417.
      The use of this title by the author of the *Gesta* may assist in dating the chronicle, although it
      appears from the administrative records of the campaign that Holland was already allowed the
      title by courtesy (*CP*, V, 205–11).

16   Cornwall, aged around forty, was married to Henry IV's sister, Elizabeth, mother of the earl by
      her first marriage, and had the added distinction of being born at sea off St Michael's Mount (*CP*,
      V, 253–4). Umfraville (b.1390) was one of Henry's knights of the chamber (*CP*, I, 151–2). From
      1403 Porter was an esquire of Prince Henry and had served in Wales. He was also around forty
      in 1415, and was knighted on 11 September when, still serving under the Earl of Huntingdon,
      he drove back a sortie made by the defenders of Harfleur (*History of Parliament. The Commons
      1386–1421*, ed. J.S. Roskell, L. Clark, and C. Rawcliffe, 4 vols (Gloucester, 1992), iv, 118–21). John
      Grey (of Ruthin) was married to Huntingdon's sister (*CP*, VI, 159–50). Steward (or Stuard) was
      later the master of horse under Henry VI.

17   The buildings of the priory of Graville are largely intact and open to the public, lying on the side
      of the hill above the village of that name to the west of Harfleur.

18   J-L Dufresne, 'La délinquance dans une region en guerre: Harfleur-Montivilliers dans la première
      moitié du XVème siècle', *Actes du cent cinquième congrès des sociétés savantes* (Caen, 1980), 181.

19   BN Clairambault 21/1480, 7480, 23/1672, 92/3969.

20   Not Sire de Gaucourt at this point but his son. For his career, see *Gesta*, 32 n. 1. His brother,
      Guillaume, died at Agincourt. Monstrelet puts the figure of Raoul jnr's troops at 400.

21   BN Clairambault 92/3909, 3911.

22   *Brut*, 553.

23   BN Clairambault 5/241, 26/1897.

24   Nicolas, Appendix, 24–6.

25   In the pro-Burgundian *Chronique anonyme*, de Gaucourt is named as responsible for the surren-
      der as captain, being described as an adherent of the Orléans party (*Sources*, 115).

26   For details of the later captivity of twenty-four of the garrison, see Wylie, *Henry V*, ii, 252. On 9
      October Charles VI issued an order in favour of Jeanne de Chaumont, whose husband, Baudrain
      de la Heuse, died at the siege (BN pièces originales 1522 Heuse 71–2).

27   Lyonnet de Bracquemont was the younger son of the lord of the fief of Bracquemont just
      outside Dieppe. His elder brother, Robert, had been chamberlain to Louis, Duke of Orléans in
      1405.

28   Rouen, AD Seine Maritime 100J 35/9, 10, 11 (the last to a semi-circular tower near the chapel of
      Notre-Dame des Villettes).

29   BN manuscrit français 26040/4971, printed in full in *Chronique de Perceval de Cagny*, ed. H.
      Moranville (SHF, Paris, 1902), 95–6.

30   See below, 99.

31   BN manuscript français 25766/714 (298), 26040/4981: muster on 21 September of Jean Duseau
      and nine other esquires.

32   BN manuscrit français 26040/4989 and 4991 on defensive measures in Rouen at this time.

33   BN manuscrit français 26040/4971

34   E101/47/1 (Arundel), 101/47/40 (York).

35   A. Curry, 'Towns at War. Relations between the towns of Normandy and their English rulers
      1417–1450', *Towns and Townspeople in the Fifteenth Century*, ed. J.A.F. Thomson (Gloucester, 1988),
      149–53.

36   I am grateful to Dr Richard Jones for information. See www/arch-projects.org.ac.uk/harfleur.
      htm.

37   *Sources*, 444-5.

38   Fusoris, 205-8.

39   BN pièces originales 496 Breban 30 (12 September).

40   BN pièces originales 573 de Calbrille 41 (*quittance* of 12 September for journey to Brittany): BN manuscrit français 25766/715 (297); BL Additional Charters 68, 259 (for Sluys); BN pièces originales 2289 Piquet 49, 51.

41   BN pièces originales 2268 Piquet 7.

42   Taylor, 'Chronicle of John Streeche', 152.

43   Nicolas, Appendix, 25.

44   Bourchier, who was probably in his mid-forties, was one of Henry's household knights as prince and king, and was appointed constable of the Tower shortly after the return of the expedition: *CP*, V, 176-8.

45   BN manuscrit français 26040/4974, 4980.

46   *Sources*, 441-2, with the original in the London Letter Book I, folio cxliiib.

47   There was variety of practice over whether they were allowed to keep their armour and personal weapons. The Burgundian chroniclers mention that they came in their *pourpoints*, implying they had been required to give up their plate.

48   On 3 January 1416 Henry presented Jean de Bourdin (or Bordilli) to its parochial benefice of St Martin (*French Rolls*, 576).

49   *PPC*, ii, 147-8.

50   H. Lamotte, *Antiquités de la ville d'Harfleur* (Paris, 1799), 64.

51   London Letter Book I, 159.

52   *French Rolls*, 577.

53   'Rôles normands et français et autres pièces tirées des archives de Londres par Bréquigny en 1764, 1765, et 1766', *Mémoires de la Société des Antiquaires de Normandie*, 23 (1858), 234-6.

54   London Letter Book I, 161.

55   *CPR 1413–16*, 364.

56   For eighteen gunners, forty-two carpenters and twenty masons there, see BL Additional Manuscript 4601/99 cited in Wylie, *Henry V*, ii, 63 n. 8.

57   *PPC*, ii, 184. For fuller discussion of the post-siege period, see A. Curry, 'Harfleur et les Anglais 1415–1422', *La Normandie et l'Angleterre au Moyen Âge* (Caen, 2003), 249-63.

58   *PPC*, ii, 196-7.

59   *Gesta*, 144-9.

60   *PPC*, ii, pp. 184-5. The first muster to survive is that for the first quarter of 1416 (E101/47/39).

61   B. Le Cain, 'Les fortifications de Harfleur au début du XVe siècle. Les années de l'occupation anglaise', *Les fortifications Plantagenêt*, ed. M-P. Baudry (Poitiers, 2000), 103-10.

CHAPTER 5. TO FIGHT OR NOT TO FIGHT? 22 SEPTEMBER–8 OCTOBER 1415

1   Monstrelet, iii, 69-70.

2   BN manuscrit français 26040/4971, printed in full in *de Cagny*, 95-6.

3   BN manuscrit français 25709/725 (order of the *bailli* of Caen to the *vicomte* of Falaise); BL Additional Charter 3464 (order of the *bailli* of Caen to the *vicomte* of Bayeux).

4   BN manuscrit français 25709/722.

5   Archives de la Prefecture de la Police, Livre vert vieil premier, folio 54v, cited in Famiglietti, 165.

6   Famiglietti, 165; Contamine, *Guerre, état et société*, 214, 220.

7   P. Contamine, *War in the Middle Ages* (English translation by M. Jones, Oxford, 1980), 153.

8   BN manuscrit français 25709/726. Contamine, *Guerre, état et société*, 223 misreads this document as meaning that the French intended to raise another 9,000 men. The text does not say this but rather that more taxation needed to be levied for the army which the king was raising ('mis sus') of 6,000 men-at-arms and 3,000 archers.

9   Rouen, AD Seine Maritime 100J6, no. 40 (receipt of 5 July by the *gens des comptes* at Paris for 1,500 *livres tournois* delivered by Cardot de Laitre, *commis* in the *élection* of Caen, as part of the aide 'to resist the English'). He paid in a further 500 *livres tournois* on 28 July (no. 41).

10 See, for instance, Rouen, AD Seine Maritime 100J8, no. 1 (receipt dated 16 September 1415 of payment for carriage of 3,000 *livres tournois* from St Lô to Rouen to Macé Heron).

11 BN pièces originales 423, du Boscaule 2.

12 J. Shirley, *A Parisian Journal 1405–1449* (Oxford, 1968), 94.

13 Religieux, v, 538-9, 285-6; Famiglietti, 277 n. 83.

14 Des Ursins, 507.

15 BN manuscrit français 26040/4974, 4980. The Religieux (v, 540-1) also tells us that on several occasions the besieged sent representatives to the Dauphin, even giving us their supposed words to him – that they were in a parlous state and feared they might have to surrender, which would be to the detriment of the kingdom given the importance and renown of their town.

16 Religieux, v, 540-1. Des Ursins (507) speaks of the Sire de Hacqueville being sent by the Harfleurais around 15 September to the king in Mantes and to the Dauphin in Vernon, but that they could do nothing 'since the army of the French was not strong enough to raise the siege'. This is a likely confusion with his mission to alert them to the treaty of composition.

17 *Chronique de Bec et Chronique de François Carré*, ed. Abbé Porée (SHF, Paris, 1883), 81-2.

18 BN manuscrit latin, 13,905 (mémoires de Dom Jouvlin).

19 What follows is derived from an analysis of all the surviving materials in the Bibliothèque Nationale: Collection Clairambault. Given the quantity of documents involved and the wide range of volumes in which they are found, it is impossible to give specific references. For instance, the material on the garrison of Valognes for the month of July is found in at least thirty-two different documents.

20 As expressed in a payment to a company of thirty mounted crossbowmen based in Valognes, 24 July 1415 (BN Clairambault 54/4113). For the Dauphin's appointment on 30 April, see Chapter 4 n. 2.

21 BN Clairambault 15/5049, 3/104.

22 BN Clairambault 53/4029.

23 BN Clairambault 53/4055 (quittance of 30 September), but Clairambault 24 suggests they were in service around 20 September.

24 BN Clairambault 103/99.

25 *Le Fèvre*, i, 227; Waurin, ii, 184, without giving the name of the Sire de Hacqueville.

26 *Sources*, 276.

27 BN manuscrit français 6748, p. 109, 132.

28 Des Ursins, 509.

29 BN pièces originales 1522 Heuse no. 71 (Vernon); BN manuscrit français 6748 p. 115 (Rouen).

30 A. Chéruel, *Histoire de Rouen sous la domination anglaise* (Rouen, 1840, repr., 1970), pièces justificatives, 2-3. For a letter of Charles VI received at Noyon on 14 July saying that 'the English were ready to invade the kingdom', see J. La Fons-Mélicocq, *Noyon et le Noyonnais au moyen age* (Noyon, 1841), 24.

31 BN manuscrit français 26040/4989-91, 4993 (king's house), 4996 (Pont-de-l'Arche).

32 A. Hellot, *Récit du siege d'Harfleur en 1415 par un témoin oculaire* (Rouen, 1881), 99.

33 *Sources*, 445.

34 For instance, BN Clairambault 30/2249 (Jean de Chaule, Sire de Brétigny).

35 BN Clairambault 83/6491 (Renard de Torcy under Guichard Dauphin). See below, 000.

36 BN manuscrit français 6748, p. 115.

37 Wylie, *Henry V*, ii, 104. For his troops, see for example BN Clairambault 44/3287 (le bâtard d'Estaconnes).

38 C. Du Fresne de Beaucourt, *Histoire de Charles VII* (Paris, 1881–91), i, 17.

39 BL Additional Charter 2607. A Milanese merchant in Paris had already supplied him with a helmet (*bavière/beavoir*) and pieces of plate in early August (BN pièces originales 158 Ayrolde 2).

40 Champion, *Vie de Charles d'Orléans*, 668.

41 *Chronique des Pays Bas, de France, d'Angleterre et de Tournai*, Recueil des Chroniques de Flandres, vol. 3, ed. J.-J. Smet (Brussels, 1856), 354. This was probably written in the 1460s. The king allegedly greeted them with 'my children of Tournai, I am overjoyed that you have come'.

42 Des Ursins, 506-7. The letters are also referred to but not dated in Religieux, c, 534-5.

43 Des Ursins, 511.

44   Des Ursins, 510-12.

45   Des Ursins, 516-7; AN K61/2, although a modern copy which therefore does not solve the
      problem of des Ursins's reliability.

46   E30/1597. This document is damaged but orders the marshals to carry out muster and reviews of
      the men-at-arms and archers.

47   Vaughan, *John the Fearless*, 208, citing AD Nord B17618 (letters of 10 October); AD Nord B17620
      (letters from Robert Bourée in Paris); AD Nord B4090, f. 106b, U. Plancher, *Histoire générale
      et particulière de Bourgogne*, 4 vols (Dijon, 1739–81), iii, 438. The Religieux also claims that he
      raised troops in Burgundy, Savoy and Lorraine but that the king was advised not to summon his
      assistance since the other princes did not have affection towards him and preferred to finish the
      campaign in full honour without him. The locations of recruitment are somewhat whimsical
      but the overall message that the duke was not asked to come in person fits with the letters in des
      Ursins.

48   Des Ursins, 513-5.

49   *Sources*, 141-3.

50   *Sources*, 143, wrongly gives this as Melun.

51   *Ordonnances*, x, 247. The English invasion is mentioned.

52   *Sources*, 177.

53   *Sources*, 102.

54   These are to be found in BN pièces originales, using the *fichier chronologique* from 1 October
      onwards. See for instance the muster of Pierre (Poton?) de Xaintrailles and his nine *escuiers* at
      Paris on 27 October, BN pièces originales 2356, Ponton-Xaintrailly 2.

55   G. Knowlson, *Jean V, duc de Bretagne et l'Angleterre* (London and Rennes, 1964), 84-96.

56   Dom Morice, *Mémoires pour servir de preuves à l'historie de Bretagne* (Paris, 1744), ii, 924-5.

57   To avoid repetitive referencing, the page ranges in *Sources* are as follows: *Gesta* (26-7); *Liber
      Metricus* (42-3); Titus Livius (56-7); Pseudo-Elmham (65); Religieux (101-2); Berry Herald (179);
      Monstrelet (144-5).

58   *Sources*, 442.

59   *Foedera*, IV, ii, 147, but incorrectly dated to 16 September. Translated in Nicolas, Appendix, 29-30,
      and in C. Hibbert, *Agincourt* (London, 1964), Appendix V.

60   Brown, 'English campaign', 43.

61   *Le journal de Nicholas de Baye, greffier du parlement de Paris, 1400–1417*, ed. A Tuetey (SHF, 1885-8), ii,
      231-2.

62   Fenin, 68.

63   Fusoris, 236.

64   C. Given-Wilson, *The Chronicle of Adam Usk 1377-1421* (Oxford, 1997), 257. Deserters were
      sometimes tracked down, as happened to two men recruited from Kidwelly for this or a later
      campaign (DL 7/1/25 document D).

65   Nicolas, Appendix, 24-8.

66   *Sources*, 445-6.

67   E101/47/1 (retinue list submitted with post-campaign account).

68   Fusoris, 247-9.

69   The Scottish chronicler, Walter Bower, writing in the 1440s, comments that 'he planned to move
      with his army of 12,000 men to England for a time to recover themselves', although he does not
      mention Calais (*Scotichronicon by Walter Bower*, vol. 8, ed. D.E.R. Watt [Aberdeen, 1987], 85).

70   The *Chronique de Ruisseauville* (*Sources*, 125) notes that Henry could not return from Harfleur
      because the ships from Holland and Zealand had returned to their own lands and English ships
      has been scuttled at sea by heavy rain and storms.

71   E101/47/37.

72   E101/44/30 m.16.

73   London Letter Book I, 159.

74   E403/622, m.3 (entry under 23 October).

75   Deseille, 422.

76   E403/621 (Gilbert, Lord Talbot, Humphrey Stafford, Roger Leche, Thomas Clarell and others).

77   *PPC*, ii, 147-8.

78   For eighteen gunners, forty-two carpenters and twenty masons there, see BL Additional Manuscript 4601/99 cited in Wylie, *Henry V*, ii, 63 note 8.

79   For fuller discussion see *Sources*, 426-34. Enrolled accounts for fifty-nine retinues are in E358/6, with others in E364. Particulars of account are grouped in E101. In some cases the particulars are accompanied by a retinue list with details of what happened to each man.

80   Sir Hugh Stafford (Lord Bourchier) (60), Thomas Carew (36), Sir William Grauntson (8), Sir John Skidmore (16), Lewis John, esquire (8), John Louthe, esquire (8), John Blaket, esquire (8), John Radcliffe, esquire (24), John Montgomery, esquire (4, but he himself was invalided home before the end of the second quarter).

81   See his particulars of account in E101/47/7. He had failed to provide one further knight and four archers at the initial muster and had been excused five men-at-arms.

82   E101/47/39.

83   These include Bourchier, Carew, Grauntson and Ecton, as well as Skidmore, Radcliffe, Blaket and John who had all now achieved the status of knight.

84   Dorset had indented to serve on the 1415 campaign with 400 men, Clinton with sixty men. Hastings did not indent for the campaign but may have been the baron serving within the retinue of Dorset.

85   E101/44/30, roll 1, m. 9; *French rolls*, 577. Basset (*Sources*, 87) notes that Sir John Fastolf 'had a noble retinue of 1,500 knights and 35 esquires and other men of war for the defence of Harfleur', giving the names of Carew, Sir Hugh Luttrell, John Standish and Thomas Lord. Although following mention of the siege this refers to later years when Fastolf was lieutenant of Harfleur for the absent Dorset/Exeter. There is no evidence that Sir Hugh Luttrell served on the 1415 campaign, although he was on the 1417 expedition (PRO E 101/51/2).

86   Particulars of account: E101/46/24.

87   E358/6, m. 4.

88   E101/47/1.

89   Other deaths can be traced from additional sources. For instance, Joan Elwick sued in Chancery for the lands of her husband, William, of Elwick, Northumberland (Wylie, *Henry V*, ii, 66 n. 4).

90   Wylie, *Henry V*, ii, 68, 71.

91   E101/44/30, E101/45/1. There is also a signet letter of the king permitting the repatriation of those whose names appeared on attached schedules (E101/45/14, reproduced as the frontispiece to J. Otway-Ruthven, *The King's Secretary and the Signet Office in the XVth Century* [Cambridge, 1939]).

92   The particulars of his post-campaign account are at E101/47/1, with the list of sick in E101/44/30, m.6-7.

93   E101/44/30.

94   For example, one of the archers from Lancashire under Sir John Southworth who died at the siege was placed in the company of William Phelip (E358/6 m.4).

95   E403/21, m.7. The account of the receiver-general of the Earl Marshal also shows food being brought from Bosham.

96   E403/622 (accounted under 23, 26 and 30 October).

97   *Sources*, 446-7. The entry for Richard, Earl of Warwick in the *New Dictionary of National Biography* that claims that 'he was at the siege of Harfleur in 1415 but, having been sent to Calais with prisoners, missed the battle of Agincourt' (http://www.oxforddnb.com/view/article/1838). I have not found proof of his presence at the siege and he certainly did not indent for the campaign.

98   Belleval, 66.

CHAPTER 6. FROM HARFLEUR TO THE CROSSING OF THE SOMME, 8–19 OCTOBER 1415

1   The relevant sections in *Sources* are as follows: *Gesta*, (27-32); *Liber Metricus* (43-4); Walsingham (50); Hardyng (80, 82); Titus Livius (57-8); Pseudo-Elmham (66-8); Religieux (103-4); Fenin (117); *de Cagny* (121); *Ruisseauville* (124); Des Ursins (132); *Monstrelet, Waurin* and *Le Fèvre*, 145-55); Basin (179-80).

2   Deseille, 421. Subsequent information concerning Boulogne is derived from this article.

3   This is given in the administrative records as either 5 or 6 October, the divergence arising from whether the ninety-one days of a quarter were taken to include the first and last days or not. Wylie, *Henry V*, ii, 88 n. 3 is mistaken in believing that the second quarter began on 8 October.

4   The dead included Geoffrey Blake (Nicolas, 361), Richard Curson in the retinue of Gregory Benet (E101/45/13). Roger Robert (man-at-arms) and Richard Turnour (archer) of the retinue of Michael de la Pole, Earl of Suffolk, were taken prisoner (E101/46/24).

5   BN Clairambault 65/5063, 60/4623, 113/128.

6   BL Cotton Cleopatra CIV claims that Henry rode through Fécamp although the list of places it gives for the march – including Honfleur and Barfleur – is so incorrect as to be untrustworthy (*Chronicles of London*, 119).

7   BN manuscrit français 25708/631, 635, 639.

8   Deseille, 418.

9   E101/45/1: William Bramshulf (man-at-arms), Edward Legh and John de Rede (archers).

10   Belleval, 59, suggests that Henry went first to Fauville and then turned towards Fécamp to launch an attack but the timings make this unlikely.

11   BN Clairambault 15/977.

12   There is evidence of repairs in 1398 and 1407 (Rouen, AD Seine-Maritime 100J, no. 32 and 34). For an order of 22 December 1415 to put the castle into a defensive state, see BN manuscrit français 26041/5018.

13   S. Deck, *Une commune normande au moyen âge. La ville d'Eu* (Paris, 1924), 99.

14   Deseille, 422.

15   Clignet as admiral had certainly been active during the siege and would have therefore been in a position to join Boucicaut's company. It is not wholly clear who is meant by the bastard of Bourbon. Duke John had an illegitimate brother called Hector but he was apparently killed at the siege of Soissons in 1414 (Vaughan, *John the Fearless*, 147).

16   Belleval, 65.

17   BN Clairambault 46.

18   Jean Froissart, *Chroniques, Livres I et II*, ed. P. Ainsworth and G.T. Diller (Paris, 2001), 563.

19   *De Cagny*, 17, 97.

20   Archives Communales d'Amiens BB2 f. 67, cited in Godard, 'Quelques precisions', 131; Wylie, *Henry V*, ii, 112.

21   BL Cotton Caligula DV, fols 43v-44r, printed in C.J. Phillpotts, 'The French plan of battle during the Agincourt campaign', *English Historical Review*, 99 (1984), 64-6, and translated in *Sources*, 468-9.

22   Morice, ii, col. 902.

23   E. Cosneau, *Le Connétable de Richemont. Artur de Bretagne, 1393–1458* (Paris, 1886), 39.

24   There are several quittances for his company at the siege of Parthenay in BN Clairambault for June and July.

25   BN Clairambault 69; Belleval, 177. He died at Agincourt.

26   Famiglietti, 102, 130.

27   BL Additional Charter 3466.

28   BL Additional Charter 3470-71.

29   BN Clairambault 46.

30   Belleval, 244-5.

31   As discussed in Chapter 5.

32   Godard, 'Quelques précisions', 132.

33   *Sources*, 121.

34   *St Albans Chronicle*, 93; *Sources*, 50 (taking 'assis carnibus' to mean dried meat rather than, as in the translation there, as roast meat).

35   John, Lord Ferrers of Groby, Ralph de Greystoke, Peter Tempest, Christopher Moresby, Thomas Pickering, William Hodelston, John Hosbalton, John Mortimer, Philip Halle and William Halle, James Ormond and others: *Sources*, 88 from College of Arms MS 9 fol. xxxii.

36   BN Clairambault 109; Belleval, 296-7.

37   Archives municipales d'Amiens CC 16, f. 75v, cited in Godard, 'Quelques précisions', 132.

38   Wrongly given as Pont-Audemer in *Monstrelet*: Wylie, *Henry V*, ii, 113, n. 10.

39   The *Gesta* has it that it belonged to the duke himself. Count Ferry of Vaudémont was the second
      son of Jean, Duke of Lorraine (d.1390).

40   Wylie, *Henry V*, ii, 114, although the source for this is rather dubious.

41   The point of this remark is not clear. I have not found evidence that he served at Agincourt.

42   Belleval, 71.

43   *Sources*, 77.

44   The supposed grant is printed in full in Nicolas, 228-9. For a brief biography of Sir Hugh, who
      was the younger brother of Edmund, 5th Earl of Stafford (d.1403), see *CP*, II, 247-8, and C.
      Rawcliffe, *The Stafford, earls of Stafford and dukes of Buckingham 1394–1521* (Cambridge, 1978), 9,
      106, 109. His widow later married another veteran of Agincourt, Lewis Robessart (d.1431).

45   E101/47/6 (particulars of account, with retinue roll). He had indented to serve with nineteen
      men-at-arms and forty archers, along with himself paid as a baron (E 404/31/152). He was still
      serving in Harfleur in April 1416 (E101/47/39).

46   *Agincourt 1415*, 49.

47   P. Champion, *Vie de Charles d'Orléans 1394–1465* (Paris, 1911), 668.

48   Godard, 'Quelques précisions', 132.

49   *Chronique des Pays Bas, de France, d'Angleterre et de Tournai*, Recueil des Chroniques de Flandres,
      vol. 3, ed. J.-J. Smet (Brussels, 1856), 355.

50   *Cartulaire des comtes de Hainault ed 1337 à 1436*, ed. L. Devillers, vol. 4 (Brussels, 1889), 46.

51   Wylie, *Henry V*, ii, 117-8. The Burgundian chroniclers also have Henry pass by Nesle but do not
      mention any interaction with its inhabitants.

CHAPTER 7. FROM THE CROSSING OF THE SOMME TO THE EVE OF BATTLE, 19–24 OCTOBER 1415

1   The chronicle sources for this chapter are as given in note 1 of Chapter 6.

2   Godard, 'Quelques précisions', 133.

3   The prose account in Hardyng adds William Porter and William Bourchier to Cornwall and
      Umfraville, making the group even closer to that at the landing. These men appear to have been
      Henry's equivalent of the SAS!

4   Dynter, 298-9; *Sources*, 172.

5   Hardyng also has Henry passing Péronne close by on the left, but dates this to 22 October.

6   BN manuscrit français 6748, p. 115.

7   C. Du Fresne de Beaucourt, *Histoire de Charles VII* (Paris, 1881–91), i, 17.

8   Wylie, *Henry V*, ii, 104.

9   Champion, *Vie de Charles d'Orléans*, 668.

10   Waurin also mentions Miraumont but has it rather as the river on which Monchy-Lagache was
      situated, although that is an error since the river there is the Omignon. Wylie, *Henry V*, ii 119 sug-
      gests that by the river Miraumont Waurin meant the river on which Miraumont lay, i.e. the Ancre.

11   *Cartulaire des comtes de Hainault de 1337 à 1436*, ed. L. Devillers, vol. 4 (Brussels, 1889), 47.

12   Titus Livius speaks of a battle with the French over a bridge, dating this to 22 October, but also
      naming the day as the feats of St Romanus, which would make it 23 October. It is not clear
      where this was.

13   This may be the engagement to which the Venetian, Morosini, refers: 'we learned that the
      English had been trapped at the crossing of a bridge and that they could not escape from the
      French and were therefore compelled to give battle' (*Sources*, 193).

14   For instance, seven of the Lancashire archers under Sir Richard Kyghley (E101/44/29).

15   I have discounted here the possibility of a Somme crossing at Eclusier-Vaux.

16   Dead: Geoffrey Blake (Nicolas, 361). Richard Curson, an archer in the retinue of the master
      cordwainer, Gregory Benet (E101/45/13), Roger Robert (man-at-arms) and Richard Turnour
      (archer) of the retinue of Michael de la Pole, Earl of Suffolk, were taken prisoner (E101/46/24).

17   The following were taken prisoner: William Bramshulf (man-at-arms), Edward Legh and John
      de Rede (archers) (E101/45/1).

18   John Relverge, man-at-arms of Michael de la Pole jnr (E101/46/24 m. 4).

19   An unnamed Lancashire archer who had crossed with Sir John Southworth but had been re-
      assigned after the latter's death at Harfleur to William Porter (E358/6 m. 4).

20   E101/44/29. One of Erpingham's archers, Richard Charman, was captured at some point
      between Harfleur and Agincourt (E101/47/20).

21   E101/45/2. This also refers to men being taken prisoner but does not give any dates.

22   E101/47/37 (retinue of Earl Marshal, which had 138 men and 345 horses on the march, includ-
      ing twenty-four which belonged to the earl who had himself been invalided home).

23   Partly revealed by the release given on 1 June 1416 to John Hargrove, sergeant of the pantry,
      concerning what was lost from the royal baggage when it was raided at the battle (*Foedera*, IV, ii,
      163).

24   The relevant passage is 'in tam longa distancia eorum patriam populantem', which Roskell and
      Taylor translated as 'laid waste their country at so great a distance from it'.

25   The issue of ordinances is also mentioned in Titus Livius and the Pseudo-Elmham.

26   British Library Additional Manuscript 33,191. One of their clauses speaks of 'this viage the
      which oure foresaid soverayne lord the Kyng maketh in his owne persone', which is highly
      reminiscent of vocabulary used in relation to the 1415 campaign. Many of the clauses echo those
      in the first known text of disciplinary ordinances issued in French for the Scottish campaign of
      1385, printed in *The Black Book of the Admiralty*, ed. T. Twiss (London, 1871), i, 453-8, The 1419
      ordinances are printed in Nicolas, Appendix, 31-40, and C. Hibbert, *Agincourt* (London, 1964),
      Appendix IV.

27   It is also interesting to note that in negotiations with the Duke of Burgundy in the summer of
      1414, the king had his envoys ask how the duke would treat any Armagnac territories which any
      Anglo-Burgundian army passed through in victory. The answer was 'in an orderly and peaceful
      way, paying for all victuals' (Vaughan, *John the Fearless*, 207).

28   Numbers 25:14.

29   Outlined in C. J. Rogers, 'Edward III and the dialectics of strategy, 1327–1360', *Transactions of the
      Royal Historical Society*, 6th series, 4 (1994), and more fully developed in his *War Cruel and Sharp.
      English Strategy under Edward III, 1327–1360* (Woodbridge, 2000).

30   For comparison see H.J. Hewitt, *The Black Princes' Expedition of 1355–1357* (Manchester, 1958),
      Rogers, *War Cruel and Sharp;* M. Livingstone and M. Witzel, *The Road to Crécy. The English
      Invasion of France 1346* (London, 2004).

31   A. Ayton, 'The Crécy campaign', in Ayton and Preston, *The Battle of Crécy*, quote at 66. Parts of
      Edward's march in 1346 were quicker than others: A. Burne, *The Crécy War* (London, 1955), 154,
      notes an average of 14.5 miles (23km) per day after the crossing of the Seine. See also his map on
      p. 141.

32   BN manuscrit français 25709/725.

33   Des Ursins, 510.

34   BN manuscrit français 25709/728. On 12 November enquiry into their complaints was ordered
      (British Library Additional Charter 6799).

35   *Chronique du Bec et Chronique de François Carré*, ed. Abbé Porée (Société de l'Histoire de France,
      Paris, 1883), 81-2.

36   *Sources*, 143.

CHAPTER 8. THE ARMIES ASSEMBLE, 24–25 OCTOBER 1415

1   The relevant sections in *Sources* are as follows: *Gesta* (34-8); *Liber Metricus* (46-7), Walsingham
     (51-2); Titus Livius (59-62); Pseudo-Elmham (71-4); *Brut* (92-6); Religieux (104-8); *Chronique
     anonyme* (115); Fenin (118-9); *Ruisseauville* (124-6); Des Ursins (1329-34); *Monstrelet, Waurin* and
     Le Fèvre (156-65); Dynter (173-4); Bourgeois of Paris (177-8); Berry Herald, (180-1); *Chronique de
     Richemont* (184); *Chronique de Normandie* (187); Basin (190).

2   Wylie, *Henry V*, i, 135, note 11.

3   *Sources*, 51.

4   I am grateful to Dr Clifford Rogers for his advice on the order to keep silence. He has pointed

out to me that similar orders are seen in Thucydides and in the American Civil War.

5   Dr Rogers suggests that 'a night attack is not an uncommon maneuver for a small army facing a large one', pointing to the example of the Earl of Northampton's attack on La Roche Derrien in 1345.

6   See above 140-2.

7   *Sources*, 132.

8   See above 156-7.

9   *Sources*, 151.

10   The Bourgeois of Paris claims that on 20 October the French lords heard that the English were moving through Picardy and 'my lord of Charolais was pressing so hard upon them'.

11   Information given in a talk by Professor Betrand Schnerb at Azincourt in October 2005.

12   *Monstrelet*, iii, 7.

13   *Sources*, 181.

14   BN manuscrit français 25709/726.

15   Edward, Duke of Bar had succeeded to the title in 1411 and is known to have made his will on 7 October, implying preparation for hostilities (Wylie, *Henry V*, ii, 180).

16   *Sources*, 34. The *Liber Metricus* also says the van was foot and the rearguard mounted, adding that the French were in many companies, which may be an allusion to squadrons on the wings.

17   Contamine, *Guerre, état et société*, 225. See for instance the fifty-seven-strong company of crossbowmen of Jean de Seville within the command of the Count of Vendôme (BN Clairambault 103/99).

18   BN manuscrit français 25709/726

19   Vendôme: BN Clairambault 53/4029; Berry: BN Clairambault 53/4055; de Ligne: BN Clairambault 15/5049, 3/104.

20   Des Ursins, 510-2.

21   V. Grave, *Archives municipales de Mantes. Analyse des registres des comptes de 1381 à 1450* (Paris, 1896), 14.

22   S. Boffa, 'Anthoine de Bourgogne et le contingent brabaçon à la bataille d'Azincourt (1415)', *Revue belge de philologie et d'histoire*, 72 (1994), 255-84. See also the useful overview for a slightly earlier period in S. Boffa, *Warfare in Medieval Brabant 1356–1406* (Woodbridge, 2004).

23   Contamine, *Guerre, état et société*, 216.

24   J. Flammermont, *Institutions municipales de Senlis* (Senlis, 1881), 234-5. In 1410 they had been asked for thirty crossbowmen but only sent eight (230-1).

25   V. Gay, *Glossaire archéologique du Moyen Age et de la Renaissance*, 2 vols (Paris, 1887–1928), ii, 429, col. A.

26   A. Janvier, *Notices sur les anciennes corporations d'archers, d'arbalétriers, de couleuvriniers et d'arquebusiers des villes de Picardie* (Amiens, 1855), 98-9. Wage rates in 1401 had been 24 *livres parisis* per month for their captain, 6 *sous parisis* per day for each crossbowman, and 4 *sous 6 deniers parisis* per day for each *pavesier* (Contamine, *Guerre, état et société*, 222, note 81).

27   L. Mirot, 'Lettres closes de Charles VI conservées aux archives de Reims et de Tournai', *Le Moyen Age*, 29 (1917–18), 309-38, 30 (1919), 1-44, no. XXVIII; Contamine, *Guerre, état et société*, 217. See above 101.

28   One of the companies mustering at Rouen on 17 October under Bourbon's command apparently included eight men-at-arms provided by Isabel de Harcourt, Dame de Villars of the county of Dombes near Lyon (J.M. Le Mure, *Histoire des ducs de Bourbon*, 4 vols [Paris, 1860–97], ii, 130). There is also a story that Bernard d'Auvergne, marching north for the campaign, burned villages where he lodged (cited in R.A. Newhall, *The English Conquest of Normandy 1416–24* [New Haven, 1924], 239 n. 241). The Burgundian chroniclers include a lord of Auvergne in the list of dead. Further research on the geographical origins of the dead and prisoners would be extremely useful.

29   Contamine, *Guerre, état et société*, 223.

30   Vaughan, *John the Fearless*, 139.

31   For biographies see the *New Oxford Dictionary of National Biography* as well as *The Complete Peerage*.

32   For a useful discussion on the problem see M. Bennett, 'The Battle', *Agincourt 1415. Henry V, Sir Thomas Erpingham and the triumph of the English archers*, ed. A. Curry (Woodbridge, 2000), 25-30.

33   M. Bennett, 'The development of battle tactics in the Hundred Years War', *Arms, Armies and Fortifications in the Hundred Years War*, ed. A. Curry and M. Hughes (Woodbridge, 1994), 15-16.

CHAPTER 9. THE FIGHT, 25 OCTOBER 1415

1   The relevant sections in *Sources* are as follows: *Gesta* (34-8); *Liber Metricus* (46-7), Walsingham (51-2); Titus Livius (59-62); Pseudo-Elmham (71-4); *Brut* (92-6); Religieux (104-8); *Chronique anonyme* (115); Fenin (118-9); *Ruisseauville* (124-6); Des Ursins (1329-34); *Monstrelet, Waurin* and *Le Fèvre* (156-65); Dynter (173-4); Bourgeois of Paris (177-8); Berry Herald, (180-1); *Chronique de Richemont* (184); *Chronique de Normandie* (187); Basin (190). For Chartier, 'Livre des Quatres Dames', see *Sources*, 344-7.

2   Bennett, 'The Battle', 31.

3   It later adds 'and this battle will have half of the *varles* of the company mounted on the best horses of their masters', which suggests again that this plan was drawn up at a time when the French resources needed to be maximised.

4   I am grateful to Dr Rowena Archer for sharing her thoughts on the problem of the stakes.

5   In May 1414, during the civil war, Hector and Philippe de Saveuse had raided Blangy as the royal army had moved northwards, and were again active in the counties of Eu and Aumale under the Burgundian flag in 1416 (Deck, *La ville d'Eu*, 28, 30).

6   Waurin and *Le Fèvre* suggest actual numbers for those guarding the baggage, saying that the king ordered a gentleman with ten lances and twenty archers to the task, along with pages of noble rank and others who were sick and could not be of help.

7   What was lost can be reconstructed from the release given on 1 June 1416 to John Hargrove, sergeant of the pantry (*Foedera*, IV, ii, 163).

8   It was through Monstrelet that this link was drawn in the histories of Hall and Holinshed and found its way into Shakespeare.

9   E101/47/40. Of the 400 troops with which he sailed, 374 were at the battle, but only 283 returned to England.

10   E101/46/24, 45/7, 44/29 respectively.

11   *Oeuvres de Ghillebert de Lannoy*, 49.

12   *Oeuvres de Ghillebert de Lannoy*, 50.

13   E358/6 m.1.

14   *Oeuvres de Ghillebert de Lannoy*, 49.

15   *Sources*, 288-98 for these poems.

CHAPTER 10. THE AFTERMATH, 26 OCTOBER–16 NOVEMBER 1415

1   The relevant sections in *Sources* are as follows: *Gesta* (37-40); *Liber Metricus* (47-8), Walsingham (53); Titus Livius 62-3); Pseudo-Elmham (74-5); Religieux (108-10); Fenin (119); *Ruisseauville* (126-7); Des Ursins (133-5); *Monstrelet, Waurin* and *Le Fèvre* (164-71); Dynter (174-5); Bourgeois of Paris (177-8); *Chronique de Richemont* (184-5); *Chronique de Normandie* (187).

2   *Sources*, 263-5, 279, 284, 335. For further discussion on naming, see Wylie, *Henry V*, ii, 178-9.

3   Godard, 'Quelques précisions', 135.

4   York's body was taken to London and then for burial at Fotheringhay; Suffolk was buried at Ewelme (Wylie, *Henry V*, ii, 269-71).

5   Belleval, 118, Wylie, *Henry V*, ii, 216.

6   *Le Fèvre* and Waurin make no mention at all of the burials.

7   Bacquet, *Azincourt*, 83, citing Bibliothèque municipale de Besançon Collection Chifflet MS 64.

8   Wylie, *Henry V*, ii, 218 note 12. For what follows, see *ibid*, 219-23

9   Further examples: in St-Omer, Philippe de Wissoc at the church of St Aldegonde; Jean de Croy and Archembaud de Croy at the abbey of St Bertin, and Guillaume d'Avroult in a chapel of the parish of St Denis. Gilles de St-Aubert, Sire de Chin, at Busigny in Hainault; Henry de Gavre in the cathedral of Cambrai; Colart de Mailly in the church of St Nicholas at Arras.

10   The *Chronique de Normandie* also credits Charolais, then said to be at Arras, with causing the field to be consecrated and the dead to be interred, save for the bodies of the nobility, 'which he caused to be carried each to his own territory'. On 28 October a messenger had been sent from Boulogne to Charolais at Ghent with news of the battle and 'in order to have comfort and aid

for fear of the king of England who was in the area' (Deseille, 155).

11 Fenin mentions only the Bishop of Thérouanne.

12 Godard, 'Quelques précisions', 135.

13 The Bourgeois of Paris names the *baillis* of Vermandois, Mâcon, Sens, Senlis, Caen and Meaux, but further research in office holders using the lists in *Gallia Regia* is needed to substantiate this. Pierre de Hellenviller, *bailli* of Evreux, was believed to be a prisoner in England in May 1416 when his wife appealed for permission to hold lands in his absence (BN pièces originales 1504 de Hellenvillier, en Normandie, 56).

14 Of the Lancashire archers, four in Southworth's company, four in Kyghley's (Calais E358/6 m4, E101/44/29). One archer in the late Earl of Suffolk's retinue (E101/46/24); E101/45/7 (Huntingdon, 5 archers and Strete); E101/47/20 (Erpingham, one archer and Aungers). The information in Wylie, *Henry V*, ii, 188 is not wholly to be trusted.

15 E101/47/40.

16 *PPC*, ii, 226; *Sources*, 448

17 *Sources*, 269–70, from *Rotuli parliamentorum*, iv, 62.

18 For repairs to the bridge for the entry, see E101/187/6.

19 Calais may have continued to commemorate the battle on an annual basis. In the late 1530s or early 1540s a text encouraging Henry VIII to inaugurate annual triumphs against the Pope cited the annual celebrations of Agincourt at Calais as an example of the kind of event envisaged (*Sources*, 278).

20 E403/622 m. 2 (payments to Roger Leche under 30 October).

21 E403/622 m.3 (accounted under 23 November).

22 E101/46/36.

23 Seventeen were certainly lodged at Calais from 17 November to 10 December (E406/29) but de Gaucourt himself was taken to England with the king.

24 *Oeuvres*, 50.

25 Wylie, *Henry V*, ii, 243, n. 8.

26 The identification of Tromagon is uncertain. A Gascon of that name commanded Pontoise in 1417, but a Louis Tromagon of Breton origin fought in the French army in the raising of the siege of Orléans in 1429 (P. Contamine, 'Les armées française et anglaise à l'époque de Jeanne d'Arc', *Revue des sociétés savantes de Haute-Normandie. Lettres et sciences humaines*, 57 [1970], 17). Guillemette de Tresmagon was one of the ladies in waiting of the Duchess of Orléans in 1394 (Wylie, *Henry V*, ii, 245, n. 6).

27 E101/47/35, *PPC*, ii, 205. Wylie, *Henry V*, ii, 252–3 also notes the use of other places of safe-keeping such as the castles of Conway and Caernarvon.

28 Babthorpe's men took a further prisoner, Phelip is an unknown number. The others accounting for ransom income are the Duke of Clarence, members of whose retinue were at the battle although the duke had been invalided home; the executors of Michael de la Pole, Earl of Suffolk, senior, whose archer Edmund Bland, had captured several men; the executors of Michael de la Pole, Earl of Suffolk, junior, whose archer, John Killebury, had taken one unnamed prisoner; Thomas, Lord Camoys; the Duke of Gloucester; and Robert Lawrence, esquire. This information is derived from E358/6.

29 These are calendared in the *Annual Report of the Deputy Keeper of the Public Records*, 44 (1883). The French prisoners taken at Agincourt are currently under investigation by Rémy Ambühl at the University of Nottingham.

30 E101/48/2, seventy-three bonds covering eighty-nine prisoners; E101/46/4, bond of Sir Henry Husee to pay 200 marks to the king for the ransom of nine French prisoners from Beauce, Eu, Vimeu, Beaugency and Abbeville; E101/45/13 bond of William Trussell for nine prisoners.

31 E358/6 m.8d.

32 *Sources*, 451, from *Select Cases in Chancery 1364–1471*, ed. W.P. Baildon (Selden Society, 10, 1896), item 112.

33 No chronicler gives names for those present but it was most likely the lords who were accommodated at Windsor from 11 December: Orléans, Bourbon, Richemont, Eu, Vendôme, Boucicaut, Raoul de Gaucourt and the Sire d'Estouteville.

EPILOGUE: BATTLE OR MURDER?

1   *Gesta*, 150-1.
2   Du Fresne de Beaucourt, *Histoire de Charles VII*, i, 177-8.
3   A. Leguai, 'Le problème des rançons au XVème siècle: la captivité de Jean I, duc de Bourbon',
     Cahiers d'histoire, 6 (1961), 43-4; Cosneau, *Le connétable Richemont*, 58-60.
4   Newhall, *English Conquest of Normandy*, 17-18. The first chapter of this book shows clearly fears
     in Normandy of another attack after the victory at Agincourt.
5   Vaughan, *John the Fearless*, 215.
6   A recent discussion of Crécy emphasises the heaping-up effect there too, although also involv-
     ing horses (A. Ayton and P. Preston, 'Topography and archery: further reflections', in *The Battle of
     Crécy*, 373-4).
7   C. Given-Wilson, 'Edward's III's prisoners of war: the battle of Poitiers and its context', *English
     Historical Review*, 116 (2001), 803-5.
8   *Sources*, 275.
9   *Gesta*, 112-3; G. Kipling. *Enter the King. Theatre, Liturgy, and Ritual in the Medieval Civic Triumph*
     (Oxford, 1998), 208. From 1417 onwards, coinciding with his second invasion, Henry aban-
     doned the use of Latin and French in his correspondence, turning instead to the vernacular (M.
     Richardson, 'Henry V, the English Chancery and Chancery English', *Speculum*, 55 [1980], 727).
10   A contrast can be drawn with Edward III, who had been king for almost twenty years when he
     won his victory at Crécy. Henry needed only another five years after his victory to be named
     heir of France, Edward a further fourteen to give up his claim in return for a territorial settle-
     ment.
11   *Waurin* and *Le Fèvre*: 'In addition the king told them that the French had boasted that if any
     English archers were captured they would cut off the three fingers of their right hand so that
     neither man or horse would ever again by killed by their arrow fire' (*Sources*, 155). See also
     Walsingham: 'the French had published abroad that they wished no one to be spared save for
     certain named lords and the king himself. They announced that the rest would be killed or have
     their limbs horribly mutilated. Because of this our men were much excited to rage and took
     heart, encouraging one another against the event' (*Sources*, 51).
12   Alain Chartier calls it this in his 'Livre des Quatre Dames' (1416–18), not being able to bring
     himself to mention it by name. In the early sixteenth century, Philippe de Metz reports that it
     was popularly known by this term (*Sources*, 345).

Appendix A: Distances on the march

Route	Distance (km)	Cumulative	Day (8 Oct = 1)
Harfleur–Montivilliers	4	4	
Montivilliers–Fauville	33	37	
Fauville–Arques	51	88	4
(Montivilliers–Fécamp)	(29)	(33)	
(Fécamp–Arques)	(69)	(102)	
Arques–Eu	35	123	5
Harfleur–Eu		**123 – 137**	5
Eu–Blanchetaque	28	151 – 165	
Blanchetaque–Pont-Rémy	16	167 – 181	
Pont-Rémy–Boves along Somme	43.5	210.5 – 224.5	9/10
(Pont-Rémy–Airaines)	(9.5)	(176.5 – 190.5)	
(Airaines–Boves)	(29)	(205.5 – 219.5)	9/10
Harfleur–Boves		**205.5 – 224.5**	9/10
Boves–Corbie	21	226.5 – 265.5	
(Boves–Harbonnières)	(21)	(247.5 – 245.5)	
(Harbonnières–Nesle)	(20)	(267.5 – 265.5)	
Corbie–Nesle	33	259.5 – 273.5	
Nesle–Bethencourt (Somme crossing)	7.5	267 – 281	12
Harfleur–Somme crossing		**267 – 281**	12
Bethencourt–Péronne	17	284 – 298	
(Bethencourt–Athies/Monchy-Lagache)	(9)	(276 – 290)	
(Athies/Monchy–Miraumont)	(34)	(310 – 324)	
(Miraumont–Ancre)	(15)	(325 – 339)	
(Athies/Monchy–Ancre)	(36)	(312 – 333.5)	
(Ancre–Forceville)	(10.5)	(322.5 – 349.5)	
(Forceville–Lucheux)	(20)	(342.5 – 369.5)	
Péronne–Doullens/Lucheux	55	339 – 353	
Doullens/Lucheux–Blangy	35	374 – 388	
(Ancre–Acheux)	(12.5)	(324.5 – 346)	
(Acheux–Frévent)	(33)	(357.5 – 379)	
(Frévent–Blangy)	(19)	(376.5 – 398)	
(Lucheux–Frévent)	(13)	(352 – 382.5)	
Blangy–Maisoncelle	4	378 – 402	17
Harfleur–Maisoncelle		**378 – 402**	17
		22.2 – 23.6 km per day	

Fenin
Corbie–Miraumont via Eclusier   51   277.5–291.5 (310 by other route)

Berry Herald
Eclusier–Doullens via Beauquesne   49.5   306–320 (339 by other route)

Stage 1 Harfleur–Eu 123-137 km. Day 1 to 5: 5 days = 24.6–27.4
Stage 2 Eu–Boves 82.5-96.5 km. Day 6 to 9/10: 4 days = 20.6 – 24.1 3.5 days = 23.5 – 27.6
Stage 3 Boves–crossing of Somme 61.5-83 km. Day 9/10 to 12: 3 days 20.5–27.7 3.5 days = 17.5–23.7
Stage 4 Somme–Maisoncelle 111-135 km. Day 13–17: 5 days = 22.2–27

Appendix B: Army sizes according to the chroniclers

	English	French
Gesta	300 men-at-arms, 900 archers Harfleur garrison. 5,000 invalided home. 900 men-at-arms, 5,000 archers (march) Did not exceed 6,000 (battle)	60,000 by their own reckoning. Van at a rough guess 30 times more than all our men put together
Liber Metricus	5,000 went home 900 men-at-arms, 5,000 archers (march – each day the number with him grew smaller) 7,000 (battle)	60,000
Walsingham	8,000 (march)	140,000
Otterbourne	1,500 ships	60,000
Usk	10,000 (march) Thousands went home from disease or desertion (siege)	60,000
Streeche	8,000 (march) Many thousands ill (siege)	100,000
Titus Livius	2,000 Harfleur garrison; line 4 deep (battle)	Line 31 deep Two wings of 1,000 cavalry with spears
Pseudo-Elmham	Line 4 deep (battle)	Line 20 deep. 1,000 cavalry
Capgrave, *De Illustribus Henricis*	9,000 (landing) 5,000 (march)	60,000
Capgrave, *Abbreviacion*	8,000 (march)	140,000
Hardyng prose	900 men-at-arms, 5,000 archers (march)	100,000
Basset, College of Arms MS9	1,500 kts, 35 esq + others in Harfleur garr	
	800 men-at-arms, 8, 500 lances (march)	150,000
Benet	1,500 ships. 11,000 (march)	100,000
Brut	8,000 (march, Harley MS 53) 7,000 (battle, other versions)	120,000
London Chronicles	10,000	60,000

Latin *Brut*	8,000	100,000
Salisbury register	10,000 (battle)	100,000
Religieux	12,000 archers (battle)	14,000 (w. king at Rouen). 5,000 van (battle)
De Cagny	80–100,000 (landing)	
Ruisseauville	8–9,000 (battle) 'parmi les archers'	
Des Ursins 1	4,000 men-at-arms, 16–18,000 archers (march)	
Des Ursins 2	4,000 men-at-arms, 4,000 gros valets, 30,000 archers (landing)	5,000, 3,000 in first two battles
Monstrelet	6,000 men-at-arms, 24,000 archers (siege) 2,000 die at siege 2,000 men-at-arms, 13,000 archers and no. of other soldiers (march) 13,000 archers (battle)	50,000. Outnumbered English six to one. 8,000 men-at-arms, knights, esquires, 4,000 archers, 1,500 cross-bowmen in vanguard, and as many in main battle. 1,600 wing. 800 wing
Le Fèvre	2,000 die at siege 500 went home 500 men-at-arms, 1,500 archers in Harfleur garr. 900–1,000 men-at-arms, 10,000 archers (battle)	50,000. Outnumbered English three to one. 8,000 men-at-arms, knights, esquires, and few archers in vanguard. 1,600 wing. 800 wing
Waurin	2,000 die at siege 500 went home 500 men-at-arms, 1,000 archer Harfleur garr 2,000 men-at-arms, 14,000 archers (march) 900–1,000 men-at-arms, 10,000 archers (battle)	50,000. Outnumbered English six to one. 8,000 men-at-arms, knights, esquires, 4,000 archers, 1,500 cross-bowmen in vanguard and as many in main battle. 1,600 wing. 800 wing
Bourgeois de Paris		One and a half times English
Berry Herald	1,500 knights, 15–16,000 archers (battle)	10,000 men-at-arms (4,800 in van, 3,000 main battle, 1,200 in wings)
Richemont	11–12,000 (battle)	10,000
Morosini	30,000 (landing) 6,000 dead at Harfleur	
Basin	12–15,000 (landing)	

Appendix C: Numbers of dead and prisoners according to the chronicles

	French prisoners	French dead	English dead
Gesta	6+ (6 named 'but few others of gentle birth')	5,598–5,598 3 named + 5 counts, 90 barons whose names are set down in vol. of records; more than 1,500 knights acc. to their own estimate; 4-5000 other gentlemen	13-14 York, Suffolk+ 2 newly dubbed knights + 9 to 10
Liber Metricus	8+ (1 named + 2 dukes, 3 counts + 'many other gentlemen')	9,310 A bishop, 3 dukes, 6 counts, no less than 800 barons, 1,000 knights, 7,500 men of noble rank. Later mentions 11 by name, with 1,200 barons, 1,500 knights and 7,000 other nobles and esquires	
Walsingham	700 (6 named 'and others it is said up to 700')	3,180 6 named + 5 counts and other lords numbering almost a hundred, and 3,069 knights and esquires. Of rank and file not calculated by the heralds	35 York, Suffolk, Gam 8 of rank and file
Usk	8 (2 named + 6 counts)		
Streeche	? (French dukes and many others)		3 York + 2 newly dubbed knights
Titus Livius	3+ (3 named + 'many others')	10,004 4 named + many others numbering up to 10,000	100 York, Suffolk in first fight
Pseudo-Elmham	6 (6 named)	9,011–10,011 11 named + between 9-10,000	102 York, Suffolk + about a hundred others
Capgrave, *De Illustribus Henricis*	5+ (2 dukes, 3 counts and many other gentlemen)	8,612 2 named + 3 dukes, 7 counts, 100 barons, 1,500 knights, 7,000 men of gentle birth	32 York, Suffolk + more than 30 common people

Hardyng version 1	4+ (4 named + 'many more of other prisoners that taken were, as say chroniclers')	No detail	
Hardyng version 2	6 (6 named)	1,508 3 named + 5 barons, 1500 knights and esquires	?York, Suffolk + 2 knights with others
Hardyng prose	6 (6 named)	100,000 3 named + 5 counts, 90 barons, 1,500 knights, great multitude of the rank and file acc. to heralds totalling 100,000	14 York, Suffolk + 2 newly dubbed knights, 10 others
Basset, College of Arms MS9	5 (5 named)	2,438 38 named + 2,400 acc. to declaration delivered by Mountjoye, King of Arms, but may incl. prisoners	14 York, Suffolk, Gam, Sir Richard Kyghely + about 10 archers
Benet	4+ (4 named + 'many others')		
Brut	800 (6 named + 'many others to number of 800')	12,000 (some versions give 11,000) 6+ named + (other versions named + 8 other counts, over 100 barons, 1,500 knights)	30 York, Suffolk + other yeomen to number of 28 (or 26)
London Chronicles	5 (5 named)	10,000 (Cleo CIV) 97 named + many more lords	28 York, Suffolk, Gam + 2 knights and of gentlemen no more
Salisbury register	6 + (6 named + 'other gentlemen')	4,075 75 named + 4,000 valiant knights and esquires without counting the rest	18 York, Suffolk + of lords no more but 15 of their men
Religieux	1404 (4 named + 1400 knights and esquires)	4,011 11 named + several baillis and seneschals, old knights. Later rumours more than 4,000 of the best troops of kingdom	
Geste des nobles francois	5+ (5 named +)	5 named + other noble lords	
Cochon	2+ (2 named + many other great knights)	5 named + a very lg. no. of the nobles of France	
Chronique Anonyme	4+ (4 named + some others)	14 named + all those of gentle birth who had fought at the battle of whom few escaped save those taken alive	

Fenin	4+ (3 named + 'many great lords taken there with those I cannot name')	8 named + many other great lords	
De Cagny	6+ (6 named + 'many other barons, knights and esquires')	5,010–6,010 10 named + many other barons, knights, esquires and other men of war estimated to number 5–6,000	
Ruisseauville	2, 200 (6 named + 'other great lords')	7,600–7,800	
	1,600–1,800 coats of arms + others without coat, 6,000 men	604 Bros of king and 2 or 3 great princes of England + 600	
Des Ursins 1	Several (1 named coincidentally)	4,008 8 named + kts and esqs to 4,000	York+ other deaths but 'no real comparison with French'
Des Ursins 2	6 (6 named)		
Monstrelet	1,500 + (21 named, rest 'all knights and esquires')	10,000 230 named + 10,000 of which 1,6000 varlets and rest of gentle births, 120 with banners incl. princes	York + 600 of other ranks
Le Fèvre	1,600 or thereabouts (21 named + 'and many other great lords, knights and esquires whose names I do not know'. Number 'all knights and esquires')	10,000 133 named + 10,000 of whom 7–8,000 noble and remainder archers, 100–200 men entitled to banners	York and Oxford + 1,600 of all ranks
Waurin	1,600 (20 named + 'many other great lords, knights and esquires whose names I do not know'. Number 'all men of name')	10,000 228 named + 10,000 of whom it is thought 1,600 varlets	York and Oxford + 1,600 of all ranks
Bourgeois de Paris	11+ (11 named + 'many others, knights and esquires, whose names are not known')	3,015 15 named + at least 3,000 gilt spurs	
Berry Herald	6 (6 named)	4,500–4,600 4,000 knights and esquires and 500–600 other men of war	301–401 York + 300–400
Richemont	9+ (9 named + 'many other lords and captains')	13 named	
Morosini	13 (13 named)	10,026–12,026 26 named + 10–12,000	

Basin	3+ (3 named + 'numerous counts, barons and nobles')	3 named	
Normandie	6+ (6 named +'many others')	7,005–8,005 5 named + 7–8,000 knights and esquires	York, Suffolk + of other ranks a great number not exactly known as the dead lay altogether
Dynter	7+ (7 named + 'several other great lords, several others from Brabant)	14+ 14 named + several of their servants	York brother of king, Arundel, + many other magnates and nobles

Appendix D: Men known to have taken out indentures to serve on the 1415 campaign

All listed are described as esquires unless otherwise indicated. For abbreviations of first names see Appendix E. Kt = knight.

Agarston, J.; Alcock, Wm, archer; Alderwich, Nicholas; Alkemade, Florence van kt; Anderton, Thurstan; Appulton, Thos; Arundel, Richard kt; Arundel, J.; Arundel, Thos, earl of; Asco, J.; Asenhull, Wm; Assent, Roger, archer; Assheton, J. kt; Asshton, Nicholas; Atherton, Nicholas; Athurton, Wm; Attilbrigge, J.; Babthorpe, Rbt; Bagot, J. kt; Ballard, Gregory; Bamebury, J., archer; Banaster, Roger; Bangor, Wm; Bank, J.; Barton, Randolph; Baskerville, J. kt; Beauchamp, Walter; Beaufort, Thos, earl of Dorset; Beaumond, Charles kt; Benet, J., master mason; Benet, George, cordwainer of London; Benet, Gregory; Bigge, Hugh; Birkyn, J.; Blaket, J.; Blount, James; Blount, J. kt; Blundell, Henry; Bolde, Thos de; Bolron, Rbt; Bordiu, J., clericus; Botiller, J.; Botreaux, Wm lord; Bourchier, Hugh lord (Sir Hugh Stafford); Bourchier, Wm kt; Bowet, Thos; Bowet, Nicholas; Bradshawe, Wm; Bradwardine, Wm, surgeon; Brancepath, Wm; Breuster, Richard, archer; Brokesby, Wm; Bromley, Henry; Brut, Rbt; Bugge, Baldwin; Bukeham, J., archer; Burgh, J.; Burton, Richard; Burton, Wm; Butiller, J.; Butler, Wm kt; Cambridge, Richard, earl of; Camoys, Thos lord; Carew, Thos 'baro'; Castel, Rbt, clerk of marshalcy; Castellon, Wm; Castleton, Rbt, archer; Chalons, Rbt kt; Charyng, J., gunner; Chaucer, Thos; Chaworth, Thos kt; Chenduyt, J.; Chetwynd, J.; Cheyne, J.; Chich, Roger; Clarence, Thos, duke of; Clement, J.; Clere, David; Cliff, J., minstrel; Clifford, J.; Clifford, J. lord; Clinton, Wm lord; Clux, Hartank van kt; Clynk, J.; Cobyn, J.; Colle, Frederick, master gunner; Colnet, Nicholas, physician; Coneway, J.; Corbet, Thos; Cornwall, J. kt; Courtenay, Edward kt; Courtenay, Wm; Dartas, Janico; Dederyk, Long, gunner; Dent, J., archer; Draycote, Roger; Dutton, Thos kt; Elham, J.; Elys, J., archer; Erpingham, Thos kt; Esmond, J.; Eston, Thos; Etton, Richard; Everard, Lawrence; Everdon, J., clerk; Felbrigg, Simon kt; Ferrers, Edmund, lord of Chartley; Fiennes, Roger kt; Filongley, Richard, archer; Filongley, Henry; Fitzharry, Wm; Fitzhugh, Henry lord; Foulere, Thos, archer; Fowler, Henry; France, Bertram; Gamme, David; Gardemewe, Richard; Gary, Andrew; Gascoyn, Peter, gunner; Gerard, Laurence; Gerardesson, Wm; Gloucester, Humphrey, duke of; Gloucester, Rbt; Graa, J.; Grauntson, Wm kt; Gray, Andrew; Gresley, J. kt; Gresley, Thos kt; Grey, Thos kt of Heton; Grey, J. kt of Ruthin; Grey, J. kt; Greyndor, J. kt; Gryse, Wm, archer; Hall, J., archer; Hals, Richard, clericus in legibus licentiatus; Halsam, Richard; Hampton, Thos; Hargrove, Wm; Harrington, James kt; Harrington, J. lord; Harrington, Wm kt; Hastings, Richard kt; Hatfield, Stephen; Hawley, Thos kt; Hay, Richard; Haywood, Nicholas; Henry, Thos ap; Henry, J. ap; Hervy, Thos; Heton, Rbt; Hille, J.; Hobilod, J.; Hoget, James; Holand, J.; Holand, Nicholas; Holt, Wm; Horsey, J.; Horton, Nicholas; Hudelston, Richard; Hudelston, Wm; Hungerford, Walter kt; Huntingdon, J., earl of; Ireby, J.; Isender, Wm kt; John, Lewis; Joy, Hayne, gunner; Kexby, J., archer; Kyghley, Richard kt; Kylver, J.; Kynwolmerssh, Wm, cofferer of household; Kyrton, J., archer; Lacok, Rbt; Lavender, Wm, archer; Lavender, Richard, archer; Lawrence, Rbt; Leche, Roger kt; Leche, Philip kt; Lee, Wm atte, sergeant at arms; Legh, Wm de kt; Lenthale, Roland kt; Longevyle, J. kt; Lounde, Alexander; Louthe, J.; Lovell, Rbt; Lowart, Peter; Lychbarowe, Thos; Mapurley, Thos; March, Edmund, earl of; Marchon, Richard, archer; Marshall, Wm; Mathewe, Thos, master carpenter; Matthowse, Wm, archer; Merbury, Nicholas; Merbury, J.; Meryng, Wm; Mikelfield, J., archer; Montgomery, J.; Montgomery, Nicholas kt; Morley, J.; Morstede, Thos, surgeon; Mountenay, Wm; Newman, Thos, archer; Norfolk, J., earl of; Norfolk, J.; Normanton, Henry, clericus; Northumberland, Henry, earl of; Nowell, J.; Olton, Wm; Orell, Wm; Osbaldeston, J.; Oskest, Martin van, gunner; Oxford, Richard, earl of; Parker, Richard; Passemere, Rbt; Passenham;

Ralph, archer; Payne, Stephen, almoner; Pemberton, Henry; Percevale, Griffin; Percy, Thos kt; Peryent, J.; Peterburgh, J., archer; Philip, J. kt; Philip, Wm kt; Philip, J.; Pilkington, J.; Plomaker; Dirk; Plum, Thos, gunner; Pole, Martin; Pole, Ralph del; Pope, Wm; Porter, Wm; Radcliff, J.; Radcliffe, Rbt; Radcliffe, Wm; Radcliffe, Richard kt; Rassh, J.; Raumsey, Ralph; Rempston, Thos kt; Rerisby, Nicholas; Rigmaiden, Thos; Robessart, Lewis; Robessart, J. kt; Roos, J. lord; Rothington, Rbt; Roundell, J.; Ryder, J.; Salisbury, Thos, earl of; Sandes, Walter kt; Sankey, J., archer; Scalder, Gregory, archer; Scaldere, Henry, archer; Scarisbrick, Henry; Scrop, Richard kt; Scrope, Henry lord; Seintpee, J. lord; Selby, J.; Semper, Roger; Sherard, Rbt; Shipley, Henry; Shirley, Ralph kt; Shorne, Wm, archer; Shottesbrook, Rbt; Skerbrick, Henry; Skidmore, J. kt; Skipton, J.; Smetheley, Alex, archer; Smyth, Wm; Southworth, J. kt; Spaldyng, J., archer; Spore, Rbt, archer; Sprong, Gerard, gunner; Standish, Hugh kt; Stanley, Ralph kt; Stanley, J.; Stanley, Rbt; Staunton, Thos; Staveley, Ralph kt; Steward, J.; Stokley, Wm; Strange, Ivill; Strauley, Hugh; Strikland, Thos; Suffolk, Michael de la Pole jnr, earl of; Suffolk, Michael de la Pole snr earl of; Sugewas, J.; Sweetenham, Thos, archer; Swillington, J.; Talbot, Gilbert lord; Talbot, Wm kt; Tempest, Richard kt; Temple, Wm, master carpenter; Thorp, Thos, archer; Tirwhit, Wm; Topcliffe, J.; Tropenell, Wm, sergeant tailor; Troutbeck, Wm; Trumpington, Roger kt; Tunbrigge, Thos, archer; Tunneley, Richard; Tunstall, Thos kt; Ufflete, Gerard kt; Umfraville, Gilbert kt; Vale, J.; Walsh, J. archer; Ward, Thos; Waterton, J.; Wembre, J., archer; West, Thos kt; Whitingham, Alan; Wightman, Wm; Wilcotes, Thos; Willoughby, Rbt lord; Wolde, Wm; Yedelissh, J. kt; York, Edward duke of; Zouche, Wm lord.

Appendix E: Men-at-arms and archers known to have served in the English army

This lists only those named in muster rolls and retinue lists in The National Archives and excludes the 'Agincourt roll' in Nicolas, 333-70, on which see *Sources*, 407. Abbreviations: J. = John, Wm = William, Rich = Richard, Rob = Robert, Thos = Thomas. NB More than one man may share the same name.

Men-at-arms (1,422):

Abram, Rich; Accok, Hugh; Acton, Sir Andrew; Adrya, Adam; Agarston, J.; Alaired, J.; Aldere, Rob; Alderworth, Nicholas; Aler, Thos; Alexin, J.; Alford, Adam; Allerton, Rob; Alman, J.; Alnewyk, J.; Andrewe, Rich; Andrewe, Wm; Andrieu, J.; Ap Guille, Jakke; ap Gwyllym, Willym ap Howell; ap Henry, Griffutt ap Mereduth; ap Howell, Howell ap Jenan; Ap Jar, Morgan; ap Jenan, Walter ap Griffuth; ap Lewys, Andrew; ap Madok, Jenan ap Richard; Ap meredith, Eden; ap Owen, Meredud; ap Rhys, Ricard ap Mewryk; ap Ricard, Jankyn ap Mewryt; ap Richard, Mabe Mereduth; ap Rother, Rys; ap Rys, Jankyn ap J.; ap Rys, J.; ap Thomas, Thomas ap David; ap Traharn, David ap Jenan; Appulby, Wm; Appulton, Ralph; Appulton, Thos; Arderne, Rich; Ardes, Nicholas; Argentem, Wm; Armurer, J.; Arnold, Wm; Arthur, J.; Arthur, Thos; Arundel, Thomas, earl of; Arundel herald; Arundell, Sir J.; Asheman, J.; Ashfield, Rob; Aske, Thos; Aske, Edmund; Aspur, Wm; Asshell, Thos; Assheton, John de; Assheton, J.; Asshman, J.; Astley, Thos; Atkynse, Henry; Atkynson, J.; Atle, Thos; Aultiby, Rich; Aunger, J.; Aungers, J.; Axham, Wm; Ayleward, J.; Ayleward, Wm; Aylynby, Wm; Ayscowe, J.; Aywleward, J.; Babthorp, Rob; Babthorp, Thos; Bacheler, Wm; Baker, J.; Ballard, Gregory; Ballyngborough, Thos; Ballyngborough, J.; Balne, Wm; Bambrueck, Rob; Bamburg, Wm; Banaster, J.; Banastre, Thos; Barbour, J.; Barnstaple, Thos; Barowe, J.; Barowe, Rob; Barre, Wm; Barre, J.; Barrey, J.; Bartelot, John snr; Bartha, J.; Barton, Wm; Barton, James; Barton, Oliver; Baskerville, Rich; Basset, Philip; Basset, Rich; Bawe, J.; Bawlyn, Wm; Baydell, David; Baydell, David; Bayhous, J.; Bayne, Gernonet de; Bayon, Geronet du; Beamond, Rich; Beanpee, J.; Beauchamp, Sir Wm; Beauchamp, Thos; Beauchamp, Walter; Beaumond, Thos; Beaumont, Sir Charles; Beaurepaire, Thos; Bedford, J.; Bedyngfeld, Wm; Befort, Thos; Beke, Laurence; Bekwym, J.; Belestede, J.; Belesteded, J.; Belgrave, Thos; Belle, J.; Benalua, Wm; Bere, J.; Beresby, Nicholas; Berham, J.; Berham, Wm; Berkeley, Maurice; Berkheed, Roger; Berkyry, Wm; Bernard, Thos; Bernard, J.; Bernarde, J.; Bernet, J.; Berney, Sir Louis; Berwyck, Thos; Beryton, Elis; Bilisby, Thos; Birkhed, Rich; Birston, J.; Birtby, Wm; Bitterlee, J.; Bitterley, Rich; Bitterley, J.; Blacleys, J.; Blakebourne, Wm; Blakesson, J.; Blaklowe, Ralph; Blaye, Thos; Bleyton, Thos; Blound, Rob; Bodrugan, Wm; Bokenham, J.; Boland, Richard of; Bold, J.; Bolde, Thos; Bole, J.; Bolran, Wm; Bolton, Wm; Bolton, Rob; Bonevile, Thos; Bonore, Rob; Bonvyle, Wm; Boold, Rob; Boold, Bartholemew; Borle, J.; Borlee, Hugh; Bosevile, Christopher; Boston, Thos; Boteler, J.; Boteler, Rich; Boterville, Wm; Botherforth, Wm; Botiller, J.; Boton, Roger; Botreaux, Wm; Botreaux, William lord; Bourchier, Hugh lord; Boutre, John de la; Bowe, J.; Bowet, Sir Wm; Bowys, Sir Wm; Boydell, Davie; Boys, Rich; Braas, Philip ap Gwillym; Bradeston, J.; Bradston, J.; Brakemaste, J.; Brampton, Rich; Brampton, Wm; Bran, Thos; Branche, Sir Philip; Brandasby, J.; Braunche, J.; Braunspem, Ralf; Bray, J.; Bredon, Ralph; Bredwardine, Wm; Brereton, Wm; Brereton, Randolf; Bresingham, Reynald; Bret, Wm; Breton, Wm; Breton, Thos; Breton, Robard; Brettan, Wm; Bretton, Wm; Bretton, J.; Brewes, J.; Brian, Wm; Brigeford, J.; Brigge, Baldwin; Brimwyche, Thos; Brocas, Samson; Brokel, Thos; Brokesby, Bertholemew; Brokesby, Wm; Bromeley, Wm; Bromley, Henry; Brook, J.; Broun, J.; Broune, J.; Broune, Wm; Browe, Rob; Browe, J.; Browne, Wm; Browne, J.; Brownyng, J.; Bruin, Morys; Brunwyche, Thos; Brycete, Rich; Brydport, Wm; Brygge, J.; Brymsham,

Walter; Brynyne, Thos; Bryse, J.; Bryston, J.; Brystowthe, Wm; Bukton, Rich; Bukton, Wm; Burcester, Thos; Burdet, Nicholas; Burgh, Thos; Burgoyns, Wm; Burnel, Sir Edward; Buron, Rob; Burton, Thos; Burton, Giles; Burton, Sir Thos; Burton, Wm; Burton, Rob; Burton, Walter; Buttrens, Wm; Butuelayne, Rob; Byche, J.; Bykombe, Rich; Bylam, J.; Bylle, Hugh; Bynde, Wm; Bynyshe, J.; Byron, Rob; Byry, J.; Byschypp, Rich; Byshop, Henry; Cabert, Benedict.; Calan, Wm; Calaryns, Thos; Caleys, John de; Calf, Wm; Calf, Pierires; Calf, Walter; Calf, J.; Calpok, Wm; Calston, J.; Calthorn, Wm; Calthorp, J.; Calveney, Davyd; Calveney, Hugh; Cambyle, Wm; Cammseyle, George; Camoys, Thomas lord; Camvile, J.; Camvyle, Wm; Candeler, Henry; Canford, J.; Carbet, Thos; Cardenowe, Rich; Carles, Stephen; Carmyon, Thos; Carrant, Thos; Carwen, Thos; Castell, Nicholas; Castell, Rob; Castell, J.; Castellayn, Wm; Casuall, Nicholas; Cathon, Wm; Catlynson, Rich; Catte, Hugh; Caule, Geoffrey; Cavendysh, J.; Celer, Wm; Chamber, J.; Chambre, J.; Chambre, Thos; Chambre, Roger; Chambre, Rob; Chambre, John del; Chapman, J.; Charles, Sir Thos; Charles, Esmon; Chattow, J.; Cheaumbr, Wm; Chircheman, Wm; Chokelake, Fyleyhy; Chorley, Nicholas; Clapham, Rob; Clapton, Wm; Clarence, Thomas Duke of; Clarvaux, Thos; Claryngdon, J.; Claxton, J.; Claxton, Thos; Claypole, Thos; Clement, J.; Clepam, Thancelyn; Clere, Wm; Clew, Rich; Clifford, J.; Clifton, J.; Clifton, Gerveys; Clifton, Rob; Clinton, Sir Thos; Cloneslond, John de; Clynk, J.; Clynton, J.; Clystun, Wm; Cobham, Sir Reginald; Codyngton, Simon; Cogmour, Wm; Cokeyr, George; Cokke, Wm; Cokton, Dicon; Cole, J.; Cole, Nicolas; Colerond, Rich; Coley, Wm; Colfo, Rich; Colfox, Sir Nicholas; Collan, J.; Colman, J.; Colmer, J.; Colnet, Nicholas; Colon, Peter; Colvyle, Sir J.; Coly, Wm; Colyn, J.; Colyn, Nicholas; Colyn, Walter; Colyngs, Roger; Comer, J.; Compton, Rob; Cook, Andrew; Coolpepir, J.; Coppedok, J.; Corbet, Rob; Corbet, Thos; Cornew, Rich; Cornewaill, Herand; Cornewaille, Wm; Cornysh, Walter; Cornyssh, J.; Costard, Henry; Cote, Rich; Cote, Wm; Cotegreve, Rob; Coterell, Symkyn; Cotes, Rob; Cotesmore, George; Coton, Richard de; Coton, J.; Coton, Hugh; Cotwryght, J.; Courson, J.; Courtenay, Wm; Coveley, J.; Coventre, Thos; Coverley, Thos; Covert, J.; Covyngtry, Rich; Cowper, J.; Craphull, Rob; Cressewell, Wm; Cressi, J.; Cresson, Wm; Crisacre, James; Crispyngge, J.; Croche, J.; Croft, James; Cromwell, Sir Wm; Cromwell, Ralph; Crowe, J.; Crysp, Thos; Curteys, Hugh; Curteys, Wm; Curvyle, J.; Dacre, Edmund; Dacre, Wm; Dalfanby, J.; Dalmada, Alphonso; Dam, Thos; Danzel, Lauerent; Daubeney, J.; Daubriggecourt, Sir J.; Daubriggecourt, J.; Daubryggecourt, Robynet; Davy, J.; Dayvel, Louis; Dayvyle, Thos; de la Mare, J.; de Medecroft, Godfrey; de Spayne, Wm; Dedham, George; Delahay, J.; Delcroun, Henry; Dell, Thos; Delle, Thos; Denham, Wm; Denne, Thos; Dennys, Rob; Denys, Geoffrey; Denys, James; Deram, Andrew; Derby, Thos; Derolf, Andrew; Deschalers, Thos; Destre, Wm; Devet, Roger; Devyle, Thos; Devyle, Wm; Dewer, J.; Digges, J.; Disney, J.; Dod, Utright; Dodde, Wm; Dodyngton, Wm; Doke, J.; Dole, Wm; Domerzayn, Johan; Donne, J.; Donyt, Wm; Doriset, Wm; Dowglas, Davy; Dowyll, Henry; Drake, Henry; Dryvere, J.; du Bayon, Geronet; Duckworth, Wm; Durham, Thos; Dutton, Lawrence; Dutton, Wm; Dycon, Wm; Dyngley, Roland; Dys, J.; Dytter, Wm; Ecton, Rich; Edmund, J.; Edward, Wm; Edward, J.; Eland, Rob; Elkenhed, Rob; Elman, J.; Elys, Rich; Elys, Eyon; Erdepoet, Wm; Erloffhe, John de; Erpingham, Sir Thos; Esmond, Davy; Estenay, Rich; Eston, Thos; Eston, Roger; Estot, Stephen; Estovey, Wm; Etton, Rich; Everard, Lawrence; Evere, Walter; Evere, J.; Everyngham, Wm; Eveus, J.; Ewre, Henry; Eyton, Wm; Falkes, Rich; Fannt, J.; Farnam, J.; Faryngton, David; Fastolf, Edmund; Fastolf, J.; Fayng, Thos; Fegefery, J.; Fehanery, Thos; Felbrigg, Sir Simon; Felde, J.; Felongley, Henry; Fenys, James; Ferbiy, J.; Feriby, Rob; Fermur, Thos; Ferrers, Edward; Ferrers, Thos; Ferrers, Sir Henry; Ferrers, Henry; Ferrers, J.; Ferror, Stephen; Ffehenry, Thos; Fisch, J.; Fitzharry, Wm; Fitzhenry, Thos; Fitzhugh, Michael; Fitzpiers, J.; Fitzrichard, J.; Fitzwalter, Humphrey lord (d. 1 Sept 1415); Fitzwilliam, Wm; Fiztleonis, Peter; Flaundres, Thos; Flemyng, Thos; Flompyson, Laurence; Flore, Thos; Flyntrale, Henry; Folvyle, J.; Foot, Wm; Forde, Thos; Foredn, Griffin; Forest, Henry; Forster, Rich; Forster, Thos; Fosse, J.; Fowler, Henry; Fowler, Wm; Fowne, Ralph; Frawon, Bartholemew; Fraynoh[lost], J.; Freman, J.; Fresel, James; Fresell, Robard; Fresell, Wm; Frestowe, Rich; Fulford, Robard; Fynche, J.; Fyndern, Thos; Fythian, Rich; Gabriel, Thos; Gant, Thos; Ganthorp, Alan; Gardener, Stephen; Gargrave, Thos; Garlek, Stevene; Garneys, Piers; Garston, Walter; Gatscombe, J.; Gayght, Nicholas; Gayne, Thos; Geddyng, Rich; Gegge, J.; Gegge, Rich; Gegge, J.; Geney, Thos; Gerard, Henry; Gerart, J.; Gernet, J.; Gersley, Wm; Girdelay, Wm; Gloucester, Humphrey Duke of; Gloucester, Thos; Gloucester, Rob; Gloucestre, J.; Glym, Thos; Godard, Wm; Godard, Sir J.; Godard, Henry; Gode, J.; Gode, Wm; Gode, J.; Godfrey, Stephen; Godyngton, Simon; Godyngton, Simon; Godyngton, Wm; Golde, Wm; Goldehey, J.; Goldingham, Sir Walter; Goldyng, J.; Gournay, Thos; Gower, Wm; Gowerell, Thos; Gradelyng,

Stephen; Grandicares, Wm; Granson, Sir Wm; Grantham, Wm; Gray, J.; Gregory, Thos; Grek, Wm; Grendam, Roger; Grenham, J.; Grey, J.; Grey, Andrew; Grey, Thos; Grey, Sir J.; Grey, John de; Grimwyche, Thos; Groos, Simon; Groos, J.; Groos, Oliver; Grove, J.; Grove, Rich; Gryfton, Michael; Grystowe, Rich; Guerard, J.; Gumville, Nicholas; Gunter, Roger; Gunvile, Nicholas; Gwyn, Henry ap Jenan; Gyffard, Thos; Gyffard, J.; Gyldere, Rich; Gylspyn, Thos; Haals, J.; Habmond, Philip; Hagman, J.; Haket, Rich; Halbkeslowe, Rich; Halet, J.; Halibell, Matthew; Halsale, J.; Halsham, Rich; Halsham, Hugh; Halton, Thos; Hammes, Rich; Hammond, J.; Hamond, J.; Hankeswelle, Wm; Hardewyn, Thos; Hardy, J.; Hardys, Edward; Harefeke, Brian; Hargild, Wm; Hargraove, J.; Harkes, Wm; Harley, Esmon; Harley, Rob; Harper, Nicholas; Harryngton, Wm; Hatfield, Thos; Haughton, Thos; Haughton, Edward; Haukyn, Edmund; Hawe, Arnold; Hawes, Rob; Hawgwyn, J.; Hawkes, Wm; Hawkwode, J.; Hawte, Wm; Hawte, Sir Nicholas; Hawton, Radulf; Haybergh, Henry; Haywood, Nicholas; Hegge, Jacob; Helde, Thos; Helygan, J.; Hemnale, Rob; Herbottell, Edward; Hereford, Lewes; Herny, Wm; Heron, Sir J.; Heron, Rob; Heron, Wm; Hert, Nicholas; Hervy, J.; Hervynge, Rich; Hethom[lost], J.; Heton, Rob; Hewet, J.; Hewne, Gerard; Hikedon, Laurence; Hille, John de; Hilton, Rob; Hoakk, Thos; Hobt, Wm; Hobyldon, J.; Hodelston, Wm; Hokley, Thos; Holand, J.; Holdeley, J.; Holdelyne, Geoffrey; Holder, J.; Holford, Rich; Holkam, J.; Holland, Wm; Holland, Nicholas; Holme, J.; Holt, J.; Holton, Wm; Holton, Nicholas; Holton, J.; Holwybont, Thos; Hone, J.; Hoo, J.; Hoo, Thos; Hoore, Wm; Hoore, Henry; Hootoft, Wm; Hope, Edmund; Horn, Rich; Horne, J.; Horneby, Walter; Horseles, J.; Horson, Rich; Horton, Nicholas; Hoton, Wm; Hoton, J.; Howden, Patrik; Howden, Symond; Howell, David; Huddleston, Wm; Huet, J.; Hukgin, Thos; Hunt, Rob; Hunte, Henry; Hunte, J.; Huntingdon, John, earl of; Husee, J.; Husee, Sir Henry; Huton, Thos; Hyde, Wm; Hykelyng, Wm; Hyllary, Rob; Hynkley, Thos; Hynstoke, Thos; Hyton, Thos; Ilpeston, J.; Ingilby, Rob; Intebergh, Waulter; Ippstones, Thos; Iscoid, Gruffuth ap Jenan; Jay, Thos; Jenney, J.; Joce, Wm; John, Lewis; Johne, Hankyn; Jonesson, Rob; Jonson, Simon; Jonson, Peter; Jonson, Rich; Jonyson, Gerund; Junnyng, Wm; Junyng, Wm; Kamfran, Wm; Karlyan, J.; Kay, Makyn; Kechill, J.; Kede, Wm; Kelby, Richard de; Keleryan, J.; Kely, Henry; Kemscote, Wm; Kendale, J.; Kennale, Robertt; Kenre, J.; Kent, Hugh; Kentyng, J.; Kenynton, J.; Kerwitham, J.; Kilkenny, Henry; Killeran, J.; Kirkeman, Rich; Knaky, Thos; Knottyng, J.; Kyghley, Wm; Kylver, J.; Kynes, J.; Kyng, Nicholas; Kyngeston, Rob; Kyngeston, Rob; Kyngges, J.; Kynwolmersh, Wm; Kyrcbryd, Edward; Kyrkeby, Wm; Kyrkeby, Richard de; Kyrkham, Wm; La Waryn, Wm; Lacok, Rob; Lacon, Rich; Lacre, Rob; Lacy, Thos; Lampelove, Thos; Lampet, George; Lande, John de la; Langare, Wm; Langeston, Wm; Langford, Thos; Langford, Rob; Langlegh, J.; Lano, J.; Larendon, J.; Lary, Nichol; Lathbury, Rob; Laughton, George; Laurence, Rob; Laveney, J.; Lawther, Hugh; Lawton, Henry; Lawyer, Thos; Lay, Roulant du; Layland, Rich; Layng, Peter; Le Melon, Walter; Leder, Thos; Ledes, Wm; Ledes, Alexander; Ledyngton, J.; Lee, James; Lee, Hugh; Lee, Peter; Lee, Robard; Leget, Thos; Legh, Sir Wm; Lenham, Wm; Lenthale, Rouland; Lewkenore, Thos; Lloit, Llewellyn ap Gwlim; Lloyt, Walter; Lommesdon, Thos; Longestchawe, Wm; Loryn, J.; Louth, J.; Love, J.; Love, Wm; Loveday, Rich; Lovel, Nicholas; Lovell, Rich; Lovell, William lord; Lovell, Thos; Lovelych, Rich; Lowe, Wm; Lowher, Geoffrey; Lowngesby, Rob; Lowther, Rich; Lowtrie, J.; Lumley, William de; Lumley, J.; Lychbarowe, Thos; Lymbury, J.; Lyndesey, J.; Lynfrothe, Wm; Lynne, Thos; Lynton, J.; Maictagn, J.; Manghfeld, J.; Manston, Roger; Manyngham, J.; Mapurely, Thos; Marian, J.; Marley, J.; Marnam, Wm; Marney, Thos; Marshall, Michael; Marton, Rob; Massy, Nicholas; Massy, Nicholas; Mathy, J.; Maun, J.; Mayle, Wm; Mayn, J.; Mayn, Jamys; Medecroft, Gerard; Medees, Lowas; Medelham, J.; Medes, Lewis; Meek, J.; Menston, Thos; Merbury, Nicholas; Mering, Wm; Merlote, Wm; Mewes, Wm; Mewys, Lewes; Meylor, J.; Michelgone, John snr; Michell, J.; Middleton, Charles; Middleton, Rich; Middleton, J.; Mighelstowe, J.; Moaland, Ralph; Mompager, Bartre; Mordan, Piers; More, J.; More, J.; More, J.; Moreys, Rob; Morley, Sir Rob; Morley, Sir Thos; Morley, Thos; Morstede, J.; Mortimer, Sir J.; Morton, Sir Rob; Morton, Hugh; Morton, Rob; Morton, Thos; Mortymer, Owen; Moryell, Henry; Mossyn, Rob; Motlow, Mayow; Motoun, Rich; Moubray, Rob; Mounde, Thos; Mountray, Thos; Moutenaz, Wm; Mowbray, Wm; Moyle, Wm; Moyner, Rich; Mulgrave, Thos; Mulso, Henry; Mundeford, Osbern; Mungomere, J.; Myddleton, Thos; Mylbourne, Rob; Needham, Rob; Neele, Thos; Nesmyth, Sir Thos; Nevile, Rob; Neville, Ralph; Neville, Rob; Nevyle, Hames; Newbryge, Hugh; Newcomb, Thos; Newmarche, Thos; Newmarche, Rob; Newton, J.; Nichaas, Seynt; Nonngyll, J.; Noon, Henry; Norfolk, John, earl of (earl marshal); Norton, Jannos; Norton, J.; Norton, Thos; Norton, James; Norwich, Wm; Norwych, Wm; Nowby, J.; Nyter, Wm; Ocle, Thos; Oderne, J.; Ogan, Wm; Oke, J.; Okeman, Thos; Oldebef, Wm; Oliver, Ralph; Ormesby,

Arthur; Osborne, Roger; Ostell, Thos; Oturbens, Rob; Oudebu, J.; Ouyngton, Wm; Oxford, Richard, earl of; Oyldebeef, Wm; Pakeman, Thos; Palmer, Rob; Palmer, Phythian; Palmer, Thomas snr; Palmer, J.; Palmer, J.; Parker, Laurence; Parker, Rich; Parker, Lawrence; Parker, Thos; Parr, Gilbert; Pashale, Nicholas; Passmere, Rob; Passy, J.; Paternoster, Wm; Pateyngton, J.; Patrych, Jamys; Pavy, Rich; Pawlyn, Wm; Pawlyn, Thos; Paybne, Stephen; Payn, Thos; Payn, Thos; Pekirke, Rob; Pekke, Wm; Pelham, J.; Pensors, Peter; Percy, Wm; Percy, Thos; Perebolt, Wm; Peret, J.; Permans, Rich; Permans, Walter; Perot, Wm; Person, Wm; Person, J.; Peryn, Thos; Peshale, Nicholas; Petybon, Wm; Petyrsson, Jacob; Peverell, J.; Philip, Sir Wm; Phillip, J.; Philypp, J.; Phyllip, Rob; Pigeon, J.; Plosans, J.; Pluland, Edward; Podesey, J.; Podesey, Sir J.; Polay, Thos; Pole, Ralph; Pole, William de la; Poley, Thos; Polglasse, Thos; Poling, J.; Polmer, J.; Ponnt, John de; Pope, Ralph; Pope, Wm; Popham, J.; Popham, Stephen; Porter, J.; Porter, Wm; Potman, Laurence; Poulle, Alart de la; Powcher, J.; Power, J.; Poy, Rich; Prestempde, Rich; Preston, Edmund; Preston, Wm; Prideaux, Rich; Pruet, Rich; Prylle, J.; Pryne, J.; Pudsay, Wm; Pulteney, Thos; Purchace, ?; Puryan, J.; Puslynch, Edward; Pyd, J.; Pygot, Thos; Pympe, J.; Pyrley, Wm; Pyxton, J.; Quykkesley, Rob; Radcliff, Henry; Radcliffe, Wm; Radclyff, J.; Radclyff, Henry; Radclyff, Sir J.; Radyngton, Rob; Ralham, J.; Ramfer, Ralph; Ramsell, Nicholas; Ramsey, Rich; Rasche, J.; Rasyn, Wm; Raynston, J.; Redewelle, J.; Reede, J.; Relverge, J.; Rephyngham, Thos; Reston, Rich; Reymys, J.; Reynes, J.; Ripon, Gibbon; Robert, Roger; Robessart, Sir J.; Rokell, Rob; Ronde, J.; Roos, Rob; Roos, Thos; Ros, Wm; Rosmeryn, Jacob; Rothyng, J.; Rotlyng, John de; Rouff, J.; Roundell, J.; Rous, J.; Routh, J.; Russell, J.; Rutherfoys, Michael; Rygelyn, J.; Rynder, J.; Ryslorpe, J.; S[lost], Rob; Sagars, J.; Saint George, J.; Sala, Rob; Salcock, Sawayn; Salmon, Thos; Saltmarsh, Rob; Salver, J.; Sampston, [ ]; Sanderyson, J.; Sans, Peter; Sanstun, J.; Sareth, J.; Sauxton, J.; Sauxton, Rauf; Sayer, Bartholmew; Sayntquyntayn, Rob; Sayvill, Bernard; Scarburgh, J.; Scargill, Thos; Scarlet, J.; Scekesbay, Rob; Schelton, Oliver; Schotilworth, Wm; Schyryngton, Walter; Scogan, Rob; Scott, Stephen; Scudamore, J.; Secheford, Edmund; Seintjust, Aleyn; Selby, Thos; Selby, Hugo; Selby, J.; Sencler, Thos; Sencourt, Alan; Sengleton, Bernard; Sengyton, Thos; Sentcler, Wm; Sentlow, Edward; Sewale, Thos; Seymer, J.; Seymer, Nicholas; Seynesbury, J.; Seyntabyn, J.; Shaffe, Alexander; Shakene, Thos; Shapwyk, J.; Shawe, J.; Sheffield, Wm; Shepewke, J.; Shille, Wm; Shirboris, Rich; Shirley, Ralph; Shirmore, Dipart; Shobdon, Walter; Shottesbrook, Peter; Shyngolton, Wm; Sicton, Wm; Silles, Rich; Skavesbreke, J.; Skavesbreke, Rich; Skelton, J.; Skelton, Rich; Slegill, Walter; Slowby?, J.; Smethwyk, Roger; Smyth, Hugh; Smyth, Wm; Smythes, J.; Solomon,; Somanz, Wm; Somerley, J.; Somerset, Henry, earl of; Somerton, Hogekyn; Somerton, J.; Sonde, J.; Southek, J.; Southek, Rich; Sowbley, J.; Spayne, Sir Wm; Spencer, Rich; Spens[er?], Jacob; Spernore, Wm; Spofford, Rob; Spore, J.; Spycer, Thos; Stafford, J.; Stallworth, Rich; Stampford, J.; Standish, Gibbon; Stanely, Rich; Stanlake, Rob; Stanley, Rich; Stapp, Thos; Stapulton, Thos; Stapulton, Brian; Stapulton, J.; Starlyng, J.; Staunton, Thos; Stebynton, Wm; Stele, Patrick; Stenenessons, Thos; Sterki, Rich; Sterlyng, J.; Stokes, J.; Stokton, Thos; Stonynges, Thos; Stormestre, J.; Stradlyng, Edward; Strange, Ibel; Strangrond, J.; Strangwas, Thos; Stratton, Augustinus; Stratton, Auston; Straunge, Sir Hamo; Straunge, Leonard; Straunge, Hamo; Stretchely, J.; Strete, Henry; Streyn, Wm; Strickland, Walter; Stroner, Rich; Stubber, J.; Stubbler, J.; Stulworth, Wm; Stunden, Wm; Sturston, Wm; Style, Wm; Styrop, Rob; Styward, J.; Suffolk, Michael, earl of snr; Suonman, Rob; Sutton, Hugh; Sutton, J.; Swenerton, Edmund; Sweppston, J.; Swylington, Rob; Swynford, Thos; Swynsheade, J.; Swynsyn, Wm; Sydnam, Rob; Symon, Henry; Symson, Thos; Tailard, Rich; Tailfier, Eustace; Talbot, Rich; Talbot, Wm; Talbot, J.; Talbot, Thos; Taverham, J.; Taylor, Edmund; Tebbe, Rob; Teesdale, J.; Tendryng, J.; Teryk, J.; Thomas, Michael; Thorley, Peter; Thornburgh, J.; Thorndam, Giles; Thornton, J.; Thorp, J.; Thrnburgh, Rob; Thrygston, Rich; Thursen, Rob; Thwayt, Thos; Thwayt, Oliver; Thweny, Rich; Tildesle, Edmond; Todenham, Rob; Tomson, Davi; Toner, J.; Tonge, Wm; Topcliff, J.; Topclyf, Thos; Toppyfeld, Franc; Towrney, J.; Travas, J.; Treganon, Wm; Tregonwall, Wm; Tremlyn, Thos; Trenewith, Michael; Trenewyth, J.; Trevaignon, Thos; Trevour, Reginald; Trevry, Nicholas; Trevysdale, J.; Trewethelek, Rich; Trewman, Clement; Trewynnard, Henry; Trussell, J.; Trussell, Wm; Tryll, Wm; Tryngham, Thos; Tryskebetys, Thos; Twhyng, Rich; Twyford, J.; Twyford, Wat; Twyford, Robard; Tybba, Stephen; Tylbute, Thos; Tyrell, J.; Tyrell, Walter; Tyrell, Wm; Udell, Thos; Ugan, Henry; Ugan, J.; Unneslawe, Roger; Ussher, Rich; Vachan, Rys ap Llellewyn ap Griffuth; Vaughan, Rob; Vaughan, Meredith; Vaughan, J.; Vawre, J.; Veer, John de; Vele, Henry; Venables, Raduf; Venys, J.; Virlawtresson, Wake; Viston, Thos; Vrpath, J.; Walesse, Wm; Waleys, Wm; Waleys, J.; Walgrance, Waren; Waller, Wm; Waller, Wm; Waller, Rich; Wallselde, Wm; Walshe, J.; Walton, Rob; Walweyn, Edmund; Warborton, Hugh; Wardale, J.; Wardale, Ralph; Warde, Thos; Warde, J.; Warde,

Edmond; Warde, J.; Warner, J.; Warnier, Gilles; Waryn, J.; Wasdall, J.; Waslyn, Rob; Wastnes, Wm; Wate, Wm; Wate, J.; Waterman, J.; Waterton, J.; Watford, Wm; Watford, Pierres; Wath, Robard; Watson, Rob; Watton, Richard of; Wauton, Wm; Wayte, Thos; Webbe, J.; Welby, Rich; Welle, Thos; Wellyng, Rob; Wenne, J.; Wenynglon, Wm; Werk, J.; Werk, Rob; Werton, J.; Werweton, Wm; Wessyngton, J.; West, Stephen; West, Wm; West, Rob; West, J.; Westan, Thos; Whalton, George of; White, Rob; White, J.; White, J.; Whitehead, Rich; Whitle, John de; Whitton, Rich; Whityngton, Wm; Whyteney, Thos; Whytington, Guy; Whyttyngton, James; Whytuey, Thos; Wightman, Wm; Willeson, J.; Willeson, Thos; Willeson, J.; Willson, Alaxander; Wiltshire, J.; Windesor, Henry; Wisse, Thos; Wittington, Reginald; Wodwharpole, Thos; Wolde, Wm; Wolf, J.; Wolf, Wm; Wolveston, Wm; Woolf, Rob; Worcester, Rich; Worde, J.; Worseley, Charles; Worslegh, Elys; Worslegh, Rich; Worsleyn, Ambros; Wortley, Nicholas; Wrothe, Wm; Wulwyn, Thos; Wybbury, J.; Wyche, Rich; Wyche, Roger; Wyclif, Henry; Wygonale, Wm; Wykehurst, Wm; Wykham, Rob; Wylcok, Rob; Wyllaby, Thos; Wyllysone, J.; Wyllysone, Thos; Wylton, Hugh; Wylughby, Hugh; Wymondeswold, Wm; Wynge, Thos; Wynnesbury, J.; Wynslowe, J.; Wyntrishill, Thos; Wynvale, Rob; Wyseman, Nicholas; Wytewyk, Henry; Yarmin, J.; Ylloyt, Owen ap Jankyn; Yonge, J.; York, Edward, duke of; Young, Walter.

Archers (5,116):

Abbot, J.; Abbot, Thos; Abbot, J.; Abel, Thos; Abram, Bartholomew; Abyndon, J.; Abyrcourt, Stephen; Adam, J.; Adam, Thos; Adammes, Rich; Adammessone, Gibonn; Adamson, J.; Adamsone, Thos; Aderston, Dycon; Adlard, J.; Adryston, Wm; Aissbey, Wm; Akthorn, J.; Alan, J.; Alan, J.; Albirbury, Lewys; Aldeborne, Wm; Aldeken, Rich; Aldyrbury, Rich; Alechom, J.; Aleyn, J.; Aleyn, J.; Aleyn, Stephen; Aleyn, Wm; Aleyn, Esmond; Aleyn, J.; Aleyn, J.; Aleyn, Thos; Aleyn, J.; Aleyn, Thos; Alisandre, J.; Alman, J.; Alred, Edward; Alrede, Edmund; Alyday, Thos; Alysaunder, Rob; Ambaston, J.; Ambrate, J.; Ancell, Andrew; Andrew, Thos; Andrew, J.; Andrew, Thos; Andrews, J.; Andrews, Rob; Ankyr, J.; Annow, J.; ap ?dagon, Trahan ap Res; ap [lost], David ap Trahan; ap [Sir] David, Llewellyn; ap Adam, Llewellyn ap Jenan; ap Adam, Lewys; ap Adda, Mered ap Jenan; ap Aron, Jenan ap Jenan; ap Artha, Philip; ap Atha, Howell ap Jenan; ap Atha, Philip; ap Atha, Philip; ap Atha, David ap Llewellyn ap Jenan; ap Bynon, David ap Jenan ap Howell; ap Cadagan, Jena ap Llellewyn; ap Cadogan, Rosser ap Jenan; ap Cadogan, Howell ap Jena; ap Cadogan, David ap Griffith ap Llewellyn; ap Cadogan, Jenan Lloyt ap David; ap Cochyn, Llewellyn; ap Coffe, David ap Jenan; ap Coghyn, Jenan; ap Coyge, Griffith ap Gwillym; ap Crahan, Howell ap David; ap David, Trahan ap Gwlim ap Howell; ap David, Gr[uffth] ap Jena; ap David, Llewellyn; ap David, David Duy ap Rys ap Jenan; ap David, John ap Llewellyn; ap David, David ap Jenan; ap David, Philip ap Llewellyn; ap David, Gwillym ap David ap Jenan; ap David, Mathew; ap David, David ap Llewellyn; ap David, Llewellyn; ap David, David ap Res; ap David, Gwillym ap Jenan; ap David, Clement; ap Davy, Jenan; ap Duy, Jena Goche; ap Edmound, David; ap Ethell, J.; ap Ethell, J.; ap Eyvon, Gwallter ap Gwlim ap Howell; ap Eyvon, Jankyn; ap Eyvon, Philip ap Jena; ap Eyvon, Griffuth; ap Eyvon, Howell ap Griffuth ap David ap Eyvon; ap Eyvon, Eyvon ap Griffith ap Jenan; ap Eyvon, Jenna ap David; ap Eyvon, Jenan ap Howell; ap Eyvon, Philip ap Jenan; ap Eyvon, Griffuth Vachan; ap Eyvon, Jenan; ap Eyvon, David ap Howell; ap Eyvon, Griffith Lloyt; ap Eyvon, Med[erud?] ap Jenan; ap Eyvon, Philip ap Eyvon; ap Eyvon, Rys ap Llewellyn; ap Gilbert, Jenan; ap Goboule, Jenan; ap Gr[uffth], Morgan; ap Gr[uffth], Morgan ap Jena; ap Gr[uffth], Gr[uffth] ap Jenna; ap Gr[uffth], Richard ap J.; ap Griffith, Jenan ap Atha; ap Griffith, Jenan ap Howell ap Jenan; ap Griffith, Mered ap Howell; ap Griffith, Mered ap Jenan; ap Griffith, Griffith ap Adda ap Jenan; ap Griffith Gogh, Thos; ap Griffuth, Morgan ap David; ap Griffuth, Howell ap David; ap Grono, Howall ap Mered; ap Gruffith ap Madduk ap Meredith, Yenan; ap Gruffuth, Gruffuth ap Jenan; ap Guill, Hoghwel; ap Gurgene, J.; ap Gwallter, Jenan ap Trahan; ap Gwalter, Jen ap Gr[uffth]; ap Gwalter, Gwillym ap Rys; ap Gwalter, Mereduth ap Jenan Duy ap Llewellyn; ap Gwalter, Philip ap Griffith; ap Gwalter, Walter ap Jorum; ap Gwalter, Jenna ap David; ap Gwalter, Jenan ap David; ap Gwalter, Philip; ap Gwalter, David ap Gwillym ap Griffith; ap Gwalter, Griffin ap Eyvon; ap Gwalter, Gwalter ap Jankyn; ap Gwillym, Gwillym ap Griffuth; ap Gwillym, Griffith; ap Gwillym, David ap Llewellyn ap David; ap Gwillym, Griffith ap Jenan ap Griffith; ap Gwillym, David ap Gwillym ap Griffith; ap Gwillym, Walter; ap Gwillym, Llewellyn ap Jenan ap Gwillym; ap Gwillym, David ap Jenan; ap Gwillym, Mered; ap Gwillym, Griffith ap Jenan; ap Gwyon, David ap Llewellyn ap Howell; ap H[arry]s?, Walter ap David ap Jena; ap Henry, David; ap Henry, Ricard ap Jenan; ap Henry, Madok ap Llewellyn; ap Henry, Jenan; ap Henry, Gwillym; ap Henry, Ricard; ap

Herry, J.; ap Hochekyn, Gr[uffth]; ap Howell, Morys; ap Howell, David Maur; ap Howell, Jena ap J.; ap Howell, Jenan ap David ap Howell; ap Howell, Howell ap Griffith; ap Howell, Llewellyn ap David; ap Howell, Gwalter ap Howell ap Jenan; ap Howell, Jenan ap J.; ap Howell, Thomas Vachan ap Thos; ap Howell, David ap Gwillym ap David; ap Howell, Rys ap Griffith; ap Howell, Ricard ap Griffith; ap Howell, Yevan; ap Jak, David ap Madoc; ap Jak, David; ap Jake, Howell ap David Lloyt; ap Jankyn, Llellewyn; ap Jankyn, Gwillym; ap Jena, J.; ap Jena, David ap Gr[uffth]; ap Jena, Jenan ap Llewellyn; ap Jenan, Jenan Melyn; ap Jenan, David Lloyt; ap Jenan, Griffith ap David Vachan ap David; ap Jenan, Jenan ap David; ap Jenan, Willym ap Llewellyn; ap Jenan, Reynold ap Rosser; ap Jenan, Griffith Goch; ap Jenan, Walter ap Jenan ap Llewellyn; ap Jenkyn, Gr[uffth] ap Jenan ap Howell; ap John, Robyn; ap John, David ap Phelpot; ap John, Rys; ap John, David ap Gwillym ap David; ap Jon, Howell; ap Jorum, J.; ap Jorum, David; ap Jorum, David ap Rys ap David; ap Jorum, Jenan ap David ap Llewellyn; ap Jorum, Gwillym ap Jenan; ap Kenwrec, Griffith ap Eyvon; ap Kenwrec, Griffith ap Griffith ap Llewellyn; ap Llelewyn, J.; ap Llelewyn Guynva, Deyow; ap Llewellyn, Rhys ap Philip; ap Llewellyn, Jankyn; ap Llewellyn, David ap rean?; ap Llewellyn, Jenan Dew ap Jenan; ap Llewellyn, Griffith ap Jenan; ap Llewellyn, Gwillym ap Jenan; ap Llewellyn, David; ap Llewellyn, Jankyn ap Jenan; ap Llewellyn, Llewellyn ap Griffith ap Gwillym; ap Llewellyn, Griffith ap Jenan; ap Llewelyn, Griffith; ap Llonyth, Llewellyn ap Jenan; ap Lloydyn, Yentyn; ap Lloyt, Jenan ap Griffith; ap Mad, David Dew ap Howell ap Gr[uffth]; ap Madoc, Jenan ap Jankyn ap Gr[uffth]; ap Madoc, Trahan; ap Madoc, Morgan; ap Madoc, David ap Howell; ap Madoc, Thomas ap David; ap Madoc, Thomas ap Gr[uffth]; ap Madoc, Griffith ap Llewellyn Duy; ap Madoc, Jenan Vachan ap Jenan; ap Madok, Madoc ap Jenan; ap Madok, Howell; ap Madok, Jenan ap Jenan; ap Mered[ud?], Gwillym ap Philip; ap Mered[ud?], Rys ap Howell; ap Mered[ud?], Griffith; ap Meredith, J.; ap Mereduth, Jenan ap Llewellyn; ap Mereduth, Mereduth ap Jena; ap Mereduth, Jenan ap Thomas; ap Merik, Roger; ap Meruryk, Llewellyn ap Howell; ap Mewryk, Gwillym ap David; ap Mewryk, David ap Jenan Vachan ap Jenan; ap Mewryk, Lewys; ap Mewryt, Jevan ap Morgan ap David; ap Morer, Thos; ap Morgan, Llellewyn ap Jenan; ap Morgan, Mered; ap Morgan, Meredudd; ap Morgan, Morgan ap Jenna; ap Morgan, Philip; ap Morgan, Thos; ap Morgan, Griffin; ap Morgan, Griffith Moell ap Llewellyn; ap Morgan, Jorum; ap Morgan, Jenan ap Jenan; ap Morgan, Mered ap David; ap Morgan, Llewellyn; ap Owen, Jenan; ap Pentreth, Philip ap Grono; ap Phelip, Morgan; ap Phelpot, David; ap Philip, Deyow; ap Philip, David; ap Philip, David ap Jenan; ap Philip, Howell; ap Philipp, Howell; ap Philipp, Morgan; ap Raulff, Jenan ap Howell ap Gr[uffth]; ap Rees, Howell ap Jennan; ap Res, Gr[uffth] ap Gwallter; ap Res, Llewellyn ap Howell ap David; ap Res, Gr[uffth] ap Gwlim; ap Retherech, Griffuth ap Griffuth; ap Ricard, Howell; ap Ricard, David ap Gwillym; ap Richard, J.; ap Richard, Thos; ap Richard, Sympkyn; ap Richard, Henry; ap Robyn, Llewellyn; ap Roger, Howek; ap Rosser, Jenan Duy; ap Rosser, Llewellyn ap Llellewyn; ap Rosser, Jenan Gwyn; ap Rustogyn, Llewelyn; ap Rydderch, Jenan ap Griffith ap Jenan; ap Ryddredd, David Lloyt; ap Rys, Richard ap Griffuth; ap Rys, Gwillym ap Llewellyn; ap Rys, Jankyn ap Griffuth; ap Rys, Jenan ap Phili; ap Rys, Eyvon; ap Rys, Aaron ap Jenan; ap Rys, Rys ap Eyvon; ap Rys, Jenan; ap Rys, Philip; ap Rys, David ap Llewellyn ap Griffuth; ap Rys, Jenan; ap Rys, Jenan ap Jenan; ap Rys, Rys ap Howell; ap Rys, Rys ap Griffith; ap Rys, Llewellyn ap Atha; ap Rys, Atha ap Mered; ap Thomas, Willym ap David; ap Thomas, Howell ap Gwillym; ap Thomas, Owen; ap Thomas, Res ap David; ap Thomelyn, J.; ap Trahan, Howell; ap Traharn, Rys ap Jenan; ap Traharn, Rys ap Griffuth ap Rys; ap Traharn, Traharn ap Jenan; ap Traharn, Philip ap Jenan; ap Troydu, Rys ap Jenna Duy; ap William, Jenna; ap Yen'n, Davy; ap Ygof, David; ap Yperson, Howell; Appelby, Rob; Appelby, Thos; Appelton, Rob; Apslonde, Rich; Arche, J.; Archebald, J.; Archebold, Thos; Archere, J.; Archibold, Hnd'. Hernand?; Archure, J.; Arglas, J.; Arlee, Wm; Armerar, J.; Armere, Wm; Armerer, Thos; Armerer, Laurence; Armerer, J.; Armetredyng, Rich; Armorer, Gerard; Armorer, J.; Armorer, Wm; Armorer, Henry; Armoyeur, Rich; Armurer, J.; Armurer, George; Armygrove, Thos; Arnald, Rich; Arnald, Wm; Arnold, Wm; Arnold, Rich; Arston, Thos; Arundell, Hugo; Arusmyth, Thos; Arusmyth, Laurence; Aryngton, J.; Asfordby, Thos; Askam, J.; Aske, J.; Askham, J.; Aspall, J.; Aspell, J.; Asperner, J.; Aspore, J.; Assent, Roger; Asshal, Rich; Asshe, Thos; Asshe, Thos; Asshe, Thos; Assheberner, Rich; Assherst, Thos; Asshewell, J.; Asshfeld, J.; Asstel, J.; Astel, J.; Asteley, Thos; Aston, Wm; Astyn, J.; at Hull, Neel; at Hurst, Rich; at Lane, J.; at Mer, J.; at Nelme, Wm; at Wodde, Symond; Atforton, J.; Athyrfalle, Wm; Atkyn, Rich; Atkynson, J.; Atkynson, Adam; Atkynson, Ralph; Aton, Rob; atte Causey, Rob; atte Causey, Rob; atte Ford, Rob; atte Gale, Maykyn; atte Gate, Wm; atte Gate, J.; atte Hale, Wm; atte Hall, J.; atte Halle, J.; atte Halle, Wm; atte Hirst, J.; atte Nede, J.;

atte Ryge, Henry; atte Stone, Wm; atte Well, Wm; atte Well, Rich; atte Well, Robard; atte Welle, Wm;
atte Wode, Wm; atte Wode, J.; atte Wode, Wm; atte Wode, Thos; atte Wode, Rob; atte Wode, Perot; atte
Wode, Henry; atte Wood, Arthur; Attekynson, Thos; Attilbrigg, J.; Atwode, Walter; Audley, J.; Audneye,
J.; Auger, J.; Austyn, Hugh; Austyr, Hugh; Avener, George; Axebryg, J.; Ayleward, J.; Aylmer, J.;
Aynesworth, Thos; Ayssch, J.; Ayssh, J.; Ayston, J.; Ayston, J.; B?rook, J.; B?roud, Rich; B[?], Adam;
Babyn, J.; Bach, Jenan ap Gr[uffth]; Bach, Jenan; Bach, Llewellyn; Bachan, Trahern ap Gwalter;
Bachan, Philip ap Jenan; Bacher, Thos; Bachyler, Thos; Badby, Thos; Badstok, Thos; Badwe, Edmund;
Baggele, J.; Bailif, J.; Baille, Roger; Bailly, Nicholas; Bailly, J.; Bailly, Philip; Bailly, J.; Bailly, de Bacesseye,
J.; Bailton, J.; Baily, Rich; Bakare, J.; Bakenald, J.; Bakenale, J.; Baker, Thos; Baker, Thos; Baker, Rob;
Baker, J.; Baker, Rich; Baker, Rich; Baker, Robyn; Baker, Henry; Baker, Wm; Baker, Thos; Baker, Wm;
Baker, Rob; Baker, J.; Baker, J.; Baker, J.; Baker, Rob; Baker, J.; Baker, Rich; Baker, J.; Baker, Yolyn;
Baker, J.; Baker, Thos; Baker, Jankyn; Baker, Rich; Baker, J.; Baker, Walter; Baker, Rob; Baker, J.; Baker,
Thos; Baker, J.; Baker, Thos; Baker, Rob; Bakere, Rob; Bakere, Rob; Bakere, Thos; Bakere, Stephen;
Bakere, Thos; Bakere, Walter; Bakere, Thos; Bakere, J.; Bakere, Nicholas; Bakere, Wm; Bakere, J.;
Bakere, Wm; Bakster, J.; Bala, J.; Balerell, Roger; Balham, J.; Ball, J.; Ball, Vap'Wm; Ballard, Wm; Balle,
J.; Balle, Wm; Balle, Henry; Balle, J.; Balle, Wm; Balle, Rich; Balsham, Wm; Balster, J.; Balyevue, J.;
Bambery, Wm; Bamforth, Hugh; Banaster, Wm; Banastre, J.; Banastre, J.; Banastre, J.; Banbery, Wm;
Banbery, Perys; Banbery, Andrew; Banbury, Roger; Banestere, Wm; Banke, J.; Banke, Wm; Banke, J.;
Bannam, J.; Bansforth, J.; Barber, Henry; Barbor, Wm; Barbor, J.; Barbor, Adam; Barbor, J.; Barbor,
Rob; Barbor, J.; Barbor, Wm; Barbor, Wm; Barbor, Thos; Barbor, J.; Barbor, Rob; Barbor, Rich;
Barbor, Rich; Barbor, Edmund; Barbor, J.; Barbor, Rich; Barbor, Cok; Barbor, Symond; Barbor, J.;
Barbor, J.; Barbor, Nicholas; Barbor, Rich; Barbor, Nicholas; Barbor, Wm; Barbor, J.; Barbor, Henry;
Barbor, J.; Barbor, Wm; Barbor, J.; Barbor, J.; Barbor, J.; Barbor, Rich; Barbor, J.; Barbour, Wm;
Barbour, Roger; Barbour, J.; Barbour, J.; Barbour, J.; Barbour, J.; Barbour, Godfrey; Barbour, Rich;
Barbur, Andrew; Baret, J.; Baret, Geffrey; Barhede, Thos; Barkare, Robard; Barker, Godfrey; Barker,
Hugo; Barkere, J.; Barkere, Wm; Barlo, J.; Barlow, Wm; Barneby, Wm; Baroby, J.; Baron, J.; Baronn,
Wm; Baronn, Wm; Barre, J.; Barre, Rich; Barry, Rob; Barry, J.; Barton, Roger; Barton, Rich; Barton,
Rich; Barton, Wm; Barton, Hugh; Barton, J.; Bartram, J.; Bartylot, Thos; Bartyndale, J.; Barwe, Thos;
Barynger, J.; Baryngton, J.; Baryngton, J.; Basage, Wm; Baso, J.; Basse, Thos; Basset, J.; Basset, J.; Basset,
Thos; Basset, Rich; Bassyngborne, Wm; Bassyngbourne, J.; Bate, Rich; Bate, Thos; Bate, Rich; Bate,
Thos; Bateman, Rob; Bateman, Rich; Batesun, J.; Batman, J.; Batteford, Blank; Battele, Rob;
Bawdewyn, Thos; Bawtre, Roger; Baxter, J.; Baylly, J.; Bayllyf, Walter; Bayly, Wm; Bayn, Ric[hard];
Bayn, Rich; Baystow, J.; Beauchamp, J.; Bedenhale, Nicholas; Bedford, J.; Bedman, Thos; Bedon, Rich;
Beerde, J.; Beeston, Wm; Beget, Thos; Bekfield, J.; Bekford, J.; Bekinyffeld, J.; Bekkle, Wm; Bekwith,
Wm; Bekynfeld, George; Bekynshawe, Edward; Bekynswyke, Thos; Bele, J.; Belgrave, Thos; Bell,
Rob; Bell, Rob; Bell, Wm; Belle, Wm; Belle, Wm; Belle, Rich; Belle, Rich; Beller, Wm; Bellowe,
Roger; Belton, J.; Belyngham, Alayn; Bemond, John snr; Bendyssh, Thos; Bene, Rob; Bene, Stephen;
Bene, Wm; Benet, J.; Benet, J.; Benet, Davy; Benet, J.; Benet, Wm; Benet, Thos; Benet, J.; Benet, Wm;
Benet, Philip; Benet, Rob; Benette, J.; Benkyng, Rob; Benny, Thos; Bennyngton, Stephen; Bensey,
Wm; Benson, J.; Bentley, J.; Benyng, J.; Berche, Wm; Berd, J.; Berde, Rob; Bereham, Wm; Berkmastede,
J.; Berlay, Thos; Bernard, J.; Bernard, Wm; Bernard, David; Bernard, Hugh; Bernarde, J.; Bernarer, J.;
Berne, Rob; Bernerd, Wm; Bernier, Jacat; Beron, Wm; Bert, J.; Bertelot, J.; Bertram, J.; Bery, J.; Beryl,
J.; Beryngton, Stephen; Berysby, J.; Beseley, Thos; Best, J.; Bethessone, Thos; Bette, J.; Beuchamp,
Nicholas; Beverle, Wm; Beverley, Rich; Beverley, Thos; Beverly, Edward; Bewly, Jacob; Bewsale, J.;
Bewyk, Wm; Bich, Jevan ap Eyvon; Bilisby, Thos; Billesthorp, Rich; Billing, J.; Bircestre, J.; Birchere,
Peter; Birkyn, J.; Bischop, J.; Bisshop, J.; Bissley, Wm; Bitterle, J.; Blaby, Wm; Blade, J.; Blakburn, J.;
Blakby, Wm; Blake, Wm; Blake, Wm; Blake, Patryk; Blakeman, J.; Blakemore, Wm; Blakeston, J.;
Blakhyll, Saundre; Blakson, Rich; Blakwell, J.; Blakwell, J.; Blande, Edward; Blank, Gruff[uth?]; Blank,
Howell; Blaunchard, Wm; Blecke, David; Blencowe, Thos; Bloith, Thomas ap Gruffth; Blomelegh,
Rich; Blondell, Wm; Bloundell, Rob; Bloundell, Thos; Blower, J.; Bluet, J.; Blunndy, Rich; Blythe, J.;
Bocher, Andrew; Bocher, J.; Bocher, Thos; Bochier, J.; Bodener, Wm; Bodman, J.; Body, J.; Boge, J.;
Bokyngham, J.; Boland, Henry; Bolard, Richard, of; Bole, J.; Bolepayt, Henry; Bolsor, J.; Bolter, Wm;
Bolton, Roger; Bolton, Rob; Bolton, J.; Bolton, Wm; Bolton, J.; Bolton, Wm; Bolton, Wm; Bolton, J.;
Bolton, J.; Bone, J.; Bonhure, Roger; Bonle, David ap Griffith ap Llewellyn; Booke, Thos; Boold,
Rob; Bordduw, Philip ap Jenan; Bornage, Wm; Boron, Rob; Borton, J.; Bosevyle, J.; Bosevyle, J.;

Bosewele, Rob; Boston, Rob; Bosy, J.; Boteler, Wm; Boteler, John snr; Boteler, John jnr; Boteler, J.; Boteler, Thos; Boteler, Wm; Boteler, Thos; Boteler, Thos; Boteler, J.; Boteler, Roger; Boteler, J.; Botelier, Thos; Botelier, Thos; Boteller, Thos; Botiller, J.; Botiller, Rob; Botillier, Wm; Botler, J.; Boton, J.; Bougent, J.; Bougent, Thos; Boule, David ap Meredudd; Boules, Thos; Boules, Grenow; Boure, J.; Bourgh, Wm; Bowede, Rob; Bower, Wm; Bowier, Hugo; Bowman, Rob; Bowthe, Thos; Bowyar, Robard; Bowyer, J.; Bowyer, J.; Bowyere, Reginald; Boynton, J.; Bracy, J.; Bracy, Wm; Bracy, Nicholas; Bradely, J.; Bradfeld, Thos; Bradford, J.; Bradhurst, Walter; Bradley, Wm; Bradley, Rich; Bradley, Wm; Bradley, Rob; Bradschawe, Rob; Bradshawe, Hugh; Bradshawe, Rich; Bradwell, Rob; Brake, Thos; Brakley, J.; Bramfeld, Mathew; Brampston, J.; Brampston, J.; Brandesby, Wm; Brandesby, Rich; Branton, J.; Brantyngham, J.; Brasele, J.; Braserton, Thos; Brawby, Nicholas; Bray, J.; Bray, J.; Bray, Peter; Bredyng, Wm; Brees, Wm; Brekefaste, J.; Bremelcombe, Stephen; Bremer, Rich; Brent, Benet; Brereton, J.; Brerreton, Wm; Brese, J.; Breton, J.; Bretonn, Wm; Bretton, J.; Bretwell, J.; Brews, J.; Brewster, Rob; Brewster, J.; Brian, Godfrey; Bride, Thos; Bridsale, J.; Brigford, J.; Brigge, Wm; Briggeman, Walter; Briggeman, Wm; Brigges, Wm; Brightlede, Rob; Brikill, J.; Bristow, Rich; Broke, J.; Bromfeld, Davy; Bromfeld, J.; Bromfeld, Matthew; Bromfeld, J.; Bromley, Wm; Bromley, Thos; Bromley, J.; Bromsly, Enos?; Bron, Roger; Broun, Rich; Broun, Rich; Broun, J.; Broun, J.; Broun, J.; Broun, Rich; Broun, J.; Broun, J.; Broun, Wm; Broun, J.; Broun, J.; Broun, J.; Broun, Wm; Broun, Nicholas; Broun, Lambert; Broun, Thos; Broun, J.; Broun, Henry; Broun de Aler, J.; Broun, del chamber, J.; Bround, J.; Broune, J.; Broune, Rich; Broune, Nicholas; Broune, J.; Brounfeld, Rich; Brounfelde, J.; Brounfield, Rich; Brounhuls, Rich; Brount, J.; Brounyng, J.; Browe, Davy; Brugg, J.; Brugge, Matthew; Brugges, Wm; Brummer, Rich; Brun, J.; Brunham, J.; Brutte, Thos; Bruyn, Thos; Bruyne, Rob; Bryan, J.; Bryan, J.; Bryan, Nicholas; Bryd, Simon; Bryd, Laurence; Bryd, Laurence; Bryd, Hawokyn; Bryde, Rich; Brydych, Howell; Bryggeman, J.; Brygges, J.; Bryghemer, Henry; Bryghton, Rich; Bryghtwell, Adam; Brygnell, J.; Bryham, Watkyn; Brynsoppe, J.; Brysche, Rich; Brystow, Wm; Brythwell, Thos; Bryton, Wm; Bryton, J.; Buckeby, J.; Buckynham, J.; Budde, Wm; Bugys, Wm; Bukstones, J.; Bule, Wm; Bulkeley, Philippot; Bull, Dicon; Bullyngbrok, J.; Bulman, Geffray; Bungey, J.; Buntingforde, Thos; Burbroke, J.; Burdon, J.; Burdon, Rich; Burdon, Nicholas; Burford, J.; Burgate, Wm; Burgays, J.; Burgeys, J.; Burgh, Roger; Burgh, Roger; Burghull, J.; Burgoch, Madoc; Burgon, Hugo; Burn, Wm; Burne, Wm; Burnet, J.; Burry, J.; Bursecer, Nicholas; Burseon, Rob; Burton, Davy; Burton, Davy; Burton, J.; Burton, Wm; Burton, Nicholas; Burton, Wm; Burton, J.; Burton, Nicholas; Burton, Rich; Burton, Wm; Burtons, Rich; Burwell, J.; Bury, J.; Bussh, Rich; Busveld, Symond; Butte, Wm; Butteler, Wm; Butteler, J.; Butteler, Thos; Buttiler, Rob; Butyler, Thos; Byby, Roger; Byfeld, Symkyn; Byfeld, Roger; Byfelde, Roger; Bykcombe, Ralph; Bykeldy, Lewes; Bykerstathe, Rob; Byll, J.; Bylter, J.; Bylton, Edward; Bylton, Wm; Bymon de Sebold, Wm; Bymson, Thos; Byngle, Thos; Bynglee, J.; Bypon, Wm; Byrch, J.; Byrcote, Wm; Byrlancessone, J.; Byrstal, Thos; Byspam, Rich; Byspam, Wm; Bysshop, J.; Bysshopp, Thos; Bystestre, J.; C[?]tor, Wm; Caaarpenter, Philip; Cabet, Peter; Caddenay, J.; Cadewold, J.; Cadogan, Thos; Cadwell, Roger; Cage, Thos; Cakker, Rob; Caldebek, Thos; Caldecotes, J.; Cale, Wm; Calkewell, J.; Callod?, Wm; Callowe, Wm; Cals?, Roger; Cals?, Wm; Calton, Nicholas; Calverley, Wm; Camel, J.; C--ami-?, J.; Campyon, Wm; Can[er?]o, J.; Candeler, Piers; Candiler, J.; Canon, Robard; Caperon, Thos; Cardemaker, J.; Cardemaker, Wm; Careswald, Wm; Careswell, Wm; Carlanchek, Odo; Carnaby, Henry; Carok, J.; Carpenter, J.; Carpenter, Hugh; Carpenter, Rawlyn; Carpenter, Roger; Carpenter, Roger; Carpenter, Wm; Carpenter, Thos; Carpenter, Philip; Carpenter, Jenan ap Res; Carpentier, Thos; Carpentier, Martin; Carre, J.; Carro, Saunder; Carselak, Roger; Carter, J.; Carter, J.; Cartwreth, Wm; Cartwryght, Thos; Carvile, Thos; Castell, Rich; Castell, Rich; Castell, Rich; Castell, Clement; Castell, Thos; Castell, Nicholas; Castell, Wm; Castelton, Rob; Castowe, J.; Catelowe, J.; Catelyn, Nicholas; Caterton, J.; Cateryke, J.; Catteworth, Wm; Caucefeld, Wm; Caumbryg, J.; Caunttbrigge, J.; Caus, Phelpot; Cauthorn, Rob; Caux, J.; Cave, J.; Cawerenn, Owen; Cawerenn, David; Cawod, Rich; Cawtes, J.; Caxston, J.; Cayley, Henry; Celer, Wm; Ceman, Thos; Cepland, Wm; Cester, Rob; Chalston, Wm; Chalstud, Simon; Chalton, Wm; Chamber, Rich; Chamber, Rob; Chamberlayn, Rich; Chamberlayn, Wm; Chamberlayn, Wm; Chamberlayn, Wm; Chamberlein, J.; Chamberleyn, Wm; Chamberleyn, Wm; Chamberleyn, Henry; Chamberleyn, Rob; Chambr, J.; Chambre, J.; Chamburleyne, J.; Champeyne, J.; Chapeleyn, Geffrey; Chapell, Wm; Chapman, Rob; Chapman, J.; Chappe, Henry; Charer, Andrew; Chareter, Wm; Charietter, J.; Charietter, Thos; Chariotter, Simion; Charyot, Thos; Charyour, Thos; Charytor, J.; Chatton, J.; Chaukyn, Rich; Chaumber, Wm; Chaumberlayn, J.;

Chaumberler, Wm; Chaumberleyn, Olyver; Chaumberlyn, Thos; Chaundler, Walter; Chaunterell, Hugh; Chepe, Rich; Cherman, Rich; Chervyle, Rich; Chery, Wm; Cherye, J.; Chesman, Rich; Chest, J.; Chesterfeld, J.; Cheston, Wm; Cheston, Wm; Cheswyse, Davy; Cheveley, J.; Cheyne, Nicholas; Chichestre, J.; Chienhall, Rich; Childe, Roger; Chilton, Wm; Chippe, Wm; Chirche, Wm; Chircheman, Rich; Chiswell, Henry; Chode, Rob; Cholmeley, Davy; Cholmesley, David; Chrispe, Rich; Chronesby, J.; Chubb, Thos; Chyf, Rich; Chyffe, Roger; Chygwelle, Rich; Chymecsley, Thos; Chynham, Rich; Chyveruff, J.; Clarc, Wm; Clare, J.; Clarell, Thos; Claryngdon, Thos; Clase, J.; Clement, J.; Clement, J.; Clement, Philip; Clement, Wm; Clementhorp, J.; Clerc, J.; Clerc, J.; Clerc, J.; Clerc, Thos; Clerc, J.; Clere, Wm; Clerk, Thos; Clerk, Wm; Clerk, Thos; Clerk, Wm; Clerk, Rich; Clerk, J.; Clerk, Thos; Clerk, Rob; Clerk, Thos; Clerk, Thos; Clerk, J.; Clerk, J.; Clerk, J.; Clerk, J.; Clerk, J.; Clerk, J.; Clerk, Godfrey; Clerk, J.; Clerk, J.; Clerk, Wm; Clerk, Rich; Clerk, Wm; Clerk, J.; Clerk, Laurenc; Clerk, J.; Clerk, Rob; Clerk, Marmaduke; Clerke, J.; Clerke, J.; Clerke, Rich; Clerkesson, J.; Clerkson, Wm; Clerkson, J.; Cleymond, Aleyn; Cliderow, J.; Cliderowe, Rob; Clifford, Lewis; Clifforth, Lewys; Clifton, John, de Clifton; Clifton, Roger, de Eadem; Clifton, Thos; Clifton, Edward; Clopham, Rich; Clos, Wm; Clouk, Andrew; Clune, Thos; Clustee, Llewellyn; Clyf, Rich; Clyfe, J.; Clyffe, J.; Clyfford, J.; Clyfton, Wm; Clyput, J.; Coake, Thos; Cobald, J.; Cobbe, J.; Cobbe, J.; Codyngham, Wm; Codyngton, J.; Cogell, Walter; Cok, Wm; Cok, J.; Cok, Rich; Cok, J.; Cok, J.; Cok, J.; Cokcroft, J.; Coke, J.; Coke, Thos; Coke, Rob; Coke, Wm; Coke, David; Coke, Wm; Coke, J.; Coke, Wm; Coke, Thos; Coke, J.; Coke, J.; Coke, Nicholas; Coke, J.; Coker, Symkyn; Cokerell, Thos; Cokke, J.; Cokke, J.; Cokke, Rob; Cokman, J.; Cokt, Henry; Colbrok, Rich; Colbron, Ralph; Colchestr, J.; Colchestr, Wm; Cole, J.; Colecote, J.; Colfax, J.; Colgeyn, Godfrey; Colle, Walter; Colles, J.; Colly, Peter; Collyng, Henry; Collyngge, Wm; Colman, Robard; Colman, J.; Colshalle, J.; Coltman, Wm; Colverhous, Rob; Colvylle, J.; Colwell, Wm; Colwode, Stephen; Colyar, Nicholas; Colyer, Roger; Colyers, J.; Colyn, Thos; Colyn, J.; Colyn, Wm; Colyn, Thos; Colyn, Rob; Colynson, J.; Colynson, Cristofer; Combe, Laurence; Comber, J.; Comerhall, Rich; Compton, Wm; Compton, J.; Conestable, Thos; Congulton, Wm; Coniers, J.; Connhede, Thos; Constable, Thos; Constabyl, Wm; Conyers, Jamys; Conyng, J.; Coo, Rob; Cook, Wm; Cook, Wm; Cook, J.; Cook, Thos; Cook, Wm; Cook, Thos; Cook, Thos; Cook, Rob; Cook, J.; Cook, Walter; Cook, Wm; Cook, J.; Cooke, J.; Cooke, Rich; Cooke, J.; Cooke, Wm; Cooke, Wm; Cooke, Edmonde; Cooke, Wm; Cooke, J.; Cooke, Thos; Cooke, Rob; Cookes, J.; Cookes, Rich; Cookes, J.; Copelond, J.; Copenhale, Rob; Copper, Wm; Corbet, J.; Corby, Rob; Corfill, Rich; Cornewaile, J.; Cornewayle, J.; Cornlous, Henry; Cornysh, J.; Corsant, Wm; Corsill, Rich; Cort, J.; Cort, J.; Cosham, Thos; Coson, J.; Costantyn, J.; Costard, J.; Costeseye, Wm; Costolewe, J.; Cosyn, J.; Coterell, J.; Cotes, J.; Cotom, J.; Coton, Henry; Coton, Philip; Cotyngham, J.; Cotyngham, J.; Couk, Henry; Couk, Thos; Couk, Thos; Couk, Rich; Couke, Roger; Couke, J.; Couke, Hugh; Couper, J.; Couper, Wm; Couper, Wm; Couper, Rob; Couper, Rob; Couper, Wm; Coupere, Wm; Coupere, Wm; Coupere de Wyrlyngwort, Wm; Courteney, Wm; Couton, J.; Couver, J.; Cove ?, Walter; Coventre, J.; Coventre, Wm; Coventre, J.; Covieshale, Simon; Cowhird, Rob; Cowper, J.; Cowper, Thos; Cowton, J.; Coyll, J.; Crabbe, J.; Craddok, Wm; Cradok, Wm; Cradok, Rich; Craft, J.; Cranhaw, J.; Cranswych, J.; Crede, Wm; Crem, Rob; Cren, Rob; Cressy, Wm; Cresty, J.; Creswell, J.; Creswell, J.; Creswell, Wm; Creswell, Wm; Crethoor, David Wellc; Crispe, Henry; Croft, Symond; Crofton, Wm; Croke, J.; Croke, Nicholas; Crokere, Wm; Crokkere, Wm; Cromer, J.; Cromer, J.; Croos, Hugh; Croppere, Thos; Cropshowe, ?; Crosby, Rich; Crosby, Rich; Crosby, Adam; Croster, J.; Croston, Thos; Croston, Wm; Crouch, Rich; Crouch, Thos; Crouch, J.; Crouche, J.; Crouche, J.; Crowcher, J.; Crowe, J.; Crowland, Thos; Croysour, J.; Cruyer, Christofer; Cryse, Wm; Cuirteys, Wm; Cuke, Mathew; Cuke, J.; Culcheth, Henry; Culver, J.; Culvercok, J.; Cunstede, Thos; Cuollys, Wm; Curlewe, Wm; Curll, J.; Curson, Wm; Curson, J.; Curson, Thos; Cursone, Robard; Curteys, Wm; Curteys, Stephen; Curteys, J.; Curteys, Mereduth ap Trahan ap David; Curteys, Jankyn; Cussham, J.; Cusshni, J.; Cutrard, J.; Cuw?arrte, Wm; Daa, Thos; Dabiston, Wm; Dacre, J.; Daker, Thos; Dalam, J.; Dalcok, Rich; Dalderby, J.; Dale, J.; Dale, J.; Dale, Wm; Dale, of the, Wm; Dalgyen, J.; Dalton, J.; Dalton, Thos; Daly, J.; Dalycot, Wm; Dalyeit, J.; Damber, Rob; Damport, Thos; Danber, Thos; Danhurst, Rich; Dannyngs, Hugh; Danyel, J.; Danyele, Thos; Danyell, J.; Danyell, Wm; Danyell, Emond; Darley, Roger; Darundell, J.; Dator, Simon; Daukyns, J.; Dauncer, Rob; Daunesby, Wm; Dauson, J.; Dautre, Wm; Davey, J.; Daviport, Laurence; Davy, J.; Davy, J.; Davy, Cok; Davy, J.; Davy, Rich; Davy, Rob; Davy, Mathew; Davy, J.; Davy, Wm; Davy, J.; Davyson, Wm; Dawe, Ralph; Dawe, Wm; Daweson, J.; Dawn, Perkyn; Dawson, Rob; Dawson, Wm; Dawson, J.; Daycote, ?; Daydore,

Geoffrey; Daykham, Rich; Dduy, Merudth ap Llewelyn ap Jenan ap Llewelyn; de [?]lkrys, Wm; de Alamby, J.; de Arkelode, Thos; de Awine, J.; de Bathowa, J.; de Berwyke, J.; de Blumpton, Thos; de Boaldon, Wm; de Bolton, Rich; de Borowdale, Wm; de Boterye, Rich; de Bouke, Rob; de Briseter, J.; de Burton, J.; de Burton, Christopher; de Bury, J.; de Calverlay, J.; de Car, Thos; de Chambre, Janyn; de Chauntrye, Clement; de Clif, Rich; de Cravene, J.; de Crayke, Rob; de Croxston, Rob; de Dilworth, Adam; de Drayton, Thos; de Ellell, Rich; de Forde, Rob; de Garderobe, Yevan; de Gayn, Roger; de Graston, David; de Grenehals, Wm; de Halghton, J.; de Hauden, J.; de Hawardthyn, Wm; de Hawe, Coke; de Hilton, Rich; de Hirelon, J.; de Holand, Charles; de Holyns, Wm; de Hore, J.; de Huls, Herman; de Hulse, J.; de Hylle, Thos; de Kent, J.; de Kery, Howel Dewgh; de Kirketon, Wm; de Kychyn, John junior; de Kyrk, J.; de la Barre, Rich; de la Boutre, J.; de la Chamber, Thos; de la Launde, Wm; de la More, Rich; de la Parke, Rob; de la Pole, Lewes; de la Strode, Gerard; de Lamson, Hengo; de Lay, Doncaid; de le Chambre, Reynold; de Ledys, Thos; de Lee, Piers; de Leylond, Thos; de Lymdeley, Thos; de Lyndley, Wm; de Manchester, J.; de Manne, Gilbert; de Matreste, J.; de Middelton, J.; de Neuporte, J.; de Pilkenton, J.; de Plomude, Thos; de Rilay, Nicholas; de Saintalbone, Watkyn; de Sandall, Wm; de Seint Albans, J.; de Seler, Rich; de Selere, J.; de Shepley, Rich; de Skyrawe, J.; de Stable, J.; de Stable, Benet; de Stanestrete, Rich; de Stapelfforde, Llewelyn; de Stocchelache, Jacob/ James; de Stravely, Roger; de Sutton, Rich; de Sutton, J.; de Sutton, Rob; de Swynton, J.; de Tawnton, Jacob; de Thornton, Wm; de Tildesley, Seth; de Tildesley, J.; de Tildesley, Henry; de Trescont, John Seys; de War, J.; de Wassyngton, Rob; de Wodde, Wm; de Worsley, Jurdan; de Wyght, Wm; de Yate, Rob; Debet, Jenan; Dedell, Andrew; Dederyk alias Brid, J.; Dedyngheyst, Rob; Deine, Amary; Deka, Morgan ap Jenan; Deke, J.; Dekene, Rich; del Butre, Rob; del Chamber, David; del Chamber alias Coupere, Rob; del Chambere, Thos; del Chambr, Walter; del Chaundre, Roger; del Chauntrye, Robard; del Forest, Thos; del Halle, Wm; del Halle, Wm; del Howe, Wm; Del L?, J.; del Lawe, Hugo; del Mare, Thos; del Pantrie, Matheus; del Pantrye, J.; del Sauserye, Roger; del Shagh, J.; del Wode, J.; Delynnor, Jenan Gethyn; Denaston, J.; Dene, Rich; Dene, Rob; Denet, Walter; Denforde, J.; Denham, J.; Denston, J.; Dent, Wm; Denton, J.; Denton, J.; Denton, J.; Denton, J.; Denton, J.; Deny, J.; Deny, J.; Denyas, J.; Depdale, J.; Deram, J.; Derant, Roger; Derby, J.; Derby, J.; Dercy, Walter; Derham, J.; Dert, Wm; Deve, Geffrey; Devenes, Wm; Devlyn, Thos; Dew, John ap David; Dew, Eyvon ap Gr[uffth]; Dew, Willym; Dew, Jenan ap David; Dewe, Llellewyn ap Jena; Dewent, George; Dewhurst, Raulyn; Dey, Roger; Deyg, Nicholas; Deygmore, Walter; Diconson, J.; Diconson, Thos; Diconsone, Thos; Dicson, Rob; Digore, J.; Dikson, J.; Dilworth, Nicholas; Dippyng, Thos; Disell, J.; Dixton, Rob; Dobackws, of, J.; Dobbes, J.; Dobmagh, Henry; Dobson, Wm; Dod, Rob; Dodde, Thos; Dodford, Thos; Dodynghurste, Rob; Doide, J.; Dokun, Rob; Dolphyn, Rich; Don, Maurice; Don, David; Don, Hopkyn; Don, Mered; Don, Wm; Donet, Wm; Donkastre, Henry; Donnaton, Rich; Donnys, J.; Donyngton, Rob; Dorande, Peter; Dorchester, Thos; Dore, Thos; Dorent, Peter; Douglas, Thos; Dounstabyll, Thos; Dounthorp de Routh, Rich; Dovnam, Nicholas; Dowke, J.; Downald, Rob; Downe, Rob; Doxey, J.; Doxndesore, J.; Doynald, Adomare; Drake, J.; Draps, J.; Draughton, J.; Drawtton, J.; Draycot, Roger; Drayton, J.; Drayton, J.; Dream?, Symond; Dremesgone?, Griffith; Drewry, J.; Driby, Thos; Dryffeld, J.; Dryvere, J.; Duch, Stephen; Dudill, Christopher; Duffeld, Nicholas; Duffeld, Henry; Duffeld, Piers; Duke, Adam; Duke, J.; Dun, J.; Dunbar, Rich; Dune, J.; Durant, Rob; Durant, Rob; Durbulby, Adam; Durham, Rich; Durnor, J.; Durnwell, J.; Duruyng(sic), J.; Dutre, J.; Dutton, Wm; Dutton, Nicholas; Dutton, J.; Dutton, Thos; Duy, Gwlym Dew ap David; Duy, Rys ap J.; Duy, Gwillym ap Gwillym; Duy, Llellewyn ap David; Duy, Howell ap Res; Duy, Morgan ap Llewellyn; Duy, Rys ap Griffuth ap Jenan; Duy, Jenan ap Jenan ap Griffuth; Duy, Llewellyn ap Madok; Duy, David ap Madok; Duy, Jenan ap Griffith ap Jennan; Duy, Howell ap David; Duy, Llewellyn; Duy, Jenan Gwyn ap Jenan; Duy, David ap Jenan; Duy, Mered; Duy, Thos; Duy, David ap Ygwas; Duy, Llewellyn ap Griffith; Duy, Llewellyn ap David ap Llewellyn; Dwareden, J.; Dyard, Rich; Dyare, Wm; Dyare, Rich; Dyare, Thos; Dyconson, Thos; Dyer, Simon; Dyer, Rob; Dyer, Rob; Dyer, J.; Dyer, Laurence; Dyffurthe, Wm; Dyghton, Rob; Dyldorp, J.; Dymney, J.; Dymnord, J.; Dyndale, J.; Dyneley, Rich; Dyngylwode, J.; Dyruyng (sic), Rich; Dysard, Thos; Ebchester, Thos; Ecles, J.; Edarsh, Wm; Ede, J.; Edeward, J.; Edmund, Thos; Ednenet, J.; Edward, Wm; Edward, J.; Edy, Rob; Edymond, (blank); Ekyngton, Wm; Elande, J.; Elarcon, J.; Elemeham, Thos; Elianore, Thos; Elkyn, J.; Ellerton, Hugo; Elles, J.; Elman, Rich; Elman, Rich; Elsewyke, J.; Elsham, J.; Elyettes, Rich; Elyngton, Rich; Elyot, Rob; Elyot, Elyas; Elyotston, Symond; Elys, not given; Elys de Ware, Wm; Embrok, Wm; Emely, Thos; Emely, J.; Emryson, Rich; Endurgate, J.; Engelond, J.; Englyssh, J.; Eppill, David; Erbery, Thos;

Ereby, Wm; Eresby, J.; Erith, Wm; Ermyce, Wm; Ermyger, Thos; Est, J.; Estby, J.; Estby, J.; Estmonw,
Wm; Eston, J.; Esyk, J.; Esyngwold, Thos; Ethersed, Thos; Eton, J.; Eton, Rich; Evelgold, Thos; Everard,
Ralph; Everrard, Rob; Everrard, Rob; Everwyk, Thos; Everwyke, Thos; Ewre, Henry, of the; Ewrych,
Philip ap Griffith ap David; Ewyas, Jankyn; Exale, Thos; Exham, Wm; Exmor, Wm; Eynham, Wm;
Eyre, Rich; Eyre, Rich; Eyston, Thos; Eyvon, David ap Eneyt; Fabkyner, J.; Fadyr, Regulus; Fadyre,
Wm; Fage, Walter; Fage, Walter; Fairchild, Wm; Farefeld, J.; Farleton, Thos; Farleton, Rob; Farley, Rob;
Farman, Thos; Farman, Henry; Farman, Peter; Farman, Thos; Farman, J.; Farman, Henry; Farmer, J.;
Farnam, Nicholas; Farnham, Walter; Faucon, Arnold; Fawcun, Rob; Felde, Thos; Felde, Walter;
Felstede, J.; Fenart, James; Fender, Thos; Fenne, Rob; Fens, Rich; Fenton, Wm; Ferby, J.; Ferby, J.;
Fereror, Nicholas; Ferman, Wm; Fermer, Thos; Fermor, Thos; Fermor, Thos; Fernchilde, Thos; Fernyll,
Roger; Feror, Rob; Feror, Rob; Feror, Thos; Feror, Rob; Feror, Wm; Feror, Lewys; Feror, J.; Feror, J.;
Feror, Blethyn; Feror, Rob; Feror, J.; Feror, Wm; Feror, Wm; Ferour, Jenan; Feroweby, J.; Ferreur, J.;
Ferriby, J.; Ferror, Rich; Ferror, J.; Ferror, Phelip; Ferror, Rich; Ferror, J.; Ferror, J.; Ferror, J.; Ferror,
Rob; Ferror, J.; Ferror, Rich; Ferror, J.; Ferror, Symond; Ferror, Howell; Ferror, J.; Ferror, Wm; Ferror,
Walter; Ferror, Wm; Ferror, Wm; Ferror, Rich; Ferror, J.; Ferror, J.; Ferror, James; Ferror, Thos; Ferror,
J.; Ferror, Rob; Ferror, Rob; Ferror, J.; Ferror, J.; Ferror, Rich; Ferror, Rich; Ferror, J.; Ferror, Wm;
Ferror, Harry; Ferror, Laurence; Ferror, Rob; Ferror, David; Ferror, Mungeham; Ferror, J.; Ferror, J.;
Ferror, J.; Ferror, Wm; Ferrour, Wm; Ferrour, J.; Ferrour, Wm; Ferrour, Rich; Ferrour, J.; Ferrour,
Henry; Ferrour, J.; Ferrour, Rees; Ferrowre, Rob; Fewy, J.; Feyreffax, J.; ffachel, J.; ffalcorue, Thos;
Ffale, J.; ffalks, J.; ffaryngton, J.; fferror, J.; fferror, J.; fferror, Thos; fferror, Rich; fferror, Wm; ffevene,
Hugh; fflavan, Wm; fflemyng, Wm; ffletch, Hugh; ffletch[er], J.; fflete, J.; fflete, Esmon; fflynt, Thos;
fforster, Wm; fforster, J.; fforster, Wm; fforstere, J.; ffrankeleyne, Nicholas; ffrankleyn, Wm; ffreman,
Rob; ffresser, Wm; ffrowyk, Rich; ffynton, Wm; Filkyn, Morgaunt; Fisher, Wm; Fissche, J.; Fissche, J.;
Fissher, Jeffrey; Fissher, Wm; Fissher, J.; Fitzaberley, Symond; Fitzwalter, Hugh; Fleccher, Wm;
Flecchere, Rich; Flecham, J.; Flecher, J.; Flegcher, Henry; Fletcher, Rich; Fletcher, Wm; Fletcher, Wm;
Fletcher, Simon; Fletcher, Wm; Fletcher, Thos; Fletchere, Wm; Fletchere, J.; Fletchere, J.; Flete, J.;
Flour, J.; Fode, J.; Foke, J.; Foldere, Thos; Folstede, J.; Forbor, Walter; Forbor, J.; Forder, J.; Fordyn,
Gr[uffth]; Forest, Rich; Forest, Adam; Forest, J.; Forest, J.; Forestier, J.; Forster, Roger; Forster, Wm;
Forster, J.; Forster, J.; Forster, J.; Forster, Godfrey; Forster, J.; Forster, Ralph; Forster, J.; Forster, J.; Fort,
Rob; Forte, Rob; Forthyngham, Rich; Foster, J.; Foster, J.; Fote, J.; Fotman, J.; Foucher, J.; Foul[er?], J.;
Fouler, Raulyn; Foune, Thos; Founteyns, J.; Fourbor, J.; Foweler, Thos; Fowlmere, J.; Fowne, Nicholas;
Fowne, Thos; Fox, J.; Fox, Wm; Fox, Thos; Fox, J.; Fox, J.; Fox, Rich; Foxe, J.; Foxe, Thos; Foxle, Wm;
Frampton, J.; Francleyn, Wm; Frangleyn, Wm; Fraunceys, J.; Fraunceys, Symond; Fraunk, Wm;
Fraunke, J.; Fraunseys, Rob; Fraynkelayn, Wm; Freman, Wm; Freman, J.; Freman, Wm; Freman, Rob;
Freman, J.; Frenche, J.; Frenssh, Stephen; Frenssh, Stephen; Frer, Rob; Fressh, Wm; Frie, J.; Frithby,
Edward; Fromward, Thos; Fronlond, J.; Fryseles, J.; Fuller, J.; Fuller, J.; Fuller, Nicholas; Fuller, Rob;
Fulschawe, Maykyn; Furbor, Thos; Furbor, Peter; Furbor, Hugh; Furnays, Robard; Fyche, Wm; Fygge,
J.; Fyket, Roger; Fylkyn, Philip; Fylyngley, Rich; Fymber, Wm; Fysher, Edmund; Fysher, Rich; Fyssh,
Thos; Fysshelake, J.; Fysshere, Edmund; Gabilwright, Wm; Gabygherd, Wm; Galdny, J.; Gall, Thos;
Galley, Wm; Galton, Wm; Galum, Wm; Galyzard, Nicholas; Gam, Thomas ap John ap Jake; Gam,
Jankyn ap Howell ap Griffuth; Gam, Howell; Game, Stephen; Gamell, J.; Gamell, J.; Gammesley, Wm;
Gamul, Stephen; Ganshulle, Rich; Gardiner, Matheus; Gardiner, J.; Gardyner, Roger; Gardyner,
Thomas junior; Garlond, Nicholas; Garlowe?, Wm; Garstange, Henry; Gassgill, Wm; Gate, Wm; Gate,
Symond; Gate, J.; Gates, Walter; Gatun?, Wm; Gauder, J.; Gaunsonn, Rob; Gaunt, J.; Gawunn, Thos;
Gawyn, Robard; Gaylon, Wm; Gayne, J.; Gaynesburgh, J.; Gaynsford, Rob; Geall, Edmund; Geffray, J.;
Geffre, J.; Gelyan, Peter; Genewe, J.; Geodchap, J.; Gerard, Rich; Gerard, J.; Gerard, Henry; Germyn,
Rob; Gertaen, J.; Gervex, J.; Geryng, Stephen; Gethyn, Davy; Gethyn, David ap Jena; Gethyn, Rys;
Gethyn, Rys; Gethyn, Mereduth ap Howell; Gethyn, Morgan ap Howell; Gethyn, Madok ap Madok;
Gethyn, Gwillym ap Jenan; Gethyn, Griffuth ap David; Gethyn, Gwillym; Geye, Wm; Gibonson,
Rob; Gibson, Rich; Gilder, Roger; Gilkyn, Henry; Gladewyn, Wm; Glads, Morgan ap David;
Glanton, J.; Glayser, Thos; Glayve, Thos; Glede, Simon; Gledwyk, not given; Gleter, Thos; Glosinbury,
J.; Glover, J.; Glover, Thos; Glover, J.; Glover, J.; Glover, J.; Glovere, J.; Glovere, J.; Glovere, Wm;
Glovere, Wm; Glyn, Wm; Glynwyn, David; Go[g]h, Wm; Gobald, Roger; Gobbsell, Thos; Gobld?, J.;
Goch, Walter ap Llewellyn; Goch, David ap Gr[uffth]; Goch, David; Goch, Jena ap Morgan ap Jena;
Goch, Rosser ap David ap Howell; Goch, David; Goch, David Vachan ap David; Goch, J.; Goch,

Philip Lang; Goche, Jena ap Gr[uffth]; Godechild, Wm; Godewyn, Rich; Godewyne, Rob; Godfray, Rich; Godfray, Stephen; Godhyne, Rob; Godlowe, Robard; Godsalffe, J.; Godston, Wm; Godwyn, Henry; Godwyne, Rich; Goffayre, J.; Gogh de Hudcote, J.; Golclif, J.; Golde, Wm; Golde, J.; Goldene, Wm; Goldryng, Henry; Golofre, Wm; Golynch, J.; Gomeray, J.; Gondour, Jenan Bach ap Gwlym; Good, J.; Goode, Thos; Goolde, Henry; Goore, Thos; Goos, Henry; Gorlegh, Robaard; Gouldei, Thos; Gowen, Thurstan; Gower, Thos; Grafton, Thos; Granyn, Rich; Grart, J.; Grasham, J.; Gratedew, J.; Grauntt, J.; Graveson, Edmund; Gray, Wm; Gray, Rob; Gray, J.; Gray, Rob; Gray, Wm; Grayeson, Wm; Grayeson, Wm; Grays, Wm; Grege, Philip; Greges, J.; Gregg, J.; Grenclef, Alexander; Grene, Wm; Grene, Wm; Grene, J.; Grene, Thos; Grene, Thos; Grene, Wm; Grene, J.; Grene, Rob; Grene, Wm; Grene, Wm; Grene, Rich; Grene, Rob; Grene, Rich; Grene, J.; Grene, Wm; Grene, Wm; Grene, Ralph; Grene, Rich; Grene, J.; Grene, Edmund; Grene, Rich; Grene, Wm; Grenefeld, Thos; Grenehull, J.; Grenelef, J.; Grenelef, Matheus; Greneok, J.; Greneway, Henry; Grenewod, Rich; Grenewode, J.; Grenhale, Wm; Grenley, J.; Gresels, Robard; Greudon, J.; Greve, J.; Grey, Rob; Grey, Wm; Grey, J.; Greye, Wm; Greyeson, Dunn; Greyge, J.; Groom, J.; Gropton, J.; Gross?, J.; Grosse, Wm; Grossell, J.; Grove, Thos; Grover, Rich; Grow, Bernard; Gruge, Rys ap Llewellyn ap Gr[uffth]; Grull, J.; Gryce, Wm; Grygeri, Rich; Grygge, J.; Grygges, J.; Gryseley, J.; Grysey, Thos; Gulle, J.; Gulsowe, Nicholas; Guy, J.; Guype, Thos; Gvyn, Wm; Gwlim, Res; Gwlim, Mered ap Jena; Gwyn, Wm; Gwyn, Jenan ap David; Gwyn, Jenan ap Jenan; Gwyn, Eyvon ap David; Gwyn, Gwillym ap Jenan; Gwynnow, Benedict; Gybbe, J.; Gybbes, J.; Gybbes, Wm; Gybbson, J.; Gybson, J.; Gybson, Wm; Gydale, J.; Gyffray, J.; Gyldene, J.; Gyles, J.; Gyllyot, J.; Gylmyn, Thos; Gylys, Thos; Gylys, Thos; Gynnys, J.; Gynnys, J.; H[?], Wm; Hablot, Thos; Habmond, Thos; Hacket, J.; Hacokes, J.; Hacton, Wm; Hacun, Rich; Haddon, Rich; Haddylsay, Rob; Hagh, J.; Hake, Rich; Hakebeche, J.; Hakkewode, Walter?; Halbard, Robard; Hale, Thos; Hales, Geffray; Halghton, Thos; Halifax, Thos; Halifax, Thos; Halkeborwe, J.; Hall, J.; Hall, J.; Hall, J.; Halle, Edward; Halle, Thos; Halle, Ralph; Halley, Wm; Halley, J.; Halley, J.; Halman, Thos; Halman, J.; Halman, Thos; Halt, Rob; Halveld, Robard; Halyday, J.; Halyngest, Thos; Halys, Rich; Halys, Rich; Haman, Thos; Haman, Thos; Hambold, Thos; Hamme, J.; Hammylby, Thos; Hamond, Wm; Hamond, J.; Hamond, J.; Hampton, Thos; Hampton, Thos; Hampton, Rob; Hampton, Raulyn; Hampton, Rob; Hamson, Henry; Hamson, Thos; Hamyldon, Edward; Hamys, Wm; Hanam, J.; Hancocke, J.; Hancok, Walter; Hancok, Rob; Hande, Walter; Hanewell, Thos; Hankyn, J.; Hanley, Symkyn; Hanson, J.; Hanson, Rob; Hanyn, Reginald; Hanyton, J.; Harby de Depyng, J.; Hardegate, J.; Hardy, Wm; Hardyng, J.; Hardyng, J.; Hardyng, Rob; Hare, Wm; Hare, J.; Hare, J.; Harecroft, Henry; Harewell, J.; Harewell, Wm; Harewode, J.; Harewode, Rich; Harewode, J.; Harman, J.; Harper, Wm; Harpere, Rich; Harry, J.; Harryes, J.; Harswell, Jacob; Hary, Wm; Haryn, Wm; Haryngton, Thos; Harysone, Thos; Haseyng, J.; Hasilwode, J.; Haslarton, Wm; Hastynge, Wm; Hasylwode, Rob; Hatton, Wm; Hauchyn, J.; Hauke, Wm; Haukeswell, J.; Haukyn, J.; Hauneley, J.; Hausman, Wm; Hauthorn, J.; Hawes, Rob; Hawkeswell, J.; Hawkyn, Rob; Hawkyn, Henry; Hawkyns, J.; Hawlowes, J.; Hawlowes, Rob; Hawmond, Thos; Hawys, Wm; Hax, J.; Hayburgh, Thos; Haydok, Robard; Haye, Davy; Haygarth, Thos; Hayl, J.; Hayteley, Hugyn; Hayward, J.; Hayward, Wm; Hayward, Rich; Hayward, J.; Hayward, Wm; Hebbe, Wm; Hedlamp, Wm; Hedon, J.; Hedson, J.; Heed, Rich; Hegge, J.; Hegge, Jacob; Heggeman, J.; Heiley, J.; Hekeman, Rich; Heland, Simon; Helde, Wm; Helman, Walter?; Helme, Rich; Helonde, Rob; Helyar, Piers; Hemmyng, Rob; Hemyngton, J.; Hencok, J.; Henries, Ralph; Henrison, J.; Henryson, Thos; Henryson, J.; Hensman, J.; Hensman, Thos; Henywood, Wm; Herde, J.; Hereford, J.; Hereforth, J.; Herford, Roger; Herman, J.; Herman, J.; Herman, John jnr; Herny, Rich; Heron, Lyell; Herre, Thos; Hersile, Roger; Herskysman, J.; Hert, J.; Hert, Rob; Hert, J.; Hert, J.; Hert, Roger; Hert, Nicholas; Herte, Wm; Herteshorn, Laurence; Hertford, J.; Hertishorn, Laurence; Hervy, Walter; Hervy, Thos; Hervy, J.; Hervyessone, Thos; Herworth, J.; Heryng, J.; Heryng, Wm; Heryng, J.; Hesam, Wm; Hesey, Godfrey; Hesilwode, J.; Hesketh, Thos; Hesybryg, Nicholas; Hether, Wm; Heton, J.; Heton, Edmund; Hewell, J.; Hewetson, Thos; Hexham, Wm; Heyles, Mayew; Heyll, Thos; Heymyf, Jenan ap Gwas; Heyne, Thos; Heyward, Wm; Heywey, Rich; Hicke, J.; Hickes, Thos; Higdon, Thos; Hill, J.; Hill, J.; Hille, Wm; Hille, Roger; Hille, Rich; Hille, J.; Hilton, Wm; Hipstun, J.; Hir, Madoc ap Llellewyn ap Jena; Hochekynsone, Thos; Hochonn, Rob; Hodeleston, Christofur; Hodenet, Philip; Hogekyn, J.; Hoggard, J.; Hogge, J.; Hoggehird, Roger; Hogges, J.; Hoggessone, Thos; Hoghton, Rich; Hoghton, Rob; Hoiskyn, J.; Hoiskyn, Rich; Hoke, Nicholas; Holare?, Thos; Holbek, Wm; Holbroke, J.; Holder, Rich; Holder, Rob; Holder, Rich; Holdernesse, J.; Holgreve, Thos; Holkote, Thos; Holme, Reginald; Holme, Thos; Holond, J.; Holond, Thos; Holt, Thos; Holte, Mathew; Holte, Thos; Holwell,

Thos; Holwell, Stephen; Holyer, J.; Hombrisley, J.; Homel, J.; Homond, Rich; Homwode, Godfrey; Honter, Wm; Hoo, Henry; Hoo, J.; Hoo, Wm; Hoode, Wm; Hook, Nicholas; Hoole, at ye, Rich; Hope, Thos; Hope, Wm; Hope, Thos; Hoper, J.; Hopkyn, Rob; Hopton, Walter; Hopton, Walter; Horde, J.; Hordern, Wm; Horle?, Wm; Horn, Rob; Horn, Rob; Horn, J.; Horneby, Henry; Horshenes, J.; Horslowe, Nicholas; Horspase, J.; Horton, Philip; Horton, Wm; Hosteler, J.; Hosteler, J.; Hosyer, J.; Hosyere, Thos; Hoton, Wm; Hoton, Wm; Houchonson, Wm; Houghton, Henry; House, Rob; House, Rob; Howdon, Thos; Howe, J.; Huby, Thos; Huchonson, Roger; Huddessone, J.; Huddilston, Nicholas; Hudelston, Rich; Huden, Rich; Hudhill, Rich; Hudson, J.; Huet, Roger; Huetson, J.; Huge, J.; Hughson, Rob; Hughson, Geffray; Hugyn, J.; Hugyn, Wm; Hukeham, Thos; Hull, Roger; Hull, Wm; Hulle, Henry; Hulle, Henry; Hulle, Sympkyn; Hulot, Rob; Hulton, Thos; Hundescrer, Wm; Hundeslane, Thos; Hunsterton, J.; Hunt, Thos; Hunte, Wm; Hunte, Wm; Hunte, J.; Hunte, Henry; Hunte, Lewis; Hunte, Peter; Hunte, Walter; Hunte, Rob; Hunte, Rich; Hunter, J.; Hunter, Rob; Hunter, Rob; Huntt, J.; Huntte, Thos; Hure, Rich; Hurlebat, J.; Hurlebat, J.; Hussher, Wm; Hussher, Wm; Huwet, J.; Huwett, J.; Huwett, Wm; Hycke, J.; Hycke, Thos; Hyde, Wm; Hyde, Rob; Hygkys, Joyk; Hygyn, Philip; Hykke, J.; Hylle, J.; Hylton, J.; Hylton, J.; Hynebest, J.; Hynemersch, Wm; Hyngham, Henry; Hynton, Rich; Hyre, Jenan Lloyt; Hyre, Griffith; Hywell, David ap Mereduth; Ildregat, Rich; Ile, Wm; Illez, Wm; in the Okes, J.; Iovenesse, Wm; Ireland, Wm; Iremonger, Wm; Ireton, Rich; Irroyr, Jennan Duy; Iseby, J.; Ive, J.; Ive, J.; Jackson, Thos; Jackson, J.; Jacson, Thos; Jacson, Rob; Jakelyng, Walter; Jakkysone, Henry; Jakson, J.; Jakson, J.; Jakson, John jnr; Jakson, Rich; James, Thos; James, Thos; James, Andrew; Jamessone, Rob; Jamys, Rich; Janes, Wm; Jankenesse, J.; Jannys, Porys; Jannys, Piers; Janynsone, Robard; Jaqueman, J.; Jay, Wm; Jeffray, Davy; Jekys, Walter; Jemanessone, J.; Jete, Wm; Jevewe, J.; Joce, Thos; Johanson, Thos; Johebon, Peter; Johnson, Henry; Johnson, Rich; Johnson, Rich; Johnson, Wm; Johnsone, Rob; Johnsone, Rich; Johnysson, Rich; Jolby, Edmund; Jones, Wm; Jonesson, Henry; Jonesson, Thos; Jonessone, Thos; Jonessone, Thos; Jonessone, Rob; Jonson, Gilbert; Jonson, Peter; Jonson, Thos; Jonson, Wm; Jonson, Thos; Jonson, Alexander; Jonson, Rich; Jonyssone, Henry; Jordan, Stephan; Joy?, J.; Joye, J.; Joynor, J.; Jude, Rob; Jurdeyn, J.; Jurdon, J.; Justice, Walter; Juyles, Rich; K??, Rich; Karlton, Rich; Karwell, Thos; Kateryk, Rob; Kay, J.; Kaye, J.; Kays, Henry; Kayshoo, J.; Kech, Davy; Kech, Roger; Kech, Rob; Keche, Wm; Kedewyn, Godfrey; Kedewyn, Howell ap Llellewyn; Keetilby, Wm; Kegwyn, David; Kehevyn, Jena ap Philip; Kekely, Henry; Kele, Rich; Kelebray, Philip; Kelke, J.; Kellfeld, Wm; Kellow, J.; Kellowe, J.; Kelsale, J.; Kembre, Rob; Kempe, Rob; Kempes, J.; Kempley, J.; Kemsyng?, Rich; Kendale, Wm; Kendale, J.; Kendale, Thos; Kendale, Walter; Kendale, off (sic), Wm; Kendele, J.; Kene, Thos; Kene, Wm; Kenevek, J.; Keneward, J.; Kent, J.; Kent, J.; Kent, J.; Kent, Wm; Kent, J.; Kent, Nicholas; Kent, John, of; Kent, Rob; Kerlyngham, Wm; Kerreys, Thos; Kery, Hoghwel; Keston, Roger; Keteryng, Wm; Kethyn, Eyvon; Ketyn, Meredith; Kexby, J.; Kirby, Thos; Kirkele, Thos; Kirton, J.; Knappyng, Wm; Knaresdale, Rich; Knok, J.; Knolles, J.; Knoppyng, Paule; Knotte, Thos; Knowel, Rich; Knyght, Jamys; Koke, Lewes; Koke, Rich; Koke, J.; Kombe, Thos; Koper, Rich; Korby, Wm; Kot, J.; Kuyghth, Yenan; Kyborne, J.; Kydesley, Thos; Kyighlay, J.; Kylbery, J.; Kyllyngworth, Wm; Kymberlegh, J.; Kyng, Thos; Kyng, Thos; Kyng alias Gregge, J.; Kynge, Alexander; Kynge, J.; Kynge, J.; Kyngesee, Rich; Kyngeston, J.; Kyngeston, Rich; Kyngeston, J.; Kyngeston, Rob; Kyngeston, Rich; Kyngeston, Thos; Kyngierwer, Rob; Kyngston, Wm; Kyngston, Edmund; Kynton, Piers; Kypas, Thos; Kyppyng, Hugh; Kyrby, Thos; Kyrby, Thos; Kyrby, Wm; Kyrkby, J.; Kyrkeby, J.; Kyrkeby, Rob; Kyrkeby, Thos; Kyrkeby de Gayteshed, Wm; Kyrkeby de Newecastle, Wm; Kyrkehouse, Robard; Kyrkgarth, J.; Kyrkham, Robard; Kyrkman, J.; Kytchyn, J.; Labton, Thos; Laconn, Thos; Laconn, Wm; Lacy, Wm; Lacy, J.; Lacy, J.; Lacy, Rob; Lacy, Thos; Ladlon, Thos; Lake, Rob; Lakenhale, J.; Laklesford, Rich; Lalynton, Rich; Lamberd, Rob; Lamborne, J.; Lame, Wm; Lame, Wm; Lamkyn, Rob; Lampoet, Wm; Lanbert, J.; Lancastre, Henry; Lancryman, Walter; Landran, Thos; Lane, J.; Lane, Ralph; Lane, J.; Lanedissh, J.; Lang, Wm; Lang, J.; Lang, J.; Lange, J.; Langford, J.; Langfurth, Henry; Langhall, J.; Langle, Ralph; Langton, Wm; Langton, J.; Langton, J.; Langton, Henry; Langton, J.; Lankland, Thos; Lansadren, J.; Lanton, J.; Lanvort, J.; Laree, Adam; Lark, J.; Larke, Thos; Larke, Thos; Lasbe, Walter; Lasyngby, Thos; Lauerance, Thos; Launt, J.; Laurence, J.; Laurent, Hugo; Lavender, J.; Lavendre, Wm; Lavendre, Rich; Laverant, J.; Laverok, Wm; Laveroke, Symond; Lawe, J.; Lawkland, Rich; Lawrence, Lewes; Lawson, Wm; Layborn, Thos; Laykyn, J.; Laylond, J.; le Barbor, Wm; le Baxter, Edward; le Foler, Wm; le Glover, Edward(Edus); le Milner, Thos; le Parker, Rich; le Sclater, Rob; le Smyth, Roger; le Taillor, Thos; le Taillor, Wm; le Wryght, Thos; Lech, J.; Leche, Rob; Leche, Wm; Leche, Hugh; Leche, Rich; Leche, Rich; Leche, J.; Leche, Nicholas; Leche, Morgan Duy;

Lee, J.; Lee, Henry; Leeke, Thos; Lees, Thos; Leeson, Rob; left blank, Jacket; Leg, J.; Legge, J.; Leke, J.; Lellem, Thos; Leman, J.; Leman, Henry; Lemere, J.; Lenham, Thos; Leoffhot, J.; Lerwyt, Wm; Leryng, J.; Lessy, Nicholas; Lesyng, Wm; Lette, Simon; Letton, Thos; Leverour, Walter; Leveryche, J.; Leveryche, J.; Leveson, Wm; Lewys, Walter; Ley, Thos; Leya, David ap Jenan ap Traharn; Leycestr, J.; Leycestr, J.; Leye, Walter; Leykuy, Phelpot; Lillebourne, J.; Lilye, Rich; Lincoln, Wm; Lincoln, J.; Litelton, Rob; Litewode, Rich; Ll[ewlyn], David; Llewen, Walter ap Gwlim ap Trahan; Lloyd, Philip; Lloyt, David ap Howell ap Gwillym; Lloyt, Llewelyn Dduy ap David; Lloyt, Jenan ap Gr[uffth]; Lloyt, Watkyn ap Jake; Lloyt, Res ap M[ado]c; Lloyt, Gwlim ap Madoc ap David; Lloyt, Henry; Lloyt, Jenkyn; Lloyt, David ap Llellewyn; Lloyt, Griffuth ap David; Lloyt, Jenan Duy ap David; Lloyt, Jenan Leya ap David; Lloyt, Gwilly ap Llewellyn ap David ap Jenan; Lloyt, John ap Rys; Lloyt, David ap Jenan Vachan ap Jenan; Lloyt, Llewellyn ap Gwillym; Lloyt, Owen ap Llewellyn; Lloyt, Philip ap David ap Jenan; Lloyt, Jenan ap Philip ap Jenan; Lloyt, John ap David; Lloyt, Llewellyn ap David; Lloyt, Gwillym ap Jenan; Lloyt, Madoc ap Ricard; Lloyt, Llewellyn ap David; Lloyt, Jenan ap Gwas; Lloyt, Jenan ap Jenan ap David; Lloyt, Owen ap Griffith ap Jenan; Lockstton, J.; Lodepond, Hugh; Lodys, J.; Loffthous, Thos; Logeraund, Adam; Logge, Piers; Lokehwayt, Thos; Lokewodde, J.; Lokkyng, Rich; Lokyngton, Thos; Lokysby, Rob; London, J.; London, J.; London, Rich; London, Wm; Longe, Nicholas; Longe, Rob; Longe, Walter; Longe, J.; Lorymer, Rob; Loryn, J.; Lounde, Saundre; Louthe, J.; Louther, Wm; Louyth, David; Lovekyn, Rob; Lovell, J.; Lovell, J.; Lovell, Wm; Lovelok, J.; Lovelord, Adam; Lowe, Rich; Lowes, J.; Lowkerygge, J.; Lowre, Davi; Loxle, Rob; Lucet, Wm; Ludbery, Thos; Ludlowe, Rob; Luk, Phelip; Lundesson, J.; Lutterworth, Rob; Lutterworth, Wm; Lwe?, J.; Lyawyn, Thos; Lycsterre, Roger; Lyfesey, Wm; Lygatlaas, Jenan; Lyghton, J.; Lyll, John?; Lymmer, J.; Lynche, J.; Lyncholads, J.; Lyncolne, Thos; Lynde, Henry; Lynde, Henry; Lynde, Thos; Lynde, J.; Lyndesay, J.; Lyndeselle, J.; Lyndesey, Thos; Lyndeshay, Wm; Lyndsey, Thos; Lynehous, Thos; Lyngestun, Wm; Lynkesle, Wm; Lynn, J.; Lynous, Wm; Lyntoun, Walter; Lyons, Walter; Lyrbene, Wm; Lyster, J.; Lytfote, J.; Lyttilton, Jacob; Lyvermere, Simon; Macy, Wm; Madefray, Rob; Madok, Llewellyn ap Jak; Magot, J.; Magot, Walter; Maii, J.; Makefayr, Wm; Makerell, J.; Makereth, Thos; Malan, Thos; Maldenn, J.; Maldon, J.; Maldon, J.; Maleblank, J.; Malman, J.; Malpas, Hugh; Malpas, Rich; Malthous, Wm; Malver, George; Malverne, George; Man, Wm; Man, Thos; Man, Thomas; Mandffew, J.; Manfeld, Wm; Mankesfeld, J.; Manniby, J.; Mannyng, J.; Manryng, Thos; Manryng, Thos; Mantel, J.; Manyngham, J.; Mape, Morice; Mapelton, Roger; March, J.; March, J.; Marchal, J.; Marchal, Henry; Marchal, Thos; Marchal, Wm; Marchall, Nicholas; Marchall, Rich; Marchall, J.; Marchaunt, Rich; Marham, Roger; Markyndale, Rich; Marnham, J.; Marschall, J.; Marshall, Thos; Martendell, Thos; Martin, Thos; Martin, Wm; Martin, J.; Marton, Wm; Martyn, Laurence; Martyn, J.; Martyn, Robynet; Martyn, Wm; Martyn, Roger; Martyn, J.; Martyn, J.; Martyn, Rich; Martyne, Rich; Maryot, Henry; Masenger, J.; Mason, Wm; Mason, Walter; Mason, Robard; Mason, Ralph; Mason, J.; Mason, J.; Mason, J.; Mason, Rich; Mason, Wm; Masonn, Rich; Massam, Rob; Massy, Rich; Massy, Pythyan; Maswyk, J.; Maswyk, J.; Matheu, Wm; Mathew, J.; Mathew, David; Mathewssone, J.; Mathou, J.; Matson, Rob; Matteson, J.; Matthewe, Rich; Maubei, J.; Maundevyle, J.; Maundevyle, J.; Maundevyle, J.; Maundevyle, Roger; Maundevyle, Thos; Maunsell, Rob; Maunton, Morys; Maur, Howell; Maveys, J.; Mawer, J.; Mawer, Roger; May, J.; May?, Rich; Mayandeville, Wm; Maycot, J.; Mayholt, Wm; Mayland, J.; Mayler, Reginald; Mayllar, Reynald; Mayn, Henry; Mayn, J.; Maynell, Thos; Mayny, J.; Mayr, Wm; Mechell, Roger; Med, J.; Meddelstret, J.; Meddelstret, Wm; Mede, J.; Medecreste, Rob; Medewe, Wm; Medilton, J.; Medylton, J.; Megre, Walter; Meiller, Rich; Meimo, J.; Melbourne, Wattekin; Mellere, Nicholas; Mellour, Rich; Mellys, Rob; Melman, J.; Mendham, J.; Mercer, Edmund; Merden, J.; Merger, J.; Merschton, Thos; Mersh, J.; Mershall, J.; Merston, J.; Merston, J.; Message, Stephen; Messager, J.; Messager, Lowys; Messager, Rich; Messager, Edward; Messager, Cok; Messanger, Robard; Messe, Henry; Meston, J.; Methevey, David Goch ap Jenan; Meurt?, Jankyn; Meyman, J.; Meyndy, James; Michell, Simon; Michell, Hankyn; Michell, J.; Michell, J.; Michell, Rob; Michell, J.; Michelson, Leonard; Middelton, J.; Middelton, Wm; Miggylfeld, Walter; Milam, Rich; Miles, Thos; Mille, Wm; Mille, J.; Mille, Thos; Miller, J.; Millner, Thos; Millyngton, Nicholas; Milneholme, J.; Milner, J.; Milner, Wm; Milner, Wm; Mody, J.; Moell, Geffray ap Jenan; Moell, David ap Gwillym ap Jenan; Moell, Griffith ap Philip ap Griffith; Moell, Gwillym ap Jenan; Moell, Llewellyn ap Jenan; Moill, Rys ap Cadogan; Moleners, Wm; Moles, Thos; Molineux, Dicon; Molle, J.; Monford, Thos; Mongom (sic), J.; Monpisson, Robard; Monse, J.; Monse, J.; Moor, of the, Sympkyn; Moore, Thos; Moot alias Ketyll, J.; More, Rich; More, J.; More, Gregory; More, Rob; More, J.; More, Gruffuth ap Jenan ap Gwillim; Morell, J.; Morell, J.; Morell?, Peter;

Morer, J.; Mores, J.; Mores, John jnr; Mores, Wm; Mores, J.; Morethwayt, Wm; Moreys, Rich; Moreys, J.; Morgan, J.; Morley, Ralph; Mors, Wm; Morsburah, J.; Morsholt, J.; Mort[?], Hugh; Mortemere, Rich; Mortimer, J.; Morton?, Rob; Morys, J.; Mosehale, Rich; Mot, J.; Motom, Wm; Mott, J.; Mottland, Thos; Mour, Wm; Mowbray, Thos; Mowver, Wm; Moyll, Rich; Moyn, J.; Moyn, J.; Moys, J.; Moys, Peter; Muleward, J.; Mullyng, J.; Mundy, J.; Mungomeri, J.; Mungomery, Hugh; Munke, Wm; Munkton, Thos; Munnowich, J.; Mutlowe, Henry; Mychelfeld, J.; Myddelham, J.; Myddilton, J.; Myles, Thos; Myles, Wm; Myller, Thos; Myllyngton, J.; Mylner, J.; Mylner, Thos; Mylzonek, Wm; Mymer, Rob; Mymull, Wm; Myners, Wm; Mynton, Rich; Mynton, J.; Myreman, J.; Myryk, J.; Naghert, J.; Nalleston, J.; Napton, Wm; Nasshe, Rich; Nawegterr, Rich; Nayle, J.; Necold, George; Nedham, Thos; Neel, J.; Neffe, J.; Nele, Wm; Neleson, J.; Nepe, J.; Nerhall, J.; Nerhalle, J.; Nethewey, Wm; Netlam, Thos; Neulond, J.; Neuman, J.; Neusom, Wm; Neuton, J.; Neuton, Wm; Nevyle, Wm; New, Thos; Newall, J.; Newbolt, Wm; Newby, Jacob; Newdy, Geffrey; Newelond, Wm; Neweman, Robard; Neweman, J.; Neweton, Geffray; Neweton, Thos; Newhalle, J.; Newland, Simon; Newland, Wm; Newport, Wm; Newsam, Rich; Neyler, J.; Nichol, J.; Nicholas, Wm; Nicholson, J.; Nicluern?, J.; Nicoll, George; Nicoll, Esmond; Nicoll, Peter; Nicoll, Edward; Nocton, Wm; Nopton, J.; Norbury, J.; Noreys, J.; Norffolk, J.; Norice, J.; Noris, Thos; Noris, Rich; Norle, Wm; Norman, J.; Norman, Rich; North, Thos; North, Wm; Northfolk, Rich; Northwey, J.; Northwold, Rich; Northwych, Wm; Norton, J.; Norton, Rich; Norton, Thos; Norton, Thos; Norton, Rob; Norwych, Matthew; Norys, Rich; Norys, Wm; not given, Nicholas; not given, J.; not given, Lewes minor; not given, Deykyn; not given, Yanthlos; not given, J.; Notheyer, J.; Notton, Rich; Notyngham, Thos; Notyngham, J.; Notyngham, Henry; Noune?, Wm; Nowman, Davy; Nowne, Wm; Nut?, Wm; Nutell, J.; Nutteson, Wm; Oberd, J.; Ocholt, Rob; Oclee, Wm; Ocleshawe, Laurence; Ocryngham, Wm; Odhurst, Wm; of Burdews, J.; of Coventry, J.; of Derbyshir, Henry; of Derham, J.; of Grantham, J.; of Kycchyne, J.; of Langley, Henry; of Okes, J.; of Okes, Thos; of Stanestrete, Rich; of Tollay, Henry; of Van, Rich; of Wordley, J.; Ogle, Rob; Ogle, Wm; Okeley, Thos; Okers, J.; Okers, Jankyn; Oldcastel, J.; Oldham, Wm; Ollesmere, Hugh; on the Haspys, Haukn; Onaeby, Wm; Ordemere, Nicholas; Orgrave?, J.; Orkenay, J.; Orlyanes, Wm; Orwynd, Wm; Osewestre, David; Ostreger, Rob; Ostregh, Laurence; Ostroche, Lawrener; Oswastre, David; Oswertur, J.; Oswestre, Wm; Oswoster, Hugo; Othman, J.; Otys, Rob; Outtreggd, J.; Overay, Wm; Overton, Wm; Owardrop, J.; Ower, J.; Pacoke, Wm; Padle, Wm; Padley, J.; Page, J.; Page, Rawlyn; Page, J.; Page, J.; Page, Wm; Pageroun, J.; Pake, J.; Pakenham, Rob; Pakker, Wm; Pakwode, Wm; Paliewede, Wm; Palinere, Thos; Palmer, Rich; Palmer, Thos; Palmere, Wm; Palmere, Phelyp; Palmere, Wm; Palnart-?, Thos; Panter, Thos; Pape, Wm; Paradys, J.; Park, Wm; Parke, Simon; Parke, Thos; Parker, Rich; Parker, Rich; Parker, Thos; Parker, David; Parker, J.; Parker, Wm; Parker, Thos; Parker, J.; Parker, Thos; Parker, Wm; Parker, Wm; Parker, J.; Parker, Thos; Parker, J.; Parker, Thos; Parker, J.; Parker, J.; Parker, J.; Parkere, Wm; Parkere, Wm; Parlebone, Thos; Parre, Wm; Parre, Rich; Partrich, J.; Parys, Wm; Pasande, Hugh; Pascnar, Wm; Passemer, Thos; Passeware, J.; Paterykson, J.; Patonson, J.; Patryk, J.; Patryke, J.; Patryngton, J.; Paucok, Mathew; Paunchebek, Henry; Pavy, Alan; Pawlyne, Thos; Paxton, J.; Payn, Henry; Payne, J.; Payne, Rich; Payneswyke, Wm; Paytte, J.; Pecche, Wm; Pecche, J.; Pecham, Wm; Peche, Thos; Peche, Nicholas; Peckyng, Wm; Pecok, J.; Pecok, Rob; Pedlycane, Thos; Pedyngton, J.; Peeke, J.; Pege, Thos; Peggis, Rob; Peghon, Thos; Pekwode, Wm; Pemberton, Rob; Penbruk, Wm; Pendale, Thos; Penduy, Res; Penghur, Thos; Penhalow, J.; Penkeston, Rich; Penne, Henry; Penreth, Rich; Pentryth, Thos; Peper, Thos; Percyvall, Piers; Peressone, Wm; Perford, Thos; Perie, J.; Perkyn, J.; Perkyn, Randolph; Perot, Wm; Perot, J.; Perpoynte, J.; Perschowre, Rich; Persevale, Rob; Person, J.; Person, Henry; Person, Huge; Person, Thos; Person, J.; Peruant?, J.; Pery, Nicholas; Petreborwe, J.; Pettyt, Wm; Pety John, J.; Petyrsfeld, J.; Phelyp, J.; Philip, Nicholas; Philip, Edward; Philyp, Wm; Phyllyp, J.; Phyllyp, Rich; Pibam, J.; Piert, Wm; Pigconn, J.; Pik, J.; Pillar, Wm; Pillar, Philip; Piller, Thos; Pinnet, Philip; Piper, J.; Placy, Wm; Placy, Wm; Placy, Wm; Playce, J.; Playford, Rob; Plesant, Rob; Plesby, Thos; Ploghground, Rich; Plomer, Thos; Plomer, J.; Plowman, Thos; Plowman, J.; Plu[?]os, J.; Plum, Roger; Plummouth, Rob; Pocok, J.; Podlyng, Wm; Pokkeswell, Thos; Poklyngton, Wm; Pokyllyngton, Wm; Polard, J.; Pole, Wm; Polerd, J.; Poleyn, J.; Polyner, J.; Pond, J.; Pontyngton, Laurence; Pope, Thos; Popylwyk, J.; Port, J.; Porter, J.; Porter, J.; Porter, Henry; Porter, J.; Porter, Henry; Porter, Wm; Porter, J.; Porter, Aleyn; Porter, Wm; Porter, Wm; Porter, Thos; Porter, David; Porter alias Medewe, J.; Portere, Thos; Portor, J.; Postele, Simon; Postle, J.; Pottere, J.; Pouncefret, J.; Pountesbury, Thos; Povy, Thos; Powe, Rich; Power, Thos; Powis, J.; Pownchardon, Ralph; Poworell, Thos; Poyll, Walter; Prat, Wm; Pratte, J.; Prealiner, Johan; Prentys, J.; Prentys, Rob;

Presteyn, Wm; Preston, J.; Preston, Thos; Preston, Piers; Preston, Wm; Preston, J.; Preston, Rob; Preston, J.; Preston, Wm; Preston, Rich; Prestyn, J.; Pret John, Stephen; Prior, J.; Prom, Henry; Prydens, J.; Pudenis?, J.; Pulfforde, Hugo; Pulforth, J.; Pulgryng, J.; Pulpit, J.; Pulter, Gregory; Purchas, Thos; Purdu, Thos; Pure, Hugh; Purgas, Thos; Purly, J.; Purser, Wm; Pursure, Wm; Pycton, J.; Pye, J.; Pye, J.; Pye, J.; Pygot, J.; Pyke, J.; Pyken, J.; Pykeryng, Thos; Pykeryng, Thos; Pykeryng, Wm; Pykestoke, Rich; Pykot, J.; Pykstoke, J.; Pyller, Wm; Pynchebeb, Wm; Pynford, J.; Pynge, Wm; Pynke, J.; Pynketh, Rich; Pynkyn,; Pynnowe, J.; Pype, Rys; Pyper, Wm; Pyper, Rob; Pyper, Walter; Pyper, Jacob; Pyper, J.; Pyper, J.; Pyson, Thos; Pytte, J.; Qlas?, David Qlas?; Quyn, J.; Quytehede, J.; Quytenede, Thos; Rabuk, Henry; Rabyn, Roger; Rac[?], John jnr; Rachedale, Rich; Radclyf, Nicholas; Raffe, J.; Ralfe, J.; Ramyngton, Edmund; Rande, Wm; Randolf, J.; Randolf, J.; Ranham, J.; Raper, Rob; Raper, Thos; Rasch, J.; Rasse, Thos; Ratfeld, Rob; Raulff, Jenan Duy ap Howell? ap Gruffyth; Raulyn, J.; Raulyn, Thos; Raulyn, Wm; Raulyn, J.; Raulynsone, Rob; Raynald, J.; Raynforth, Ralph; Raysche, Wm; Rechefort, J.; Rechynson, George; Rede, Thos; Rede, J.; Rede, Wm; Rede, Thos; Rede, J.; Rede, J.; Rede, Rob; Redes, Wm; Redfer, Thos; Redhow, Thos; Redmayn, Thos; Redyng, J.; Redyng, Rich; Redyng, J.; Reed, Wm; Reede, Wm; Rekolsell, J.; Rempston, J.; Remyngton, J.; Reson, Thos; Retheford, J.; Reve, Wm; Reve, Wm; Reylle, J.; Reymer, Simon; Reymond, J.; Reymond, J.; Reynald, Geffray; Reynaldson, Rob; Reynam, Rob; Reynam, Thos; Reyner, J.; Reynold, J.; Reynold, Rich; Reynold, J.; Reynold, Matheu; Reynold, Richard; Reysham, J.; Reyvesby, Thos; Riall, Peter; Richard, Wm; Richard, Jacob; Richardes, J.; Richardson, Thos; Richardson, Thos; Riche, J.; Rigeley, J.; Riggemond, Wm; Ripon, Gibbon; Rispyn, Wm; Robardby, Henry; Robbun, J.; Robert, J.; Robles, Wm; Robley, Rich; Robmessone, Rich; Robson, J.; Robyn, J.; Robyn, J.; Robyn, Edmund; Robyn, Philipot; Robynhode, J.; Robyns, J.; Robynson, Gilbert; Robynson, Gilbert; Robynson, J.; Robynson, J.; Robynson, Dicon; Robynson, Henry; Robynson, J.; Robynson de Hedon, Wm; Robynsone, Thos; Robynsone, Thos; Rocheford, J.; Rocheforde, Roger; Roculby, Wm; Rodheng, Alexander; Roger, J.; Rogerson, J.; Rogerson, Nicholas; Rogerson, Thos; Rogerston, Wm; Roke, Thos; Rokele, Rob; Rolo, J.; Rook, J.; Roos, Rob; Roos, Rob; Roos, Thos; Roos, J.; Roos, Wm; Roos, J.; Roose, Wm; Rosawen, Michael; Rose, J.; Rosley, J.; Rosser, ap Howell ap Gr[uffth] ap Madoc; Rotherangh, Rees; Rotherfeld, J.; Rotherford, Henry; Rotherham, Wm; Rothewell, Henry; Rougham, Adam; Rouley, J.; Roulston, Wm; Round, Thos; Round[qil/], Henry; Rounton, Dyow; Rous, J.; Routh, Jenan Tew[dar?] ap Gr[ufft?]h; Rowchestre, Rich; Rowe, J.; Rowes, J.; Royok, Thos; Roys, J.; Roysaresse, Wm; Rrys, J.; Ruddok, J.; Ruddok, J.; Rudham, Mathew; Rufford, J.; Rumpe, Rob; Russbroke, J.; Russell, Thos; Russell, Rich; Russell, Rich; Russell, J.; Rydale, J.; Rydele, Henry; Ryder, J.; Rygge, J.; Rygge, Rich; Rygge, J.; Rykby, Henry; Rykevere, Thos; Rylay, Rich; Ryngedale, Wm; Rypon, Wm; Ryppele, Thos; Rys, J.; Ryse, J.; Ryssheworth, J.; Ryver, J.; Sadeler, J.; Sadeler, J.; Sadeler, Rich; Sadeler, Mathew; Sadeler, Nicholas; Sadeler, Wm; Sadeler, Wm; Sadelere, J.; Sadelere, Rich; Sadelier, Thos; Sadeller, Wm; Sadeller, Wm; Sadler, Andrew; Sadler, Thos; Saer, J.; Sai, J.; Sale, Gilbert; Salesbery, Thos; Saller, Rob; Salman, J.; Salmon, Rich; Saltemersch, Walter; Saltmersch, J.; Salysbery, Simon; Sam, J.; Sampson, Rich; Sampson, Thos; Sampson, Thos; Samson, Patrik; Sander, J.; Sandersone, J.; Sandesby, Thos; Sandon, Hugh; Sandre, Hugh; Sandton, Wm; Sanewell, Wm; Sanke, J.; Sanky, Geffrey; Sarteryn, Wm; Saterwayte, J.; Saucemore, Thos; Saul, Wm; Saunderson, Wm; Saundre, Rob; Saunford, J.; Saunton, Rich; Sauxton, Thos; Savage, Walter; Sawer, J.; Sawyer, Hugh; Saxilby, J.; Saxston, Thos; Saxton, J.; Saxton, J.; Sayton, J.; Scarlet, Thos; Scarlet, J.; Schaddle, J.; Schagh, Elye; Scharisdorill, Thos; Scharlet, J.; Schastesbery, Walter; Schawe, J.; Scheffelde, J.; Scheffelde, J.; Schephey, J.; Schephurd, Nichol; Scher, Wm; Schere, Thos; Schetton, Roger; Schipton, Wm; Schirwod, Thos; Schirwode, Ralph; Schoreswode, J.; Schortrede, Rich; Schotisbrok, J.; Schotte, Rob; Schrote, J.; Schuter, J.; Schyrle, Rob; Schyrley, Roger; Sclate, Wm; Scolaik, Philip; Scoperell, Wm; scored out, Martyn; Scot, Wm; Scot, Thos; Scot, Rich; Scot, Rob; Scote, J.; Scote, J.; Scotson, Thos; Scott, Rich; Scott, J.; Scott, J.; Scoyle, Peter; Scroby, J.; Scut, Rich; Sebyste, Wm; Sedborugh, Wm; Segge, Thos; Seggesley, Rich; Seggeswikham, Rob; Selby, Thos; Selby, Peter; Seldard, Thos; Semper, Roger; Sente, Adam; Sentte, J.; Senys, J.; Ser?, J.; Serle, J.; Serll, J.; Serteyn, J.; Servaunt, Adam; Seton, J.; Sevyngton, J.; Seward, J.; Seward, J.; Sewell, J.; Sexteyn, J.; Seybe, Wm; Seymour, Stephen; Seyne, Llewellyn ap Gr[uffth] ap Llellewyn; Seys, Willym ap Jena; Seys, David ap Gwillym; Seys, Llewellyn; Seys, Rys ap Griffith; Seys, Jenan Gethyn ap Griffith; Shaket, Rich; Shaklyn, J.; Shale, Nicholas; Shalford, Rob; Share, Rob; Sharp, Rich; Sharp, Henry; Sharp, Thos; Sharp, Wm; Sharp, Thos; Sharpyngton, Walter; Sharrom, J.; Shawe, Roger; Shawe, Thurstan; Shawe, Wm; Shawe, Thos; Shawe, Henry; Sheffeld, Rob; Sheffeld, Wm; Sheffeld, Wm; Shelsey, Wm; Shepley,

Henry; Shere, Thos; Sherman, J.; Sherman, Rob; Sherman, Thos; Sherwent, J.; Sherwod, J.; Sherwynd, Perys; Shillard, Thos; Shipman, J.; Shipman, J.; Shirborne, Wm; Shirborne, Laurence; Shirley, Rich; Shirley, J.; Shirwode, J.; Short, Nicholas; Short, Walter; Shorte, Henry; Shorte, Thos; Shorthale, Olyver; Shriesbery, J.; Shyngylwod, (Blank); Sibthorp, Edward; Siewcom, J.; Silbertyn, Wm; Silbys, Henry; Simond, Wm; Simonde, Adam; Simour, Thos; Sityngborn, J.; Skales, J.; Skarlet, Wm; Skarlet, Wm; Skedemor, J.; Skelton, J.; Skelton, Wm; Skenit, Geffrey; Skenyngton, J.; Skidmore, Reginald; Skipmore, Wm; Skipton, Rich; Sklather, J.; Sklattere, J.; Skodier, Stephen; Skolys, Robard; Skolys, Wm; Skonwoder, Walter; Skot, Thos; Skott, Rob; Skowce, J.; Skruvene, Walter; Skuddere, J.; Skydmore, Thos; Skylly, J.; Skynner, Aleyn; Skynner, Wm; Skynner, Wm; Skynner, J.; Skynnere, Wm; Skyrmore, J.; Skyrwhit, J.; Slak, Rob; Slak, Rich; Slegh, Wm; Slowley, Wm; Slyngesby, J.; Smalbone, Wm; Smalgrave, Robard; Smalwode, J.; Smert, Benet; Smethley, Alexander; Smyth, Roger; Smyth, Roger; Smyth, Rich; Smyth, James; Smyth, Rich; Smyth, Nicholas; Smyth, J.; Smyth, Wm; Smyth, Wm; Smyth, Wm; Smyth, Thos; Smyth, Raulyn; Smyth, Thos; Smyth, Wm; Smyth, J.; Smyth, Raulyn; Smyth, Hankyn; Smyth, Rich; Smyth, Henry; Smyth, J.; Smyth, Maddok; Smyth, Rich; Smyth, Edward; Smyth, J.; Smyth, J.; Smyth, J.; Smyth, J.; Smyth, Wylcok; Smyth, J.; Smyth, J.; Smyth, Wm; Smyth, Thos; Smyth, J.; Smyth, J.; Smyth, Rich; Smyth, J.; Smyth?, Thomas?; Smythe de Stradbrook, J.; Snayth, Nicholas; Sneton, J.; Snoball, Wm; Snow, Roger; Snowe, Rob; Sohs, J.; Sohyrewynd, Wm; Solacun, Philip; Somer, J.; Somer, J.; Somerby, Walter; Somercotes, Wm; Somnor, Thos; Sompterman, Wm; Sompterman, Henry; Sonbage, Rob; Sotbery, Rich; Sotherton, J.; Sourby, Rob; Soureby, J.; Soureby, Thos; Southam, J.; Sowdeor, David; Spalden, Thos; Spaldyng, J.; Spalryk, Roger; Sparcheforthe, Wm; Spark, J.; Spark, Wm; Sparke, J.; Sparke, Wm; Sparke, Roger; Sparkmam, Thos; Spencer, Cok; Spenser, Wm; Sperk, Jacob; Sperlyng, J.; Speryer, Wm; Spicer, J.; Spienne, Laurence; Spofford, Wm; Spore, J.; Sporle, J.; Sporyer, J.; Spray, Nicholas; Sprent, Rich; Sprig, Wm; Spruce, Nicholas; Sprugalt, Wm; Spryng, Rich; Spryng, Rich; Sprynge, Roger; Spryngholt, Rob; Spycer, Henry; Spycer, J.; Spyre, J.; Spyucer, Raulyn; Sqwyer, Philip; Sryght, J.; Stabele, J.; Stabills, John, of ye; Stabull, Thos; Staffe, Piers; Stafford, Rich; Stafford, Rich; Stakier, Thos; Stalkere, J.; Stalward, J.; Stalworth, Rich; Stanbank, J.; Standbank, Wm; Standirwyk, Wm; Standwich, Henry; Standyshe, David; Stanisby, Wm; Stanlas, J.; Stanlawe, Nicholas; Stanle, Wm; Stanley, Rich; Stanley, Rich; Stanly, J.; Stapele, Hamond; Stapill, J.; Stapulton, Roger; Statfeld, Nicholas; Staunton, Henry; Staunton, Wm; Staunton, J.; Staynton, J.; Staynware, J.; Steffyn, Thos; Stempedale, J.; Stenaux, Peryn; Stenynfule, Wm; Stephann, J.; Steredale, Rich; Sterke, Rich; Sterke, David; Stetfeld, Thos; Stevenes, Wm; Stevens, Rich; Stevenson, Rob; Stevenson, Rob; Stevenson, J.; Stevenys, Thos; Stevyns, Walter; Stipsot, J.; Stirop, Thos; Stodeley, Wm; Stokdene, J.; Stokes, J.; Stokeslay, Henry; Stokesley, J.; Stokke, J.; Stokkys, Rob; Stone, J.; Stonweder, Walter; Storke, Rob; Storke, Wm; Stotfold, Thos; Stoute, Thos; Stow, Jena ap Gr[uffth]; Strangrose, Wm; Strauton, Rob; Strene, J.; Strode, Wm; Strong, Thos; Stryght, J.; Strynger, Rob; Sturgys, Wm; Sturmy, Rob; Stury, Perys; Styf, Rob; Styklawe, Thos; Style, Raynale; Suarston, J.; Suelston, J.; Suker, Rich; Sunnyng, Robard; Sureby, Rich; Suthcote, Wm; Suthewyk, Henry; Sutton, J.; Sutton, J.; Sutton, Wm; Sutton, Wm; Sutton, Thos; Sutton, Wm; Sutton, Adam; Sutton, J.; Sutton, J.; Sutton, Wm; Sutton, Rich; Sutton, Wm; Sutton, Rich; Sutton, Hugo; Sutton, Wm; Sutton, Thos; Sutton, J.; Swaldale, Wm; Swale, J.; Swan, Wm; Swan, Simon; Swan, J.; Swenge, Wm; Swetenham, Thos; Swetnam, J.; Swyft, J.; Swyft, Peter; Swylyngton, J.; Swynford, Wm; Swynford, Norman; Swynford, J.; Sy, J.; Sygor, Edmund; Sylham, J.; Sylver, J.; Sylvestre, Thos; Sylvestre, J.; Sylvestre, Thos; Symes, J.; Symmesone, Thos; Symond, Wm; Symond, Wm; Symond, J.; Symondson, J.; Symson, Rich; Syngelton, Matheu; Syngisby, Wm; Syngleton, Wm; Syvyer, Walter; T?wene, Wm; Taalyor (sic), Henry; Taaylor (sic), J.; Taberd, J.; Tabur, Wm; Taillor, Wm; Taillor, Wm; Taillor, J.; Taillor, Rich; Taillor, Wm; Taillor, Wm; Taillor, J.; Taillor, Denys; Taillor, David; Taillor, Rich; Taillor, Laurence; Taillor, J.; Taillor, Jordan; Taillor, Rob; Taillor, Rich; Taillor de Inkypen, Wm; Taillour, Rob; Taillour, Thos; Taillour, Stephen; Taillour, Roger; Taillour, Thos; Taillour, Gr[uffth]; Tailor, Peter; Tailor, Rich; Tailor, J.; Tailor, Thos; Tailor, J.; Tailor, Rob; Tailor, Godfrey; Tailor, J.; Tailor, Edmond; Tailor, Jankyn; Tailor, David ap Jenan; Tailor de Ormeskirk, Wm; Tailour, J.; Tailour, J.; Tailyor, Wm; Tailyor, Thos; Tailyor, J.; Tailyor, Edward; Tailyor, Wm; Talgarth, Hugh; Talket, Rich; Talle, Rich; Tanjels, Robard; Tankerle, J.; Tannerer, Wm; Tatton, J.; Tavland, Rob; Tawe, Rich; Taylghowy, Rich; Tayllor, J.; Tayllor, Symond; Tayllor, Henry; Tayllor, Wm; Tayllour, Rich; Taylor, Rich; Taylor, J.; Taylor, Llellewyn ap Jena ap David; Taylor, Jenan Bach; Taylor, J.; Taylour, Sandr; Taylour, Rich; Tedenhale, J.; Tege, Jenan; Tell, Trahan ap David; Temple, Rich; Temple, Rich; Terell, J.; Terry, Piers; Tesdale, Wm; Tesdale, Ralph; Teteborth, J.; Tew, Jena ap David Jena; Tew, J.; Tewle, J.; Tewyford, Wm; Thakstede, Rich; Therr, Rob; Thetforde, David; Thewe?, Godfrey; Thirslee, Rich; Thoma, J.; Thoma, Stephen; Thomaeson, J.; Thomas, Wm; Thomas, Rich; Thomas, J.; Thomas, Davy; Thomas, Rich; Thomas, Wm; Thomas, David; Thomas, J.; Thomasson, Wm; Thomessone, Rich; Thompson, Rob; Thomsone, J.; Thoresby, Wm; Thorn, Roger; Thornage, J.; Thornel, J.; Thorneton, Thos; Thornham, Robard; Thornor, Henry; Thornton, Wm; Thornton, Wm; Thornton, Wm; Thorp, Wm; Thorp, Wm; Thorp, J.; Thorpe, Thos; Thropp, Walter; Thruston, Wm; Thryngton, Thos; Thurkild, J.; Thurkyld, Wm; Thurlewynd, J.; Thursteyn, J.; Thwaites, Wm; Tillyng, Peter; Todd, Rob; Todde, J.; Todde, J.; Todde, Rich; Todde, Rich; Tomessone, Wm; Tomson, J.; Tomson, Wm; Tomson, J.; Tomson, Rob; Tomson, Wm; Toppcliff, J.; Torner, Thos; Tornor, J.; Tornour, David; Torre, Rich; Torte, J.; Toteas, Rob; Totenhale, J.; Toucker, Walter; Towker, David; Towky, Thos; Trafford, Christopher; Traharn, David ap Jenan; Trapper, Olyver; Tredrue, J.; Tredyng, Rich; Trefeals, Henry; Tregee, Walter; Tregene, Peter; Trego[?], Thos; Tregold, Nicholas; Trelagarthan, Rob; Trelelban, J.; Tretonale, Wm; Trevley, Wm; Trevranek, Rich; Trewe, Wm; Trewe, Wm; Trewelove, Wm; Treygold, Thos; Triclose, Lambert; Trippe, J.; Trogge, J.; Trum, Wm; Trumpet, Wm; Trumpett, Wm; Trumppett, Laurence; Trumppett, Walter; Trumppett, Lodewic; Trusbut, Edmond; Trusslor, J.; Tryer, Thos; Tryer, Thos; Tuchett, Wm; Tuke, J.; Tunbrigg, Thos; Tundewe, J.; Tunwell, Rob; Tupe, Rob; Turell, J.; Turgys, J.; Turndale, J.; Turnemore, Thos; Turner, Wm; Turner, Nicholas; Turnor, J.; Turnor, Thos; Turnor, Rich; Turnor, J.; Turnor, Jacob; Turnor, Thos; Turnor, Wm; Turnor, Roger; Turnour, J.; Turnyn, Roger; Tuwe, J.; Twycroft, Wm; Twyforde, J.; Tybton, Rich; Tychill, Wm; Tye, J.; Tyler, J.; Tyler, J.; Tyler, Philip; Tyler, J.; Tyler, J.; Tyler, Thos; Tylere, J.; Tylle, J.; Tylle, Rich; Tyllet, Rich; Tylley, Rich; Tymbole, J.; Tympurley, Wm; Tyndale, Wm; Tynton, Rich; Tynwell, Wm; Tyson, Nicholas; Tyssyngton, Thos; U[ton, Rich; Ufflete, Thos; Ulskelf, J.; unnamed, x15; Uphouse, J.; Urpath, Thos; Ussher, Roger; Ussher, Thos; Ussher, Thos; Utton, Thos; Vachan, Howell ap M[ado?]c ap Gr[uffth]; Vachan, Mereduth ap Trahan ap Jenan; Vachan, Jenan ap Henry; Vachan, Griffuth ap Jenan; Vachan, Jenan ap Jenan Lloyt ap Jenna; Vachan, Jenan ap Philip ap Jenan; Vachan, Jowell ap David ap Jenan; Vachan, Rys ap Jenan; Vachan, Jenan ap Howell; Vachan, Jenan ap David; Vachan, Jenan ap Jenan; Vachan, Jenan ap Griffith; Vachan, Llewellyn ap Madok; Vachan, Jenan ap Jenan Lloyt ap Llewellyn; Vachan, Jenan ap Howell ap Jenan; Vachan, Mered ap Llewellyn; Vachan, Griffith ap Jenan; Vachan, Rys ap Gwillym; Vadyn, J.; Vaghan, Johan; Vaghan, David; Vaghan, David ap Jenan; Vaghan, Llellewyn ap Jena; Valler, Rich; Vantarde, Wm; Varnor, Deycons; Vaughan, Gruffyth ap Jenan; Vaux, Thos; Vawre, Griffith ap Rys; Vayse, Wm; Veel, J.; Veel, Wm; Veisy, Wm; Vele, Wm; Venter, Rich; Verley, J.; Vernon, Wm; Vernon, Stephen; Veyn, Gruffth ap Renan ap Howell; Veyn, Jena ap Howell; Veyn, Gr[uffth]; Vikers, Ralph; Ville, J.; Voile?, David ap Jenan ap Howell; Vougann, Jenan Lloyt ap Jenan ap David; Voya, Jenan ap Jenan Lloyt; Vuwyn, J.; Vykery, Rob; Vyncent, Gebon; Vynter, Rob; Vyse, Rich; Westwode, J.; Wach, Wm; Waddlacy, Wm; Waddysle, J.; Wadle, Thos; Wakefeld, Thos; Waker, J.; Walas, J.; Waldebesse, William; Wale, Thos; Walesse, J.; Waley, J.; Waleys, Wm; Waleys, J.; Waleys, Rich; Walker, Wm; Walker, J.; Walker, Hugo; Walker, Thos; Walker, Wm; Walker, Rich; Walker, Rob; Walker, Andrew; Walker, J.; Walker, Thos; Walker, J.; Walkere, Rob; Walkrue, Walter; Walkyngton, J.; Waller, Hugo; Walls, Thos; Walo?, Thos; Walsh, Wm; Walsh, Thos; Walsh, J.; Walsh, Rich; Walsh, David; Walsh, Wm; Walsham, Edward; Walsheman, Gregor; Walshman, Huge; Walslond, Thos; Walsor, Thos; Walssh, Ralph; Walssh, Wm; Walssh, J.; Walssh, Thos; Walssh, J.; Walsshman, Howell; Walsshman, Gregor; Walter, Wm; Walter, Thos; Walter, Thos; Waltham, Thos; Walton, Rich; Walton, Henry; Walys, J.; Walysch, J.; Walyson, J.; Wandesford, Thos; Warchill, Robard; Warde, Rob; Warde, J.; Warde, Rich; Warde, Rob; Wardeyn, Rob; Wardeyn, Rob; Wardon, Henry; Wardropp, J.; Ware, J.; Ware, Walter; Ware, J.; Ware, Walter; Waren?, Rob; Wareyn, Wm; Warmouthe, J.; Warner, Cok; Warnere, J.; Warnere, J.; Warrewyke, J.; Warwod, J.; Waryk, Rob; Waryn, Wm; Waryne, J.; Wase, J.; Watele, J.; Waterfalle, J.; Waterman, J.; Waterman, J.; Waterton, J.; Watford, Wm; Wathylond, Gilbert; Watkynsson, Roger; Watle, Rob; Watson, Thos; Watson, Thos; Watson, J.; Watte, Rich; Wattes, J.; Watton, Rich; Watton, Rich; Watton, Rob; Wattson, Rob; Wauk, Peter; Wautord, Wm; Wawe, Wm; Wayke, Rob; Wayte, J.; Wayte, J.; Wayte, J.; Webbe, J.; Webbe, J.; Webbe, Roger; Webbe, Walter; Webbe, J.; Webbe, J.; Webbe, J.; Webster, Thos; Webster, Henry; Webstre, Wm; Wederard, J.; Wedhak, J.; Welburn, J.; Welby, Nicholas; Welcom, Thos; Welcome, Thos; Welde, Thos; Weldon, J.; Well, at ye, Henry; Welles, Wm; Welles, J.; Wellington, Hew; Wellys, J.; Went, Godfrey, snr; Went, Godfrey jnr; Wenyngton, Wm; Werett, J.; Weryngton, J.; West, Wm; West, Wm; West, Henry; West, Rob; West, Lucas; Westby, J.; Westcot, J.; Westfeld, J.; Westley, Wm; Westlond, J.; Westlond, Wm; Weston, Thos; Weston, Thos; Weston, Thos; Weston, J.; Weston, J.; Weston, J.; Weston, J.; Weston, Hugo; Weston, J.; Wetheryk, J.; Wethip, J.;

Wetnall, Ralph; Wetryk, J.; Wevley, J.; Weyche, Res; Weye, Rob; Weymunde, J.; Whawdy?, Rich; Wheler, Walter; Wheler, J.; Wheler, John; Whelere, J.; Whetieacre, Rich; Whiston, Rob; Whit, J.; Whit, Geffrey; Whit, David; Whit, Rich; Whitcherche, David; Whitchode, Rich; White, Thos; White, J.; Whitebrok, Rich; Whithe, Jenan Moell ap Llewellyn; Whithede, Rob; Whitley, J.; Whittledale, Edward; Whitton, Rich; Whityng, Hugh; Whityngton, Rich; Whyte, J.; Whyte, Wm; Whyte, Wm; Whyte, Wm; Whyte, Wm; Whyte, J.; Whyte, Simon; Whyte, J.; Whyte, Rob; Whythand, Thos; Whythe, Llewellyn; Whythull, J.; Whytmersh, Wm; Whytte, Nicholas; Whytyngton, J.; Wichenore, Rob; Wigan, Peres; Wilcok, Thos; Wildgrys, Wm; Wilkoc, Thos; Wilkynson, Thos; Wilkynson, Rich; Willekin, Wm; Willeson, Rob; Willeson, J.; Willeson, Wm; Willeson, J.; William, J.; Williamson, J.; Willofer, J.; Willson, J.; Willson, J.; Willy, Thomas Philip; Willy, Wm; Willyam, Hugh; Willyam, Rich; Wilson, J.; Wilson, J.; Wilthorp, Thos; Wirmyngham, J[ohn?]; Wither, Rich; Withman, Henry; Witton, Thos; Witton, J.; Wodd, Thos; Wode, Wm; Wode, J.; Wodecok, Thos; Wodecok, Hugh; Wodegrave, J.; Wodehache, Roger; Wodestoke, J.; Wodeward, Thos; Wodeward, J.; Wodhous, Wm; Woloy, Thos; Wolston, J.; Wolverle, J.; Wolyff, Wm; Wombewell, Wm; Worcester, Rich; Worsell, Thos; Worslegh, Gebon; Worsseley, Rich; Worth, J.; Wrenne, Wm; Wrenne, Nicholas; Wresill, J.; Wribber, Henry; Wright, J.; Wright, Rich; Wright, Robyn; Wright, Wm; Wright, Rob; Wrothe, Thos; Wryesdale, Wm; Wryght, Rich; Wryght, Wm; Wryght, Rich; Wryght, Thos; Wryght, J.; Wryght, J.; Wryght, J.; Wryght, Wm; Wryte, Thos; Wyat, J.; Wyberden, Thos; Wybur, Roger; Wycceryk, J.; Wych, Adam; Wych, Adam; Wyche, Watkyn; Wyde, Thos; Wydensone, Henry; Wyet, Rich; Wygan, Peter; Wygan, J.; Wygge, William; Wyghm[faded], Thos; Wygmor, Wm; Wygott, J.; Wygston, Thos; Wykam, Henry; Wykes, J.; Wykes, Thos; Wykham, Wm; Wyldon, Wm; Wylghby, Roger; Wylkys, Stephen; Wyllessone, Wm; Wylliamsone, J.; Wylly, J.; Wylton, Robard; Wyltschyre, J.; Wymond, Wm; Wyn, Piers; Wynard, Henry; Wynborne, J.; Wyncote, Ralph; Wyne, Jankyn ap Gr[uffth] ap David; Wyng, Henry; Wyngate, Wm; Wynselowe, Rich; Wynter, J.; Wynter, J.; Wynter, Rob; Wynter, J.; Wynter, Wm; Wyntercotes, J.; Wynwryght, J.; Wynwyk, J.; Wynwyk, J.; Wyrcestre, J.; Wyrley, Cornyus; Wyrley, J.; Wyrlyngworde, Rob; Wyrlyngworth, Wm; Wyrtestre, J.; Wyse, Wm; Wyse, Rich; Wyseman, J.; Wyssyngden, J.; Wyte, Thos; Wyte, J.; Wythe, Llewellyn ap Jenan; Wyther, J.; Wytlesey, Rob; Wytlok, J.; Wytte, J.; Wytyngham, Rich; Yale, Rob; Yalston, Thos; Yarble, Vrchan ap Llewellyn; Yarneswode, Wm; Yarum, Thos; Yates, Henry; Ycomme, Griffith ap David; Yervale, J.; Ygoch, Rys ap Jenan Duy ap Jenan; Yngrem, Wm; Yoman, J.; Yon, J.; Yong, J.; Yonge, Adam; Yonge, Wm; Yonge, J.; Yonge, Rich; Yonge, Rich; Yonge, J.; Yonge, Simon; Yonge, Wm; Yonge, J.; Yonge, J.; Yons, Thos; York, J.; York, J.; York, Wm; York, of, J.; Ysaak, J.; Yvyan, Wm; Zelden, J.; Zerward, Phelip; Zevan, Phylip.

Maps and Genealogical Tables

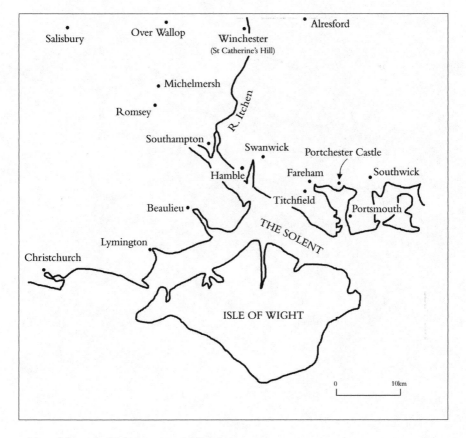

1 Map of the embarkation area around Southampton.

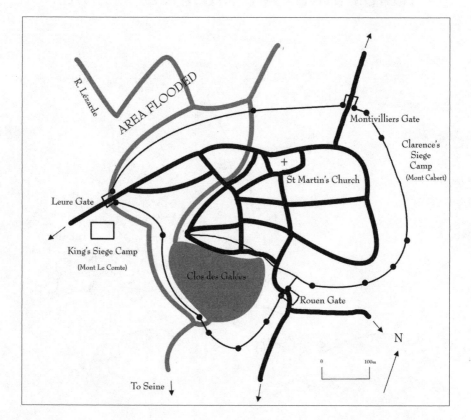

2 Harfleur.

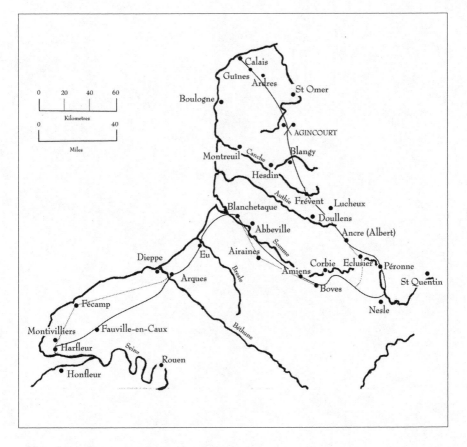

3 Henry's march – an overview.

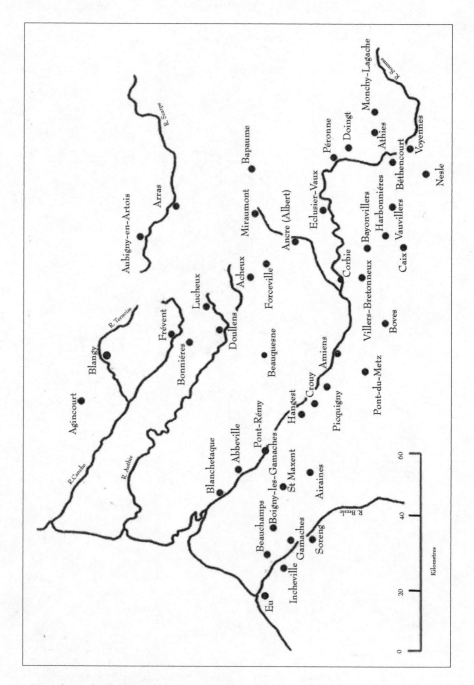

4 Henry's march – between the Somme and Agincourt.

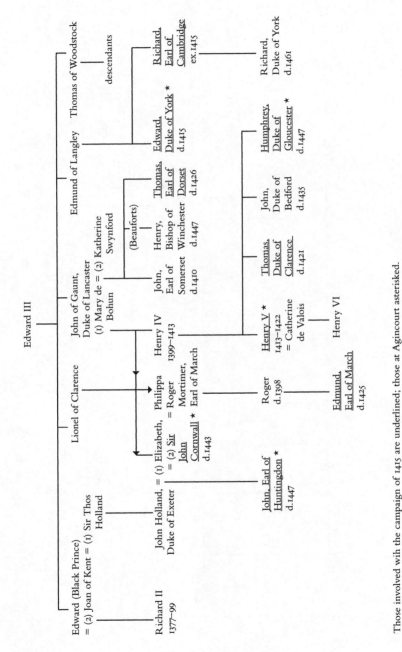

5. The English Royal Family

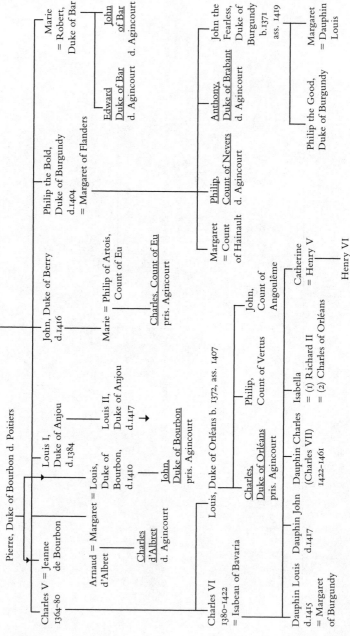

6. The French Royal Family

Bibliography

The first part of this bibliography lists all of the chronicle and administrative sources that have been printed. Many extracts are printed in my *The Battle of Agincourt: Sources and Interpretations*. Given-Wilson and Gransden, whose works are listed in the second part, provide useful introductions to the nature of medieval chronicles. For Henry's reign as a whole, Allmand's biography of Henry V is excellent; Dockray's puts chronicle sources to good use. Many of the works on Agincourt are now rather dated but are interesting in showing how the subject has been studied over the years. Bennett's book on the battle includes excellent diagrams. I have edited two wide-ranging collections of essays (*Agincourt 1415* and *Arms, Armies and Fortifications in the Hundred Years War*) which summarise recent research.

PUBLISHED PRIMARY SOURCES

Archives Municipales de Bordeaux, vol. 4. Registres de la Jurade. Déliberations de 1414 à 1416 et de 1420 à 1422 (Bordeaux, 1883)

Thomas Basin, *Histoire de Charles VII*, vol. 1, ed. C. Samaran and H. De Saint-Rémy (Paris, 1934)

The Brut, or the Chronicle of England, vol. 2, ed. F.W.D. Brie (Early English Text Society, original series, 136, London, 1906–1908)

'Calendar of French Rolls' in *Annual Report of the Deputy Keeper of the Public Records*, 44 (1883)

Calendar of Letter Books preserved among the archives of the Corporation of the City of London. Letter Book I, ed. R.R. Sharpe (London, 1909)

John Capgrave, *De Illustribus Henricis*, ed. F.C. Hingeston, (Rolls Series, London, 1858)

Cartulaire des comtes de Hainaut de 1337 à 1436, vol. 4, ed. L. Devillers (Brussels, 1889)

Choix de pieces inédites relatives au règne de Charles VI, vol. 1, ed. L. Douët d'Arcq (SHF, Paris, 1863)

The Chronicle of Adam Usk 1377–1421, ed. C. Given-Wilson (Oxford, 1997)

Chronique d'Antonio Morosini, vol. 2, ed. G. Le Fèvre-Pontalis and L. Dorez (SHF, Paris, 1899)

Chronique d'Arthur de Richemont par Guillaume Gruel, ed. A. Le Vavasseur (SHF, Paris, 1890)

La Chronique d'Enguerran de Monstrelet, vols 2 and 3, ed. L. Douet-d'Arcq (SHF, Paris, 1858–9)

Chronique de Jean Le Fèvre, Seigneur de Saint Remy, vol. 1, ed. F. Morand (SHF, Paris, 1876)

Chronique de Perceval de Cagny, ed. H. Moranville (SHF, Paris, 1902)

Chronique des ducs de Brabant par Edmond Dynter, vol. 3, ed. P.F.X. De Ram (Brussels, 1858)

Chronique des Pays Bas, de France, d'Angleterre et de Tournai, Recueil des Chroniques de Flandres, vol. 3, ed. J.-J. Smet (Brussels, 1856)

Chronique de Bec et Chronique de François Carré, ed. Abbé Porée (SHF, Paris, 1883)

Les Chroniques du roi Charles VII par Gilles le Bouvier dit le héraut Berry, ed. H. Couteault and L. Celier with M. Jullien de Pommerol (SHF, Paris, 1979)

Chronique normande de Pierre Cochon, ed. C. de Robillard de Beaurepaire (Société de l'Histoire de Normandie, 1870)

J. Delpit, *Collection générale des documents français qui se trouvent en Angleterre* (Paris, 1847)

Gesta Henrici Quinti. The Deeds of Henry the Fifth, ed. F. Taylor and J.S. Roskell (Oxford, 1975)

V. Grave, *Archives municipales de Mantes. Analyse des registres des comptes de 1381 à 1450* (Paris, 1896)

The Great Chronicle of London, ed. A.H. Thomas and I.D. Thornley (London, 1938)

John Hardyng, *Chronicle (to 1461)*, ed. H. Ellis (London, 1812)

Thomas Hoccleve, *Works, iii. The Regement of Princes, AD 1411–12*, ed. F.J. Furnivall (Early English Text Society, 1897)

Jean Juvenal des Ursins, *Histoire de Charles VI, roy de* France, Nouvelle collection des mémoires pour servir à l'histoire de France, ed. Michaud & Poujoulet, series 1, vol. 2 (Paris, 1836)

Journal d'un Bourgeois de Paris de 1404–1449, ed. C. Beaune (Paris, 1990)

Lettres des rois, reines et autres personages des course de France et d'Angleterre, vol. 2, ed J.J. Champollion Figeac (Paris, 1847)

'*Liber Metricus* de Henrico Quinto' by Thomas Elmham, *Memorials of Henry the Fifth, King of England*, ed. C.A. Cole (Rolls Series, London, 1858)

Mémoires de Pierre de Fenin, ed. E. Dupont (SHF, Paris, 1837)

Memorials of London and London Life in the xiiith, xivth and xvth centuries, ed. H.T. Riley (London, 1868)

Oeuvres de Ghillebert de Lannoy, voyageur, diplomate et moralist. Recueillies et publiées par Charles Poitvin (Louvain, 1878)

Ordonnances des rois de France de la troisième race, 21 vols (Paris, 1723–1849)

A Parisian Journal 1405–1449, ed. J. Shirley (Oxford, 1968)

Proceedings and Ordinances of the Privy Council, vol. 2, ed. N.H. Nicolas (London, 1834)

[Pseudo-Elmham] *Thomae de Elmham Vita et Gesta Henrici Quinti*, ed. T. Hearne (Oxford, 1727)

Receuil des Croniques et Anchiennes istories de la Grant Bretagne a present nomme Engleterre par Jehan de Waurin, vol. 2, ed. W.L. Hardy and E.L.C.P. Hardy (Rolls Series, London, 1864)

Le Religieux de Saint-Denis, *Histoire de Charles VI*, vols 4 and 5, ed. L. Bellaguet (Collection de documents inédits sur l'histoire de France, Paris, 1839–44)

'Rôles normands et français et autres pieces tirées des archives de Londres par Bréquigny en 1764, 1765, et 1766', *Mémoires de la Société des Antiquaires de Normandie*, 23 (1858)

Rotuli Parliamentorum, ed. J. Strachey et al (London, 1767–77)

T. Rymer, *Foedera, conventions, litterae et cuiuscunque generis acta publica*, 3rd edn (The Hague, 1739–45)

F. Taylor, 'The Chronicle of John Streeche for the reign of Henry V (1414–1422)', *Bulletin of the John Rylands Library*, 16 (1932)

Scotichronicon by Walter Bower, vol. 8, ed. D.E.R. Watt (Aberdeen, 1987)

Titi Livii Foro-Juliensis Vita Henrici Quinti, ed. T. Hearne (Oxford, 1716)

Thomas Walsingham, *The St. Albans Chronicle 1406–1420*, ed. V.H. Galbraith (Oxford, 1937)

SECONDARY WORKS

C.T. Allmand, *The Hundred Years War* (Cambridge, 1988)

C.T. Allmand, *Henry V* (London, 1992)

A. Ayton, *Knights and Warhorses. Military Service and the English Aristocracy under Edward III* (Woodbridge, 1994)

A. Ayton and P. Preston, *The Battle of Crécy, 1346* (Woodbridge, 2005)

G. Bacquet, *Azincourt* (Bellegrade, 1977)

A.R. Bell, *War and the Soldier in the Fourteenth Century* (Woodbridge, 2004)

R. de Belleval, *Azincourt* (Paris, 1865)

M. Bennett, *Agincourt 1415. Triumph Against the Odds* (London, 1991)

M. Bennett, 'The development of battle tactics in the Hundred Years War', *Arms, Armies and Fortifications in the Hundred Years War*, ed. A. Curry and M. Hughes (Woodbridge, 1994)

S. Boffa, *Warfare in Medieval Brabant 1356–1406* (Woodbridge, 2004)

S. Boffa, 'Anthoine de Bourgogne et le contingent brabaçon à la bataille d'Azincourt (1415)', *Revue belge de philologie et d'histoire*, 72 (1994)

A.L. Brown, 'The English Campaign in Scotland, 1400', *British Government and Administration. Studies presented to S.B. Chrimes*, ed. H. Hearder and H.R. Loyn (Cardiff, 1974)

A. Burne, *The Crécy War* (London, 1955)

A. Burne, *The Agincourt War* (London, 1956)

A.D. Carr, 'Welshmen and the Hundred Years War', *Welsh History Review*, 4 (1968)

A. Chéruel, *Histoire de Rouen sous la domination anglaise* (Rouen, 1840, repr, 1970)

P. Contamine, *Guerre, état et société. Étude sur les armées des rois de France 1337–1494* (Paris/The Hague, 1972)

P. Contamine, *War in the Middle Ages* (English translation by M. Jones, Oxford, 1980)

P. Contamine, 'Les armées française et anglaise à l'époque de Jeanne d'Arc', *Revue des sociétés savantes de Haute-Normandie. Lettres et sciences humaines*, 57 (1970)

E. Cosneau, *Le Connétable de Richemont. Artur de Bretagne, 1393–1458* (Paris, 1886)

A. Curry, *The Battle of Agincourt. Sources and Interpretations* (Woodbridge, 2000)

A. Curry (ed.), *Agincourt 1415. Henry V, Sir Thomas Erpingham and the triumph of the English Archers* (Stroud, 2000)

A. Curry, *The Hundred Years War*, 2nd edn (Basingstoke and London, 2001)

A. Curry, 'Towns at War. Relations between the towns of Normandy and their English rulers 1417–1450', *Towns and Townspeople in the Fifteenth Century*, ed. J.A.F. Thomson (Gloucester, 1988)

A. Curry, 'English armies in the fifteenth century', in *Arms, Armies and Fortifications in the Hundred Years War*, ed. A. Curry and M. Hughes (Woodbridge, 1994)

A. Curry, 'Lancastrian Normandy: the jewel in the crown?', in *England and Normandy in the Middle Ages*, ed. D. Bates and A. Curry (London, 1994)

A. Curry, 'Isolated or Integrated? The English soldier in Lancastrian Normandy', in *Courts and Regions in Medieval Europe*, ed. S. Rees Jones, R. Marks and A.J. Minnis (York/Woodbridge, 2000)

A. Curry, 'Harfleur et les Anglais 1415–1422', *La Normandie et l'Angleterre au Moyen Âge* (Caen, 2003)

A. Curry, 'Personal links and the nature of the English war retinue: a case study of John Mowbray, earl marshal, and the campaign of 1415', *La table ronde de Glasgow*, ed. E. Anceau, V. Gazeau and F.J. Ruggiu (Publications de la Sorbonne, Paris, forthcoming, 2005).

R.R. Davies, *The Revolt of Owain Glyndŵr* (Oxford, 1995)

S. Deck, *Une commune normande au moyen âge. La ville d'Eu* (Paris, 1924)

E. Deseille, 'Étude sur les relations des communes du Nord lors du désastre d'Azincourt', *Mémoires de la Société Académique de l'arrondissment de Boulogne-sur-Mer* (1879)

K. Dockray, *Henry V* (Stroud, 2004)

J.-L. Dufresne, 'La délinquance dans une region en guerre: Harfleur-Montivilliers dans la première moitié du XVème siècle', *Actes du cent cinquième congrès des sociétés savantes* (Caen, 1980)

R.C. Familgetti, *Royal Intrigue. Crisis at the Court of Charles VI 1392–1420* (New York, 1986)

J. Flammermont, *Institutions municipales de Senlis* (Senlis, 1881)

C. Given-Wilson, *Chronicles. The Writing of History in Medieval England* (London, 2004)

C. Given-Wilson, 'Edward III's prisoners of war: the battler of Poitiers and its context', *English Historical Review*, 116 (2001)

J. Godard, 'Quelques précisions sur la campagne d'Azincourt tirées des archives municipales d'Amiens', *Bulletin trimestre de la Société des Antiquaires de Picardie* (1971)

A. Gransden, *Historical Writing in England, ii. c. 1307 to the Early Sixteenth Century* (London and Henley, 1982)

R. Griffiths, 'Prince Henry, Wales and the Royal Exchequer, 1400–13', *Bulletin of the Board of Celtic Studies*, 32 (1985)

R. Griffiths, 'Prince Henry's war: armies, garrisons and supply during the Glyndŵr rising', *Bulletin of the Board of Celtic Studies*, 34 (1987)

G. Harriss, *Cardinal Beaufort. A Study of Lancastrian Ascendancy and Decline* (Oxford, 1988)

D. Hay, 'The division of spoils of war in fourteenth century England', *Transactions of the Royal Historical Society*, fifth series, 4 (1954)

H.J. Hewitt, *The Black Prince's Expedition of 1355–1357* (Manchester, 1958)

C. Hibbert, *Agincourt* (London, 1964)

A. Janvier, *Notices sur les anciennes corporations d'archers, d'arbalétriers, de couleuvriniers et d'arquebusiers des villes de Picardie* (Amiens, 1855)

J. Keegan, *The Face of Battle. A Study of Agincourt, Waterloo and the Somme* (London, 1976)

G. Kipling, *Enter the King. Theatre, Liturgy and Ritual in the Medieval Civi Triumph* (Oxford, 1998)

J. Kirby, 'The financing of Calais under Henry V, *Bulletin of the Institute of Historical Research*, 23 (1950)

G.A. Knowlson, *Jean V, duc de Bretagne, et l'Angleterre (1399–1442)* (Cambridge and Rennes, 1964)

J. La Fons-Mélicocq, *Noyon et le Noyonnais au moyen age* (Noyon, 1841),

D. Lalande, *Jean II le Meingre dit Boucicaut (1366–1421). Étude d'une biographie héroïque* (Geneva, 1988)

H. Lamotte, *Antiquités de la ville d'Harfleur* (Paris, 1799)

B. Le Cain, 'Les fortifications de Harfleur au début du XVe siècle. Les années de l'occupation anglaise', *Les fortifications Plantagenêt*, ed. M.-P. Baudry (Poitiers, 2000)

A. Leguai, 'Le problème des rançons au XVème siècle: la captivité de Jean I, duc de Bourbon', *Cahiers d'histoire*, 6 (1961)

F. Lehoux, *Jean de France, duc de Berri. Sa vie. Son action politique*, 4 vols (Paris, 1968)

M. Livingstone and M. Witzel, *The Road to Crécy. The English Invasion of France 1346* (London, 2004)

P. McNiven, 'Prince Henry and the English political crisis of 1412', *History*, 65 (1980)

P. McNiven, 'The problem of Henry IV's health, 1405–13', *English Historical Review*, 100 (1985)

L. Mirot, 'Le process de maître Jean Fusoris', *Mémoires de la société de l'histoire de Paris et de l'île de France*, 27 (1900)

L. Mirot, 'Lettres closes de Charles VI conservées aux archives de Reims et de Tournai', *Le Moyen Age*, 29, 30 (1917–19)

Dom Morice, *Mémoires pour servir de preuves à l'historie de Bretagne*, vol. 2 (Paris, 1744)

N.H. Nicolas, *History of the Battle of Agincourt*, 3rd edn (London, 1833)

C. Phillpotts, 'The French plan of battle during the Agincourt campaign', *English Historical Review*, 99 (1984)

C. Phillpotts, 'The fate of the truce of Paris, 1396–1415', *Journal of Medieval History*, 24 (1998)

U. Plancher, *Histoire de duché de Bourgogne*, 3 vols (Dijon, 1739–48)

J. Poquet de Haut Jussé, 'Une renaissance littéraire au cour d'Henry V', *Revue historique*, 224 (1960)

E. Powell, *Kingship, Law and Society. Criminal Justice in the Reign of Henry V* (Oxford, 1989)

M.R. Powicke, 'Lancastrian captains', *Essays in Medieval History presented to Bertie Wilkinson*, ed. T.A. Sandquist and M.R. Powicke (Toronto, 1969)

M. Prestwich, *Armies and Warfare in the Middle Ages. The English Experience* (New Haven and London, 1996)

T.B. Pugh, *Henry V and the Southampton Plot* (Southampton Record Series, 1988)

M. Richardson, 'Henry V, The English Chancery, and Chancery English', *Speculum*, 55 (1980)

C.J. Rogers (ed.), *The Wars of Edward III. Sources and Interpretations* (Woodbridge, 1999)

C.J. Rogers, *War Cruel and Sharp. English Strategy under Edward III, 1327–1360* (Woodbridge, 2000)

S. Rose (ed.), *The Navy of the Lancastrian Kings. Accounts and Inventories of William Soper, Keeper of the King's Ships 1422–1427* (Navy Records Society, 1982)

J.S. Roskell, L. Clark, and C. Rawcliffe (ed.) *History of Parliament. The Commons 1386–1421*, 4 vols (Gloucester, 1992)

T.A. Sandquist, 'The holy oil of St Thomas of Canterbury', *Essays in Medieval History presented to Bertie Wilkinson*, ed. T.A. Sandquist and M.R. Powicke (Toronto, 1969)

J. Sherborne, 'Indentured retinues and English expeditions to France, 1369–80', *English Historical Review*, 79 (1964)

J.A. Tuck, 'Henry IV and Europe: a dynasty's search for recognition', *The McFarlane Legacy. Studies in Late Medieval Politics*, ed. R.H. Britnell and A.J. Pollard (Stroud, 1995)

C. Tyreman, *England and the Crusades 1095–1588* (Chicago and London, 1988)

M.G.A. Vale, *English Gascony 1399–1453* (Oxford, 1970)

R. Vaughan, *John the Fearless* (London, 1973)

C. de Vic and J. Vaissète, *Histoire générale de Languedoc*, 16 vols (Toulouse, 1872–1905)

S. Walker, 'Janico Dartasso: chivalry, nationality and the man-at-arms', *History*, 84 (1999)

J.H. Wylie, *History of England under Henry IV*, 4 vols (London, 1884–9)

J.H. Wylie and W.T. Waugh, *The Reign of Henry V*, 3 vols (Cambridge, 1914–29)

List of Illustrations and Figures

ILLUSTRATIONS

MAPS AND GENEALOGICAL TABLES

Index

Since Henry V, Agincourt, and the various chroniclers are mentioned passim, they are excluded from this index of names and places.